Animating Truth

Edinburgh Studies in Film and Intermediality

Series editors: Martine Beugnet and Kriss Ravetto
Founding editor: John Orr

A series of scholarly research intended to challenge and expand on the various approaches to film studies, bringing together film theory and film aesthetics with the emerging intermedial aspects of the field. The volumes combine critical theoretical interventions with a consideration of specific contexts, aesthetic qualities, and a strong sense of the medium's ability to appropriate current technological developments in its practice and form as well as in its distribution.

Advisory board
Duncan Petrie (University of Auckland)
John Caughie (University of Glasgow)
Dina Iordanova (University of St Andrews)
Elizabeth Ezra (University of Stirling)
Gina Marchetti (University of Hong Kong)
Jolyon Mitchell (University of Edinburgh)
Judith Mayne (The Ohio State University)
Dominique Bluher (Harvard University)

Titles in the series include:

Romantics and Modernists in British Cinema
John Orr

Framing Pictures: Film and the Visual Arts
Steven Jacobs

The Sense of Film Narration
Ian Garwood

The Feel-Bad Film
Nikolaj Lübecker

American Independent Cinema: Rites of Passage and the Crisis Image
Anna Backman Rogers

The Incurable-Image: Curating Post-Mexican Film and Media Arts
Tarek Elhaik

Screen Presence: Cinema Culture and the Art of Warhol, Rauschenberg, Hatoum and Gordon
Stephen Monteiro

Indefinite Visions: Cinema and the Attractions of Uncertainty
Martine Beugnet, Allan Cameron and Arild Fetveit (eds)

Screening Statues: Sculpture and Cinema
Steven Jacobs, Susan Felleman, Vito Adriaensens and Lisa Colpaert (eds)

Drawn From Life: Issues and Themes in Animated Documentary Cinema
Jonathan Murray and Nea Ehrlich (eds)

Intermedial Dialogues: The French New Wave and the Other Arts
Marion Schmid

The Museum as a Cinematic Space: The Display of Moving Images in Exhibitions
Elisa Mandelli

Theatre Through the Camera Eye: The Poetics of an Intermedial Encounter
Laura Sava

Caught In-Between: Intermediality in Contemporary Eastern Europe and Russian Cinema
Ágnes Pethő

No Power Without an Image: Icons Between Photography and Film
Libby Saxton

Cinematic Intermediality: Theory and Practice
Kim Knowles and Marion Schmid (eds)

Animating Truth: Documentary and Visual Culture in the 21st Century
Nea Ehrlich

Visit the Edinburgh Studies in Film website at www.edinburghuniversitypress.com/series/ESIF

Animating Truth
Documentary and Visual Culture in the 21st Century

Nea Ehrlich

EDINBURGH
University Press

For Sebastian, for making me laugh when I least expect it

Edinburgh University Press is one of the leading university presses in the UK. We publish academic books and journals in our selected subject areas across the humanities and social sciences, combining cutting-edge scholarship with high editorial and production values to produce academic works of lasting importance. For more information visit our website: edinburghuniversitypress.com

© Nea Ehrlich, 2021, 2022

Grateful acknowledgement is made to the following sources for permission to reproduce material previously published elsewhere. Every effort has been made to trace the copyright holders, but if any have been inadvertently overlooked, the publisher will be pleased to make the necessary arrangements at the first opportunity.

Edinburgh University Press Ltd
The Tun – Holyrood Road
12(2f) Jackson's Entry
Edinburgh EH8 8PJ

First published in hardback by Edinburgh University Press 2021

Typeset in Garamond MT Pro by
Servis Filmsetting Ltd, Stockport, Cheshire

A CIP record for this book is available from the British Library

ISBN 978 1 4744 6336 2 (hardback)
ISBN 978 1 4744 6337 9 (paperback)
ISBN 978 1 4744 6338 6 (webready PDF)
ISBN 978 1 4744 6339 3 (epub)

The right of Nea Ehrlich to be identified as the author of this work has been asserted in accordance with the Copyright, Designs and Patents Act 1988, and the Copyright and Related Rights Regulations 2003 (SI No. 2498).

Contents

List of Illustrations   vi
Acknowledgements   viii

Introduction   1

Part I Starting Points: The Evidentiary Status of Animation as Documentary Imagery

1. Why Now?   27
2. Defining Animation and Animated Documents in Contemporary Mixed Realities   54

Part II Animation and Technoculture: The Virtualisation of Culture and Virtual Documentaries

3. Screens, Virtuality and Materiality   87
4. Documenting Game Realities   111
5. In-game Documentaries of Non-game Realities   135
6. Interactive Animated Documentaries: Documentary Games and VR   150

Part III The Power of Animation: Disputing the Aesthetics of 'the Real'

7. Encounters, Ethics and Empathy   177
8. Conflicting Realisms: Animated Documentaries and Post-truth   199

Epilogue   223
Filmography   244
Bibliography   247
Index   264

Illustrations

FIGURES

I.1	Screenshot from *Kill Bill*, directed by Quentin Tarantino, 2003	1
I.2	*Waltz with Bashir*, animated by David Polonsky and directed by Ari Folman, 2008	4
I.3	*Tower*, directed by Keith Maitland, 2016	5
1.1	Screenshot of Donald Trump and Xi Jinping sunbathing, *TomoNews*, 2017	28
1.2	Screenshot from *One Iranian Lawyer's Fight to Save Juveniles from Execution*, *The Guardian* and Sherbet, 2012	33
2.1	*Slaves*, directed by David Aronowitsch and Hanna Heilborn, 2008	55
2.2	*Flight Patterns*, a time-lapse animation artwork by Aaron Koblin, 2011	70
2.3	*Powering the Cell – Mitochondria*, BioVisions Program and XVIVO Scientific Animation, 2012	71
3.1	*Do It Yourself*, directed by Eric Ledune, 2007	98
3.2	*Second Bodies*, directed by Sandra Danilovic, 2009	104
3.3	*Serious Games: Immersion*, artwork by Harun Farocki, 2009 Copyright Harun Farocki GbR, Berlin.	105
3.4	*Reenactment of Valie Export and Peter Weibel's Tapp und Tastkino*, Eva and Franco Mattes, 2007. Online performance, Galleria Civica di Trento.	106
4.1	*Molotov Alva and His Search for the Creator*, directed by Douglas Gayeton, 2007	118
5.1	Avatar in three modes of animation, from *Stranger Comes to Town*, directed by Jacqueline Goss, 2007	142
5.2	*World of Warcraft* avatars incorporated into the *US Visit* rotoscoped video, from *Stranger Comes to Town*, directed by Jacqueline Goss, 2007	142
6.1	Continuum of vividness	152
6.2	Mob gathering outside the photography studio, from *September*	

	1955, an installation by Cagri Hakan Zaman, Deniz Tortum, Nil Tuzcu, 2016	160
6.3	Screenshot from documentary game *9/11 Survivor*, by John Brennan, Mike Caloud and Jeff Cole, 2003	162
7.1	Screenshot from *Darfur is Dying*, Take Action Games, 2006	187
7.2	*Music & Clowns*, by Alex Widdowson, 2018	191
7.3	*Slaves*, directed by David Aronowitsch and Hanna Heilborn, 2008	192
8.1	*Snack and Drink*, directed by Bob Sabiston, 1999	208
8.2	*The Simpson Verdict*, video installation by Kota Ezawa, 2002	217
E.1	*Another Planet*, an animated documentary by Amir Yatziv, 2017	226
E.2	Screenshot from *Black Mirror*, 'Fifteen Million Merits' episode, created by Charlie Brooker, 2011	236
E.3	*Trump Dreams*, animated by Ruth Lingford, 2017	240

TABLE

E.1	Comparison of animation in the past with animation today	229

Acknowledgements

It would not have been possible to write this book without the generous help and support of many individuals. I would like to emphasise my deep gratitude to Kriss Ravetto and Angela Dimitrakaki for their unparalleled guidance and lasting influence on my thinking. My warm thanks also to Richard Williams, Suzanne Buchan, Paul Wells, Paul Ward, Gabriel Motzkin and Shai Lavi for their academic and intellectual support along the way.

I'd like to thank the team at Edinburgh University Press, and especially Gillian Leslie and Richard Strachan. The University of Edinburgh was instrumental in providing the resources and support necessary to complete this project and the Animated Realities conference I co-organised, thereby bringing together practitioners and researchers of animated documentary and allowing me to learn from the people in this emerging field. Important in my academic path was also the Van Leer Jerusalem Institute, for providing me the opportunity to develop the ideas in this book. I'm also grateful to my colleagues and students at the Department of the Arts at Ben-Gurion University of the Negev and would like to specifically thank Ruth Yurovski for her help on this project.

I'd also like to acknowledge the members of the Society for Animation Studies for proving to me I was in the right field and that I had found 'my people', and for being a source of friendship, discussions, good advice and collaboration. Thank you also to all the animators who shared their practical knowledge, work and perspectives on the field; the animation community's endless creativity and enthusiasm for their research have been contagious and motivational. The many scholars whose work is quoted and referenced in these pages have inspired my thinking.

Many thanks to all the artists and individuals who generously gave me permission to use their work in my book: Amir Yatziv, Ari Folman and Yael Nahlieli, Keith Maitland, Jonathan Bairstow and Ben Sayer, Michael Astrachan, David Aronowitsch and Hanna Heilborn, Alain Viel, Aaron Koblin, Eric Ledune, Eva and Franco Mattes, Sandra Danilovic, Douglas Gayeton, Jacqueline Goss, Cagri Hakan Zaman, Deniz Tortum, Nil Tuzcu, Susana Ruiz, Alex Widdowson, Bob Sabiston, Kota Ezawa, Ruth Lingford and Antje Ehmann of the Harun Farocki GbR.

I owe a debt of gratitude to my friends, for their endless support. Thank you, Lauren Pyott, for being the first to listen. Thank you Ayelet Carmi, Claire Benn and Benjamin Dahlbeck, for everything. Thank you, Sivan Balslev, Zohar Gotesman, Oded Erell, Yaara Ilan, Ruthi Aladjem, Carmel Vaisman, Alexandra Antoniadou, Lara Aranson and Nicholas Miller for your intellectual feedback, incisive critique and stimulating conversations. Thank you also Cristina Formenti and Jonathan Murray for wonderful collaborations. Thank you, Lesley Marks, for meticulous editing but also for ongoing good advice.

Finally, I would like to thank my parents and partner, unwavering sources of support. Elana and Avishai, your different approaches, endless thoughtfulness and wisdom made this possible. And beyond everything else, Sebastian, for encouraging me in the first place and enduring everything it entailed, and for making me realise that some things are beyond words.

Introduction

This book was born out of the powerful experience of watching Quentin Tarantino's film *Kill Bill* (2003).[1] This is how I remember it: 'W-h-i-m-p-e-r . . .' the animated letters escape the child's mouth. Hiding under the bed as her parents are attacked, a single tear forms as she watches the mattress above her slowly become soaked with blood, which then drips down onto her face, replacing the tears on her cheeks. In this sequence, a child witnesses the cruel murder of both her parents. There is so much blood; like steam rising, the red haze covers the screen, engulfing the scene in a way that no live-action footage could have done. Later, the girl takes her triumphant revenge through deadly sexual intercourse with the paedophile who slaughtered her mother and father.

The bold graphics with the slow-motion choreography present a surreal dance, aesthetically beautiful and yet, simultaneously and perhaps consequently, horrible. Not being familiar with Japanese anime and manga at the time, I felt the shock of the juxtaposition; it made me see animation as I had never seen it before. At the time, for me, animation had been all about fantasy, humour and memories of TV cartoons on Saturday mornings. This one scene showed me that now the potential capabilities of animation were limitless. I realised that the shocking use of animation in this particular case

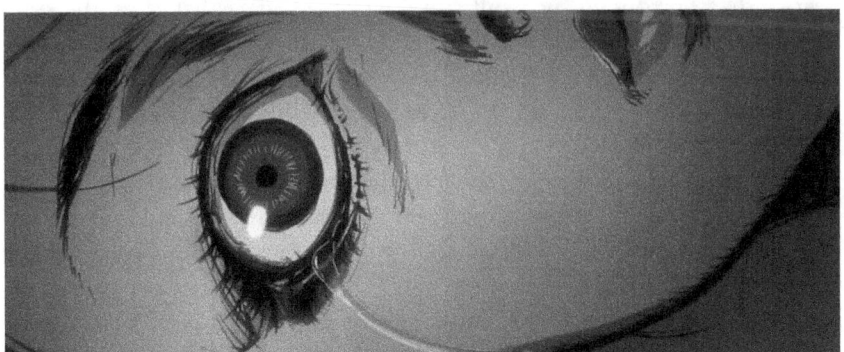

Figure I.1   Screenshot from *Kill Bill*, directed by Quentin Tarantino, 2003.

reflected a much broader and deeper change in the uses of animation today. This is what this book is about.

Even though animation has a complex, varied history, Disney's pivotal role in creating animated content meant that it was culturally understood as removed from 'the real'.[2] It was frequently associated with childhood entertainment, fantastical content, and simplified or safeguarded educational matter with which to treat 'difficult' subjects like sexual education in the 1940s, as seen in Eddie Albert's *Human Growth* (1947),[3] Disney's *Family Planning* (1968),[4] and Les Clark's *VD Attack Plan!* (1973)[5] Or the visual signification of psychological states like the nightmare sequence in Alfred Hitchcock's *Vertigo* (1958),[6] in which the spiral-themed animated sequences symbolise the protagonist's despair, repeatedly circling back to the same moment. The animated *Kill Bill* scene, however, does not symbolise a fantastical dream; it is intended to jolt viewers, making the violence so graphic that it seems almost more than real. Using animation to portray 'the real' reflects a cultural shift whereby animation departs from childhood- or fantasy-oriented imagery, to engage increasingly with factual content. This trend is most obvious in the field of animated documentaries, which has grown rapidly since 2008 when the Oscar-nominated *Waltz with Bashir*[7] gained wide critical acclaim.[8] Before 2009, contemporary examples of animated documentaries were scarce, and limited to works like *Ryan* (2004),[9] *Persepolis* (2007),[10] *Chicago 10* (2007),[11] and *Waltz with Bashir*. In 2008, animated documentary still sounded like something of an oxymoron.[12] However, since 2009, the medium has proliferated widely and as this book was going to press, a keyword search for 'animated documentary' videos on Google rendered 29.5 million results and included wide-ranging topics and media.

Animating Truth seeks to understand the reasons for this proliferation of animated documentaries. I propose that the shift in the imagery used to depict factual content is an essential aspect of what we now call the era of post-truth. Confronting such shifts in the status and aesthetics of 'the real', this book examines the rise of animated documentary in the twenty-first century, and addresses how non-photorealistic animation – that is, animation that does not attempt to look real or to resemble photographic imagery – is increasingly used both to depict and shape reality. In order to demonstrate this change, I map out the two parallel trends in animation: the expanded use of animation within documentary or non-fiction contexts, and the increasingly pervasive use of non-photorealistic animation within digital media. *Animating Truth* analyses the ways in which contemporary technoculture has transformed the relation of animation to documentary. (Technoculture indicates the co-dependence between society, culture and technology while emphasising issues of representation.)

I refer to documentary by recognising that today the boundaries between documentary and different fields of non-fiction such as journalism, forensics, education and information, are blurred.[13] Moreover, animated documentary is not a contemporary invention, and the categorisation of individual films as animated documentary depends on different, often competing, critical definitions and classificatory criteria.[14] Writing in 2005, Sheila Sofian defined animated documentaries as 'any animated film that deals with non-fiction material'.[15] This definition raises the murky issue of 'non-fiction', and points back to the blurred boundaries mentioned above.

As technology shapes culture, contemporary virtual realities – ubiquitous screens and the centrality of online platforms – require new visualisation methods. Once virtual screen worlds become interactive, the *on*-screen world becomes an *in*-screen world, in which the viewer/user plays an active role. Animation has become central as a virtual aesthetic because it uses dynamic moving imagery that can respond in real time to user input. Since our contemporary mixed reality includes the virtual as well as the physical, new theorisations of documentary that transcend the capacity of photography are required; for photography both resembles and relies on material reality.[16]

This book defines three key areas relating animation to documentary: the evidentiary status of animation as documentary imagery, the relationship between animation and the prevailing technoculture, and the aesthetics of 'the real'. My aim is to understand how this visual paradigm shift influences viewers both ethically and politically, and what epistemological ramifications this transformation in non-fiction aesthetics may evoke.

Waltz with Bashir – about Israeli soldiers' recollections of war – was an important trigger for this study because it is a contemporary example of animated documentary that stimulated much academic research.[17] It is also a good starting point to interrogate animation's evidentiary value, the kind of realities it portrays, and its conventions of documentary aesthetics. The film addresses trauma, memory loss and reconstruction, and ends with the animation dissolving into live-action photographic footage of the aftermath of the Sabra and Shatila massacre during the 1982 Lebanon War. This move from animation to live action in the final scene is similar to the animated opening scene in *Kill Bill*, for it acts as a visual bombshell. However, the significance is quite different. Whereas some may see the last scene in *Waltz with Bashir* as validating the otherwise animated film's documentary value, others may see it as having the opposite effect. By using photographic footage at the end of the film as evidence of 'the real', the constructed nature of the animated representation is emphasised, and the reality portrayed in the rest of the film is potentially undermined. The changing documentary aesthetics also question the nature of the reality with which the film engages, accentuating the personal

Figure I.2 *Waltz with Bashir*, animated by David Polonsky and directed by Ari Folman, 2008.

exploration of the protagonist's lost memories rather than any objective search for facts. Furthermore, the animated imagery in *Waltz with Bashir* is indirectly used to question the difference between animation and photography, and to reflect upon different modes of representation that are accepted as credible, legitimate documentation. 'It's fine as long as you draw, but don't film', retorts one of the characters when asked about the possibility of recording their meeting. The imperative 'don't film' articulates an ironic and central theme of the work, namely, that photography is 'real' whereas animation is not. Not only has animation been historically linked to the portrayal of fantasy worlds, it is often stylised very differently from photorealism, and its production is based on the construction rather than the capture of imagery. These features have contributed to animation's reputation for artificiality, and thus explain why it may be considered as beyond the borders of 'the real'.

Almost a decade later, these issues persist, as seen in the award-winning animated documentary *Tower*[18] about America's first mass shooting in 1966 at the University of Texas, Austin. Here, too, animation is combined with live action to interrogate the difficult question of memory and to emphasise the trauma and surreal quality of the events, like the portrayal of war in *Waltz with Bashir*.[19] Soldiers who were interviewed as part of the research for this book, reported that the representations of war in *Waltz with Bashir* actually seemed to them more, rather than less, realistic in comparison to live footage. They explained that only unconventional representation can come close to embodying the extraordinary and bizarre emotions inherent in these horrific events that cannot be compared to anything else, and they can only be understood by those who have experienced them personally. In this sense, the realism of both films inheres in their success in enabling viewers to grasp some aspect of reality that would otherwise be inaccessible.

However, in contrast to *Waltz with Bashir*, the varied documentary aesthetics in *Tower* continually change, shifting between black and white photographic footage of the actual event, contemporary photographic colour footage of the location today, rotoscoped animation based on actors portraying the survivors' experiences and interviews with survivors, to name but a few. Thus, in *Tower* the distinction between animation and photography is blurred from the start, demonstrating the diversity and cross-pollination of documentary aesthetics today, as opposed to the stark contrast in *Waltz with Bashir* that underscores the assumed contradiction between fantasy-animation and fact-photography. It is noteworthy that Maitland described his apprehension about reaching out to survivors with: 'Hey, you don't know me, but I want to make a movie about the worst thing that ever happened to you 50 years ago, and it's going to be a cartoon. Let's talk!'[20] His unease about people's reactions to the portrayal of tragic events in animated form reveals that despite the recent rise of animated documentaries – and the vast range of topics animation now covers – something of animation's assumed link to fiction, childhood, humour and light-heartedness persists.[21] Thus, questions related to the nature of the reality being depicted, and the most suitable means for its truthful portrayal, play a central role in these two films. Similar themes underpin the theoretical basis of *Animating Truth* and the rise of animated documentary in contemporary culture.

Figure I.3 *Tower*, directed by Keith Maitland, 2016.

I will paint a broad picture in order to contextualise this book. While the debates of the twentieth century involved the crisis of representation, it is now less clear where or if any boundaries exist between what is 'real' and what is represented. In today's visual culture with its rapidly changing imaging technologies, the role of the visual requires reconsideration. For example, when people rely on animated gifs and emojis to communicate, they replace their actual physical appearance and facial expressions with simplified, cartooned, clichéd representations. As such, users amplify the role of animation in their daily interactions by using animation to symbolise 'the self' and various modes of self-expression. Similarly, in the era of Snapchat filters, many choose to represent themselves as a cuddly animal, or an airbrushed perfect self, differentiating their actual physical appearance from these online visual portraits. The proliferation of such representations has even developed into 'Snapchat dysmorphia', a surprisingly common phenomena whereby millennials are seeking surgery to help them appear like the filtered, or 'perfect', versions of themselves, thus replicating image-manipulation techniques in real life. In the past, the physical appearance of referents influenced what was deemed to be a realistic visual representation, but today it is no longer clear what is shaping what. The changing relations between imagery and the reality it claims to depict are rapidly transforming. This is the result of contemporary technoculture where omnipresent screens prize visual means of communication and create dual or multiple realms of activity so that the physical domain, and the way it looks, becomes just one among many. The ubiquity and mundane use of non-photographic animated imagery to engage with current realities is also a result of constantly evolving imaging technologies, such as Nvidia's 2018 GeForce RTX graphics chips, which create real-time, highly realistic animation that could be confused with photographic footage. Such technologies blur the boundaries between more traditionally accepted aesthetics of 'the real', like photography, and what animation has become today. Finally, the wider informational media environment of post-truth also contributes to these transformations in visual culture. When information overload prevails, animated imagery, which summarises and simplifies information and processes it through stylisation – even in exaggerated or inaccurate ways – has a growing place in today's visual depictions of actual events. Why not trust animated documentary to portray current events when 'news' falls victim to disinformation, poor images and image manipulation, often resulting in the ubiquitous claim of 'fake news'? Is animation in these cases any less real or credible than alternative depictions?

Realism is the believable articulation of 'the real', highlighting the fact that the status of representations' veracity is in constant flux. What is deemed appropriate and reliable representation is a fundamental motif in documentary studies. Documentary is a genre that emerges in a time of crisis[22] and it is therefore no surprise that documentary is prevalent in today's rapidly changing technological world characterised by post-9/11 surveillance, the refugee crisis, global pandemics, rising nationalism and unstable geo-political alliances, among many others. The continuing interest in documentaries shows that, despite the haziness of their claims to 'truth', there is still a belief that they are a credible way to search for meaning in troubled times. It therefore also makes perfect sense that realism is not only an aesthetic approach but also a political goal that aims to shape realities rather than merely reflect them. Many of the works discussed in this book are cinematic rather than film *per se*. The complexity and multiple uses of animation in contemporary culture demonstrate that animated documentary must be understood in proximity to other disciplines. *Animating Truth* therefore draws together film, art, cultural and media studies, posthumanism, gaming studies, semiotics and philosophy to shed new light on the topic of animated documentary, and underscore the fact that this interdisciplinary analysis benefits from a mix of media and fields.

The goal of the book is to advance the perspectives through which animated documentary is studied by presenting it in a way that differs from previous analyses, and by reaching into other fields of cultural enquiry by examining animation as a visual language that appears in various fields of non-fiction in contemporary visual culture. This ubiquitous use of animation results in its changing status as believable representation in documentary contexts since viewers have become accustomed to receiving factual content in animated form in a wide variety of fields, and they now rely on such content in their daily lives.

What follows includes a theoretical discussion of realism and the evidentiary status of animation through its technological, aesthetic, and narrative uses in contemporary documentary and non-fiction rather than the presentation of a historical model or argument as provided, for example, in Annabelle Honess Roe's excellent 2013 book on the topic. As technological developments change the production and uses of animation in documentary, new theorisations are necessary. Interestingly, although the topic of experimental documentary has received scholarly attention in the fields of contemporary art and journalism, the related topics of animation, digital gaming and virtual culture are often overlooked.[23] At a time when both animation and documentary are changing, they transcend their emergent status as documentary animation cinema, and operate across broader platforms and contexts of digital expression, application and exhibition, thus further underscoring the need for new approaches. Although the scope may be ambitious, by extending the discussion across many disciplines and using a cross-platform analysis, the definitions of both 'animation' and 'documentary' are rethought, and the topic of animated documentary as a dominant form of non-fiction visualisation becomes pertinent to a variety of contemporary debates.[24] The parameters of this research include animated documentaries of physical events, those that focus on virtual realms, and works that reflect upon the combination of documentary and animation in varied ways.[25]

In today's visual culture, animation is at an interesting turning point, poised between fiction and fact, perhaps combining the two. We are confronted with ubiquitous animated images, videos and gifs, for example, on smartphones, computers, in airplanes, doctors' offices, schools, and many more, that are all used uncritically to represent or express real events, feelings, processes and interactions. This makes the topic important and timely. Animation's traditional association with fiction has become less dominant, but that does not mean that animation is no longer a form of escapist, artificial, spectacular and often child-oriented entertainment.

In-flight safety films offer an example of the unique capabilities of animation to cross between fact and fiction. They are a useful means of conveying information and dealing with critical issues in a way that is clear, memorable and easily digestible.[26] However, they also highlight the possibility of a plane crash, yet no one reacts to them as such. Why? The reception of in-flight safety films illustrates how viewing animated non-fiction can isolate the cognitive internalisation of information (how to act in an emergency) from the emotional reaction (panic) to that information. Since animation is still associated with fantasy, it can be stylised in a particular way to appear friendly and unthreatening. In the context of international travel, which caters to various cultures and languages, animation more readily conveys the message. In today's globalised, highly visual culture, new forms of imagery are needed to handle the avalanche of data we continually encounter, and thus the animation of data (or data visualisation) becomes a regular feature of contemporary information culture. In other words, animation today embodies a double allusion to both fiction and fact.

This mixture of fact and fiction is also apparent in recent fictional entertainment-based animated films that involve varying degrees of factual data visualisation. This is the case in Pixar/Disney's *Inside Out* (2015),[27] which personifies emotions and artistically visualises the structure of the mind, innovatively if loosely based on different psychological theories and neuropsychological findings.[28] Similarly, Disney's *Ralph Breaks the Internet* (aka *Wreck-It Ralph 2*) (2018)[29] visualises the internet in a spatial–urban–architectural mode for the sake of the film's narrative. Since animation excels at visually simplifying complex systems and processes, it is used pervasively as a means of data visualisation. These cinematic examples demonstrate how fiction, fused with factual infographic data visualisation, is expanding the borders between fact and fiction. This is particularly evident in animated documentaries.

Ralph Breaks the Internet is also a compelling example of the multi-layered use of animation in visual culture in which multiple realms are each depicted in a different animated style: (1) the supposedly non-animated 'real' world of people using the internet; (2) the users' online animated representations portrayed as box-headed avatars; (3) the well-known fictional animation characters, such as Ralph himself or Disney's princesses. It is worth noting that the princesses are quickly redressed less formally, thus distancing them from their fictional worlds through visual choices that represent them in a more contemporary manner, and thus also bearing closer resemblance to the internet users depicted in the film, and to the viewers themselves. Comparably, *Ralph Breaks the Internet*'s illustration of Twitter resembles the bluebirds in Disney's 1937 *Snow White and the Seven Dwarfs* (1937),[30] merging recognisable fictional animated imagery of the past with contemporary animated data visualisation and popular logos. This complex use of animation blurs the difference between the representational choices most often used in the past and thus differentiates between the fantastical animated world and the live-action portrayal of the viewers' world. In earlier examples, such as *Mary Poppins* (1964)[31] and *The Water Babies* (1978),[32] the break between fantastical worlds and the so-called 'real' was well-defined and stylistically unmistakable. By contrast, there is a merging of multiple animation styles that symbolise the physical 'real' world of the viewer, viewers' online virtual actions and fantastical content, complicating the many uses, significations and meanings of animation. *Ralph Breaks the Internet* is but one example.

Although 'animated documentary' may still sound like a contradiction in terms to some, animation has often been used to illustrate what cannot be seen. Animation literally means 'bringing to life' and thus it expands the aesthetics of documentary by giving life to sounds and images that cannot be recorded, such as memories, subjective perspectives, nano-particles, scientific visualisations, censored events or non-physical online realities. Animation extends the boundaries of moving-image visual culture by providing the visual means for what may otherwise remain unrepresentable. In response to scholarly debates regarding the definition of animation, I define animated imagery as 'movement only visible on-screen', as explained in detail in Chapter 2. Some may criticise this definition for sidestepping the specificities of animation techniques and styles. I agree that specific styles matter, but they are not the emphasis of this book since they are as varied as the animators' methods and levels of creativity. Rather than a semantic argument, this purposely broad view of animation emphasises the fact that it can no longer be considered from a narrow perspective since it is now visible in innumerable cultural fields. This definition aims to incorporate the many technologies and fields relevant to the topic, such as digital and data-driven art, gaming, architectural, scientific or forensic visualisations, virtual reality (VR) and augmented reality (AR) research, to name just some of the often under-represented fields in animation studies; it also includes the wider philosophical questions that these related disciplines raise. In other words, this definition intentionally expands the research paradigms involved in animated documentary analysis in an era when animation has become truly 'pervasive', to borrow from Suzanne Buchan's 2013 aptly named book.[33] *Animating Truth* is not about sub-cultures of animation such as anime, which clearly influenced the above-mentioned films of Tarantino and Folman; rather, it explains how animation has been reinterpreted on a global mainstream level, becoming ubiquitous in everyday visualisations. The book focuses on the rise, and growing truth-value, of non-photorealistic animation in the form of diverse new digital imaging techniques that function as a stylistically diverse alternative to photorealism, with a shifting relationship to photography as the more traditional documentary aesthetics.

I recognise this is a broad visual paradigm shift in contemporary visual culture. Since animation can only be seen on screen rather than in the physical realm, it is ostensibly distinguished from photography: the argument follows that animation is generated while photographs are recorded. However, my central topic is the relation between the concurrent rise of animated documentary and of animation in digital media; my focus is on the technocultural context for the increase in, and changing believability of, animated images. Taken together with my definition of animation as movement that is visible only on screen, I situate screen culture and the moving-image nature of animation centre stage and choose to focus on the complex convergence of animation and photography, rather than on the historical correlation between animation and other visualisation methods, which would require an entirely separate project.

In fact, my definition points to the complex contemporary convergence of animation *with* photography. Digital imaging technologies blur distinctions between animation, live-action cinema, synthetic performances, post-production visual effects and digital puppetry, among others. For example, James Cameron's *Avatar* (2009)[34] used photorealistic synthetic CG sets/environments into which live performances recorded through MoCap were incorporated, complicating the connection between the animated on-screen world, the off-screen world and the physical referent. This is also the case with animation techniques such as machinima and real-time animation, which all modify the relationship between animation and photography, and between animation and physical referents. These developments in image-production technologies potentially alter animation's evidentiary status and resulting believability, requiring new theorisations of the topic and redefinitions of animation.

Animating Truth focuses on animated documentary because it is here that an enduring tension exists between animation as it was most often used in the past, in relation to fiction, and its growing use today, in non-fiction. Aware of such culturally conceived biases, many animated documentaries supplement novel animated imagery with supporting materials associated with documentary conventions, for example, audio interviews and/or photography, in an apparent effort to garner viewer acceptance. Understanding the proliferating uses of animation and its uncertain position as credible visualisation demands a reconsideration of the status of animation in contemporary visual culture.

Animation was considered a niche field, mostly associated with the film industry and the Disney/Pixar animation studios. However, it has expanded exponentially into myriad non-fiction fields, and is now ubiquitous – on our GPS systems,[35] in film, journalism, forensics, online gaming, data and scientific visualisations and more.[36] Full coverage of these multiple and varied non-fiction fields is beyond the scope of this research, but wider visual culture acts as a context for the rise and reception of animated documentary. That said, my focus is on how technological innovation affects documentary aesthetics, using all the above to expand the way animation is analysed and to understand its implications for theorisations of documentary. The widespread use of non-naturalistic animation in varied fields of non-fiction suggests that the signification of 'the real' is no longer tethered to photorealism, and that animation may be deemed real and believable even if its appearance belies this.

Today animation is often used to depict data, to re-enact events, such as in journalistic coverage, or to simulate scientific theories. It is sometimes referred to as theoretical photorealism since it is based on accurate data and calculations but involves unobserved occurrences or otherwise un-visualisable content, for example, phenomena in space.[37] In short, animation is often used by authoritative sources to depict 'dry facts'. This diminishes a sense of the constructedness of animation and encourages uncritical acceptance. Many viewers watch animated sequences without questioning what they actually depict, how, why they were made to appear as they do, and what truth-value they actually contain. In an era of rising populism and politics often based on misinformation, this has huge implications. Animated images that might be attention-grabbing and easily stylised for maximum effect are capable of informing and documenting, but can also sway opinion through their emotional impact. Despite animation's complex history, does its enduring relation to childhood entertainment infantilise serious content, as in Disney's 1941 *Seven Wise Dwarfs*,[38] which features the dwarfs of Disney's 1937 *Snow*

White and the Seven Dwarfs marching to the post office in order to purchase war savings certificates? Or does the discrepancy between so-called 'childish' aesthetics and potentially difficult subject matter strengthen our reactions of horror, as could be argued about the animated adaptation of Martin Rosen's 1978 *Watership Down*?[39] How may this influence viewers ethically and politically? Non-photorealistic animation can aestheticise violence and overshadow urgent content, relegating actual horrific events to the realm of fantasy. Alternatively, animation can do just the opposite by jolting viewers out of their numbness, provoking a fresh response to, and new insights into, a well-worn topic. Animation can also be seen to anonymise people by portraying protagonists without identifying them. Sometimes it may be a conscious choice to respectfully conceal the identity of individuals, especially when their traumatic experiences are depicted; but it can also have potentially dangerous ethical ramifications when real people are visually reduced to cartoons. This book examines the complex uses and possible implications of using animation in non-fiction, demonstrating that an in-depth analysis is needed in order to properly understand this newly proliferating form of imagery increasingly used to depict and consequently shape current reality.

All these examples illustrate the changing relations between ideas of reality and representation, or, in other words, how the concept of realism has been transformed. The collapse of what we consider realism into what we regard as fantasy is a central motif in this book and a recurring theme in documentary discourses. Animation embodies this transformation of aesthetics of 'the real' in an era preoccupied with the nature, importance, depiction and misuse of facts.[40] Rethinking what animation is and how it is used in documentary today is a perfect lens through which to examine bigger current questions about the credibility of imagery, image referentiality and realism. The three parts of the book are organised according to these themes: (1) the evidentiary status of non-photorealistic animation as documentary imagery; (2) the relationship of animation to technoculture, and (3) disputing the aesthetics of 'the real'.

STARTING POINTS: THE EVIDENTIARY STATUS OF ANIMATION AS DOCUMENTARY IMAGERY

Dai Vaughan claims that '[w]hat makes a film a "documentary" is the way we look at it; and the history of documentary has been the succession of strategies by which filmmakers have tried to make viewers look at films this way'.[41] The active role of the viewer as arbiter of what constitutes a documentary thus becomes paramount, shifting the focus to the viewer's persuasion and experience of the work. What, then, establishes an image's truth-value? Part I sets the stage and introduces the topic of animation's truth-value by providing historical and theoretical context. Chapter 1 takes up the question of animation's recent proliferation and current technoculture's effects on the believability of documentary imagery in relation to shifting conceptualisations of visual realism. Here I engage with various philosophical, technological, ontological and epistemological aspects of the immense discourse on realism but mainly approach the theorisation of realism from the perspective of art, film and animation studies in order to examine its relation to animation and the fluid credibility ascribed to changing documentary aesthetics. Chapter 2 discusses animation's changing relation to photography and the evidentiary status of imagery in an era of mixed realities.

The assumed 'artificiality' of animation rests on its comparison with photography since animation is generally seen to break the physical link with, and likeness to, the represented physical object embodied in analogue photography. Part I, therefore, begins by focusing on the relation between animation and photography, the contested yet persistently leading aesthetic of documentary. Through numerous debates in media and animation circles, it has become clear that in digital culture, the binary between animation and photography no longer holds;[42] Chapters 1 and 2 focus on the blurred and fluid boundaries between the two. Nonetheless, a certain duality between animation and photography acts as a structuring element throughout the book, and is used to highlight two major criteria for the acceptance of photography: I use visual realism in Chapter 1 and indexicality in Chapter 2 to analyse how they relate to contemporary animation in documentary and its apparent believability.

The discourse surrounding indexicality, which relates to questions of evidence and is grounded in photography, has been highlighted by theorists such as Rosalind Krauss, James Elkins and Mary Ann Doane. Indexicality has been used in theorisations of photography and animation before, but I engage with it in a new way that includes both the trace and deictic index in relation to physical and virtual realities. Thus, what is offered is an expanded view of animation's evidentiary status and the translation of off-screen movement into on-screen movement. Placing this work within discussions of visible evidence, as well as debates surrounding new imaging techniques by media, science and technology theorists, I refer to a *post-photographic documentary aesthetic* in Chapter 2. In contemporary non-fiction animation, the logic of the analogue photographic evidentiary status based on the indexical trace of the physical referent (as a link between the image and what it represents) is maintained, though not the photographic aesthetics of photorealism that rely on resemblance to the physical referent. In other words, the importance of the link between image and physical referent persists while new and diverse aesthetic styles are used;

this is post-photographic since it relies on evidentiary assumptions of the past while incorporating new visualisation techniques and styles.

To illustrate the above, a 2018 advert for the online world of *Second Life* (*SL*) features an image of fairly realistic-looking animated avatars kissing, and includes a credit that states 'photo by . . .'. Is this indeed a photograph, as the credit asserts? Does this image function in the same way that a photo may have done in the past, as a document? If so, what exactly does it document? Is it a photo of an animated scenario, or is animation now photographic because it can both achieve hyper-realistic imagery and capture footage of what happens on screen, capturing people's actions that are now regularly mediated through screens and graphic interfaces? Does this animated image/photo depict an actual experience, albeit not in the physical world but rather online; and can such differentiations be upheld in an era of mixed realities? The many questions that such visualisation raises demonstrate the blurred boundaries that exist today. Not only are real and virtual experiences combined in these contexts, the aesthetics used, how they are defined and how this influences viewer expectations regarding the imagery's functions and believability are also unclear. New debates are thus clearly essential.

ANIMATION AND TECHNOCULTURE: THE VIRTUALISATION OF CULTURE AND VIRTUAL DOCUMENTARIES

Which aspects of today's realities require new visualisation methods, and why? *Animating Truth* is a study of the credibility of contemporary animated documentary in a culture that is increasingly virtualised and dependent on animated information. Part II examines present developments in technoculture, focusing on how these changes have influenced our understanding of evidence, documentation and new uses of animation in documentary. The current virtualised computer culture uses various forms of animated imagery to render abstract data and processes visible. As daily actions are increasingly screen mediated, new visual representations are needed to construct and transmit information in these digital-virtual worlds, as discussed in Chapter 3. This not only explains animation's proliferation, but also impacts the reception of similar imagery in non-fiction contexts. Additionally, in today's mixed realities, the physical itself becomes less central in virtualised digital culture since a substantial part of contemporary experience takes place through computerised interfaces and networked platforms based on code, rather than material actions.[43] Chapter 3 engages with central elements of digital culture that have changed the face of contemporary realities, which now include both the physical and the virtual. This part of the book includes the theorisations of virtuality, the changing characteristics of screen culture, the shifting status of materiality in digital culture and the growing field of online games.

It is worth clarifying how gaming fits into the topic of animated documentaries. The field of gaming has grown exponentially in recent decades. Beyond being the leading form of popular entertainment today, it has evolved into a rich and complex medium that encompasses vast fields ranging from experimental art, scientific research, military training, education, journalism, economics, psychology, anthropology and more. Gaming's main visual language is animation since animation enables moving imagery that can respond in real time to user input, essential for an interactive, screen-mediated field. It is no surprise, then, that animation studies, and film studies more generally, have in recent years begun to overlap with the field of gaming. This is evident, for example, in the proliferation of games symposia, scholarly interest groups for animation and video games and the fact that many film festivals also include gaming or VR segments. Clearly, there has been a cross-pollination and blurring of boundaries that reflect the larger phenomenon whereby fields of study traditionally situated within film, such as animation, have extended beyond these confines and now require a reconsideration of their traditionally demarcated disciplines. Furthermore, the huge popularity of gaming means that animation production has been developing exponentially within these industries and, as a result, is also influencing research into animation. These production methods include virtual puppeteering, MoCap or machinima, which are all relatively new and have emerged from – or are closely related to – the gaming industries that, in turn, have influenced the production of animation and animated documentary today. The relation of contemporary games to the field of animation is, therefore, characterised by a growing convergence. It would be impossible to cover the vast current research into gaming, and that is not the intention of this book. However, approaching gaming from the perspective of animation and documentary leads to new insights into the changing uses, production and interaction between the fields, shedding new light on wider issues in contemporary digital culture.

Animating Truth discusses pictorial worlds that use real-time animation to reflect interactive user input, such as online games, which are fully animated realms of virtual activity. The book's innovation inheres in the claim that animation now functions in a way that departs from previous theorisations. It is no longer a visual interpretation for personal states of mind (as in *Waltz with Bashir*), nor does it only depict events that could have been photographed but were not (such as *The Sinking of the Lusitania*, 1918).[44] Rather, it is a direct capture of these virtual worlds as they appear to users. An example is *Molotov Alva and His Search for the Creator* (2007)[45] about an avatar's/player's experience in the *SL* online world.

I have identified three kinds of virtual documentaries that demonstrate the new uses and need for animation as a documentary language in today's virtualised culture, and blur the boundaries between today's mixed realities: (1) documenting animated virtual game realities (Chapter 4) by following the historical progression of animation in games and offering a more up-to-date historical perspective to animated documentary that is not provided by existing historical surveys; (2) the in-game/virtual depiction of physical realities that show how the two converge (Chapter 5); (3) the use of virtual aesthetics, such as interactivity and real-time animated visualisation, to depict physical events for example in documentary games and VR documentary simulations (Chapter 6). These three categories demonstrate the immense influence of wider technocultural characteristics on changes to animation in documentary production and theory.

THE POWER OF ANIMATION: DISPUTING THE AESTHETICS OF 'THE REAL'

Part III discusses the status of truth as a discourse, and assesses the potential political and ethical implications of using animation in contemporary documentary, taking into account viewers' increasing familiarisation with such visualisation in non-fiction contexts. What exactly are the aesthetics of documentary, and how do they relate to current debates surrounding realism and post-truth? Since 'the real' is always mediated through representation, realism is always based on convention. Whereas theorists such as Bill Nichols and Michael Renov have engaged with the problematic nature of documentaries and their fluid forms of realism, these questions persist and have become more urgent in an era of post-truth. Documentary studies are a way to approach the relation between reality and realism as representations of 'the real', by questioning what aesthetics of 'the real' were, what they are and what they may become. Since realism is linked to credibility but also relates to viewers' understanding of reality as shaped by documentary representation, this has various ethical, epistemological and political ramifications. This book engages with the technologised realities and 'realism(s)' of today and aims to understand the forms that realism takes in animated documentaries.

Animation's relation to realism is complex. On one hand, animation's break with visual realism is a recurring theme that supposedly problematises animation's realism and truth-value. It is, therefore, necessary to engage with visual realism, or mimesis, in order to understand how it relates to animation's growing visibility in contemporary documentary. This is the technological context for such developments and consequent changes in theorisations of realism and documentary today (Chapter 1). On the other hand, realism extends beyond mimesis and photorealism. Therefore, animation's relation to, and referencing of, the reality portrayed has been defined in various ways.[46] Stephen Rowley, for example, lists various types of realism in animated depictions, including visual and aural realism, as well as the realism of motion, narrative and character, and social realism.[47] Most commonly, animation has been used in documentaries to depict personal perspectives, feelings and memories that cannot otherwise be represented in a moving image, thus exposing the myriad ways in which reality can be seen, and demonstrating diverse perspectives. Examples include *Snack and Drink* (1999)[48] about autism; *An Eyeful of Sound* (2010)[49] about synaesthesia; *Last Day of Freedom* (2015)[50] about battle-worn soldiers and mental health, and many others. But what about other contemporary phenomena that shed new light on the realism inherent in animated depictions, both as an aesthetic and as a sociopolitical goal? Viewing this issue from a technological and philosophical perspective means taking account of the wider cultural context that explains changes in what constitutes a believable representation of 'the real'. Accordingly, this book argues that the proliferation of non-naturalistic animation in contemporary documentary and non-fiction is a consequence of various defining features of the networked information age. Contemporary phenomena such as virtuality, interactivity, machine vision, surveillance culture, wearable technology and the augmentation of human perception, the changing role of the physical in digital culture, new representational technologies, and suspicion of information in an era of 'fake news' make animation in documentary realistic in new ways, despite its non-mimetic appearance. Examining the unresolved and multiple nature of realism illustrates the many potential forms it might take in animated documentary. Rather than producing a defence of animation's realism, however, my goal is to track the ways in which that realism may be positioned in relation to past and new theorisations of what amounts to an ever-changing framework of representation.

As animation flourishes in documentary and covers challenging content such as war (*Samouni Road*, 2018, about Gaza),[51] the plight of refugees (*It's Like That*, 2003,[52] about refugee children, and *1000 Voices*, 2010,[53] about asylum seekers), two salient questions arise: (1) Will animation de- or re-sensitise viewers, as discussed in Chapters 7 to 8? (2) If animation's links to actuality are fluid and often unclear, will viewers potentially believe nothing or everything? And can these binaries be broken down as representations continually change, as argued in Chapter 8? I propose that animated documentaries are masked, self-reflexive documentary aesthetics that can both hide and expose information, foregrounding issues of truth verification versus disinformation, and thus acting as a perfect form of representation for the zeitgeist. Does the power of animation lie in its ability to evoke reflection and critical contemplation in viewers, and what must occur for this potential to persist?

Although documentary conferences and film festivals have included screenings and sessions devoted to animated documentary since the early 1990s, academic research on animated documentaries has only recently gained momentum.[54] Earlier research was mostly written from the perspective of animation rather than documentary studies.[55] Since 2011, however, a number of publications and events may be considered indicative of a growing academic interest in the topic.[56] As this interest expands, so too does the range of questions being asked. To date, research into animated documentaries has included the history of animated documentary,[57] contemporary production, animation's ability to stand in for un-photographed or un-photographable footage of real-world events, and its inclusion of subjective or fantastical accounts of a range of experiences.[58] By contrast, this book offers a new look at animated documentaries as a sign of the times.

Focusing on the technocultural reasons for this shift towards pervasive animation in documentary aesthetics, *Animating Truth* specifically examines how the virtualisation of culture fundamentally impacts the rise and theorisation of animated documentaries. It is impossible to comprehend animation's use and role in documentary today without considering the technological modifications in new media that have reshaped the contemporary world and the wider depiction of non-fiction information.[59] By evaluating animation's intersection with varied fields of contemporary visual culture, my goal is to expand the theoretical scope for analysis of animation as documentary visualisation, and introduce new approaches to the meaning and impact of the animated image in our time. Animation serves as an interface for our increasingly complex relations to data and thus becomes part of a constitutive change in ways of seeing one's world. As imagery of 'the real' and theorisations of realism change, competence in image analysis is essential to enhance our understanding of how technologies have changed realities, referentiality and reception. *Animating Truth* is an invitation to engage with – and a critical tool for understanding – emerging forms of informational representation and their wide-ranging epistemological and ethical implications, as they shape and are shaped by contemporary culture.

Notes

1. *Kill Bill*, film, directed by Quentin Tarantino (USA: A Band Apart, 2003).
2. For theorists who engage with animation's assumed fictitious nature, see Ward, 'Animating with Facts', p. 294; Skoller, 'Introduction to Special Issue', p. 207; Cavell, *World Viewed*, p. 167. See also Holliday and Sergeant, *Fantasy/Animation*. It

may be argued that animation has concerned itself with the 'real' for a long time and in varied ways, as seen in examples such as Norman McLaren's *Neighbors* (1952), Disney's *Seven Wise Dwarfs* (1941), which featured the *Snow White* (1937) dwarfs marching to the Post Office to purchase wartime savings certificates, or Jimmy Murakami's *When the Wind Blows* (1986), based on Raymond Briggs's graphic novel of the same name. Esther Leslie's *Hollywood Flatlands: Animation, Critical Theory and the Avant-Garde*, about animation, politics and modernist criticism is an important book to mention in this context. That said, these examples (1) emphasise the blurred boundaries between the representational, the fantastical, the educational, interpretive, documentary, propaganda, etc., and (2) are the minority in a field that has more commonly been considered niche, associated with fantasy and researched under that guise.
3. *Human Growth*, film, directed by Eddie Albert (USA: Wexler, 1947).
4. *Family Planning*, film, directed by Les Clark (USA: Walt Disney, 1968).
5. *VD Attack Plan!*, film, directed by Les Clark (USA: Walt Disney, 1973).
6. *Vertigo*, film, directed by Alfred Hitchcock (USA: Alfred J. Hitchcock Productions, 1958).
7. *Waltz with Bashir*, film, directed by Ari Folman (Israel, Germany and France: Bridgit Folman Film Gang, Les Films d'Ici and Razor Film Produktion, 2008).
8. The film won a Golden Globe Award for Best Foreign Language Film, an NSFC Award for Best Film, a César Award for Best Foreign Film and an IDA Award for Feature Documentary, and it was nominated for an Academy Award for Best Foreign Language Film, a BAFTA Award for Best Film Not in the English Language and an Annie Award for Best Animated Feature.
9. *Ryan*, film, directed by Chris Landreth (Canada: Copperheart Entertainment, 2004).
10. *Persepolis*, film, directed by Marjane Satrapi and Vincent Paronnaud (France and Iran: Celluloid Dreams, CNC, France 3 Cinéma, The Kennedy/Marshall Company and Région Ile-de-France, 2007).
11. *Chicago 10*, film, directed by Brett Morgan (USA: Consolidated Documentaries, Participant Productions, River Road Entertainment and Curious Pictures, 2007).
12. This is not to say that animated documentaries do not have an earlier history, they do. However, in a wider cultural sense, the rise in mainstream attention that animated documentaries received after *Waltz with Bashir* was unprecedented. See for example, Scott, 'Inside a Veteran's Nightmare'.
13. See Balsom and Peleg, *Documentary across Disciplines*.
14. In attempting to offer a critical overview of an emerging and increasingly complex field, it is useful to begin by considering how definitions of animated documentary have changed and shifted. For more on attempts at definitions see Skoller, 'Introduction to Special Issue', p. 208.
15. Sofian, 'Truth in Pictures'.
16. It is important to clarify that I am not discussing techniques such as cel animation or experimental film whereby the relationship between the photographic

aspect and the capture of physical referents may vary. Instead I refer to the manner in which photography was used in the more traditional sense within documentary contexts as a counterpart to the recent rise of non-photorealistic animation as documentary imagery.

17. For more information see Honess Roe, *Animated Documentary*; Morag, *Waltzing with Bashir*; Stewart, 'Screen Memory'; Peaslee, 'It's Fine as Long as You Draw'; Murray, 'Waltz with Bashir'; Landesman and Bendor, 'Animated Recollection'; Stav, 'Nakba and Holocaust'; Ten Brink, 'Animating Trauma'; Land, 'Animating the Other Side'; Kraemer, '*Waltz with Bashir* (2008)'; Bolaki, 'Animated Documentary'.
18. *Tower*, film, directed by Keith Maitland (USA: Go-Valley and ITVS, 2016).
19. This may explain the use of the film *Waltz with Bashir* as part of a training program of Natal, Israel's Trauma Centre for Victims of Terror and War. Therapists specialising in war trauma watch the film to better understand their patients' experiences and use it as part of their treatment. See Schäuble, 'All Filmmaking', p. 211.
20. Ebiri, 'Keith Maitland'.
21. The longstanding assumption that animation must stand in complicated relation to documentary stems from a persistent bias associating animation with fantasy and humour, due to the worldwide dominance of American commercial animation. See Strøm, 'Animated Documentary', p. 48.
22. Lind and Steyerl, *Greenroom*, 12.
23. See, for example, Lind and Steyerl, *Greenroom*; Cramerotti, *Aesthetic Journalism*.
24. See Bruckner *et al.*, *Global Animation Theory*.
25. This research examines a broad range of visual material from around the world, including North America, Australia, Europe, Asia and the Middle East, and looks at examples from the fields of art, film, gaming, scientific visualisation and news coverage. Although I aim to introduce a corpus of relevant works, this is not intended as a geographically comprehensive review or an attempt to form a 'typology' of contemporary animated documentaries. The examples chosen illustrate specific points of my argument about animation's changing role in today's visual culture and its ramifications in the field of documentary.
26. For more information on animation's ability to create memorable and captivating depictions see Ostherr, *Medical Visions*, p. 35.
27. *Inside Out*, film, directed by Pete Docter (USA: Walt Disney and Pixar, 2015).
28. Judd, 'A Conversation'.
29. *Ralph Breaks the Internet*, film, directed by Rich Moore and Phil Johnston (USA: Walt Disney, 2018).
30. *Snow White and the Seven Dwarfs*, film, directed by David Hand (USA: Walt Disney, 1937).
31. *Mary Poppins*, film, directed by Robert Stevenson (USA: Walt Disney, 1964).
32. *The Water Babies*, film, directed by Lionel Jeffries (UK and Poland: Ariadne Films and Studio Minitaur Filmowych, 1978).
33. Buchan, *Pervasive Animation*.

34. *Avatar*, film, directed by James Cameron (USA: Lightstorm Entertainment, Dune Entertainment and Ingenious Film Partners, 2009).
35. GPS stands for Global Positioning System, a satellite-based navigation system.
36. This raises the murky issue of 'non-fiction', and points in turn to the blurred boundaries between documentaries, journalistic, informational, educational, and even propaganda works. Although the terms 'fiction' and 'non-fiction' are usually associated with literature, in this study 'non-fiction' refers to an expansion of the documentary field to include other disciplines that engage with factual content and its varied visual representations, such as journalism, serious games, data and scientific visualisations. For more on contemporary documentary practices that reach across media and disciplines see Erika Balsom and Hila Peleg, *Documentary across Disciplines*.
37. See Warburton, 'Goodbye Uncanny Valley'.
38. *Seven Wise Dwarfs*, film, directed by Richard Lyford (Canada: Walt Disney, 1941).
39. *Watership Down*, film, directed by Martin Rosen (UK: Nepenthe Productions, 1978).
40. Clearly, animated documentaries have an earlier history, as described by Annabelle Honess Roe in her excellent book *Animated Documentary*, but the recent rise of the sub-genre and the current technocultural setting shed new light on the use of animation in non-fiction contexts.
41. Vaughan, *For Documentary*, pp. 84–5.
42. For more on these debates see Paul Wells (*Basics Animation*, p. 12); Lev Manovich (*Language of New Media*, p. 295; *Software Takes Command*, p. 294); Alan Cholodenko ('"First Principles" of Animation', p. 99); Tom Gunning (2014: 37–53).
43. This is not to say that reality is always solely physical. Chapter 1 deals with aspects of this discourse although it is a vast ontological-philosophical realm of research that is beyond the scope of this study. Nonetheless, in a culture mediated by screens where interactivity is possible, the role of the physical and one's physical surroundings constitute one sphere of action among many, as discussed in Chapters 3–4.
44. *The Sinking of the Lusitania*, film, directed by Winsor McCay (USA: Jewel Productions, 1918).
45. *Molotov Alva and His Search for the Creator*, film, directed by Douglas Gayeton (USA: Submarine Channel and VPRO, 2007).
46. In 1997, Paul Wells outlined four modes of categorisation for animated documentaries and their relationship to reality: the 'imitative mode', the 'subjective mode', the 'fantastic mode' and the 'post-modern mode'. See Wells, 'Beautiful Village and True Village'. In 2004, Eric Patrick proposed four different categories of animated documentaries' capacity for storytelling: The 'illustrative structure' depicts 'events based on historical or personal evidence'. The 'narrated structure' uses a script and voiceover to narrativise the events represented. The 'sound-based structure' also relies on an aural link to the depicted reality but, unlike the narrated structure, uses found or unmanipulated sound recordings as a basis for representation. The 'extended structure', in line with Wells's

postmodern approach, emphasises subjectivity, the symbolic, the surreal and metaphoric in order to consider traditional storytelling techniques in animated documentaries, expanding the epistemological possibilities through creative approaches. See Patrick, 'Representing Reality'. In 2011, Honess Roe proposed three key functions of animated documentaries: Mimetic and Non-mimetic Substitution, and the Interpretive Function. See Honess Roe, 'Absence, Excess and Epistemological Expansion', p. 215. For more information on categorisations of animated documentary see Honess Roe, *Animated Documentary*. Whereas these theorisations demonstrate animated documentary's varied relation to the reality it depicts, the emphasis in this book is on the technocultural context of this question that sheds new light on the topic.
47. Rowley, 'Life Reproduced in Drawings', pp. 70–1.
48. *Snack and Drink*, film, directed by Bob Sabiston (USA: Flat Black Films, 1999).
49. *An Eyeful of Sound*, film, directed by Samantha Moore (Canada, Netherlands and UK: Sapiens Productions, 2010).
50. *Last Day of Freedom*, film, directed by Dee Hibbert-Jones and Nomi Talisman (USA: Living Condition, 2015).
51. *Samouni Road*, film, directed by Stefano Savona (France and Italy: Dugong Production, Picofilms and Alter Ego Production, 2018).
52. *It's Like That*, film, directed by SLAG (Australia: SLAG, 2003).
53. *1000 Voices*, film, directed by Tim Travers Hawkins (UK: Ctrl.Alt.Shift, 2010).
54. It is important to mention Otto Alder, program curator of international animation festivals and director of the animation programme from 1993 to 2007 at the Leipzig Festival, where he established the animated documentary (Animadoc) section. For more information on film festivals that spearheaded the inclusion of animated documentaries in their repertoire, see Strøm, 'Animated Documentary', p. 48.
55. Earlier research on the topic, between the years 1997 and 2005, includes (in chronological order): Wells, 'Beautiful Village and True Village'; DelGaudio, 'If Truth Be Told'; Renov, 'Animation: Documentary's Imaginary Signifier'; Strøm, 'Animated Documentary'; Patrick, 'Representing Reality'; Ward, *Documentary*.
56. A partial list of these would include the following. In 2011, Suzanne Buchan and Jeffrey Skoller edited a special issue of *Animation: An Interdisciplinary Journal* dedicated to animated documentary. Also in 2011, the first conference on animated documentary, 'Animated Realities' (a collaboration between the University of Edinburgh, Edinburgh College of Art and the Edinburgh International Film Festival) was organised by Jonathan Murray and myself in Edinburgh, including presentations by over forty international speakers. In 2012, filmmakers Alys Scott-Hawkins and Ellie Land set up the regularly updated Animated Documentary blog (www.animateddocumentary.com, accessed 4 August 2020) about the production and research of the sub-genre. In 2013, Annabelle Honess Roe published the first scholarly monograph on the topic of animated documentaries. In 2016, the *International Journal of Film and Media Arts* was launched with a special issue dedicated to animated documentary and the Society for Animation

Studies blog also focused on the topic. In 2016 and 2017, the Royal College of Art in London hosted 'Ecstatic Truth', a symposium on animated documentary. The first anthology of essays on the topic, *Drawn from Life*, edited by Jonathan Murray and myself, was published by Edinburgh University Press in 2018.

57. Wells, 'Beautiful Village and True Village'; DelGaudio, 'If Truth Be Told'; Strøm, 'Animated Documentary'; Patrick, 'Representing Reality'; Honess Roe, *Animated Documentary*; Mihailova, 'Before Sound, There Was Soul'.
58. Annabelle Honess Roe describes how animation is used to represent subjective experiences and memories, for example, and Lilly Husbands explains animation as a means of representing otherwise un-photographable science. See Honess Roe, *Animated Documentary*; Husbands, 'Meta-physics of Data'. It is also important to note that varied representational devices, such as writing, painting and drawing, can also depict what is unrepresentable in photography. However, the uniqueness of animation is movement, which bestows a sense of 'life' and a form of realism to the representation. This topic will be further developed in Chapters 1, and 4–6.
59. This research thus refers to the technologised world and digital cultures available to those with access to lithium-based internet technology. The fact that billions of individuals around the globe still have no access to these technologies only accentuates the potential schism that may develop between those with and those without such technology, based on the changes I claim are developing in ways of perceiving, believing and conceptualising realities through changes in visual information. This topic also raises additional environmental, economic, political and cultural issues associated with global capitalism – issues that are crucially important but beyond the scope of this project.

Part I

Starting Points: The Evidentiary Status of Animation as Documentary Imagery

CHAPTER ONE

Why Now?

In tandem with the huge proliferation of animated documentaries since 2008, there has also been a significant rise in the creative practice, academic study and distribution of this medium.[1] This chapter explains why this shift in visual culture is occurring *now*, and how it shapes viewership.

Most obviously, a framework of representation purporting to tell 'the truth' raises questions about what that truth is, what reality is being presented, how, and why; and what (if any) modes of communication can potentially make viewers accept the work as credible. This leads us to realism, which, as the articulation of 'the real', or what is accepted as a believable delivery of 'the real', is central to the study of the documentary field.[2] Critic and filmmaker John Grierson's primary definition of documentary was 'the creative treatment of actuality',[3] which notes the tension between 'aesthetics' or 'representation' and 'reality' or 'actuality'. The growing use of animation in documentary can be considered as one particular form of creative treatment of actuality, similar to countless other experimental and aesthetic choices used in documentary production.[4] Nonetheless, although animated documentaries have proliferated, there is still a tension between sceptics who view animation in documentary as inaccurate and less 'real', and those who take a more inclusive view of the field, celebrating its expansion and diversity.[5] Animated documentaries' break with visual realism – photorealism – and their unclear ontological and epistemological nature, which influences their perceived credibility and evidentiary status, present a conundrum. Despite the digitalisation of culture and widespread changes in the photographic field and its credibility (not to mention its long history of fabrications), familiar paradigms that privilege photography as a documentary aesthetic still persist.[6] Considering animation's shifting relationship to photography, I emphasise the crossover but also use the dichotomy between the two to analyse two benchmarks for the acceptance of photography: visual realism in this chapter, and indexicality, the link between image and referent, in the next, in order to understand how they shape contemporary animation's apparent believability. There are three questions to consider: (1) What makes the animated documentary a contemporary or new phenomenon regardless of its older historical roots?[7] (2) How does contemporary technoculture make viewers more comfortable with non-photorealistic animated imagery as valid visualisations of non-fiction? (3) What do these shifts in non-fiction imagery reveal about the conceptions of visual realism and changing notions of truth?

ANIMATED NON-FICTION AS A CONTEMPORARY PHENOMENON

Animation has become 'the dominant contemporary media', claim Esther Leslie and Joel McKim.[8] In this context and in order to explain the recent emergence, popularity and reception of animated documentary and non-fiction, the expanding trend of animated news is a valuable case study. Animated news is a close cousin of animated documentaries, but due to its more mainstream visibility and ostensibly authoritative journalistic sources, it is also more familiar – and hence, potentially more acceptable – to viewers. A good example is *TomoNews* by Next Media Animation (NMA), a Taiwan-based broadcasting channel launched in 2009 that produces more than thirty computer-animated dramatisations of news events every day, ranging between the humorous and the informational. Imagine, for example, that you have just watched their animated coverage of Donald Trump's 2017 trip to Japan, which included depictions of Trump sashaying in a kimono and varied

Figure 1.1 Screenshot of Donald Trump and Xi Jinping sunbathing, *TomoNews*, 2017 (source: https://www.youtube.com/watch?v=RS6KSIwzgtg, accessed 4 August 2020).

news channels portrayed as babies crying in a playpen or his visit with Xi Jinping of China at Mar-a-Lago, where the leaders are depicted sunbathing in a swimming pool together. Is this a joke, or is it the current incarnation of the news? It may actually be up to you to decide.

The demand for documentaries to present facts while their very ability to do so and their integrity are simultaneously thrown into doubt reflects contemporary culture in which the surplus of continuous information has created pressure for exposure and demand for knowledge along with a persistent sense of uncertainty and distrust. Indeed, as noted earlier, Dai Vaughan claims that '[w]hat makes a film a "documentary" is the way we look at it; and the history of documentary has been the succession of strategies by which filmmakers have tried to make viewers look at films this way'.[9] So what is it about contemporary culture that explains this current state of affairs, and what is the viewer's role in this context?

There are various ways to define the contemporary,[10] but what is clear is that the new information and communication technologies of the internet, and the ensuing shift from analogue to digital, play a central role in the post-1989 era.[11] The rise of digital culture informs our understanding of the present since it generates an ontological anxiety about the loss of the real through the loss of indexicality,[12] which was previously understood as a more reliable marker of 'the real' in analogue photographic imagery.[13] This anxiety about the stability of truth claims and representations also explains truthiness, which was Merriam-Webster Dictionary's 2006 word of the year, reverberating as a sign of the times.[14] The American Dialect Society defines truthiness as 'the quality of preferring concepts or facts one wishes to be true, rather than concepts or facts known to be true'.[15] Similarly, 'post-truth', the Oxford Dictionary's 2016 word of the year, has been defined as 'relating to or denoting circumstances in which objective facts are less influential in shaping public opinion than appeals to emotion and personal belief'.[16] The tension between knowledge and belief means that the role of the viewer as judge of what is believable becomes central, both in documentary spectatorship and in today's mediascape more generally. This shifting notion of 'truth' is evident, for example, in Wikipedia's criterion for its entries to be defined as 'true enough', thus embodying today's unclear degree of epistemological diligence.[17] Something acknowledged as 'true enough' merely means that the viewer/user has been convinced, accepting the information given and choosing not to follow the next link for additional information, perspectives and analysis. As defining aspects of the fake-news era, these concepts illuminate the current tension between knowing and not knowing, and the rising role of the belief and persuasion of the viewer. *TomoNews* highlights this situation and the related tangential debates.

Initially targeting the Hong Kong and Taiwanese markets, by 2010 NMA's *TomoNews* videos averaged more than 4.1 million hits a day, making NMA the second-most-watched news channel in Hong Kong.[18] Since 2015, the channel's audience has expanded to US and English-speaking world markets.[19] Most of the videos incorporate animation, giving *TomoNews*'s online broadcasts a visual edge. The use of animation enables the visual inclusion of what is not photographed, and it plays an important marketing role as the website can claim that you will 'never watch boring news again'.[20] From conception through production to publication, each news story uses motion-capture technology and takes less than four hours to create in animated form, accentuating the development of once time-consuming animation techniques that now allow a rapid, unlimited visualisation of rolling content.[21]

Despite their evident local success, *TomoNews*'s signature tactics have been frequently criticised and still engender an ambivalent reception that illustrates the nature of many contemporaneous debates and assertions regarding the in-between nature of animated non-fiction. In 2010, Howard Kurz, *Washington Post* media critic and host of CNN's *Reliable Sources*, remarked, 'Let's not confuse a bunch of cartoons with what people in the news business do'.[22] However, *Next Media*'s Jimmy Lai argued that, despite certain details appearing visually inaccurate, the images in much of *TomoNews*'s output were based on other media reports, and thus maintained the 'integrity of the news' and the content depicted.[23] How far details may be changed and representations altered while still maintaining a sense of content integrity is a question that resonates with Grierson's definition of documentary as the 'creative treatment of actuality'. This is all the more relevant today, when fake news and documentary hybrids such as docudrama, mockumentaries and reality TV have become conventional, and shows such as *The Colbert Report* (2005–14),[24] *The Daily Show* (1996–present),[25] or *Last Week Tonight with John Oliver* (2014–present)[26] emphasise the growing inclination towards infotainment, the convergence of information and entertainment. In fact, comments on CNN reportage on NMA reflected unfavourably upon the sensationalism of many other (non-animated) news channels, claiming that 'news is a joke', 'journalism is dead anyway' and that 'facts are a thing of the past'.[27] It is hardly surprising, then, that animated news has emerged out of such widespread allegations against the regular channels, changing conceptions about what realism may actually be.

In a discussion of documentary practice in the field of contemporary art, Maria Lind and Hito Steyerl suggested that there is an ongoing 'documentary quest for ever more authentic representations of the real'.[28] As technologies and forms of representation change, mediations of realities change as well, and convention and trust outweigh privileged access to any truth claim. Paul

Ward explains that realism is a difficult concept to determine because it is often understood in relative rather than absolute terms. Realism can refer to the capturing of 'a close approximation of ... the world exterior to the representation'; or it can be judged against what 'has already gained the status of the "realistic" (a particular form of cinematography, for example)'.[29] In other words, realism can be understood in terms of its relation to direct vision, technology or ideology, and thus realistic representation must always be in flux.[30] In this regard, it is important to distinguish between realism as an aesthetic style, and realism as a social-political objective in varied forms of representation; this is discussed further in Chapters 7 and 8.[31] Different forms of realism embody different relationships to 'the real'; thus cultural paradigm shifts and the trends that generate them dictate what is deemed believable and why. This is why it is important to understand current technocultural developments, and explore how they help transform ideas about imagery's credibility.

Before photography, the representation of realities was obviously not mimetic, but rather constituted varying degrees of resemblance to visual appearance through a vast range of styles. Stylised representation was thus 'real enough' in order for it to be believed and accepted as true. Nevertheless, with the advent of photography, imagery of the past slowly came to be seen as less precise, and therefore less credible; photography achieved the privileged status of being an accurate and believable aesthetic. The realism of photography and cinema were more convincing as documentation than painting because they captured reality and produced imagery that was closer to what the human eye perceived. André Bazin, who examined the ontology of the photographic image, claimed that film, more than the other plastic arts, was destined to realism because of its photographic basis, which transfers 'the reality from the thing to its reproduction'.[32] For Bazin, the photographic image is, therefore, 'the object itself'.[33] However, like Grierson's definition of documentary, Bazin also noted that realism was only attained through artifice since 'some measure of realism must always be sacrificed in the effort of achieving it'.[34] The remarkable similarity between the world seen through the camera lens and the photographic image is photography's major achievement, creating a fascination with mimetic technologies and their spectacularly successful illusionism, demonstrating that resemblance is indeed a central aspect of documentary aesthetics.[35] However, while realism has been prominently related to the mimetic representation of the physical, mimesis, mimicry and illusionism have been criticised as naïve, misleading, insufficient representations of reality. Ever since Aristotle's discussion of mimesis and later *trompe l'oeil* modes of realism, attempts to touch the real have raised questions about imitation and the deception inherent in hyper-real copies.[36] Realism cannot, therefore, be reduced to mimesis. The difficulty of relinquishing these cultural assumptions about mimesis are deeply ingrained, despite photography's long history of being manipulated and the debates in recent decades about its evidentiary value.

The complexity of realism is indicated by the myriad philosophical questions it raises, from the ontological to the epistemological, moral, semantic, physical, technological and many more.[37] While realism as the depiction of 'real life' may be regarded as an attempt to present objective reality without interpretation, this assumes that such a reality exists as ontologically independent of human perception – a view deemed naïve by numerous philosophical and political thinkers.[38] Nonetheless, as an aesthetic, realism is often based on precise and accurate visual representation of the physical world, also called 'realistic', 'naturalistic', 'mimetic' or 'illusionistic'. Mimesis is understood to be an imitation of the real world, which assumes that the 'real' world looks a certain way, that it is physical and therefore photographable. The strong correspondence between visual realism and mimesis highlights the reliance on materiality, and human perception of it, as a basis for actuality and naturalism. In other words, visual realism is a form of visual aesthetic, based upon the way in which the human eye perceives the physical world.[39] John W. Yolton describes an 'epistemic shift' emphasising objects as they are perceived and accentuating the perceiving subjects and representation, just as both documentaries and truths are currently defined by the degree to which they persuade viewers.[40] The rise of animated non-fiction expresses contemporary changes in documentary representation, the central role of the viewer as arbiter of truth claims, and a break with visual mimesis; but it also exposes contradictions regarding the acceptance of animation and photography, thus exemplifying the transforming nature of realism.

TomoNews is important not only because it demonstrates how extensive the contemporary use of animation is for non-fiction purposes, but also because it exposes some of the central theoretical themes related to popular reception of this kind of animated work and, through a discussion of changing believability, current conceptions about visual realism. This form of news reportage is described as 'a bunch of cartoons', 'lacking in accuracy', and possessing 'comical overtones'.[41] Even *TomoNews* itself alludes to animation's historical association with entertainment and humour by stating on its website that 'TomoNews animates without fear or favour. If you do something stupid, you're going to get animated', suggesting that animation is automatically linked to foolishness.[42] Ironically, however, the NMA news agency was also fined for *TomoNews*'s coverage being overly graphic and exposing themes that might offend and wrongly influence viewers.[43] If *TomoNews*'s animated news sequences are so obviously fictitious and comical, how can they also be seen as 'true enough' to offend and/or influence public opinion about the so-called 'real'?

The way in which animation is used and received depends on changing cultural conventions. On one hand, a 2012 study about the effects of animation in news reports found that animated formats neither enhance nor dampen news credibility.[44] On the other hand, around the same time, an NMA official said 'we're still being laughed at', while also predicting that by 2012 their clips would not only be known abroad as amusing novelty animations, but would become the norm for TV news.[45] Such predictions have come true: the use of animation in factual reporting is increasingly a journalistic norm, not a marketing scam or quirky choice (think of the animated visualisations and simulations often used on the news as re-enactments of unfilmed events, like military operations, for example). NMA has, for instance, worked with the BBC and Reuters on joint animation projects, mostly on the topic of refugees, in order to maintain anonymity and provide 'a strong sense of visual metaphor about the experiences they've had, but can't film'.[46]

The increasing visibility of animated journalism is an important case study to consider for the rise of animated non-fiction. Since 2012, *The Guardian* website, which is more mainstream and authoritative than NMA, has included animated reports about the lawyer Mohammad Mostafaei's battle against executions of juveniles in Iran in *One Iranian Lawyer's Fight to Save Juveniles from Execution* (2012)[47] and in 2013 it featured the video animation *Guantánamo Bay: The Hunger Strikes*,[48] based on personal statements of detainees at Guantánamo

Figure 1.2 Screenshot from *One Iranian Lawyer's Fight to Save Juveniles from Execution*, The Guardian and Sherbet, 2012.

Bay. In 2014, as part of *The Guardian*'s coverage of human trafficking in the Thai fishing industry, the online newspaper produced an exposé consisting of long animated sequences based on testimonies, titled *Globalised Slavery: How Big Supermarkets are Selling Prawns in Supply Chain Fed by Slave Labour* (2014).[49] Significantly, *The Guardian* was involved in the *production* as well as the online hosting of these videos, demonstrating increasingly widespread professional and popular acceptance of animation as another form of legitimate news reportage and investigation.

When considering the evolution of animated documentaries, their relation to journalism and their perceived truth-value, it is useful to turn to Winsor McCay's *The Sinking of the Lusitania*,[50] made in 1918, which is considered the first animated documentary. The film portrays the torpedoing of a British ship by a German submarine in 1915. Depicting an event that was not recorded photographically, McCay, a newspaper illustrator, used animation to provide visual imagery based on survivors' testimonies.[51] Like the examples from *TomoNews*, the obvious creative and experimental aspects of *The Sinking of the Lusitania* complicate its assumed documentary status. As Annabelle Honess Roe notes, this film turns journalism into hyperbole through the use of intertitles and its depiction of the 'cold-hearted and callous' Germans celebrating the event.[52] In addition, the imaginary perspective is heightened by animation of an underwater scene of frightened fish avoiding the approaching torpedo. Paul Wells concludes that the film shares characteristics with tabloid journalism and propaganda, rather than the more objective approach expected of conventional documentary.[53] Thus the classification of such films fluctuates between fiction and fact.

However, the film also includes an intertitle stating 'from here on you are looking at the first *record* of the sinking of the Lusitania'.[54] In *The Sinking of the Lusitania*, the allusion to a 'record' of the events indicates that animation was considered suitable as a live-action technique for news imagery.[55] In fact, the graphic style of the animation mimicked newspaper illustrations of the period,[56] demonstrating the changing conventions of non-fictional visual presentation. Nevertheless, this example was considered insufficiently believable, so additional markers of authenticity were used to enhance the credibility of the representation. The inclusion of still photographs of well-known personalities who perished on the ship – often used in contemporary animated documentaries as well – weakens the assertion that animation was accepted as documentary representation since photographs were added to justify the work's documentary status.

Remarkably, almost 100 years after *The Sinking of the Lusitania*, many animated documentaries still use the same tactics, incorporating photographs, stylising the animation according to photographic aesthetics, including audio recordings that link to the physical world portrayed (compensating for the perceived artificiality and/or lack of indexicality of the animation), and documentary conventions such as voice-overs and interviews. In *The Guardian*'s animated videos, for example, photographs are used as in *The Sinking of the Lusitania*, but tellingly, they illustrate nothing of the content described, nor do they offer any substantive corroboration; they merely show the faces of people identified as the protagonists. The truth-value of these photographs relies on assumption and convention, and is linked to the habitual identification of photography with visual evidence. This highlights the transitional status of animation today: increasingly used as a credible form of news reportage and non-fiction, yet still subject to longstanding assumptions about the existence of more worthy, credible and established modes of documentary representation. Animation's intermediate status, as an aesthetic linked both to fiction and fact, is what marks its uniqueness in today's visual and informational landscape. This is also exemplified by *TomoNews* and the expansion of its once-ridiculed visual strategies. Animation's traditional popular association with fiction is less dominant since it is increasingly being used in non-fiction contexts while, simultaneously, it is also widely employed as a form of escapist spectacular entertainment that has yet to be fully accepted as a credible visual means of depicting factual information. The transformation of animation from imagery associated with fiction to an aesthetic increasingly used in non-fiction is thus ongoing, and this transitional status not only holds the promise of animation's potential power, but also elucidates its contemporary newness.

This begs the question: since animation was used in early non-fiction filmmaking for education and propaganda purposes, though in a somewhat marginalised capacity,[57] what makes today's animated documentaries 'new' or 'contemporary' as an aesthetic of factual information?

First, Boris Groys explains newness as context-based and demarcated as recognisably different from what went before.[58] In other words, the new and contemporary is novel, original and unusual, something that breaks with past traditions, making us notice and reflect upon them, and signalling a shift from past to future. The 'in-between' or contradictory nature of animated documentary, so obvious in the reception of *TomoNews*, indicates this shift by breaking with past conventions of documentary aesthetics based on photography, and introducing a new form of representation to the field.

Second, the recent staggering growth in the quantity of animated documentaries demonstrates that the collective creative recourse to animated modes and imagery is more characteristic of the current era than any earlier period. The numbers are indicative: although the Internet Movie Database (IMDB) website lists only twelve animated documentaries by July 2019,[59] Wikipedia listed fifty-three items under the category Animated Documentary

Films;[60] the Doco-anim channel on the Vimeo website, created in 2012, listed 172 videos;[61] the Animated Documentary Facebook discussion group created in 2011 had almost 2,000 members by 2017;[62] and a search for the keywords 'animated documentary' on YouTube in January 2017 led to 12.6 million results.[63] The search results included the documentary *Life, Animated* (2016)[64] about how Disney animations helped an autistic boy learn to communicate with the outside world; an *Animated Introduction to Cancer Biology*(2013),[65] labelled as a 'full documentary', which teaches how cancer forms and spreads; and *Nowhere Line: Voices from Manus Island* (2015),[66] an award-winning documentary about asylum seekers detained in Australia, based on interviews with them. Whereas Honess Roe defines animated documentary as any film that: '(1) has been recorded or created frame by frame; (2) is about *the* world rather than *a* world wholly imagined by its creator; and (3) has been presented as a documentary by its producers and/or received as a documentary by audiences, festivals or critics',[67] Sheila Sofian has defined it more expansively as 'any animated film that deals with non-fiction material'.[68] The online search results for 'animated documentary' reveal a leaning towards much wider and inclusive definitions. Moreover, the category 'animated documentary' comprises works that engage differently with animation: in *Life, Animated*, animation is used as the topic of the film and as a way to depict subjective perspectives; in *Animated Introduction to Cancer Biology* it is deployed as an informative/educational visualisation of scientific content; and in *Nowhere Line* it provides visual imagery for audio interviews. This elucidates both the various ways animation is engaged in non-fiction as well as the blurred boundaries between documentary and different fields of contemporary non-fiction.

Animated documentaries are also seen in numerous display contexts today: in public spaces,[69] cinemas,[70] museums and art galleries,[71] on artists' personal websites, video sharing websites,[72] databases specifically devoted to animation and animated documentary works,[73] and, as discussed, even on online newspaper websites.[74] Since animation is also closely linked to gaming, some animated documentaries are experienced as interactive simulations, or displayed as artworks in both the physical space of art galleries and as in-game virtual art.[75] The sheer numbers and omnipresent visibility of the sub-genre speak volumes about its current prominence and shift from its earlier cultural status.

Third, whereas past uses of animation in non-fiction often relied on animation's traditional association with fiction and fantasy, as seen in the inclusion of the fish's perspective in *The Sinking of the Lusitania*, today there are far fewer such allusions. This is seen in recurring uses of animation to re-enact unfilmed news events, such as the visualisation of complex political or financial processes, where no allusion is made to animation's historical use in fictional or humorous contexts.

Fourth, the technological evolution of animation production essentially changes the nature of animation, creating a real-time newly indexical visual language, as explained in Chapter 2. This distinguishes today's animation from that of earlier periods, making it truly contemporary and qualitatively different, and thereby altering animation's relation to documentary theorisations and evidentiary status.

Two trends in visual culture explain animated documentary as a rising cultural phenomenon and highlight some of the reasons why animation is sufficiently, if not yet comprehensively, mainstream in contemporary non-fiction contexts. The first concerns the demise of the traditional documentary aesthetic, that is, the photographic and the mimetic, while the second addresses the consequent rise in non-mimetic forms of visualisation, such as animation.

CONTEMPORARY TECHNOCULTURE AND CHANGING DOCUMENTARY AESTHETICS

Diminishing Truth-Value: The Demise of the Photographic and the Mimetic

In 2015, artists David O'Reilly and Kim Laughton published a series of incredibly vivid 'computer-generated images' on their blog, Hyper Real CG, under the title 'You Won't Believe These Images Aren't Photographs'. Indeed, you shouldn't, since they were in fact photographs.[76] This did not prevent multiple media outlets being fooled, and using the photographs as examples of hyperrealist, CG images. O'Reilly and Laughton commented on the inability to decipher the source of images and on the need for scepticism *vis-à-vis* photorealism today. This gains in relevance when one considers that graphics and animation can now achieve hyper-realistic visuals that can easily be mistaken for photographic footage.

Photography's perceived strength lies, *inter alia*, in mimesis (the accurate capture of the physical appearance of referents) and indexicality (the physical connection between a sign and its referent, often associated with analogue photography). These characteristics link non-fiction photographic depictions to the world beyond and, consequently, have often been used in documentaries to validate their claims to truth. The assumed 'artificiality' of animation often rests on its comparison with photography, but the notion of 'artificial' suggests a contrast with 'natural' or 'not artificial'. However, something can only be deemed fictional in comparison to that which is not deemed so. Once the two are confused, any comparison of the two as opposites fails; thus, it is essential to identify and examine photography as the focus of comparison with animation in documentary. Despite the pervasive presence of photography in everyday life, and its long-privileged claim to documenting the 'truth', in fact its authenticity (as opposed to animation's so-called artificiality) has been questioned and theorised in many different ways. Photography's status as a privileged mode of conveying information has been in decline since the 1970s and this process has accelerated with the development of digital photography.

Image production, rendering and manipulation have become so advanced that viewers are fully alert to possible manipulations. The website created by Uber software engineer Phillip Wang, www.thispersondoesnotexist.com, offers an interesting example. It is based on artificial intelligence (AI), which can create ultra-realistic photos of non-existent people. The uncanny feeling it generates in viewers reinforces the mistrust of images that may have once seemed credible. Whereas in this case the fabrication is highlighted by the website's name, it is obvious that even if something looks real, viewers are aware that it may not be. Another telling example is the spread of DeepFake videos, in which the facial expressions of a target person are animated by using a source actor. The fact that it is now possible to create realistic-looking footage of people saying something, whether they actually said it or not, has huge ramifications in this era of fake news.[77] New video and audio manipulation tools enabling real-time facial capture and re-enactment re-render manipulated videos in a highly photorealistic fashion, casting doubt on photographic footage of people's actions and speech. These tools are becoming increasingly sophisticated and their implications are alarming because photographs, and visual mimesis in general, cease to be reliable criteria of truth, and the reliability of contemporary photography is diminished.

In other words, although 'credible' visual documentary depictions are traditionally more often associated with photography, current cultural, epistemological and technological circumstances paint a more complex picture. In the context of animation as an alternative to photography in documentary representation, once photography's believability is destabilised, so too is animation's artificiality. Awareness of the widespread manipulation of images influences the changing believability of representations that do not strive for visual mimesis or transparency; this is evident in the rising interest in precarious aesthetics. Gemma Sieff asks:

> Why is it that images we trust are now most often the lowest resolution or blurred images, so-called poor images? Perhaps it's because there seems to be a trade-off inherent in these images: a compromise on quality (resolution, composition, focus) for speed and authenticity.[78]

Although Sieff is clearly referring to photography, her remarks are relevant to animated documentaries. Depending on the degree of its blurriness and/or stylisation, this kind of so-called 'poor' image could potentially be placed on a continuum between photorealism and the abstract, since it differs in varied ways from mimesis. Non-mimetic 'deficient' images could signify referents in varied ways, looking nothing like them yet still evoking credibility, which is exactly the case in animated documentaries. To conclude, photography's diminished truth-value as a documentary aesthetic makes way for new aesthetics of documentary and non-fiction that break with photorealism, such as animation.

Interesting Alternatives: The Rise of Non-Mimetic Imagery in Non-Fiction

A parallel trend that explains the contemporary rise of non-photorealistic animated documentary is the growing visibility of non-fiction imagery that does not resemble human perception and is not based on mimesis. The more familiar modes of representation are, the easier they are for viewers to accept, and the more realistic they seem. I will elaborate on this in Chapter 8. This rising visibility of varied representations also contributes to greater acceptance of animated documentaries. Several aspects of contemporary visual culture explain why animation is less associated with fiction, increasingly received as a familiar and therefore less artificial form of representation in non-fiction. These are set out in the paragraphs below.

Changing image-production technologies have resulted in animated works being produced by non-professional animators who no longer require the artistic and technological know-how once necessary for creating such imagery. These emerging animation techniques offer greater flexibility and lead to wider experimentation with animated visuals, enriching and broadening their usage and contributing to their growing visibility. *The Late Show with Stephen Colbert* (2015–present),[79] for example, began experimenting with Adobe Character Animation in 2016, enabling the creation of real-time animation in which characters interacted with live actors.[80] Thus, Stephen Colbert hosted cartoon versions of Donald Trump and Hillary Clinton, which were created in an expressive, nimble fashion that allowed for improvisation. Although far from being the first example of combining animation with live action, getting used to interacting with cartoons (especially in non-fiction contexts such as politics) blurs the boundaries between animated and non-animated worlds, and the difference between live footage and animated visuals – between fact and faction.

Documentary and surveillance culture have intensified viewers' expectation of imagery and visual footage of reported events since omnipresent cameras have accustomed viewers to visual footage even if involving mundane events or such that would probably not have been captured in the past. But in cases where such imagery does not exist, animation is ideal since it enables the unlimited visual representation of events without the limitations inherent in photography. As is the case with *TomoNews*, animation can generate quick visualisations that cut production costs, grab viewer attention, and liberate news media from the need to acquire actual footage, while providing visual materials in situations where footage may be expensive, dependent on copyright, dangerous, censored or otherwise hard to obtain. This reinforces the increasingly significant role played by animation.

The information age has seen a rise in visual representations of information. The exponential growth in available information engenders new ways of presenting and receiving that information.[81] Animation condenses and simplifies vast amounts of data and, as constructed moving imagery, is ideal for the representation of processes and change. Additionally, through its infinite array of styles, animation is a potentially attention-grabbing feature in an era of data saturation. It links animated non-fiction with data visualisation and thus manages the overabundance of information; this also helps to explain the enhanced visibility of animation today. Moreover, as viewers are surrounded by information that is mediated by screens and visualised in many different ways, there is a marked shift away from mimetic and naturalistic modes of representation. Animation is central in data-driven artworks and interfaces based on code, blurring the boundaries between art, digital and interactive design and infographics.[82] Digital media artists such as Aaron Koblin or Chris Milk, who create data-driven art, often overlap with 'information visualisation experts', as the Wikipedia page defines them, showing a growing intersection between the fields.

Machine vision is a phenomenon defined by Paul Virilio that has developed into the entire field of computer vision.[83] It occurs when machines that are independent of human operators 'see', record and then share data with other machines, until an image of the world is constructed entirely outside human experience. Drones, surveillance cameras, robotic vision and AI, products of infographic software and data visualisation that lead to a process of computer-aided design, all fall within this category. Although new sources of imagery may expand visuality – as I claim is the case with animation – what occurs for viewers as a result of machine vision is 'synthetic vision, the automation of perception … [a] doubling of the point of view'.[84] Or, as James Bridle describes it, a growing reliance upon technology and value of big data where we model our minds on the understanding of computers and the belief that automatically generated data can provide an understanding of the world (and appropriate solutions), actually results in incomprehension due to the impenetrability of these synthetic minds.[85] What are the ramifications of having become accustomed to seeing the world through perspectives other than our own and how does this contribute to the debate about shifting notions of aesthetic/visual realism? As technologies that do not require human operators proliferate, viewers become accustomed to receiving information and images of reality in styles that do not reflect human vision, yet are accepted as believable, neutral and objective – sometimes more so than styles that are human vision-oriented, such as photorealism, since the machine is seen as a more neutral witness to events and therefore more reliable.[86]

Exploring focus points that are not human-centred relates to the way technology influences realities and our perception of them. Seeing events as visually translated by sensors, satellites and automated surveillance involves viewing reality differently to humans. Such depictions of reality cause a 'splitting of the reality principle' through a 'splitting of viewpoint, the sharing of perception of the environment between the animate (the living subject) and the inanimate (the object, the seeing machine)'.[87] Machine vision relates to naturalism and so-called transparency as a realist aesthetic because it questions the superiority of mimesis, which reflects only human vision.[88] These new representations of reality, like non-photorealistic animation, take on myriad visual forms.

Neil Harbisson, who has an antenna implanted in his skull, is a good example.[89] Born colour-blind, Harbisson's antenna functions as a sensory organ that enables him to feel and hear colours as audible vibrations inside his head, creating an extended range of colours that includes those invisible to the human eye, such as infrareds and ultraviolets. This may sound like a strange sci-fi scenario but it is not. Harbisson, a British Catalan artist, is the first person to be officially recognised as a cyborg by a government.[90] Since wearable technology enables the augmentation of human perception, recent technological developments (whether connected to our physical body or not) have transformed all of us into cyborgs. Importantly, this questions what 'human vision' is today, and consequently what visual realism is becoming. The technical progress that augments and/or changes the conception of 'human', and consequently what human perception is and could become, relates these philosophical ideas to contemporary technological realities and to fields such as trans-humanist or post-humanist studies, which suggest that technology will engender a perceived progression from human, through trans-human, to post-human.[91]

Accordingly, within the discussion of shifting notions of visual realism, the recent theoretical-realist turn has sparked lively discussions and new directions in philosophical debates about realism. These include speculative realism, object-oriented ontology (aka Triple O) or object-oriented philosophy (OOP), which overturns forms of philosophy that privilege human beings, claiming that the human–world relation is insufficient as a basis for ontology and epistemology. Using different approaches, these philosophical debates place non-human phenomena at the centre of being, on a more equal footing with humans, thus de-centring human thinking in philosophy.[92] Realism based on object-oriented rather than human-oriented perception, may seem far-fetched. However, as the Internet of things (IoT) and AI develop and attract attention, non-human perspectives and observation become increasingly relevant. Film historian Thomas Elsaesser uses similar ideas in his theorisation of what he terms 'new realism' films, in which objects have agency that aims to produce a perceptual insecurity, which develops into ontological doubt.[93] These ideas are highly relevant to the study of animation, which is recognised for its ability to give agency to objects and non-human subjects, thus creating elaborate worlds that are different from those of the viewer, yet nonetheless consistent. Thus visual realism can no longer be based on human perception, for we are increasingly exposed to images of the world that break with and expand beyond human vision. Although a more detailed consideration of these ever-expanding fields of thought falls outside the scope of this book, it is important to consider how changes in the way human perception – and the status of the human – are understood and in turn influence the way the world is represented.

Viewing the world through non-human visual perception questions how things are 'really' seen, and thus how they 'should' be depicted if the perceiver is no longer human and the criterion for 'realistic' representation is not solely the human eye. This demonstrates how varied stylisations may be, and already are, and how they are considered believable in many different contexts. Thus, we see the rise of non-photorealistic imagery as increasingly acceptable imagery being used to engage with factual content, even if it doesn't look 'real', as is the case with animation.

The virtualisation of culture requires omnipresent screens through which all digitally virtual actions and spaces are mediated. Screens thus act as a portal into 'other', extended aspects of today's real, which is increasingly a mixed reality combining the virtual with the physical. Daily actions are progressively screen mediated, and new visual representations are needed to construct and transmit information in these digital-virtual worlds. Under these conditions, can we expect naturalistic depictions in mixed realities that involve non-material digital virtual phenomena? This and similar questions are explored in Chapter 2. Many aspects of contemporary digital virtual culture appear only on screen and, since they reflect actions and input, must include moving imagery such as animation. Thus, participants/inhabitants of digital worlds are increasingly familiar with an assortment of moving imagery that represents their actions and presence in online realms, and diverges from photorealism because the actions and places depicted are not physical. I will elaborate further on these ideas in Part II of the book and explain how the growing virtualisation of culture illuminates the rising role of animation as a signature visual language of twenty-first century realities.[94]

What are some of the implications of these shifts in contemporary nonfiction aesthetics on animation's relation to realisms and truth claims?

REALISM(S), TRUTHINESS AND ANIMATION

Having reviewed the main technocultural elements that contribute to changes in documentary aesthetics, it becomes clear that as suspicion of photorealistic imagery grows, non-fiction imagery, such as animation, expands and becomes more diverse. We have also seen the extent to which viewers are accustomed to receiving factual information in a variety of visual forms that both enhance the familiarity and acceptance of those forms and contribute to the validity of non-photorealistic animated imagery as valid visualisations of non-fiction.

Animation's current status is interesting *because* of its contradictory nature: while the use of animation in non-fiction is a growing trend, elements of photography's status as the privileged aesthetic of non-fiction endure. Animation is therefore both increasingly used *and* persistently questioned as a visual language. This paradoxical state emphasises the status of animated documentaries as new, and highlights their 'in-betweenness': a break between past and future, somewhere between fact and fiction, or a convergence of the two. Indeed, animation was used in non-fiction in the past, but the sharp increase in its production and dissemination, and the proliferation of interest groups and academic research on the topic, place the sub-genre centre stage. We see a persistent trend within contemporary theorisations of realism that fluctuates between mimesis and the search for novel experimental imagery capable of revealing and exploring 'the real' in varied ways. Realism is multiple and fluid, and animation can no longer be regarded as non-realistic.

This chapter examined visual realism based on mimesis; the following chapter engages with indexicality and discusses definitions of contemporary animation in an era of mixed realities. Why are these such important issues to contemplate? Because we live in an increasingly visual culture where, due to technological developments' reliance on screens, visual imagery has gained vast influence. Within this context, colossal shifts are occurring in relation to the epistemological status of imagery that viewers may be neither fully aware of nor adequately equipped to manage. By focusing specifically on animation as a contemporary phenomenon, I aim to shed light on these changes and propose tools with which to rethink the surrounding debates and possible ramifications.

The fluctuating relation of images to referenced reality recalls Jean Baudrillard's theories of simulations, simulacra and hyper-reality, in which the hyper-real world of simulations suggests that images are signs of nothing but themselves, reducing truth and reality to a game of representation, and obliterating the division between reality and unreality.[95] This echoes current debates about the trustworthiness of non-fiction images and their link to the reality they claim to present. Whereas *TomoNews*, for example, is open about its use of animation, this is not always the case, and the relationship between representations and realities is blurred even further. In 2011, the UK's ITV channel premièred a new prime-time investigative show *Exposure* (2011–present),[96] which attracted more than one million viewers. The first of six documentary episodes focused on the former Libyan leader Colonel Gaddafi's links with the IRA (Irish Republican Army).[97] The documentary used clips of shaky camera footage, captioned 'IRA film 1988', which claimed to show the IRA shooting down a British Army helicopter using Libyan weapons.[98] However, a small number of viewers who recognised the hoax exposed the fact that the footage was CG imagery from someone's gameplay experience of *Arma II*, a tactical shooter game.[99] Thus, animated documentation of game experiences masqueraded as photographic footage of the physical. An ITV spokesman claimed that the network had the correct footage of the event, but because of 'human error' the video game footage had been incorporated in the editing process instead.[100] So, either the editors, like so many unsuspecting viewers, could not decipher the imagery's source, or they made an intentional decision to use game visuals that looked 'real enough' to deceive viewers. This example epitomises the unclear truth status of images, rattles the fundamental believability of documentaries, and destabilises viewers' trust in visual representation. Thus Baudrillard's theorisations are reinforced, and the declining truth status of mimetic representations explained. In this sense, the acceptance of animation as equally authentic (or inauthentic) as any other imagery explains the growing uses of animation in non-fiction today.

However, the relationship between Baudrillard's theories and current visual culture is noteworthy for its contradictions: the absence of any reality, the implosion of meaning of mediatised imagery, and the resulting passivity of viewers are all difficult to accept as characteristic of the twenty-first century, again highlighting the complex status of imagery today. First, what Baudrillard deems as the collapse of meaning and the loss of reality leads him to describe passive audiences whose sole purpose is entertainment.[101] Although audiences today may be desensitised due to an avalanche of imagery, certain images still evoke public outcry and a demand for political action, and since the internet mediascape is interactive, viewer/users are highly active in today's participative culture.[102] Second, the labyrinth of signs that Baudrillard describes as characteristic of postmodernism has led to the view that images substitute for reality and lead to its loss. However, today there is renewed interest in that reality, and in the signs that both indicate and influence it.[103] In today's uber-visual, computerised mediascape, images are used as a way to depict and shape reality, as seen in the 2010 Wikileaks release of the Collateral Murder video footage or the 2014 release of Islamic State (ISIS) videos of beheadings. Such examples offer a 'message' to America in the form of evidence of actions taken to avenge US intervention in the region. Images have not lost their significance, but rather persist as meaningful representations. Whereas postmodern theorists such as Baudrillard saw reality as image and the simulacra as the replacement of actual reality with one that is virtual, today's technologically based digital-virtual realities become *part of* reality rather than an effacement of it. This will be discussed further in Parts II and III.

Multiple 'realisms' and decoupling the believability of images from any clear criteria do not automatically signify the loss of reality or significance of representation; rather they suggest there are new aspects of visual culture that must be taken into account. Viewers' stance towards images, and images' potential to shape world views and the actions that result from them, bring the discussion back to conceptualisations of truth such as truthiness and post-truth. If the visual no longer has clear evidentiary status, representation relies on belief, persuasion and trust rather than on the expectation of gaining definitive knowledge from the visual. This opens new avenues for what realism may mean in representation. Lúcia Nagib and Cecília Mello, who engage with the multiple nature of realism in audiovisual media, suggest the more elusive notion of 'reality effects', which create a physical and emotional impact upon viewers.[104] Reality effects are not new. Patricia Aufderheide recalls that John Grierson and Robert Flaherty, the forefathers of documentary, both anchored documentary to a tradition of realism that 'creates the illusion of reality for the viewer. Thus, realism was not an attempt to authentically capture reality but an attempt to use art to mimic it so effectively that the viewer would be pulled in without thinking about it.'[105] The idea of a 'reality effect' is obscure at best, but it gains importance when trust in the visual as linked to the referent is destabilised. Such new theorisations of realism extend beyond the realms of the visual, expanding the potential variety of non-fiction imagery, and are based on viewers' general experiences with the aim of persuading them. What potentially influences viewers' ideas about an image being 'true enough', or persuading them in ways that merely pull them in 'without thinking'?

Two considerations are important: animation's changing cultural uses and migration from a predominant centrality in fiction and fantasy to non-fiction contexts, and viewers' familiarity with animation and its preconceived associations. With so much information being transferred visually, viewers have become adept at reading visual messages at a glance and picking up visual cues. That said, speed does not equal interpretation, and acknowledging a visual message does not mean critical contemplation. Although today's visual culture has produced viewers accustomed to saturation levels of visual imagery, they do not necessarily take the time or have the tools to analyse how these messages were constructed, or why. Although viewers may indeed notice excessively flattering filters and failed touch-ups in celebrities' doctored photos, the same is not necessarily true for non-photographic imagery that can be stylised in endless ways with messages designed accordingly; this makes the manipulations and ideological incentives for representational choices less evident.

The Guardian's coverage of human trafficking in the Thai fishing industry (2014) offers a useful example: the slave trader resembles a typical Disney villain, such as Hades from *Hercules* (1997) and Jafar from *Aladdin* (1992), especially in the sneering expression and heavily lidded eyes.[106] Depicting him thus is obviously appropriate, but it exemplifies the way in which familiarity with one field of animation – fiction and entertainment – may subconsciously influence the way it is used (and perceived) in another – documentary and non-fiction. In other words, such uses and cross-influences have huge potential for the reception of information and the shaping of viewers' worldviews. Can non-villains, for example, be depicted as villains merely through representational choices in ways that viewers subconsciously detect without being aware that they are doing so? Although this book cannot cover the endless ways animation aesthetics can construct meaning, this idea affords greater power to the creators of imagery and highlights the need to focus on visual literacy tools.[107] It also corresponds to Jonathan Crary's explanation that in any analysis of spectator reception in changing regimes of the visual, it is important to understand the continuity that links novelty with older organisations of the visual so as to understand the mutation of one into the other.[108] Thus we consider animation's continued use in fiction as it also shapes its reception in non-fiction settings.

This is as true for documentary studies as it is for much wider interrogations of visual culture. The need to develop nuanced and critical visual literacy relates this topic to art history and what Manovich describes as 'the history of new [encoded] information interfaces developed by artists, and the new information behaviours developed by users [to extract the information]'.[109] Just as art history has been mapped and taught as the study of visual creations and developments in and across different cultures, eras and ideologies, the same must now be achieved in the field of animated documentaries and, more broadly, in relation to how information is conveyed visually today. Since the way information is depicted not only reflects reality but also constructs it, changes in imagery and the choices of stylisation are essential to debates about realism and what will eventually be understood as reality, making these areas of research relevant to much wider fields of study.

In an era when photorealism loses authority and a wide range of alternative non-mimetic images are habitually used to depict factual data, what, if anything, can viewers use as a basis for interpretation and authentication? This signifies a colossal shift in visual culture: image-production technologies are developing at a mind-blowing speed and viewers are at a loss to fathom the epistemological role and interpretational modes of non-fiction imagery. Complexity of imagery and visual communications have the potential to keep viewers critical, but tools for deciphering them are also needed. As imagery of the real and realism change, competence in image analysis is essential to understand how technologies have altered realities, referentiality and reception, influencing the relation between seeing, believing and visual literacy. The next chapter addresses these issues through a discussion of definitions, analysing changes in conceptions of animation and a growing convergence between animation and photography. Chapter 2 also introduces a semantic conceptual toolset in order to rethink and establish animation's link to the referents depicted in both physical and virtual environments.

NOTES

1. For more on the academic research see, for example, Strøm, 'Animated Documentary'; Sofian, 'Truth in Pictures'; Nichols, 'Documentary reenactment'; Skoller, 'Introduction to Special Issue'; Kriger, *Animated Realism*; Honess Roe, *Animated Documentary*; Formenti, 'Sincerest Form of Docudrama'. See also Murray and Ehrlich, *Drawn from Life*.
2. This is not to say that realism is exclusively related to documentary, since it is also used in fiction.
3. Grierson, *Grierson on Documentary*, p. 13.
4. See Strøm, 'Animated Documentary' and DelGaudio, 'If Truth Be Told'.
5. Honess Roe, 'Against Animated Documentary'.
6. Roberts, *Art of Interruption*, p. 2.
7. See Honess Roe, *Animated Documentary* and Cristina Formenti's forthcoming book *The Classic Animated Documentary and Its Contemporary Evolution*, to be published by Bloomsbury in 2020.
8. Leslie and McKim, 'Life Remade', p. 207.
9. Vaughan, *For Documentary*, pp. 84–5. For additional theorists who advocate a

viewer-oriented approach to documentaries see Ellis, *Documentary Idea*, p. 7; Raessens, 'Reality Play', p. 220; Odin, 'Semio-pragmatic Approach'.

10. See, for example, Smith, *What is Contemporary Art?*, p. 2; Alberro, 'Questionnaire on "The Contemporary"', p. 60 and Osborne, *Anywhere or Not at All*, pp. 18–20. Osborne's discussion of contemporary art, where he maps out several possible periodisations of 'the contemporary' include the periods since the end of World War I in 1945; since the 1960s; and since the end of the Cold War in 1989, each with its own geopolitical and aesthetic characterisations. Here I refer to the latest of the periods he defines.
11. Alberro, 'Questionnaire on "The Contemporary"', pp. 56–7.
12. Osborne, *Anywhere or Not at All*, p. 128.
13. Burnett, 'In Lies Begin Responsibilities', p. 194.
14. The word was introduced on the fake American news program *The Colbert Report* on 17 October 2005 (*The Colbert Report*, TV show, directed by Jim Hoskinson; USA: Spartina Productions, Busboy Productions and Comedy Partners, 2005–14); Armstrong, 'On the Border', p. 34.
15. Armstrong, 'On the Border', p. 34.
16. See https://en.oxforddictionaries.com/word-of-the-year/word-of-the-year-2016, accessed 29 July 2020.
17. Lambert-Beatty, 'Make Believe', p. 138.
18. Shay, 'The Taiwan Company'.
19. ABC News, 'TomoNews Uses Animation'.
20. See http://us.tomonews.com/about, accessed 8 November 2017. It is worth noting that this description actually manifests the unique historical and cultural moment where animation is situated in-between fact and fiction. As long as animation is associated with fiction, its use in non-fiction is perceived as novel or 'quirky enough' to prevent the animation itself from being boring whereas if/once animation is fully accepted as imagery of non-fiction, it too may be considered as 'boring news', potentially marking the moment for an additional and necessary change in representation. This is discussed further in Chapter 8.
21. Ibid.
22. See Boykoff, 'The Blurry Lines'.
23. Ibid.
24. *The Colbert Report*, TV show, directed by Jim Hoskinson (USA: Spartina Productions, Busboy Productions and Comedy Partners, 2005–14).
25. *The Daily Show*, TV show, directed by Paul Pennolino (USA: Ark Angel and Comedy Partners, 1996–present).
26. *Last Week Tonight with John Oliver*, TV show, directed by Joe Perota, Christopher Werner, Jim Hoskinson, Paul Pennolino and Bruce Leddy (USA: Avalon Television and Partially Important Productions, 2014–present).
27. These are all comments posted online by readers in response to Boykoff, 'Blurry Lines'.
28. Lind and Steyerl, *Greenroom*, p. 15.
29. Ward, 'Videogames as Remediated Animation', p. 125.

30. Ellis, *Visible Fictions*, p. 8.
31. Williams, 'A Lecture on Realism', pp. 63, 65; Janson, *History of Art*, p. 618.
32. Bazin, *What is Cinema?*, p. 14.
33. Ibid.
34. Ibid., p. 30.
35. Nichols, *Representing Reality*, p. 28.
36. Levy, 'From the Real to the More Real', p. 89; Jay, *Downcast Eyes*.
37. This is clearly a partial list. For more on the ontological and epistemological aspects of realism and appearances in the theories of central Western philosophers, see Yolton, *Realism and Appearances*. For a social and ethical perspective on realism through representation in recent decades, see Roberts, *Art of Interruption* and Reinhardt and Edwards, *Beautiful Suffering*. For a semantic discussion of realism, see Wollen, *Signs and Meaning*. For more on perception theory and the changing cultural role and context of the observer, see Crary, *Techniques of the Observer*. For an introduction to the discourse of humanism versus posthumanism and the role of the human–world relation versus other object-oriented ontologies, see Meillassoux, *After Finitude* and Bogost, *Alien Phenomenology*.
38. Alston, *Realism and Antirealism*, pp. 1–9.
39. Focusing on the human perceiver echoes Immanuel Kant, who claimed that the world can only be discovered by individuals and their perceptions, which means that it is based on knowledge that is grounded in thought categories, thus situating human–world relations as central: Broad, *Kant: An Introduction*.
40. Yolton, *Realism and Appearances*, pp. 134–5.
41. Boykoff, 'Blurry Lines'.
42. See http://us.tomonews.com/about, accessed 8 November 2017.
43. Ibid. For more see Lambert-Beatty, 'Make Believe', p. 138.
44. Cheng *et al.*, 'Can News Be Imaginative?'
45. Shay, 'The Taiwan Company', unpaginated.
46. Adewunmi, 'UK's Child Refugees'.
47. *One Iranian Lawyer's Fight to Save Juveniles from Execution*, film, *The Guardian* and Sherbet, 2012.
48. *Guantánamo Bay: The Hunger Strikes*, film, directed by Mustafa Khalili and Guy Grandjean (UK: Sherbet, Fonic and The Guardian, 2013).
49. *Globalised Slavery: How Big Supermarkets are Selling Prawns in Supply Chain Fed by Slave Labour*, film. (UK: *The Guardian*, 2014).
50. *The Sinking of the Lusitania*, film, directed by Winsor McCay (USA: Jewel Productions, 1918).
51. Sito, *Drawing the Line*, p. 36.
52. Honess Roe, 'Animating Documentary', p. 40.
53. Wells, 'Beautiful Village and True Village', p. 4.
54. Emphasis added.
55. Honess Roe, *Animated Documentary*, pp. 7–8.
56. Wells, 'Beautiful Village and True Village', p. 42.
57. For additional details and examples see Honess Roe, *Animated Documentary*,

pp. 8–9; Shale, *Donald Duck Joins Up*; Raiti, 'Disappearance of Disney Animated Propaganda'.
58. Groys, 'Topology of Contemporary Art', p. 78.
59. The Internet Movie Database, www.imdb.com/keyword/animated-documentary/, accessed 21 July 2019.
60. Available at https://en.wikipedia.org/wiki/Category:Animated_documentary_films, accessed 21 July 2019.
61. Available at www.vimeo.com/channels/docoanim/videos, accessed 21 July 2019.
62. Information from 'Animated Documentary', available at www.animateddocs.wordpress.com/about/ (accessed 25 April 2014) and 'Facebook Animated Documentary Discussion Group', available at www.facebook.com/AnimatedDocumentary, accessed 25 January 2017.
63. Available at www.youtube.com/results?search_query=animated+documentary, accessed 25 January 2017.
64. *Life, Animated*, film, directed by Roger Ross Williams (USA: Motto Pictures, A&E IndieFilms and Roger Ross Williams Productions, 2016).
65. *Animated Introduction to Cancer Biology*, film (USA: Cancerquest, 2013), https://www.cancerquest.org/education-centre/videos/cancer-biology-animations, accessed 4 August 2020.
66. *Nowhere Line: Voices from Manus Island*, film, directed by Lukas Schrank (Australia: Visitor Studio, 2015).
67. Honess Roe, *Animated Documentary*, p. 4.
68. Sofian, 'Truth in Pictures'.
69. *Magnetic Movie* by Semiconductor from 2007, for example, was shown in 2012 at Canary Wharf Station in London as part of Animate Projects' *Move on Up* program (*Magnetic Movie*, film, directed by Ruth Jarman and Joe Gerhardt [UK: Semiconductor, 2007]). See the event program, www.animateprojects.org/events/2012/move_on_up_at_canary_wharf_screen accessed 3 January 2013.
70. The numbers of emerging film festivals that focus on animated documentaries are slowly growing as the established festivals begin including special programs dedicated to the sub-genre. Some examples of such film festivals include: Dok Leipzig Film Festival, for documentary and animated film in Germany, www.dok-leipzig.de/home/?lang=en&; *DOCartoon* – The Drawing of Reality in Italy, www.docartoon.it; DocAviv – The Tel Aviv International Documentary Film Festival in Israel, www.docaviv.co.il/en/2012/tag/animation; Guangzhou International Documentary Film Festival in China, www.gzdoc.com/en_2012/index.asp; and *Hot Docs* – International Documentary Festival in Canada, www.hotdocs.ca/search/search.php?query=animation&search=1&x=0&y=0. In 2012 animated documentaries were the big winners at the Annecy International Animated Film Festival, with top prizes going to Anca Damian's *Crulic: The Path To Beyond* and Laurent Boileau and Jung Henin's *Approved for Adoption*, www.annecy.org/home; the Mumbai International Film Festival for documentary,

short and animation films in India, www.filmsdivision.org/miff/; *The Factual Animation Film Fuss* in the UK since 2015, www.faffuss.com/ and more. All links accessed 27 December 2012.
71. Examples of exhibitions that included animated documentaries are: *WK5* – a 2009–11 exhibition of William Kentridge's works shown at the San Francisco Museum of Modern Art; the 2011 *Watch Me Move* exhibition at the Barbican Gallery in London; the 2009–10 *Decode the Digital* at the V&A in London; the 2010–13 travelling exhibition *The Body in Women's Art Now* at Rollo Contemporary Art in London; the 2009–10 *Feedforward: The Angel of History* exhibition at the LABoral in Spain; exhibitions of the works of Kota Ezawa shown in many exhibitions including at the Metropolitan Museum of Art, New York, Seoul Museum of Art, Korea, and more.
72. Youtube and Vimeo are amongst the most popular.
73. Two recommended databases are Animate Projects, www.animateprojects.org, and the Facebook Animated Documentary Discussion Group, www.facebook.com/AnimatedDocumentary, both accessed 4 August 2020.
74. These include, for example, *The Guardian*'s 2012 Olympics video animation series, www.guardian.co.uk/sport/video/2012/aug/10/brick-behind-scenes-video-animation, or their animated shorts about the lives of five young refugees who sought asylum in the UK, www.guardian.co.uk/society/video/2012/jun/18/refugee-week-refugees, both accessed 4 August 2020. Additional examples are discussed in this chapter.
75. An example of such a work is *Gone Gitmo* (2010), a documentary game by Nonny de la Peña and Peggy Weil designed for Second Life.
76. Hanson, 'You Won't Believe'.
77. Solon, 'Future of Fake News'.
78. Sieff, 'Bertolt Brecht', p. 31.
79. *The Late Show with Stephen Colbert*, TV show, directed by Jim Hoskinson (USA: Spartina Productions, Busboy Productions and CBS Television Studios, 2015–present).
80. Cartoon Brew Connect, 'How President-elect'.
81. Lev Manovich introduces the concept of 'info-aesthetics' in this regard, explaining that the current culture of mass information requires and creates new aesthetic preferences, forms and iconologies. See Manovich, 'Introduction to Info-aesthetics', p. 340.
82. For more information on the rise of animation in digital culture and the consequent blurring of boundaries between previously distinct artistic and design practices see Leslie and McKim, 'Life Remade'.
83. Virilio, *Vision Machine*. The British Machine Vision Association and Society for Pattern Recognition defines computer vision as concerned with 'the automatic extraction, analysis and understanding of useful information from a single image or a sequence of images. It involves the development of a theoretical and algorithmic basis to achieve automatic visual understanding', and is used in varied fields such as forensics, biometrics, robotics, medical image analysis, face

recognition, augmented reality and many more. See www.bmva.org/visionoverview, accessed 15 December 2015.
84. Ibid., p. 62.
85. Bridle, *New Dark Age*, pp. 2–4.
86. Blocker, *Seeing Witness*, p. xiv.
87. Virilio, *Vision Machine*, pp. 59, 75–6.
88. See for example, Zylinska, *Nonhuman Photography*.
89. Some coverage of his case has questioned its authenticity but even as a metaphor he is a useful example.
90. See Stix, 'World's First Cyborg' and Ronchi, *Eculture*, p. 319.
91. For more on posthumanism see Hayles, *How We Became Posthuman*; Miah, 'Posthumanism'.
92. See Bryant *et al.*, *Speculative Turn*; Meillassoux, *After Finitude*; Harman, *Quentin Meillassoux*; Bogost, *Alien Phenomenology*.
93. Nagib and Mello, *Realism and the Audiovisual Media*, p. 10.
94. For more information on animation's privileged relation to computational information and representing digital data, see Leslie and McKim, 'Life Remade'; Leslie, 'Cloud Animation' and the chapter on 'Animation and Digital Media' in Furniss, *Art in Motion, Revised Edition*, pp. 173–96.
95. See Baudrillard, *Simulacra and Simulation*, pp. 1–42; Baudrillard, *Cool Memories*, p. 50.
96. *Exposure*, TV show, various producers (UK: various production companies, 2011–present).
97. My thanks to Oded Erell for bringing this case to my attention.
98. See Conlan and Plunkett, '"IRA" Footage', unpaginated.
99. Nathan and Revoir, 'ITV Admits', unpaginated. Although it was eventually recognised as false footage, it is important to keep in mind that those who called the bluff were a small percentage of viewers who spotted the imagery for what it was – game-play footage from a specific game. Others may or may not have noticed the fraud, but could not be sure without knowing the original.
100. Conlan and Plunkett, '"IRA" Footage', unpaginated. It is noteworthy that the footage was an extract from a longer clip available on YouTube, and the amount of work and editing put into making the game footage usable for the documentary sheds considerable doubt on the innocence of said 'human error'.
101. Baudrillard, 'Metamorphosis Metaphor Metastasis', p. 45.
102. Kingsley, 'Death of Alan Kurdi'.
103. See, for example, Nash, 'Reality in the Age of Aesthetics'; the special issue 'Social currency: How does art influence society?' *Frieze* issue no. 148, June–August 2012; Lind and Steyerl, *Greenroom*; Balsom and Peleg, *Documentary across Disciplines* and many publications about the documentary and art; the relation between art, imagery and socio-political realities; and the ethics of and in contemporary art.
104. Nagib and Mello, 'Introduction', *Realism and the Audiovisual Media*, pp. xv–xvi.
105. Aufderheide, *Very Short Introduction*, p. 26.

106. *Hercules*, film, directed by Ron Clements and John Musker (USA: Walt Disney, 1997) and *Aladdin*, film, directed by Ron Clements and John Musker (USA: Walt Disney, 1992).
107. For more on aesthetic issues of animation see Furniss, *Art in Motion, Revised Edition*.
108. Crary, *Techniques of the Observer*, p. 2.
109. 'Post-media Aesthetics', unpaginated.

CHAPTER TWO

Defining Animation and Animated Documents in Contemporary Mixed Realities

This chapter explores animation's changing definitions and its potential to act as a document in an era of mixed realities (where the physical and virtual converge). In addition, animation's evidentiary status is reconsidered in light of its relation to photography and live-action cinema, as well as dual aspects of the index (a central feature in photography's acceptance and credibility) that are often overlooked in documentary theory. This perspective is contextualised by the increasing uses of animation as non-fiction imagery in digital culture.[1] The chapter also engages with the question of how the animated 'world' and the world of the viewer can be brought together to enhance the credibility of animation as a legitimate documentary aesthetic in the context of developing animation techniques, contemporary mixed realities and changing documentary imagery.

The first scene in the animated Swedish film *Slaves* (2008)[2] begins with a dialogue between two interviewers about how to fix the malfunctioning microphone:

> Is it working?
> Not really. I don't know what to do.

Slaves is an animated documentary about child slavery in the civil war of Southern Sudan based on audio interviews with Abuk and Machiek, aged nine and fifteen, who talk about their abduction and enslavement by a government-sponsored militia. Owing to the dangers of filming in Sudan and the fact that the protagonists are underage and their anonymity must be protected, animation acts as a useful tool for describing the subjective nature of the children's experiences and memories. The first scene is an interesting introduction to many underlying assumptions about animation's informative capabilities, contested evidentiary status and subsequent often-used warranting devices.[3] The term 'warranting devices' was coined by Steven Lipkin to identify the ways in which docudrama 'validates ... assertions ... that "warrant" that what we are watching is (to some degree) true'.[4] These 'anchors to realities' and/or familiar stylistic documentary conventions increase a sense of truth-value and help steer the

Defining Animation and Animated Documents 55

Figure 2.1 *Slaves*, directed by David Aronowitsch and Hanna Heilborn, 2008.

viewer into a documentary 'mode of spectatorship' or 'documentarizing lecture'.⁵

While the interviewers in *Slaves* discuss the faulty equipment, the animated imagery portrays the silent children and the adults accompanying them, waiting for the technical difficulties to be resolved. This sets the stage for the viewer, highlighting a 'gap' in animated documentary whereby viewers see something that appears reasonable but for which no 'proof' is forthcoming. In this case, the interviewers offer the only aural evidence of 'the real'. The aural elements can contribute to animated documentaries' credibility, although what they create is believability rather than fact (the interviewers could have been recording in an empty room or used voice actors without the viewers being any the wiser). Audio interviews are increasingly common in animated documentaries since they ground the depiction in familiar documentary conventions and enable the soundtrack to act as link to the embodied existence and physical presence of protagonists who are not shown in their physical form.⁶ If the audio acts as a warranting device, more fluid visual depictions can be sanctioned, since they are not the only – or even the main – criteria for authentication; presence is signified by aural, not visual, elements, which contribute to the sense of the animated documentary's authenticity. Without relying on a recorded soundtrack, what exactly is animation's relation or link to the world it claims to portray when used in documentary? Can animation, as a visual signifier, embody a link to the physical reality it depicts? And what is animation's signifying role in an era of mixed realities that combine the virtual with the physical?

As animation techniques rapidly develop and the virtualisation of culture creates new connections between images and their referents, animated documentary's links to the reality it aims and claims to depict must be reconsidered.

WORLDS APART? ANIMATED WORLDS AND THE VIEWER'S SURROUNDINGS

Bill Nichols differentiates between documentary and fiction, asserting that documentary addresses '*the* world in which we live rather than *a* world imagined by the filmmaker'.[7] Suzanne Buchan defines animated 'worlds' as those 'realms of cinematic experience that are accessible to the spectator only through the techniques available in animation filmmaking'.[8] Because animation *looks* different from the physical world and is assumed to be separate from it, animation can be perceived as 'not real' when used in documentaries. The complex connection between documentary images and 'the real' they claim to depict differentiates between animation and live-action cinema. Despite photography's long history of manipulation, it is nonetheless still the privileged aesthetic most often used in documentary contexts.[9] This is most often related to (1) photography's mimetic visual style that resembles the referent portrayed (Chapter 1) and (2) photography's indexicality as a basis for its evidentiary status.[10]

To clarify, I am not interested in setting animation in opposition to photography; numerous debates in media and animation circles – including the writings of Alan Cholodenko, Tom Gunning and Lev Manovich regarding definitions of animation in relation to photography – have established that in digital culture, the binary between animation and photography no longer holds.[11] Nonetheless, a recurring point of comparison is between animation and live-action film,[12] even though the boundaries between the two are increasingly hard to delineate, on several technical, practical, aesthetic and epistemological levels:

First of all, *visual depiction is always incomplete* and thus meaning resides in interpretation.[13] Photographic imagery may surprise viewers by being used to convey information that is not necessarily visible (as in Colin Powell's testimony at the UN in 2003, which utilised satellite imagery that did not actually show weapons of mass destruction, yet provided justification for the invasion of Iraq).[14] Seeing is not necessarily understanding or knowing what exactly is being shown. If photography requires interpretation to embody meaning and animation is an interpretive visual stylisation of content, how does this affect the perceived difference between the two? The difference is that animation more obviously flaunts the incorporation of interpretative elements and practices, which is part of its inherent stylisation and blatant constructedness.[15] Once it is acknowledged that photography has multiple meanings, any direct link to realities recorded by photographic means is open to doubt.

Secondly, *photography and animation share more similarities than ever before* in their positioning within the human–technological paradigm. As recently as 2012, a special issue of *Critical Inquiry* was dedicated to the role of photography today, positioned between a (non-artistic) mechanical trace and an (artistic) representation intentionally created by the photographer.[16] This discussion emphasises the assumption that mechanical capture (by drones and satellites, for example) is a more transparent, objective and neutral representation of reality (and therefore potentially more trustworthy) than a constructed human portrayal assumed to be subjective and biased.[17] This complicates the mechanical versus human/artistic status of the photographic image all the more, since the end product may easily be a combination of the two. But is animation really so different? Since animation has no stylistic limitations, it has commonly been viewed as a subjective and interpretive art form in which the animator is omnipotent. However, animation can also be the visual end product or graphic interface of a technical apparatus or algorithm that translates data into visuals, as in data-based and AI-generated art. In these cases, although the animation is created by a designer, the changes in visualisation are nonetheless the product of an inanimate agent, an image of the world that is formed automatically. This is all the more relevant in animated scientific simulations, for example, where the scientist provides data but the imaging program selects stylistic options, unlike artists and designers who may take a more active role in the visual representation. This is similar to the way Bazin described photography's mechanical nature.[18] If we accept Bazin's viewpoint that mechanical visualisation is more neutral and transparent because it is not based on the subjectivity of its operator, automated animated visualisations may be deemed potentially valid representations of the real. In both animation and photography, however, it is the overlap between mechanical apparatus and human agent that creates uncertainty about how to define the end product. In other words, rather than viewing animation in opposition to photography, similar analytic approaches can be used for both, placing animation on a continuum with photography, rather than in opposition to it, and breaking the binary between the two. This is important in any analysis of animation's reception as a documentary aesthetic; it is another step in shattering the animation–photography binary in which animation may intuitively seem less appropriate as a documentary language.

Nevertheless, despite widespread awareness of the manipulation in photography and the many ways in which animation and photography can be seen to converge, photography is still seen as more connected to the physical world it depicts than animation; thus, photography is often used as a warranting device in animated documentaries. This is the case in *Slaves*, where photographs are included in the otherwise animated film's opening scenes. The photographs ostensibly show Sudanese children and thus legitimise the use of animation by grounding the work in more traditional documentary conventions. These scenes create a bridge between the physical world of the spectator and the animated world, encouraging the viewer to accept the work as reliable, as explained by Honess Roe.[19] The photographic silhouette of a red-tinted tree and house visible to the right of the frame are retained in the same position throughout the film's changing animated styles, evoking a sense of continuity between the initial photograph and the animation that follows.

Setting aside the discussion of animation versus photography, I want to address the evidentiary value associated with animation and the terms used to engage with it, for this is crucial to the perceived truth-value of animated documentaries and more central to the aims of this book. This is why the concept of indexicality, the signifying connection between a sign and its referent, which is still an important theoretical tool used for analysing visualisation techniques, remains relevant and needs rethinking and expanding.

Although the notion of indexicality raises many questions in relation to digital culture, it is often considered the basis upon which photography has been historically privileged as a documentary language. Roland Barthes famously explained that, unlike referents of other representational systems such as painting, the photographic referent was necessarily placed before the lens, thus confirming that the object had indeed been in the physical space before the camera.[20] This referential quality, or 'indexing', is highly valued in documentary theory, where a validation that links the referent to its sign results in a certain truth-value that is expected of the genre. As curator and art critic Okwui Enwezor has suggested, the documentary is expected to embody a direct correlation to its physical referent as an evidentiary act.[21] In comparison to photography, non-naturalistic animated imagery can be considered artificial both because it differs stylistically from the physical referents, and its production methods break with the indexical representation of analogue photography, which captures imagery rather than constructing it.[22] These characteristics support the previously mentioned gap between animation and the physical world of the spectator, strengthening the potentially problematic reception of animation as viable imagery of documentary. But what if animation has now changed to the point where (1) it is indistinguishable from photography, and (2) it embodies a physical link to its referent? This takes us back to the changing definitions of what constitutes animation today, and to a deeper exploration of animation's indexicality as a basis for its informative capacity, credibility and evidentiary status.

DEFINING ANIMATION

Animating Truth refers to animated imagery as 'movement only visible on-screen', and focuses particularly on animation that does not attempt to stylistically mimic photorealism.[23] The ongoing discussion surrounding the definition of animation is an integral characteristic of the field itself, a growing and dynamic area of theoretical and technical knowledge. There are many ways to approach the definition of animation, including techniques, styles, key studios, directors or animators, approaches to movement or visual transformation, aesthetics and spectatorship, to name but a few.[24] However, since animation is so wide-ranging and is visible across media, genres and evolving technologies, what becomes evident is that its definition requires interdisciplinary and multiple approaches. Nonetheless, a recurring point of comparison is between animation and live-action. Indeed, with the digital revolution, as cinema converges with animation on the contemporary computer screen, the meaning (and importance) of animation expands exponentially. Manovich, for example, refuses to define animation as clear-cut, and instead sees it as a combination of forms in an ever-expanding field where many post-computerised methods incorporate animation DNA to varying degrees.[25] This also explains why the screen is an essential element in the definition of animation and discussion of animated non-fiction from a technocultural perspective.

Thinking of animation as a genre or medium is a misconception, for animation can be used to depict diverse content in various styles and be viewed through wide-ranging devices.[26] It is therefore perhaps most useful to think of animation, as Paul Wells has suggested, as 'an art, an approach, an aesthetic and an application'.[27] Although the terms 'art' and 'aesthetic' may seem somewhat vague, they emphasise the fact that animation is used as a unique and exceptionally visual means of addressing a purpose or conveying meaning. Indeed, in 2003, Gunnar Strøm proposed that '"animation" is a technical term and "documentary" is a content-related approach, and ... the terms do not exclude each other'.[28]

Etymologically, the term 'animation' is derived from the Latin word *animatio*, from *animare*. Probably originating in the sixteenth century, it has two key meanings, one referring to movement and the other to bestowing life.[29] Donald Crafton explains that the earliest uses of the term were theological and referred to the union of soul and body, denoting an endowment with spirit, as in the biblical description of God giving life to Adam. The adjective 'animated' also referred to magical and supernatural beings, such as spirits and angels. Over time, the meaning expanded to reflect increasing secularisation, and incorporated different aspects of 'life forces', including 'awakening', 'becoming aroused', 'intensifying', 'reviving', 'imparting vividness' and 'giv[ing] lifelike qualities'.[30] Thus animation has two meanings: one theological, pertaining to bestowing life, and the other secular, referring to movement and change. The idea of motion is a defining element in animation theory and in the discussion of animation's realism in regard to animated documentary. Motion is also what differentiates animated documentary from graphic novels such as Art Spiegelman's *Maus* and Joe Sacco's *Palestine*, to which it is often compared.[31]

The question surrounding movement emphasises a central aspect in the discussion of animation's indexicality, for it foreshadows the issue of animation as an illusion of life or indeed life itself in new ways in digital culture. Cholodenko emphasises the illusion of life that animation creates through the successive placement of images that fool the retina by creating an effect of perfect continuity of movement;[32] but this is actually complicated by a slippage of terms. Although the terms 'life' and 'animation' may seem synonymous, according to Deborah Levitt, 'to animate' means to endow with life but also to represent *as if* alive, emphasising the illusion of life rather than life itself.[33] Levitt also claims that animation encompasses 'a wide array of cultural productions from cartoons per se to modes of simulation used across aesthetic and scientific practices', where the production of life in animation deconstructs ontology and transforms our conception of life (including artificial life), ethics and biopolitics in relation to contemporary media.[34] By analysing animation through its indexical traits in today's mixed realities, I aim to demonstrate that animation is no longer grounded in an idea of illusion of life (but rather a capture of technologically mediated presence and actions), and thus its reception as a potentially valid documentary aesthetic is established.

Just as animation transcends any specific genre or medium, it also negates any assumed link to a specific technique or visual style. In the past, definitions of animation were often technique-specific, such as films made by photographing successive scenes of inanimate objects, or series of progressively altered drawings that simulate movement.[35] However, animation is as visually varied in technique and style as fine art. The field of animation comprises sculpture, painting, drawing, photography, collage, digital art, and 2D and 3D computer imaging, and is constantly developing as a result of changing technology. Since digital animation now enables the creation of hyperrealist imagery that is often hard to distinguish visually from photography, in stylistic terms animation can be placed on a continuum ranging between *mimesis* and *abstraction*, as indicated by Maureen Furniss.[36] Animation's ability to resemble photorealism highlights the complex and continually developing relationship between animation and live-action cinema.

Definitions are important here because digital culture changes what animation is and consequently how it should be approached. Joel McKim has referred to 'artificial animation',[37] referencing 1950s' reactions to early computer art. These early explorations of CG art seemed 'artificial' to humanists, who felt that it eliminated the human element from the art experience, thus replacing feelings of wonder with cold rationality; technologists on the other hand specifically promoted computer art, seeing it within the paradigm of 'man versus machine' and situating the computer as an 'oppositional force'.[38] Although having become accustomed to computers shaping every aspect of life it is difficult to conceive of computer-based art as artificial, this discourse is currently reincarnated in the realm of art created by AI. Positioning animation within this discursive terrain shapes and constructs its reception and criticism by placing it within the competing dogma between art and science/technology. However, contemporary animation must be reconsidered because, by using new imaging technologies, it changes the relation between technological tools and human agents. Not only does this refer to new technologies of image production, as discussed below, it also incorporates the links between the stylisation of animation and machine aesthetics where the animator is no longer the omnipotent designer; this takes us into a whole new field that further expands the directions and contexts for thinking about animation.

Many animation scholars have come from film studies, but as animation becomes a dominant visual form of the twenty-first century, its very nature must be reconsidered. Suzanne Buchan's important book, *Pervasive Animation*, addressed the proliferation of animation in our times and brought together a variety of scholars from varied backgrounds to address the phenomenon. This is a work in progress, encouraged by the significant contribution of *Animation: An Interdisciplinary Journal*, but one that must be continued and pushed forward. Although animation plays a major role in myriad spheres, academically there is a certain categorisation that limits the consideration of animation's pervasive role in today's visual culture and its ramifications. For example, posthumanism, robotics, AR and VR, scientific visualisations and game studies, do consider the visual side of animation but it is less in focus than interactive storytelling structures and cultural contexts, among others, that take centre stage. Here, I will consider different uses and realms of digital culture where animation is used in relation to non-fiction, and the visual aspect of the aesthetics and how they are used. An examination of definitions, therefore, demonstrates that animation should be considered in its current, much wider cultural role, taking account of its epistemological ramifications in today's culture, changing conceptions of truth and developments in tangential image-production techniques and fields.

Some theorists claim that, through the triumph of animation over cinema and other media, the term 'animation' becomes all-inclusive and, as such, is actually reduced into nothing by becoming everything.[39] In contrast, award-winning animation artist Tom Jantol has coined the term 'anymation', which does not distinguish between varied animation techniques, and instead is entirely goal-oriented – an approach similar to my own – focusing on non-naturalistic imagery to depict reality.[40] The link between expanded conceptions of animation and the digital age become apparent in works such as those of Kenny Chow, who sees the digital environment as 'animated phenomena' because these CG visuals also include our bodily experiences through dynamic and responsive visual and audio output.[41] To summarise: digital culture shines a completely new light on what animation is, and how it should be understood.

Although the traditional, theological interpretation of animation may seem of little relevance to any study of contemporary animated imagery, nonetheless a sense of magic or wonder is still part of animation's legacy. Or, as Phillip Kelly Denslow puts it, 'what is animation if not the desire to make real that which exists in the imagination?'[42] The infinite possibilities of visual styles and content brought to life through movement, and hence different from what is perceivable in the physical world, creates a gap between the two so-called 'worlds'.[43] Brian Wells's definition of animation, which differentiates between the animated world and that of the viewer, questions whether both can exist in the same time and space, or whether animation is relegated to another dimension.[44] This gap plays an important role in differentiating animated imagery from the physical world of the viewer, and must therefore be addressed in any discussion of animation's validity as a documentary language. Animation's indexicality sheds light on the use of animation in documentary as the connection between the two 'worlds'; and the new connections between them explain animation's growing use and credibility in non-fiction contexts such as documentary in today's digital culture.

Animation and its Dual Indexicality

The growing convergence between on-screen animated worlds and the viewer's physical environment makes it essential to comprehend (1) how the changing status of the physical in contemporary culture has affected animation's relation to indexicality (often theorised only in respect to its material trace), and (2) how indexicality functions as the basis for documents, so that without it the whole concept of documentaries collapses. Although the shift from an analogue to digital visual culture could be seen as eliminating the physically indexical dimension of imagery, the issue of indexicality continues to reverberate in documentary theory.

By pursuing new connections between the animated and the physical, it becomes possible to reposition animation as potentially reliable documentary imagery. Thus we will explore multiple definitions of the concept of indexicality, evaluating the role of indexicality in digital culture, and the intricacy of contemporary referentiality as both realities and technologies of animation production are transforming. The following questions pertain: Has the index really been abolished in digital culture, or are new forms of indexicality at play? In contemporary virtual realities, what is the status of indexicality given the centrality of online platforms and the ubiquitous screen? Does a connection to the physical necessarily require visual resemblance? What, in these circumstances, becomes the basis for documentary reception?

It is also worth mentioning Mark Hansen who makes two salient points. (1) He emphasises the central role of the body and physical movement rather than visual verisimilitude in crossing between virtual and physical realms.[45] (2) He claims that 'photography – the indexical medium par excellence – simply has no purchase in the domain of the virtual'.[46] My disagreement with the second point inspired an analysis of animation's shifting relation and convergence with photography, whereas my agreement with the first statement about the role of the body and physical movement explains my focus on indexicality as a trace of the physical within virtual environments. Although photography's status and relevance must be rethought in digital culture, something of photography remains and that is the notion of indexicality as a primary marker of veracity. By discussing indexicality, I expand existing photography and animation-based scholarship to include media theory about the concept's relation to documentary representation in an era of mixed realities.

Charles Sanders Peirce's semiotic trichotomy of signs sheds light on the multifaceted relation between animated imagery and the indexical link to the real that is generally expected of documentaries. Demonstrating the complexity of the concept of the index establishes that it has an unexpected correlation with animation, raising new questions about how indexicality is used to define and theorise contemporary forms of documentary imagery.

Peirce's trichotomy comprises the icon, the symbol and the index. An *icon* is a sign that shares qualities, referred to as a resemblance or likeness, with its referent.[47] An example of an icon is a painted portrait, although an icon's likeness is not necessarily mimetic or even visually similar, opening the discussion to ever-wider possibilities and interpretations. A *symbol* is based upon arbitrary conventions that define the sign as referring to the object it denotes, such as the word 'dog', for example, which is an arbitrarily chosen sound that refers to a four-legged animal of a specific species.[48] The *index* occupies a more complex position, having a dual definition as both trace and deixis (see below). The index functions as a trace or imprint of its object when objects act as the cause of the sign, such as a footprint or bullet hole, implying a material connection between sign and object.[49] Although the index as trace received privileged status in moving-image theory, Tom Gunning has argued that it is only one genre of index, and not necessarily the most crucial or definitive, distracting attention from the index as deixis.[50] According to the Oxford English Dictionary (OED, 2012), 'deixis' denotes the cognitive reasoning processes of showing, pointing and specifying, but also proving. In other words, the deixis can demonstrate, illustrate and indicate but it does not embody a trace to the referent (as does the footprint, which is a trace of the foot), and, unlike the icon, does not *have* to be based on resemblance. Peirce's discussion of the index includes a large range of signs and indications, including 'anything which focuses attention'.[51] The index has also been defined as embodying 'the general hailing and deictic functions of language and gesture', such as the pointing finger or the denoting 'this' in the English language.[52]

The dual relation of the deixis to the symbol and the physical requires clarification. The deixis indicates and points, which infers something physical that can be pointed to. However, the deixis is also defined as denoting cognitive contents that are invisible, such as dreams or memories. Visual consideration of the deixis recalls animation's fluidity of interpretation, and its indication of elements that cannot be visualised. This takes the discussion into a broader consideration of visualisation as representations that make the invisible visible.

Significantly, Peirce himself proclaimed that there are no pure indices.[53] He regarded the photograph as an important example, since it is both iconic and indexical. The analogue photograph bears a mimetic visual resemblance to its referent, but was also fashioned in a particular way *because*, through its imprint in the photo-chemical process, the referent formed a trace.[54] In other words, the index itself can be both iconic and symbolic. As trace, the index shares a likeness to the object, becoming its iconic register. The index as deixis is symbolic, such as in 'this', 'I', or 'here', where meaning is context-dependent. The visual deixis may rely on varied degrees of recognisability to denote something, since it can also take on iconic characteristics such as shades of visual resemblances. The issue of recognisability is complex, however, since recognising a sign based on resemblance would make it iconic, whereas resemblance can be an issue of degree or even convention, such as the sign of a star, which is also symbolic. Since animation refers to many production techniques and infinite styles, it is an index that can be variously located on the continuums of trace and deixis, as well as icon and symbol. A smile emoji, for example, may be seen as an icon, since it resembles a smiling face, but also as a symbol, since it simplifies any human expression to the extent of a stick-figure diagram. Similarly, a smile emoji can be both a deictic index or, as in the latest animation techniques based on facial recognition of the app's user, a visualisation based on actual facial expression of the user, thus acting as trace.

Since animation in documentary is most often compared to photography, a discussion of animation as an emergent language of documentary further demands a consideration of indexicality in contemporary digital photography. In the digital photograph the link to the physical referent is radically redefined. Instead of containing a chemically based physical trace to its referent through its mode of production, as was the case with analogue photography, the digital photograph is based on units of data and is consequently reduced to an icon, to use Peirce's terminology, rather than functioning as an icon *and* an index. In the shift from a photographic to a post-photographic digital visual culture, the physically indexical dimension of imagery is abolished.[55] This means that as a visual language that shares a resemblance with, but lacks a physical link to, the referent, digital photography becomes similar to a drawing, painting or, for that matter, some animations.

Even though the discussion of indexicality is central to digital media, and even though animation scholarship has grown substantially in recent years, nonetheless animation has been surprisingly under-theorised in discourses of the index, which continue to concentrate on material realities. For example, in the introduction to a special issue on indexicality in the *Differences* journal, Mary Ann Doane states that, as both deixis and trace, 'the index is defined by a physical, material connection to its object'.[56] This relation to the physical is complicated for several reasons, and raises a number of questions. Does a connection to the physical necessarily require an iconic visual resemblance; that is, does a documentary image have to look like the material referent represented? How visually divergent can images be from their referents for them still to be accepted as documentary-worthy? As computerised environments and screen-based virtualisations flourish, what is the status of the physical? Can indexing even occur when reality is not material? Considering animation's dual indexicality as both trace and deixis sheds new light on animation as an index of physical as well as virtual realities, and expands the visual forms that an index takes while maintaining its status as an informative referent or evidentiary link – both vital as a foundation for documentary works.

While the centrality of the physical has been questioned in relation to contemporary technologised and virtual cultures, documentary works still appear to rely heavily on the physically indexical nature of representation to achieve trustworthiness or evaluate truth-value. This dichotomy ensures that the issue of materiality and conceptualisations of the index must be reconsidered. Thus, what follows analyses animation in relation to: (1) the index as trace of the physical; (2) the index as deixis of the physical; (3) the index as deixis of the non-physical.

ANIMATION AS INDEXICAL TRACE OF THE PHYSICAL

In the film *Holy Motors* (2012),[57] a scene depicts characters wearing motion-capture suits transformed on-screen into computerised demon snakes simulating sex. Can animated images such as these be seen as indexical, as proof of physical occurrences? Because the definition of index as trace was most commonly used in the theorisation of photographic imagery, a connection between indexicality and iconicity was established; the analogue photograph was an indexical trace of its referent as well as being similar in appearance, and was, therefore, an icon. As explained earlier, this implied relation to visual realism is not, however, part of Peirce's theory. Although animation may seem to break, or at least challenge, the link to the physical required by the index as trace, analysing various animation techniques reveals that some are directly indexical. While these methods are not necessarily reliant upon mimetic iconicity, they do demonstrate animation's varied forms of indexicality.

Some animation techniques rely on photography and thus share the dual signatory traits of icon and index, in a similar manner to the photography on which they are based.[58] So, for example, stop-motion, whereby objects are photographed and then placed in a sequence to create the illusion of movement, is based on physical objects and their photographic depiction; in rotoscoping, live-action footage is traced over frame by frame (manually or by computer). Even though the photographic imagery may be disguised, and therefore not visually mimetic, the animated imagery is not entirely divorced from the indexicality of the photographic footage from which it is sourced.

Other techniques go even further in departing from the visually mimetic conventions of realism based on similarity of appearance. While they still act as traces, they are no longer visually iconic. MoCap (motion capture) animation techniques, for example, record the actions of human actors on whose movements 2D or 3D computer animation is based. MoCap captures live movement as computer data, which is then digitally modified and finessed in post-production using animation (as in frame-by-frame techniques) into a finished product. The final imagery is both captured and generated, blurring the boundaries between photography (as recorded imagery) and animation (as generated imagery), as well as between the index as trace and deixis.[59] MoCap thus retains the performance of the recorded actor, but eliminates the camera since it does not produce video footage but spatial coordinates over time. Rose Woodcock explains that MoCap holds movement information as numeric code with no formal visual qualities, and therefore has a 'unique capacity to store motion data as potential movement: movement itself that has a life "elsewhere" and at other times, and independent of the performer's time spent in the live MoCap recording session'.[60] MoCap can thus act as a trace of physical movement, but also as a deixic index that remains 'empty', in the same way that a shifter index whose denotation is based on context (like the word 'I') is filled with meaning through the visualisation it receives. This not only demonstrates the complex nature of some of today's animation techniques, but is important when considering definitions of animation that are *not* grounded in an illusion of movement but rather capturing liveliness instead. It is also relevant to our discussion of indexicality as a trace of the physical on virtual platforms and, consequently, to their perceived evidentiary status. Chow sees the digital environment as 'animated phenomena' because 'it is "endowed with life" rather than just "movement" ... in phenomena such as motion, reaction, adaptation, and transformation ... [making us] feel that our bodies are in touch with the digital objects'.[61]

Digital technology, therefore, complicates definitions by blurring distinctions between animation, live-action cinema, synthetic performances, post-production visual effects and digital puppetry, to name but a few.[62] MoCap combines recorded and synthetic cinema, and is part of an ongoing debate about what constitutes animation in the digital age. Like rotoscoping, the basis of the image and its movements are indexical (as trace) and grounded in physical reality; however, where rotoscoping aims for a degree of visual similarity, the final image produced by MoCap does not, and actors' movements are used as a basis for anthropomorphic creatures.

Actor Andrew Clement Serkis has been critically acclaimed for his roles that comprise motion-capture acting, animation and voice work for CG characters such as Gollum in *The Lord of the Rings* (2001–3),[63] and Caesar in *Rise of the Planet of the Apes* (2011)[64] and *Dawn of the Planet of the Apes* (2014),[65] among others. In such cases the movements are the actors' own, the image thus acting as a trace of the physical movements on which it is based. But the computer-generated imagery (CGI) differs in appearance from the actors generating it. There are, of course, many such examples. Advanced MoCap techniques based on wireless technologies and 360-degree views of movement expand the uses of these methods, which are now ubiquitous in film, special effects, animation, game production and virtual reality, sport training, sport analysis and medical rehabilitation. MoCap thus combines an indexical trace with the iconic, based on similarity of movement but not necessarily of physical appearance, and also an element of what Peirce calls the symbolic because the visualisation is stylised, and in that sense arbitrary.

Machinima is another animation technique that acts as an indexical trace of the physical in yet another way. It refers to any real-time animation used in interactive platforms and is used in games and online virtual digital worlds, translating the player's commands and, increasingly, her physical actions, into animated game visuals. Recorded through varying interfaces ranging from a keyboard and mouse to motion sensors, the user interacts with and manipulates on-screen items via gesture recognition. The player's physical movements are thus captured and translated into animated visual form, maintaining a trace of the physical referent, which is then combined with different visual options ranging from an iconic avatar designed to resemble the player, to the symbolic. In this case, the symbolic refers to the endless and arbitrary options for visual imagery of an avatar, such as a dot, spaceship or humanoid, among others. On the one hand, an avatar designed to visually resemble the player may be seen as a sign that is both iconic (based on degrees of similarity) *and* an indexical trace. A cursor, on the other hand, translating the user's physical movement onto the screen, is a trace of physical movement but can take on endless visual forms, which means that it is visually arbitrary and therefore a symbolic indexical trace. In all such cases then, animation can act as an 'index as trace' of the physical, which can be placed on a continuum between iconicity and the symbolic, depending how similar it is to the referent.

Furthermore, maintaining the importance of the index as a basis for documents stimulates what I call *a post-photographic documentary mentality*. Not in the sense of a post-photographic era, when digital production methods and a growing awareness of potential image manipulation established digital photography as a new medium. Rather, that in this post-photographic aesthetic, the logic of the photographic based on indexical trace is maintained, though not the photographic aesthetics that rely on resemblance. GPS, for example, visualises the car and its movements in real-time, but translates that visualisation into a visual icon. Although Honess Roe has proposed an epistemological blurring of icon and index, whereby 'we do perhaps still take the iconic as evidence of witnessable events', I view her position as pre-photographic logic:[66] what is similar in appearance to the referent is considered sufficient, an observation that echoes the attitude to drawing and modes of visualisation that predate photography. I take a different stand, seeing animation as indexical and thus as a post-photographic documentary aesthetic, which emphasises the elements that made photography credible – specifically, its analogue relation as trace of the physical; these are maintained, while the aesthetics of photography are modified. This explains the significance of animation as physical trace in a documentary theory based on indexicality.

ANIMATION AS DEICTIC INDEX OF THE PHYSICAL

Animated explanations of complex processes are increasingly used to visualise and explain complicated and dense information in an era characterised by endless avalanches of visual data and the need to summarise and simplify information, as well as to attract viewers' attention. Esther Leslie and Joel McKim explain that, as animation's visibility proliferates in today's digital culture, 'animation is increasingly fundamental to processes of knowledge production'.[67] Consequently, as viewers we have become familiar and comfortable with varied animated data visualisations. How does this relate to animation's dual forms of indexicality?

Unlike the mimetic appearance expected of the trace's iconicity (due to its centrality in photographic theory), the power of the index as deixis is denotative. The deixis draws attention to a particular object, not by representing it visually, but by designating it and pointing 'there'.[68] The thought cloud or idea light bulb in comics and cartoons, for example, signify a thought process not in the sense of visual resemblance but in a way that calls attention to its occurrence. How, then, can animation act as deictic index to the physical world, creating a link between the two in a referential rather than visually mimetic manner?

As both imagery and the role of images change, it is necessary to challenge existing representational hierarchies and to reconsider the role and capabilities of non-mimetic representation. In our highly visual contemporary culture, images increasingly assume primacy over language as ways to convey information, and threaten to engulf us daily.[69] We are seeing an explosion of accessible information in which new representations are needed in order to visualise complex ideas, structures, and systems, and to manage vast amounts of data. It is, therefore, vital to understand the changing role of imagery in regard to the construction of knowledge. The examples of MoCap and machinima demonstrate how the visually symbolic representation of the physical world is proliferating in contemporary culture. This is important to any consideration of the relation between animated documentary and data visualisation, or non-fiction imagery more generally, because it illustrates the varied visual forms that viewers are accustomed to seeing in their consumption of information today.

Aaron Koblin's artwork *Flight Patterns* (2009), like myriad examples of data-driven art and visualisations, illustrates the multifaceted relationship between animation, symbolic and iconic imagery in the representation of factual information. *Flight Patterns* visualises the air traffic routes over North America during a twenty-four-hour period in animated colour and form. Each flight is represented by a symbolic single line, which could arguably be interpreted as an icon, resembling a flight moving from point A to point B. As the work progresses, the many lines depicting flights come to form the recognisable geographical shape of the United States. The appearance of a map acts as an icon since it shares a likeness, in this case in form, to an identifiable referent, that anchors what is on display and contextualises the information. Finally, the deictic indexing value of this work is due to the ability of the animated representation to signify more than is directly visualised. In this case the work also actually illustrates the vast amounts of people and cargo flying each day. The animated representation thus points to an occurrence in an easily understood and simplified manner, identifying the vast financial, geographic, cultural and environmental effects of such extensive air traffic.

New information about the physical world that, for different reasons, cannot be represented photographically is increasingly represented in animated form. Just as photography was once used to represent visually what was not visible to the naked eye (for example, Muybridge's depiction of movement split into single frames), animation is used today to extend visuality, and thus to expand knowledge of realities that are un-photographable. For example, a scientist may mentally 'see' something no one else can, but needs the simulating power of a computer in order to think with images, use them as cognitive tools, and to make ideas like fractals or nanotechnology visible and understandable to the rest of the world.[70] Additionally, in the *Life*

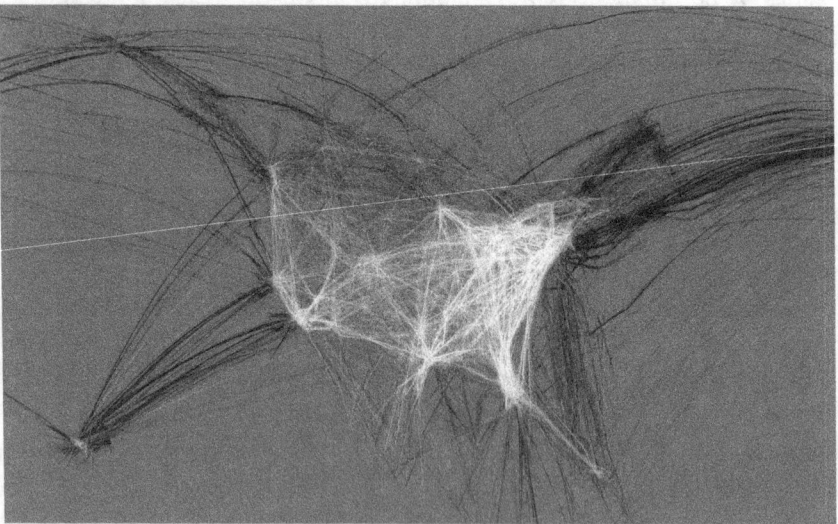

Figure 2.2 *Flight Patterns*, a time-lapse animation artwork by Aaron Koblin that employs data visualisation to display the paths of air traffic over North America visualised in colour and form, 2011.

of the Cell series, researchers in the BioVisions Program at Harvard University collaborated with the XVIVO animation company in order to make a series of highly aestheticised and compelling animated informational depictions, including *Powering the Cell – Mitochondria* (2012).[71] These animated simulations convey information that cannot be represented photographically, and represent factual data that are not otherwise available. Thus animation is expanding the epistemological framework by creating new knowledge and making it accessible. This use of imagery has been referred to as theoretical photorealism, using CGI to visualise 'unobserved but visually accurate' phenomena in scientific contexts aiming to demonstrate 'a sight beyond sight'.[72] The centrality of animation as data visualisation in varied non-fiction disciplines thus becomes clear.

The animated images in *Mitochondria* are not a trace, but they are iconic and they are an index. They are iconic because the way in which they are visualised is not arbitrary, but based on scientific research into the topic portrayed, i.e. the cell, even if the human eye is incapable of distinguishing this resemblance. Even when animation portrays the physical world, it can do so without representing anything recognisable to the human eye precisely because it acts as an innovative form of visualisation. Animation can thus be iconic (based on resemblance) but not recognisably so, introducing a gap between iconicity and recognisability. These images are also deictically indexical because, by visualising what cannot be perceived beyond a textual description, they point, thus making viewers aware. This means that viewers become increasingly

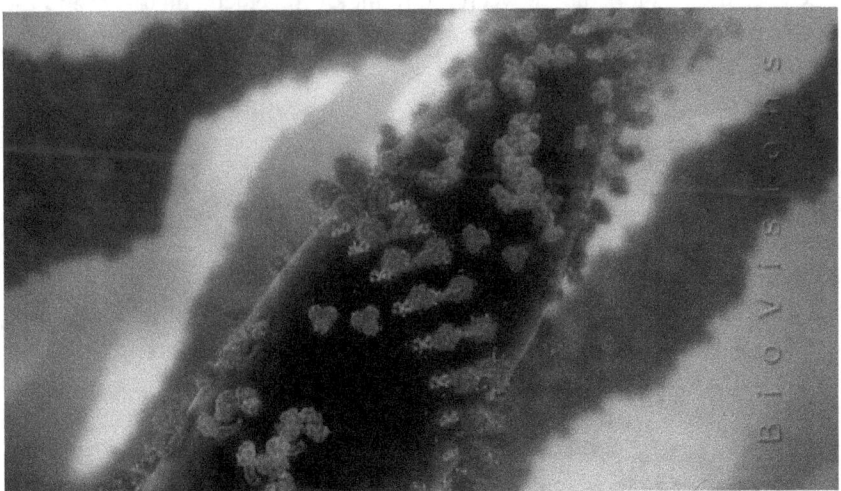

Figure 2.3 *Powering the Cell – Mitochondria*, BioVisions Program at Harvard University and XVIVO Scientific Animation, 2012.

accustomed to learning about their own world through animation, further shattering previous definitions and misconceptions about animation's separateness from the viewer's world, its artificiality or its assumed allusion to fiction.

Using documentary theory to illuminate the growing acceptability of varied non-fiction imagery resonates with Michael Renov's explanation that the etymological roots of documentary lie in the Latin *docere*, meaning 'to teach';[73] the 'documentary desire' is thus a desire to know. Using animation as representational imagery teaches viewers and fulfils their documentary desire. By drawing attention to a certain object, process or phenomenon in such a way that does not attempt mimesis, new information can be uncovered. If documentary is thus to be defined as a way to make sense of documents and to uncover otherwise unknown information, animated representations such as *The Mitochondria* certainly fulfil these criteria.

Since documentary definitions are based on conventions that are historically and culturally produced, and therefore constantly in flux, by rethinking theorisations of documentary based on indexicality, animation emerges as a new form of documentary representation. Deleuze's concept of the 'out-of-field' is useful to further consider animation's deictic capabilities and consequent validity in documentary representation that refers and points to what is not seen.

In his two *Cinema* books, Deleuze makes use of Peirce's semiotic theories. Deleuze is especially interested in the non-linguistic status of semiotics, which he uses to explain the experience and perception of film imagery. He discusses the relationship between the frame of the cinematic image and the out-of-field, that which was not photographed and which lies beyond the frame. The out-of-field signifies that which 'is neither seen nor understood, but is nevertheless perfectly present'.[74] In other words, instead of the cinematic image containing solely the environment it depicts, the out-of-field extends the cinematic image into larger sets and systems of meaning. As such, each image is not a self-contained unit of information but always exists in relation (pointing) to what is not seen, and what lies beyond its limits, making it all the more dynamic.

While Deleuze writes with specific reference to photographic imagery as deictic index, the animated image can also point to what is beyond its frame, breaking the confines of the animated world. Animation's ability to deictically refer to physical phenomena in a credible manner means that, although the physical is not seen, it remains present within the animated representation.

Whereas the index as trace is specific, the deictic index can be more fluid in its indicative possibilities. In other words, animation can be considered a deixis that points to a certain referent without acting as a trace of it. This means that animated non-fiction can point to several referents simultaneously, without necessarily relying on visual resemblance. This relates to another definition of the deixis as linked to varied denotational meanings that can only be fully understood with additional contextualising information. In Aaron Koblin's *Flight Patterns*, for example, the line mapping motion from starting point to destination partially resembles a flight, but it is nonetheless a very abstract signifier that lacks the visual features that usually denote flights, such as an airplane, the sky or a map with a dot. Nonetheless, this abstraction arguably facilitates the signification of layered meanings since it does not denote just one referent, as is made clear by the many meanings understood from *Flight Patterns* about mass travel and its economic and environmental ramifications, to name but a few. The line is mainly recognisable due to context and may not be understood as such without the work's title at the very least. The same is true of the geographical shape of the Unites States formed by the flight lines. In a different context, these might be harder to understand and could function as symbolic shifter indices that do not clearly denote anything: the further a sign is removed from recognisability, the more it is reliant upon context and narrative, which makes it symbolic.

In animated documentary and non-fiction more generally, animation points to different elements that can enhance the believability of the representation. Animation can point to an occurrence that is familiar to the viewer through inter-textual knowledge, such as an event featured prominently in the news. In other words, it is not indexicality that is being 'transferred', but a sense of credibility through interpretation and recognisability of content. Animated documentaries about Sudan or the refugee crisis, for example, can be accepted as deictically indexing subject matter known to viewers through other, more trusted, media coverage. The film *Slaves* uses such means, branding itself as an animated documentary in the opening credits so that audiences know how to receive it, and relying on documentary film conventions in order to validate its status.[75] The film opens with textual information about the civil war in Southern Sudan that would be familiar to viewers and is presented alongside photographs of (assumedly) Sudanese children, thus placing the film in its social-political context. Thus the believability of animated non-fiction pointing to actual events is based on familiarity with the subject from other sources, even if the animated form of representation is relatively new. Nonetheless, animation's ability to invoke the physical as a deictic index introduces a sense of the multiplicity of tangential worlds, easing the transition into the 'other' space of the animated world. The animated world and the material world of the viewer thus continue to converge through these inventive forms of referentiality.

ANIMATION AS DEICTIC INDEX OF THE NON-PHYSICAL

The notion of the deictic index as a form of pointing exposes assumptions about the physicality of what can be pointed to, although mental processes are also included in the OED's definition of the term 'deixis'. Animation is often used to depict what is otherwise unrepresentable visually. While animation has been widely used in documentaries in order to portray subjective accounts of events, and to explore personal interpretations of realities,[76] the non-photographable non-physical realities that now surround us are of the digital-virtual kind.

Whereas the index, as conventionally used in visual cultural theory, relies on a material connection to its referent, the digital is grounded in mathematics and code. As the world becomes increasingly computerised and digitalised, dematerialisation becomes a significant aspect of contemporary culture. This raises the central question of how these developments redefine animation's indexing status, and non-fiction imagery's truth claims more generally. German media philosopher Friedrich Kittler suggested decades ago that the digitalisation of information and rise in computer communication would reduce human-oriented interfaces,[77] themes developed by theorists such as Mark B. N. Hansen and Bernard Stiegler.[78] Joel McKim, however, suggests that:

> [R]ather than claim that representational or sensory media is becoming less relevant in a computational age, perhaps we should acknowledge instead that our contemporary media is increasingly constituted by mediations of media itself. Or, in other words, there is an increasing preponderance of media that translates digital information into a humanly perceptible form. Seen from this perspective, the relevance of digital animation, comprised of everything from data visualizations to computer-generated images, has actually expanded in our post-phenomenological or post-experiential computational environments.

While Hansen is quite right to alert us to the growth of machine-to-machine communications and the computational harnessing of pre-cognitive affects and tendencies, animation remains as a kind of representational last stand, and a viable form of resistance in relation to dehumanising forms of digital calculation.[79]

Unlike cases in which animation is used to depict the personal or the physical, in the portrayal of digital worlds animation is *not* an interpretative visual language. Animation that is used to depict the visualisation of virtual worlds is initially designed, of course, but it is not stylised according to content, like animated works about actual events. For example, Chapter 5 discusses the capture of online game activities where the animation is actually recorded directly, and portrays how the virtual events appear on screen, instead of an as interpreted visualisation of events that were actually seen differently by those who took part, as is the case when using animation to document physical events.

Animation in digital worlds portrays unplanned activity based on user input. When used in digitally virtual worlds, such as online game environments, animation is the direct visualisation of code. It provides the visual interface of the virtual world that *all* users see, and the façade through which they experience the platform – the graphic user interface (GUI) – as opposed to past visualisations of immaterial aspects of reality, such as paintings of gods as imagined by different artists. Recorded animated fragments of these digital events become more like a photographic document than interpretative documentary imagery, because they capture the only visual appearance of these online activities. In this sense, animation can be theorised as a deixis of the non-physical, or as a trace of events in the realm of code, but not as a trace of the physical.

The relation between indexicality and ontology is tricky, to say the least. Doane explains that indices are 'limited to the assurance of an existence; they provide no insight into the nature of their objects; they ... simply indicate that something is "there"'.[80] Therefore, in a virtualised culture in which non-material realities are given visual form, a new form of indication is conceived through changing uses of animation that point to the existence of such realities, though not physically, and consequently influence conceptions of these realities. These issues are central to the reconsideration of what constitutes 'the real' and its believable signification or proof in documentary works. The document, upon which the documentary is grounded, is also the basis for documentary works more generally. This begs the questions, what exactly is a document, and how does animation's role as index relate to documents as the basis for documentary representation and credibility?

RETHINKING THE INDEX AND THE DOCUMENT IN DOCUMENTARIES

How do animation's multiple forms of indexicality contribute to the theorisation of animation as a documentary aesthetic? Definitions of documentary are and always have been ambiguous. Whereas Renov's discussion of documentary's etymological roots emphasised teaching and the 'documentary desire' to know, Philip Rosen's investigation of documents' relation to documentaries produces different results.[81] According to Rosen, the etymological genealogy of the noun *document* has two chief derivations from its Latin and Old French roots, one indicating teaching or warning, and the other evidence or proof.[82] Evidence and the status of the index as trace remain central to documentary theory, but in themselves are insufficient to qualify for documentary or reliable non-fiction status. According to Rosen, an indexical image is insufficient because documentary requires a narrative that makes sense and bestows meaning upon the images seen, and is, therefore, prone to various interpretations.[83] Only through discursive intervention can a form of capture, such as a photograph, be seen as a document. This takes us back to Grierson's definition of documentary as the creative treatment of actuality, because if the expressive framing of the documents and facts is eliminated, only the documents remain and in themselves they may be too vague or open to interpretation.

Such conceptualisations of the documentary are vital to any consideration of animated documentary since they destabilise the essential role of the document-as-proof and point to the constructed nature of all documentaries, regardless of their aesthetic style. Animation merely highlights this last aspect, emphasising the constructedness rather than capture of the images themselves, forcing viewers not only to consider the truth-value of documentaries today, but also to question the truth claims of visual documents more generally. By unapologetically emphasising construction, animated documentary contributes to epistemological explorations of the documentary genre and non-fiction representations by questioning and casting new light on the capacity of the moving image to act as a record of the world. Rather than prioritising a certain form of capture as a trustworthy document, the reception of certain representations as more or less credible is accentuated. This emphasises the conventions and discourse surrounding representations and documentaries rather than documents themselves.

There is therefore a need to rethink both indexicality and documentary conventions. Since the index as proof is insufficient for documentary status, it is useful to turn to documentary theory and definitions in relation to contemporary developments of documentary imagery. According to Rosen, the 1989 revised edition of the OED notes that documentary's prime uses are for instruction or recording purposes.[84] This is similar to the index, if and only if *both* definitions of Pierce's index are accounted for, since one (the trace) acts as record and the other (the deixis) points to, instructs or informs. In revisiting Peirce's original definitions of the index, as well as the etymological roots of documentary, it becomes evident that *similar meanings reside in both*. Put simply, if the documentary aim is to record or instruct, then both forms of index – the trace as a form of record and the deixis as a form of instruction or indication – are relevant. For this reason, existing theorisations of documentary, which rely on only one aspect of the index, as trace, and which seem as a consequence to exclude animation, are insufficient. If a document both teaches and proves, and if an animated index can similarly deictically point and consequently teach, as well as act as trace, animation is itself an emerging form of document.

The relation between animation's indexicality, documents and evidence can be examined in both form and practice through forensic animation, another close cousin of animated documentaries.[85] Forensic animation uses new visualisations to create usable evidence and consequent truth claims. By merging the work of an animator with that of a forensic reconstructionist in order to portray crime scenes based on factual data, forensic animation has begun to replace the more traditional illustrations, photographs and verbal descriptions conventionally used in forensics.[86] Like animated documentaries, animation is used forensically to draw attention, simplify complex information and visualise what cannot otherwise be seen. These new forms of evidentiary graphics are 'usually classed as either substantive evidence (used to prove or disprove something) or illustrative (a demonstration or visual aid)'.[87] Like the trace as evidence and the deixis as demonstration or visualisation, forensic animation illustrates how acknowledgement of more than one kind of index might expand the exploration processes that lead to truth claims.

As documentary definitions become more fluid due to wide-ranging exploration and experimentation, one must be careful to ensure that expanding a definition does not divest it of its meaning. This has been termed by some as the 'post-documentary' moment.[88] However, by viewing documentaries as part of an epistemological exploration of realities, it becomes apparent that the OED definitions of recording or instructing still hold. Therefore, rather than abandoning or destabilising the notion of the index as a basis for the representation's epistemological stake and documentary value, accepting the index's dual definitions as trace *and* deixis maintains its relevance in today's evolving digital cultures and technologies of representation. If the multiple meanings of the index supposedly lead to its collapse, the notion of a document collapses as well, thus eliminating any base for documentary. It is therefore important to address the complexity of the concept of indexicality and its repercussions, rather than dismissing it altogether.

To conclude, as realities change due to technological developments, the referents indexed – and referentiality in general – demand attention. My analysis of the digitalisation and virtualisation of contemporary culture foregrounds the limitations of conventional theorisations of documentary imagery, which are based upon physical realities. While non-physical realities have existed throughout the history of humanity, in the shape of belief systems and constructions of knowledge, today's digital realities differ in the sense that they appear visually uniform to all who have technological access. The referencing ability of the images used thus changes accordingly.

As we have seen, the animated index, as both trace and deixis, is not only capable of indicating the mixed realities of today, it also fulfils the dual function of a document-as-proof and/or as indication, and consequently can act as a form of legitimisation and credibility for documentary works. This explains the relation between these changing modes of informational representation to one of the central aims of documentary, which is, according to Bill Nichols, to stimulate *epistephilia*, a desire to know about the world.[89] When considering animation's complex relation to indexicality, and indirectly to documents and evidence, animation's role in documentary works and its ability to strengthen their credibility become essential to acknowledge. Additionally, the animated index demonstrates the emergence of what I call a post-photographic documentary aesthetic, whereby animation can act as document, with evidentiary status, while breaking with visual photorealism. Post-photographic documentary aesthetics thus rely on indexicality as a marker of veracity but completely transform expectations regarding what such evidentiary documents may look like, raising many questions about referentiality and viewer reception today.

Chapter 1 explained the changing status of photorealism in documentary and non-fiction aesthetics, and Chapter 2 analysed the shifting conceptualisations of indexicality as a basis for imagery's evidentiary status. By demonstrating that animation can, and should, be thought of differently in relation to its truth status in contemporary mixed realities, Part II of the book considers technoculture and the emergence of varied forms of virtual documentaries and animation's central role within them as a sign of the times.

NOTES

1. For more on animation's increasingly central role in digital culture, where it is used to transform 'digital information into human-oriented visual forms' that push 'animation into the epistemic and design realms of data visualisation, modelling, simulation and rendering – forms of contemporary representation with enormous political and social resonances', see Leslie and McKim, 'Life Remade'.
2. *Slaves*, film, directed by David Aronowitsch and Hanna Heilborn (Sweden, Norway, Denmark: Story AB, 2008).
3. Animation's relation to the reality portrayed has been defined in varied ways. For examples, see sources listed in the Introduction, note 46.
4. Quoted in Ward, 'Drama-documentary, Ethics', p. 198.
5. Roger Odin has claimed that spectators can produce a 'documentarizing lecture' of films, which applies cultural constraints (rather than necessarily internal constraints in the work itself) that dictate how a work is viewed. For more on this see Odin, 'For a Semio-pragmatics of Film', p. 213. Also, Bill Nichols applies a three-part definition of documentary that relies on the way audiences engage

through a documentary mode of reading which is based on a familiarity with and acceptance of the validity and integrity of these generic modes of representation. See Craig Hight, 'Mockumentary', pp. 204–5.

6. For examples of animated documentaries that use interviews see, for example: *Snack and Drink*, animated video, directed by Bob Sabiston (USA: Flat Black Films, 1999); *Ryan*, animated film, directed by Chris Landreth (Canada: Copperheart Entertainment, 2004); *It's Like That*, film, directed by SLAG (Australia: SLAG, 2003); *Last Day of Freedom*, animated film, directed by Dee Hibbert-Jones and Nomi Talisman (USA: Living Condition, 2015); *Lip Sync – Creature Comforts*, animated video, created by Nick Park (UK: Aardman Animations, 1989); *Backseat Bingo*, animated video, directed by Liz Blazer (USA: University of Southern California, 2003); *Wonderland: The Trouble with Love and Sex*, animated TV series, directed by Jonathan Hodgson (UK: Sherbet, 2011); *Audrie & Daisy*, film, directed by Bonni Cohen and Jon Shenk (USA: Actual Film, 2016). For more on the animated interview see Honess Roe, *Animated Documentary*, pp. 74–105.

7. Nichols, *Introduction to Documentary*, p. xi. Emphasis in the original.

8. Buchan, *Animated 'Worlds'*, p. vii.

9. For more on the persistence of photography, for 'it is too disturbing to relinquish trust in what looks real because that would eliminate any basis for knowledge through vision', see Ritchin, *After Photography*, p. 180. Western culture's longstanding connection between vision and cognition reaches back to ancient Greece and persists in varying degrees to the present day, claiming that visuality is the preeminent medium of our experience of the world. For more on scholars of visual culture who deal with the history of visuality see Mitchell, *Iconology*; Mitchell, *Picture Theory*; Jay, *Downcast Eyes*.

10. Analogue photography exemplifies a connection between the physical referent recorded and the image produced since its production process is based on a chemical procedure where light causes an image – based on the material referent in front of the lens – to be imprinted on the photographic film. As such, analogue photography exemplifies a connection between the physical referent recorded and the image produced.

11. A dominant view of many media theorists is that the optical devices of the nineteenth century that synthesised the motion of drawings paved the way for cinema, which utilised similar concepts to photography. Crafton, 'Veiled Genealogies', p. 94. Before the term 'motion pictures' caught on, films were called 'animated pictures', locating film ontologically as a subfield of animation. For more on the early relationships between animation and film see Denslow, 'What is Animation', p. 4; Cholodenko, 'Animation (Theory) as the Poematic', p. 3; Cholodenko, 'Who Framed Roger Rabbit', pp. 212–13; Crafton, 'Veiled Genealogies', pp. 101, 107. Paul Wells explains that in the digital era the boundaries between animation and live action have been completely blurred: see Wells, *Basics Animation*, p. 12. Lev Manovich sees animation as now including lens-based photography, see *Software Takes Command*, p. 294 or *Language of New Media*, p. 295;

and Alan Cholodenko sees animation as the 'paradigm of all forms of cinema' in Cholodenko, '"First Principles" of Animation', p. 99.

Interestingly, the emergence of digital cinema has led to a new merging of cinema and animation. Where cinema may once have been defined by lens-based recordings of reality, the computerisation of cinema in the digital age facilitates the modification of individual frames and entire scenes so that even though the photographic appearance may be maintained in form, the images shown were never filmed. As Lev Manovich explains, this means that 'cinema can no longer be clearly distinguished from animation ... [since it] is no longer an indexical media technology but, rather, a subgenre of painting'. See *Language of New Media*, 295.

12. For different views on the comparison and convergence of animation and photography see, for example, Annabelle Honess Roe, *Animated Documentary*; Tom Gunning, 'Animating the Instant'; Frank, 'Traces of the World'.
13. See Ritchin in his aptly named book *After Photography*; Hunt and Schwartz, 'Capturing the Moment', p. 266.
14. Blocker, *Seeing Witness*, p. xvi.
15. It is noteworthy that this book engages with animation that does not attempt photorealism.
16. See Costello and Iversen, 'Introduction'; Fried, *Why Photography Matters*.
17. For more on the discussion of machine capture, see Jane Blocker's discussion of machine witnessing. Jane Blocker refers to machines that do not require human operation (such as drones and satellites) as witnesses, and argues that the fact that images have been taken by a machine 'adds considerably to their supposed neutrality, objectivity, and truth-value'. She proposes that 'the witness who is invisible, omniscient, and disembodied is more trustworthy than the witness who is visible, with finite knowledge and human limitations'. See Blocker, *Seeing Witness*, pp. xiv–xiii.
18. Bazin, *What is Cinema?*, p. 13.
19. Honess Roe, 'Interjections and Connections', p. 273. Although Honess Roe discusses an 'almost aesthetically indistinguishable' animation that aims to link the live-action footage to the animated images, the images I discuss here can also be understood as a form of 'connective tissue' despite merely having certain visual similarities and not being indistinguishable from the photographic footage, since they too act as a way to join the separate visual parts into a 'cohesive whole'.
20. Barthes, *Camera Lucida*, p. 76. On the connection between cinema and reality see also Kracauer, *Mass Ornament*.
21. Enwezor, 'Rules of Evidence', p. 10.
22. See, for example, Kim, 'Animating the Photographic Trace'.
23. This definition was part of a presentation titled 'Real-Time Animation and Data Visualization: Redefining Animation and the Animated Documentary' that I gave at the Redefining Animation Society for Animation Studies 2013 annual conference at the University of Southern California.
24. See Husbands and Ruddell, 'Approaching Animation'.

25. Manovich, 'Image Future', p. 89.
26. For more on the definitions of animation see Greenberg, 'Animated Text'.
27. Wells, *Animation*, p. 1.
28. Strøm, 'Animated Documentary', p. 47.
29. See Wells, 'Frame of Reference'.
30. This is a partial list. For an elaborated account of the term's etymology and lexicology, see Crafton, 'Veiled Genealogies', pp. 97–8.
31. For further reading on theorists who have approached the issue of movement in animation, see Wells, 'Frame of Reference', p. 17; Wells, *Animation*, p. 6; Furniss, *Art in Motion*, p. 5.
32. Cholodenko, quoted in Levitt, 'Animation and the Medium', p. 123. For a discussion of definitions based on these grounds see also Martinez, 'Criteria for Defining Animation'.
33. Levitt, *Animatic Apparatus*, p. 3.
34. Levitt, 'Animation and the Medium', p. 118.
35. Denslow, 'What is Animation', p. 1.
36. For a further discussion of animation from the perspective of representational forms, see Furniss, *Art in Motion*.
37. This was the title of Joel McKim's presentation at the Society for Animation Studies annual conference, Lisbon, 17–21 June 2019.
38. Taylor, *When the Machine Made Art*, pp. 14–16.
39. The lack of a clear definition raises questions about conceptualising animation in such a wide sense, which may be regarded as cartoons, digital arts, new media imagery, post-photography, simulations, computer graphics, multi-media and more. For more on this see Reinke, 'World is a Cartoon', p. 11. For an ongoing discussion on this topic and views about the consequential need for a new language of cinema, see Parsons, 'Why We Need a New Language'.
40. Nitsche, 'Machinima as Media', p. 114.
41. Chow, *Animation, Embodiment, and Digital Media*, p. 4.
42. Denslow, 'What is Animation', p. 4.
43. Suzanne Buchan defines animated 'worlds' as those 'realms of cinematic experience that are accessible to the spectator only through the techniques available in animation filmmaking'. See Buchan, *Animated 'Worlds'*, p. vii.
44. Wells, 'Frame of Reference', pp. 22–4.
45. Hansen, *Bodies in Code*, p. 2.
46. Ibid., pp. 8, 92.
47. Short, *Peirce's Theory of Signs*, pp. 215, 229. It is important to note the difference in how we use the word 'icon' today, and how Peirce meant it in the 1860s (today an iconised image has a readily recognisable reference attached to it).
48. Ibid., pp. 220–1.
49. Doane, 'Indexical and Concept of Medium Specificity', p. 136.
50. Gunning, 'Moving Away from the Index', p. 30.
51. Buchler, *Philosophical Writings of Peirce*, p. 108.
52. Gunning, 'Moving Away from the Index', p. 30. For further theoretical

discussions of the index, see Krauss, *Originality of the Avant-Garde*, p. 198, and Elkins, *Photography Theory*, p. 231.
53. Short, *Peirce's Theory of Signs*, pp. 218, 226.
54. Ibid., p. 215.
55. The era of post-photography is often explained as resulting from the changes in production methods of the digital revolution, and a growing awareness of the ease of manipulation of digital imagery, which lead to conceptualising digital photography as a new medium.
56. Doane, 'Indexicality', p. 2. See also Oxford English Dictionary definition of 'deixis', https://en.oxforddictionaries.com/definition/deixis, accessed 15 May 2012.
57. *Holy Motors*, film, directed by Leos Carax (France and Germany: Wild Bunch, Arte Cinema and Pierre Grise Productions, 2012).
58. This is, of course, only relevant to analogue photography.
59. Only when motion capture develops to the extent where animation is no longer needed in postproduction will it cease to fall into the category of animation. Since the definition of animation that I introduced is 'movement only visible on screen', the amalgamated image falls under this category as the final image would not be visible otherwise. Even though the movement is captured from the physical, the images undergo stylisation, which means they cannot be seen moving anywhere but on screen.
60. Woodcock, 'Capture, Hold, Release', p. 1.
61. Chow, *Animation, Embodiment, and Digital Media*, p. 2.
62. For an interesting discussion of motion capture techniques, and the on-going debate about its relation to – and status as – animation, as perceived by its changing degrees of rendering, see Freedman, 'Is it Real'. See also Chow, *Animation, Embodiment, and Digital Media*, p. 120.
63. *The Lord of the Rings*, film series, directed by Peter Jackson (New Zealand and USA: New Line Cinema and WingNut Films, 2001–3).
64. *Rise of the Planet of the Apes*, film, directed by Rupert Wyatt (USA: Chernin Entertainment, Dune Entertainment, Big Screen Productions and Ingenious Film Partners, 2011).
65. *Dawn of the Planet of the Apes*, film, directed by Matt Reeves (USA: Chernin Entertainment and TSG Entertainment, 2014).
66. Honess Roe, 'Animating Documentary', p. 142.
67. Leslie and McKim, 'Life Remade', p. 207.
68. See Hartshorne and Weiss, *Collected Papers*, p. 24; Short, *Peirce's Theory of Signs*, p. 230.
69. See Grau, *Imagery in the 21st Century*.
70. For more on the growing use of imagery across the university, in disciplines less associated with visual studies, see Elkins, 'Visual Practices'.
71. See www.multimedia.mcb.harvard.edu/ and www.xvivo.net/mitochondria-press-release/, both accessed 12 January 2013.
72. See Warburton, 'Goodbye Uncanny Valley'.

73. Renov, *Theorising Documentary*, p. 5.
74. Deleuze, *Cinema 1*, pp. 16–17.
75. Although this is an obvious though perhaps insufficient tactic, philosopher Noël Carroll claims that most films arrive already labelled so that audiences know how to receive them. See Carroll, *Engaging the Movie Image*, p. 169.
76. Honess Roe, *Animated Documentary*.
77. Kittler, *Gramophone, Film, Typewriter*, p. 1.
78. See Hansen, *Feed-Forward* and Stiegler, *Automatic Society*.
79. McKim, 'Speculative Animation', p. 294.
80. Doane, 'Indexical and Concept of Medium Specificity', p. 135.
81. Renov, *Theorising Documentary*, p. 5.
82. Rosen, 'Document and Documentary', pp. 65–6.
83. Ibid., pp. 62–76.
84. Ibid., p. 66.
85. Recently developed and publicised widely through the work on forensics and digital media by Weizman, *Forensic Architecture*.
86. Ma *et al.*, 'Virtual Reality', pp. 1227, 1229.
87. Schofield, 'Playing with Evidence', p. 56.
88. For more on the discussion of the post-documentary, see Corner, 'Performing the Real'.
89. Nichols, *Representing Reality*, p. 31.

Part II

Animation and Technoculture: The Virtualisation of Culture and Virtual Documentaries

CHAPTER THREE

The Virtualisation of Culture: Screens, Virtuality and Materiality

This chapter links the virtualisation of culture to the changes in documentary and non-fiction aesthetics discussed in Chapters 1 and 2, where I proposed that visual realism may no longer hold the same credibility once associated with it, whereas reliance on the body and physical traces still maintain their evidentiary status. These lines of thought are developed and contextualised within technoculture, most obviously through screens, virtuality, materiality and the body (and its representation) in contemporary culture, discussed in detail below.[1] Whereas screen culture defines contemporaneity and is the everyday embodiment of digitalisation, omnipresent screens also raise questions about the definition, role and so-called 'interpenetration' of the virtual with the physical and, consequently, the status and representation of material spaces and referents within this convergence of realms. I will show how these changes directly impact the study, theorisation, reception and production of animated documentaries.

The sound of your GPS calling out 'recalculating' as you drive effectively suggests that you have messed up. It evokes frustration and confusion because you know you have veered off the GPS's carefully plotted path. The fact that you know what I'm talking about demonstrates the ubiquity of GPS, and how comfortable we have become viewing and navigating our physical surroundings through their real-time animated visualisation on screen. The way animation serves as an interface for our increasingly complex relations to data changes the way we see and interact with the world.

Since GPS screens are placed just below the windshield, drivers are given a double view of their environment in both physical and animated form, generating equivalence between the two and highlighting the convergence of on- and off-screen worlds as users are simultaneously involved in both. Indeed, as early as 2006, Mark Hansen claimed that 'all reality is mixed reality'.[2] He explains that today there is an interpenetration of domains, in the sense that the virtual is no longer a distinct realm but rather an information space activated and 'transformed as the user navigates . . . real space'.[3] These ideas have expanded into more flexible terms such as XR ('cross reality'), which encompass a wide spectrum of software and hardware that bring digital objects into physical space and physical objects into digital spaces, fusing the two all the more.[4] According to Hansen, it is motor activity, rather than any representational mimesis, that enables the move between the virtual and physical worlds.[5] This entanglement of the physical with a simulated vision of the world impacts the kind of imagery viewers have become accustomed to and ultimately believe in. The proliferation of animated images means that animation is viewed less as fictional or artificial (in comparison to photorealism) and more as a significant and potentially convincing language of representation. Although GPS is a current instalment in a long history of cartographical visualisations, its uniqueness inheres in its real-time mutable depiction based on the physical presence and geographical location of the user. This form of visualisation proves relevant to our topic.

The study of animated documentary to date has included the exploration of non-physical realities that could not be photographed; the focus has been on personal perspectives and memories, or the use of animation as an interpretive representation of events.[6] However, animation's ability to visualise immaterial realities is becoming an increasingly important component of documentary practice, since it enables engagement with the virtual features of contemporary life. Digitally virtual spaces and experiences may still be seen by some as fictional, or at least less 'real' than the physical; but the virtual is an increasingly prevalent aspect of present-day culture. As more people spend more of their 'real' lives in virtual worlds, the virtual defines who they are, thus complementing, reflecting and shaping the physical, so that the virtual and non-virtual collide in various ways. Thus, the multiplicity of contemporary realities exceeds the physical and is more accurately described in terms of 'mixed realities', which embody the material and the virtual. Such mixed realities require new languages of visual documentary, bringing animation into the picture.

The digitally virtual has been defined as 3D interactive platforms available on screen that create an immersive experience of telepresence through networked communications.[7] In these computerised virtual realities, where users are active on a daily basis, pictorial imagery conveys actions and events. Media theorist Lev Manovich, in his examination of aesthetics of the contemporary computerised and networked information era, asks whether:

> the arrival of information society [has] been accompanied by a new vocabulary of forms, new design aesthetics, new iconologies? Can there be forms specific to information society, given that software and computer networks redefine the very concept of form? . . . Can information society be represented iconically, if the activities that define it – information processing, interaction between a human and a computer telecommunication, networking – are all dynamic processes?[8]

As this book demonstrates, animation is an essential part of these new aesthetics. Because animation is constructed imagery characterised by infinite styles and based on on-screen movement, it is free from the limitations of photography, which remains rooted in the physical. Animation is the ideal language for virtual worlds since it provides a means of visualisation that can represent dynamic, non-physical realities in real time that are otherwise unseen. The visual representation of the digital's physical components, such as wires, a hard drive or a person shown sitting and typing, for example, do not represent the activities and events experienced in these non-physical virtual platforms. Thomas Elsaesser and Malte Hagener explain that what users see in current computer culture is actually abstract data made visible through images and signs, not something that physically exists.[9] Animation, in other words, is the visual façade of many virtual spaces and events, converting mathematical code into dynamic visualisations that indicate users, spaces and actions. Examples might include the rotating hourglass symbolising a computerised action in progress, or a user's mouse movements shown by the cursor, indicating the user's physical movements translated into virtual space. Animation is an essential aesthetic of today's networked and computerised information society; it is a dynamic form of imagery that visualises information and procedures in the non-physical virtual realities of today. Animation also visualises user input and virtual actions within human–computer interaction (HCI), a central characteristic of contemporaneity. Animation is thus the graphic user interface (GUI) of digitally virtual activities. As viewers spend more time in virtual worlds that use animated visuals, they become increasingly accustomed to this graphic representation of daily events and activities. This makes animation's use in non-fiction settings appear more mundane, less extraordinary and less a part of fictional fantasy worlds. To appreciate how conceptualisations of virtuality have changed, and how representations of the digitally virtual contribute to documentary practice and theorisation, it is necessary to explore these issues in greater detail.

While GPS-based cartographical applications enable users to drive according to a visual translation of their vicinity on screen in animated form, Instagram filter apps allow people to modify their own images and the world around them. Thus, image manipulation is inscribed in those devices we use to present ourselves, and there is growing reliance on animated imagery that does not look 'real'. The animations used in GPS systems are stylistically simple, but they are based on real-time imaging techniques that calculate geographical positioning, which bestow an authority and evidentiary status on the images that adds to their credibility. Although a photograph offers no such calculations, it still requires the viewer to interpret the image by comparing it to what was photographed. This shift from a photorealistic depiction to one which is computationally animated demonstrates that the criteria for an image's truth-value have shifted from visual realism to, among others, interactivity and real-time visualisation of user input and/or physical location and movement.

Screen Culture

In my discussion of the multiple and shifting definitions of animation, I defined animation as 'movement that is only visible on screen'. Consequently, the screen – an essential component of animation and a divide between animated worlds and the viewer's physical environment – merits serious attention, both as physical object and cultural characteristic, and in terms of how it impacts on viewership and the credibility of imagery. Existing scholarship on animation has only briefly commented on different aspects of the screen; it has not developed the relation of contemporary screen culture with shifting documentary imagery, theorisation and reception. For example, it has been suggested that animation is closer to the computer industry than to film or graphic design because of its reliance on software innovation;[10] and that digital animation's ability to reflect technological innovation has become a way to experience technology itself.[11] Acknowledging the correlation between changing screen technologies and evolving documentary aesthetics establishes animation as a highly significant visual form in today's omnipresent computerised screen culture.

The relation between viewer and screen, or more specifically, the relation between the off-screen world inhabited by viewers and the visual on-screen world, is a persistent theme in the study of moving-image culture. Noël Carroll asserts that viewers are incapable of orienting their body towards the actual profilmic space portrayed on the screen because of the disconnection between the viewer's and the on-screen world,[12] extrapolating this to all photographic and cinematic images. But photographic imagery, on- or off-screen, unlike animation, still shares the visible properties of the viewer's world. How does the changing relation between the viewer's off-screen world with the on-screen animated world influence the study and reception of animated documentaries?

As screen technologies advance, the screen as a flat rectangle that acts as a window into the virtual world changes and, in principle, screen imagery can now appear everywhere and anywhere. Animated non-fiction can be viewed on a variety of platforms, including cinematic, private, public and various mobile screens. As types and contexts of screen display change, theorisations of the viewer's relation to what takes place on screen – once perceived as a window to other worlds – transform as well. Throughout the history of visual culture, the transformation of a three-dimensional universe into a two-dimensional representation has been significant. Classical painting since the Renaissance managed distance by using central perspective, with its attendant implications of size and the single vanishing point framing space for the spectator, and ensuring that the painting gave the illusion of being like an open window. These techniques are also used in moving-image culture where a simulated three-dimensional reality on screen can be experienced either as another coexisting world, or as a continuation of the viewer's own three-dimensional world.

Will the status of the screen as a separate entity eventually diminish, resulting in a merging of the human retina and the screen, as Manovich cautiously suggests?[13] Mobile phones and the development of Google's Project Glass augmented reality glasses (and its presumably more successful descendants), the rapid development of VR gear, and the general increase in wearable technology all lend credence to his forecast.

The screen gives access to what cannot be seen with the human eye. This is similar to the initial achievements of the photograph and the microscope – enhancing vision and revealing previously unavailable aspects of 'the real', and broadening our epistemological range. However, photography, microscopes and telescopes revealed what was physical, whereas new technologies of representation on screen reveal what is not necessarily physical and cannot otherwise be seen. Furthermore, whereas in the past, technologies of vision were available to comparatively few people, today screens enabling enhanced vision are relatively common, leading to a widespread shift in visuality and what it can encompass.

The study of screens includes the physical-technological characteristics of, and alterations to, the screen as object and investigates a wide range of related elements. These include topics of scale and technology, such as analogue cinema, electronic TVs, digital computers, cell phones and personal screens; the shape, tactility, portability and location of screens as a continuation of early pre-cinematic apparatus; different networked screens, their urban concentration and their visual consumption.[14] Contemporary computerised culture establishes screens as a fundamental characteristic of our time. However, rapid changes in contemporary screens influence the relationship between screen and viewer and the reception of the information displayed on them, as well as their definitions. The cultural implications of such changes are wide-ranging.[15]

The viewing conditions of moving imagery in traditional cinematic venues involved immobile spectatorship in an enclosed and darkened space that minimised distraction from the screen. This was meant to expedite the metaphorical dissolve of one's physical surroundings, while heightening an immersive experience in the events on screen.[16] Alongside changes in the size and portability of screens, locations of display have also multiplied: projections have left the traditional cinematic space and have been transferred to multiplexes, open-air venues and the home. These changes in screens and viewing conditions mean that on-screen and off-screen worlds coexist and constantly merge.

Separate virtual worlds, once depicted in paintings and now on screen, can be experienced differently based on their display. Frescoes and mosaics are, like large-scale contemporary screens, inseparable from their architectural surroundings. Paintings, and now personal computer screens and mobile phones, make these depictions easily accessible on canvases and portable screens, which allow viewers enduring access. Erkki Huhtamo questions how often users of mobile screens 'think about the curious shifts of perception between nothing less than ontological realms that take place when they move their gaze from the screen to other humans, to the surrounding landscape, to another screen, and back again, in rapid succession?'[17] If what transpires 'in there', on screen, is seen as related and continuous to what takes place 'out here', in the viewer's physical space, the perception of a divide between on- and off-screen worlds changes. A sense of continuity rather than innate separateness emerges, facilitating the use of one to represent the other, as happens in animated non-fiction.

A further connection between on-screen and off-screen worlds is also created by changes in the technologies of display that progressively break the confines of the screen's frame, thus 'escaping the screen' and being integrated more smoothly into existing physical environments. As IMAX gets ever bigger and 3D cinema becomes the norm, for example, they break the margins of the frame and bring viewers closer to the sense of immersion inherent in virtual reality. Projections also allow an entirely different de-framing of the image process, migrating from the screen to other physical surfaces. Advanced forms and scales of projection can similarly invade the spectator's viewing space, creating unprecedented relations between the image and the viewer's body, which may be immersive or no longer based on the viewer's verticality.

Two-dimensional animations can also escape the screen in order to infiltrate the physical world of the spectator. By creating 3D digital projections, buildings and objects, such as clothes or furniture, can become screens; what is projected onto them is enhanced by the dimensions of the projection space, and is no longer viewed merely as a 2D image. The screen, which was previously separate from viewers who sat immobilised in order to watch, is now embedded in the setting that the viewer herself inhabits. This phenomenon fluctuates between cultures, of course, but as images are increasingly projected onto the physical world, the viewer progressively finds herself in the screen. There are many examples of animation being used in live-action performances in this way, including the opening ceremony of the 2014 Winter Olympics in Russia, in which the famous animator and Oscar Award winner, Aleksandr Petrov, created four animation fragments covering the entire floor of the venue. Using 120 projectors, Petrov created a seamless display integrated with live performances, with visual amalgamations between the physical components and the animated visuals.[18] Thus the frame that previously contained the animation was broken and the image appeared to dwell in the physical world. Increasingly, artists and researchers are becoming interested in the amalgamation of animation with live performance, and interdisciplinary moving-image practice in film, theatre, dance, architecture and more.[19]

By projecting images onto 3D physical objects and through the omnipresence of portable screens, people are increasingly active within new screen spaces. The new shared space of the physical world and the screen world metaphorically locates spectators in that 'other' world too. This is a broader shift towards *life in screen*, whereby activities are increasingly based on networked interactivity and mediated through computerised screen culture. In other words, once virtual screen worlds become interactive and the screen functions as interface, the worlds it depicts no longer remain on its surface; rather, they invite the embodied viewer into a place and a role in which he or she can act dynamically. The screen as interface thus reinforces the growing convergence between on- and off-screen worlds. The environment in which contemporary users act on a daily basis is now largely computerised and virtual and consequently the *on*-screen world becomes an *in*-screen world, in which the viewer/user plays an active role. The dual phenomena of shattering screen boundaries and the vast extent of contemporary screen-based networked activities means that we increasingly live in-screen. The boundaries between off-screen and on-screen are thus persistently blurred.

Theodor H. Nelson, a pioneering sociologist and philosopher of information technology, claimed that, in order to see tomorrow's computer systems, one should look at gaming technologies.[20] In a rapidly evolving field, 'deframing' technologies such as HTC Vive and other virtual reality headsets locate the user in what was once a separate screen world. Similarly, technologies such as the Microsoft research project IllumiRoom, which uses a Kinect sensor and a projector to blend virtual and physical worlds by creating real-time projected visualisations adapted to the dimensions of the physical space, extend the screen world into the viewer's environment. Since the images on screen are no longer confined by the material screen frame, events on-screen disrupt and are disrupted by the events occurring around them in the physical world (think of your cat furiously chasing an animated car that has 'fled' the confines of the racing game on screen). The changes in screen culture and moving-imagery display thus influence the physical world as well as the virtual experience, bringing them together in new ways.

It is also important to consider augmented realities, which overlay digital data onto the physical world. Although augmented reality (AR) can include static information, animation plays a prominent role because it visualises the non-physical, which converges on screen with the physical surroundings of the viewer/user. AR is currently most relevant to mobile screens because it is used to provide additional layers of information that engage with the user's physical location; this information is layered upon that location, utilising a smartphone compass, camera and GPS system. Uses vary but augmented realities are common in games that take place in, or are layered onto, the physical world, and in tourism applications where directions to and information about physical locations are provided. The screen acts both as a window and as an interface through which the physical and the animated converge, and becomes both a means of visualising one's physical world and an augmented version of it. An obvious example would be *Pokémon Go*, one of the most popular and profitable mobile games of 2016, downloaded more than 650 million times.[21] This location-based augmented reality game by Niantic allows users to locate, battle and train virtual creatures who appear on screen in the player's real-world location. The popularity of the game highlights that what can be seen as virtual and/or fictional can have real-world consequences: such games can create a public nuisance, or generate income for local businesses at popular sites.[22]

These augmented realities not only influence actions and shape realities, they are also part of the contemporary phenomenon of 'living in-screen', whereby activities increasingly take place through screen mediation. Thus, augmented realities increasingly embody how the world is seen and experienced, with the physical simultaneously incorporating the non-physically digital. The two worlds are converging and increasingly being reconstituted as one.

THE VIRTUAL

Formerly, the image operated like the word, as a symbolic form of representation. Once photography became prevalent, the signifying relations of imagery changed, and principles of realism based on analogical mimesis were prioritised. Now, in-screen virtual worlds have departed from photorealism, and animation has taken an increasingly central role in today's virtual culture, as we shall see below.

As late as the 1990s, it would have been easier to differentiate theoretically between virtuality and reality-as-physical, and therefore photographable, but in the early twenty-first century this is no longer the case.[23] As we increasingly participate in informational environments, embodied agency transforms into a certain (technical) disembodiment, and virtuality becomes the basis of the convergence between the living and the ubiquitous information available in our world.[24] Nowadays, networked users engage with, and act according to and within, pictorial in-screen worlds that are not physical. Since mundane activities are increasingly mediated by screens, new forms of imagery are used for communication and representation. In the data-sphere of computerised networked society, icon-based and pictorial languages are used to envision abstract or non-physical concepts, constructing knowledge and allowing users to navigate in virtual space.

These non-physical or abstract computerised concepts are denoted by imagery that translates the invisible into the visible. Cubitt describes this as follows: 'peering into the space, the browser interface invites you into cyberspace ... the hardware becomes increasingly transparent as user-friendly, icon-driven designs invite you in to a space that has loosened its grip on materiality to present itself as a vast virtual playground'.[25]

In other words, aspects of contemporary digital-virtual culture appear only on screen and, as such, require representation that exceeds the photographic verisimilitude that relies on materiality. These symbolic graphic languages and, by extension, animation used in virtual spaces may not seem realistic because of their non-mimetic appearance, but as notions of realities change, the labels used to represent what was formerly branded 'not real' change as well. The idea that changes in believable visual representations are occurring due to technological shifts links the virtualisation of culture to evolving documentary imagery.

Some things about the virtual are not new at all. Rob Shields has confirmed that virtual reality has a long history in fiction, simulation and games that gave the impression the player was elsewhere, anticipating technology's capacity for bringing to life what is neither present nor 'real'.[26] Shield's definition of virtual worlds closely resembles earlier definitions of animation that also centred on visualisations of the absent and the imaginary. The digital virtual spaces and online gaming platforms discussed in this book are merely the latest manifestations of the virtual, but aesthetically they illustrate the central role animation plays in these contexts today. Since the study of virtuality is replete with notions of fiction, make believe, non-presence and deception, it is no surprise that 'the virtual' seems to have attained an unclear ontological status. Consequently, documenting contemporary digital worlds raises questions because these non-fiction works may easily seem more like fiction than fact.

The complexity of the virtual is partly due to its conflicting and changing definitions and its relationship to similarly evolving conceptions of 'the real'. Whereas some theorists have emphasised the recognition of the virtual as real because it is deeply entwined in the physical, imaginative and emotional lives of its users, this is a vast field of ontological and epistemological research. This book engages with the related discussions insofar as they are relevant to the themes of animated documentary. Focusing on central definitions of the virtual is essential. 'Virtual' has been defined as a contronym – a word that has contradictory meanings – in this case meaning both 'not really existing' and 'almost the same'.[27] As such, the virtual is seen as something similar and perhaps parallel to lived reality, but never as reality itself. Although the virtual is often contrasted with the real, an examination of other binary opposites frequently invoked in relation to the virtual can contribute to a better understanding of the ways in which virtuality has been theorised. Recurring themes in this regard include virtuality's relation to materiality, and its conceptualisation in contemporary technologised culture. Rather than maintaining binary classifications, the virtual becomes, in my reading, another aspect of contemporary realities.

First, a pairing of terms that requires critical evaluation is the opposition between virtuality and materiality. Shields adheres to this opposition proposing that 'the virtual' captures objects that are neither concrete nor tangible[28] whereas concreteness and materiality raise issues of embodiment and perception that seem to contradict the non-materiality he associates with virtuality. Indeed, the 'virtual' is commonly used to signify an absence or non-existence, whereas what is real is often equated with concreteness, material embodiment and tangible presence, suggesting that the virtual is not real. (However, non-tangible elements, such as religion or capitalism for example, can still shape aspects of 'the real'.)

As a distinctive example, and characteristic of cyberculture, online video gaming is an immensely popular virtual field of entertainment. It is fully animated and reflects on, responds to and is continuous with existing material realities. As gaming worlds evolve and multiply, their impact and significance grow, and their intersections with the more conventionally accepted 'real' also increase, for example in terms of social relations, physical effects, the economy and ecology; thus the distinctions between the virtual and the real are weakened. It is not my intention to map the whole process of how gaming culture overlaps with more traditional notions of what is 'real', or raise questions about the ontological status of online games. It is evident, however, that once virtual objects have real-world monetary value, for example, or gaming leads to child neglect, or avatars develop carbon footprints, the virtual is no longer detached from the concrete and physical.[29] Even ostensibly fictional aspects of the virtual cannot be disregarded as not 'real'; rather the virtual introduces a sense of multiplicity into the category of 'the real', which no longer only includes tangible physical reality. For these reasons, any definition of the non-physical digitally virtual as not 'real' is simplistic and inadequate.

Derrida's notion of the supplement is a useful alternative way of thinking about virtuality's ambiguous relation to 'the real'. The supplement can always be interpreted in two ways: it can be understood as fixing what is lacking in the 'original' or 'natural', adding in order to replace; or it can be seen to add to the 'natural' state in the form of multiplicity and enrichment.[30] The digitally virtual as an engaging and endless platform of possibilities is thus a potential supplement that, on one hand, offers users what is missing from their 'real' lives, at times replacing the material 'real' with the digital-virtual to varied degrees and, on the other, becomes yet another aspect of contemporary reality and contributes to its diversity. In both cases, the virtual as supplement facilitates our understanding of contemporary culture, and requires forms of documentation that break with previous documentary imagery of physical realities. The growing virtualisation of culture today leads to the virtual becoming 'more real than real', demonstrating the need to include the virtual in contemporary considerations of documentary, both in practice and theory.

Second, the discourse about virtuality must include wider consideration of the role of technology, and how the virtual is based on it. According to Benita Shaw, technology is 'the set of tools or "techniques" that serve the requirements of any given culture', thereafter emerging as more than just that, and becoming technology as culture or, as the title of her book reflects, 'technoculture'.[31] The technological developments that created the internet, cyberspace, communication networks and the resulting new virtual realities have blurred past distinctions between biological and technological, natural and artificial, human and mechanical. It is clear that technological innovations penetrate perceptions of realities, impact and shape everyday life, inevitably influencing how the world is experienced and represented.

MATERIALITY IN DIGITAL CULTURE AND EXPERIMENTAL DOCUMENTARIES

The animated documentary *Do It Yourself* (2007)[32] is based on the CIA 1970s manual on torture, and in it animated fish are used to represent people who are executed.[33] The use of fish in this example strengthens the film's anti-torture message by emphasising how the protagonists' humanity is entirely disregarded. There are many additional reasons why animated documentaries are used to disguise the appearance of the protagonists, including the need for anonymity, or the use of metaphor. However, are there wider contemporary

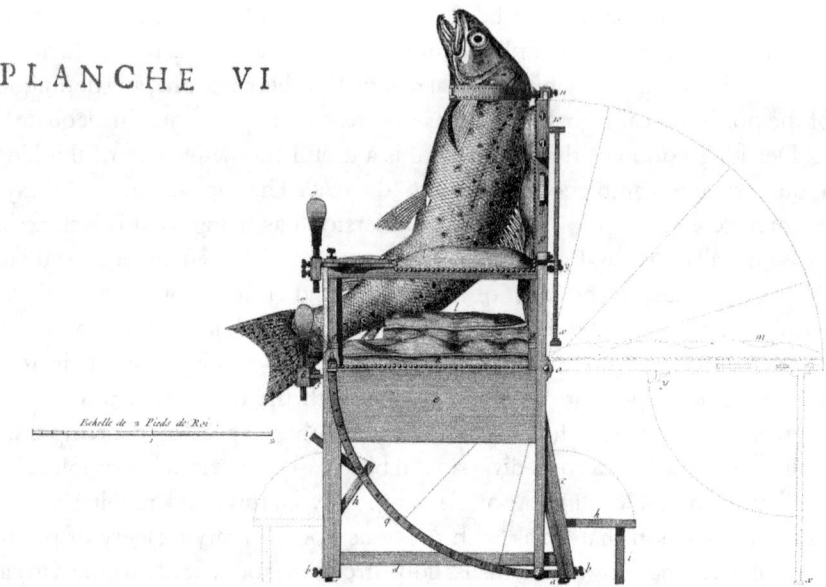

Figure 3.1   *Do It Yourself*, directed by Eric Ledune. 2007.

cultural characteristics that explain the increase in imagery that represents someone without replicating his or her physical appearance, and account for the growing acceptance of such imagery as credible?

The body does not disappear due to technological developments and digital culture but the act of conceptualising and representing the body in relation to a sense of 'self' does change. How does our shifting relation to technology influence the representation of the body, and how does this shape the perceived credibility of non-fiction imagery?

John Durham Peters explains the representation of the body as a form of visual validation: with its capacity for pain and death, the body is often used in the broadcast media as a criterion of truth and authenticity;[34] a focus on the body underscores the reality of violent or lethal events depicted.[35] While the role of the body can be an important factor in documentary viewing, I argue that today, the 'self' is represented by such varied imagery that its physical appearance is not necessarily the only way to build credibility, and that this is strongly related to techno-cultural trends, image-production methods and mediated screen realities.

The body and its relation to the sense of self is obviously a rich and complex field of study.[36] Deborah Levitt calls our time the age of the animatic apparatus, suggesting that the rise of animation and simulation releases 'images from actual and perceived ties to a real world as living bodies are increasingly untethered from determinations of biological vocation or destiny'. This, says Levitt, leads to an exploration of how transformations in the status of imagery also shape what 'life' may mean, and reflects changes in 'how we conceive, experience, and produce forms of vitality'.[37] Consequently, analysing the body's representation in contemporary digital culture and in recent experimental documentary works sheds light on the relation of the human body to contemporary technology, and explains the growing legitimisation of the use of non-physically mimetic imagery to represent people in documentaries. This is all the more so in a virtualised culture that is associated with non-materiality, in which technology alters the conceptualisation of the physical body and human perception. Recurring themes in related technology discourses include disembodiment, whereby a subject with no physical form can be linked to the technological fantasy of uploading consciousness, dispensing with the body entirely, versus new forms of embodiment through mediation, cyborgs, physical augmentation, posthumanism and re-embodiment, as an expansion of the way we think of our bodies.[38] It is, therefore, vital to examine whether and how theories about the body as validator of truth claims relate to contemporary technoculture and the widespread emergence of animated documentaries.

In 1993, Bill Nichols addressed changing conventions of documentary, and analysed how the authenticity attributed to certain practices fluctuates over time, changing the significance of signifiers in documentary filmmaking. Historically, re-enactment in documentary was considered less worthy than 'authentic' archival images. However, Nichols challenges this distinction between re-enactment and the recounting of events verbally, claiming that both can be accepted as credible documentary practice.[39] Indeed, performance and re-enactments of events have become increasingly prevalent in contemporary documentary, and are used when imagery is unavailable, or to disrupt certainties.[40] Animation functions in a similar manner.

The use of actors in re-enactments strengthens my point about the changing role of the body as a signifier of truth in several ways: the photographic image of a physical body is expected to act as legitimate documentary footage of 'somebody'.[41] In re-enactments, however, the actor becomes 'some body', merely filling in for somebody else. This trend continues in animated documentaries where the 'some body' evolves into a visual 'no body', which functions as a different kind of sign that symbolises a specific someone. If the documented character, the 'specific someone', is increasingly visually absent in live-action documentary, the question arises: do animated documentaries differ so much from live action if they merely use a different signifier for that specific someone? If signifiers and conventions change, the emphasis must shift to the viewer's reception of these signifiers, and hence to the meaning and validity the viewer attributes to them. Broader cultural trends must be taken into account, since changes in the way the body is conceptualised and represented can influence reception and credibility in documentaries. The following considers the body in contemporary virtualised culture, and its representation in recent experimental documentary works that reflect major cultural characteristics and raise meta-questions about the topic at hand.

The Body in Contemporary Virtualised Culture

In the past, animation may have seemed artificial because it appeared only on screen, beyond the physical environment of the viewer. However, once screen worlds converge with the physical world, the user's body is mediated through technology, creating various forms of embodiment, telepresence and varied on-screen representations. This altered sense of presence – of being simultaneously in more than one place – has been called 're-embodiment' by philosophers pursuing broadly conceived phenomenological analyses of human engagement with technologies.[42]

Living 'in-screen' in an increasingly networked culture involves varied forms of telepresence in which different visual signifiers can represent the absent physical body, while communication technologies sustain a sense of presence nonetheless. As Paul Virilio maintains, in an era dominated by telepresence, 'the material referent (or perhaps our belief in it), no longer exists'.[43] While I would not go so far as to suggest that the physical ceases to exist, there seem to be contradictory tendencies in regard to the physical body's relation to technology. On one hand, the body is augmented by portable technology that enhances its abilities; on the other, its centrality changes since the physical becomes only one of many realms of activity, unseen and secondary (at least in appearance) in code-based domains.

Furthermore, in the era of the 'quantified self', technological self-monitoring, biometrics, sensors and data acquisition convert the body and corporeal existence into computer information – mere additional data to be stored and analysed as if separate from the self. In other words, we have all been transformed into data and there are countless virtual profiles of users who are summarised through varied units of information that represent them in different ways for various goals and circumstances. This is similar to online profiles and avatars, which represent the user in all sorts of ways; it also explains the potential danger of identity theft, where no official relation to the body is required for one's legal, social or economic identity to be misused. Thus the role of the physical, and the authenticity associated with its visual appearance, are indeed in decline.

'Our edges are blurry', says artist Toni Dove in response to the convergence of living organism with machine, discussed in Donna Haraway's 1985 'Cyborg Manifesto'.[44] Dove points to the idea that perception of the self can extend beyond the body encapsulated by skin, and leads to the conclusion that the physical body is no longer the only visible representation of the self. Harbisson, mentioned above, is a rather extreme example, but we are all increasingly becoming one with our technologies.

For example, we are seeing a manifestation of 'nomophobia' (no mobile phobia), a contemporary term that describes the terror of being without one's phone and thus disconnected. This illustrates how the connection to, and reliance on, personal technology has developed to the point of being combined with a sense of bodily wholeness. Indeed, for Haraway, the cyborg body is not only a body extended by technology, but a transformation of the way in which the self is experienced and navigates in the world.[45] Embodiment is thus to be considered a process of construction that coordinates multiple bodies to create agency in the world.[46] This idea that the body, and thus the perception of the self, exceeds the physical flesh, is key to my discussion of animated documentary in virtualised culture, for it implies that representations that engage differently with the corporeal may be just as valid as photographic representations that are inherently linked to, and resemble, the physical. Whereas animation can allude to absence through its lack of physical capture (in contrast to photography), once animation is used in virtual worlds as an online representation of the user, it actually signifies the *presence* of the user whose actions are depicted on screen in an animated form.

As the body is mediated differently through various media, new spaces and options for embodiment and representation come into being. In computerised culture users may become embodied by handling the cursor, for example, as an extension of the hand, or by using an avatar (an icon or figure representing the user online) that is inhabited and manipulated like a digital puppet. This sense of inhabiting multiple realms of activity creates a sense of coexistence and co-presence that evokes multiple notions of the self.[47] Paul Roquet discusses the syncing of actual and virtual bodies, which results in what he calls 'the composited self' – a new form of individuation that emerges from the layers of the digital landscape.[48] In an era of increased interest in documentary works and a concurrent sense that reality ceases to make sense, many documentaries focus on the personal and the subjective. This trend, alongside changes in the sense of self shaped by vast technocultural transformations, illustrates the need to consider new forms of representation as they signify and engage with a changing sense of individuation. Elena Del Río explains that the coexistence of many different images of self turns the single 'self-possessed' body into a multiplicity of bodies that inhabit different spaces and times.[49] We thus become accustomed to the idea of electronic doubles as representations of the self, and even in our closest relationships we are used to interacting with simulacra.[50] It is evident that an altered relation to one's body is a recurring theme in visual and technological discourses, and is thus an important topic in my discussion of animated representations.

Merleau-Ponty's blind man's cane is a good example of how a technical artefact is mastered, eventually becoming part of the body schema, which implies the emergence of a renewed body with expanded perceptual powers and extended capacities for agency in the world.[51] Indeed, there is a great deal of research that shows that a sense of ownership over a different body is possible, creating perceptual illusions of body transformation and body substitution.[52] Kirk Besmer argues for a distinction between technologies that can become extensions of the body and are integrated into the body schema, and those that remain at the level of the body image.[53] The two are interrelated, but the body schema is a fusion of inputs that structures bodily activity, whereas the body image refers to self-awareness.[54] Since the avatar is never sensed tactilely, Besmer claims it is not integrated into the body schema and is thus different from the blind man's cane, its integration remaining on the level of the body image.[55] Interestingly, this suggests that as people are increasingly active in virtual worlds, their on-screen virtual representations can arguably become part of their multiple shifting body images. A sense of self is not tied to a single, unchanging body because, as science has proved, illusions of body ownership can cause the brain to accept a radically changed body, regardless of its appearance. Various body signifiers could thus potentially be accepted as representing the 'I', pointing to a more fluid sense of self through changeable body imagery, and confirming that the physical body is not the only way to depict the self.

Interesting representational examples include 'dopplebanger week', an internet meme/game that started in 2010 on Facebook, whereby users exchanged their profile pictures for those of celebrities, animation characters or anything else that supposedly bore some resemblance to the user. The 'self' was thus commonly represented by a variety of signifiers on a platform that is literally destined to project it – the name *Face*book implying reliance on the human face and physical appearance. In a similar vein, imaging advertised on Facebook between 2009 and 2013 encouraged people to 'cartoonify' themselves by means of non-photographic imagery of themselves as a form of avatar. The use of a non-photographic image as a portrait on Facebook is revealing. Personalised emoji based on the cartoonification of one's physical appearance have since become an accepted form of communication. 'Make your face into a GIF emoji' is the basis for many recent mobile phone apps such as Mojipop, Memoji or Emoji Me Face Maker, to name a few. Thus, users amplify the role of animation in their daily lives and interactions by using it to symbolise the self and, with it, various modes of self-expression.

The immensely popular mobile messaging app Snapchat, which enables communication through self-representation in visual styles that blur and camouflage one's appearance, continues these trends. Snapchat includes photos or short videos with regularly updated graphic overlays based on face detection technology that allow users to present themselves as dogs or bunnies, among others, and even includes face swapping options. Similarly, with the launch of iPhone X in 2017, Apple proudly announced the new feature of 'animoji', which uses face-scanning technology to create custom 3D animated emoji of animals (or poop) using the user's voice and facial expressions. As a new mode of communication, animoji thus makes self-representation through animated imagery, and seeing oneself and others signified by non-mimetic animated forms, increasingly commonplace. These are important cultural characteristics for an analysis and acceptance of animated documentaries, since interpretive and arbitrary depictions of the physical (characteristic of animated documentaries) are part of the myriad new ways of imaging the body and, more widely, the physical world. These trends in visual culture contribute to a changing sense of the believability of imagery in documentary contexts, strengthening the credibility of animated portrayals as a result.

A salient example is provided in Sandra Danilovic's 2009 *Second Bodies*,[56] chosen as the Best Documentary in the San Francisco New Media Film Festival in 2010. *Second Bodies* explores issues of self-image and identity, mediated through virtual world avatars and experiences.[57] Since the documentary engages with both online and offline identities, the representation of each protagonist blends real-life photographic footage with animated recordings from the virtual world of *Second Life* (*SL*). *SL* is an internet-accessed virtual world, launched in 2003 by Linden Lab. As an investigation of the body, or multiple bodies, as signifiers of the self, this documentary film, grounded in digital culture, points to the current need to surpass the photographic image's abilities (which focus on the physical referent) and extend documentary aesthetics so that new realms and mediated notions of the self may be visually explored. The film illustrates that clear delineations between online and offline identities are no longer possible.[58] Danilovic goes further and claims that by inhabiting virtual worlds, the transformation from single body to multiple bodies goes beyond the combination of player and avatar and includes the user and computer as tools.[59] In this sense, technology and the human body converge in a hybrid representation of the self.

Documentary-related artworks are useful to consider as avant-garde creations that raise relevant meta-questions about the contemporary role and representation of the human body, as well about documentary more

Figure 3.2   *Second Bodies,* directed by Sandra Danilovic, 2009.

generally. Artists have intentionally chosen to play with the body's physical appearance to demonstrate the complexity of utilising its outward appearance as a signifier of the subject. The representational fluidity of signifiers of the body has been in evidence for several years in documentary-related contemporary art, and has become even more central in technology-related projects.

Gillian Wearing, for example, continues several themes explored by Cindy Sherman since the 1970s, questioning the discrepancy between what may be photorealistic imagery of outward appearance and the inner life of the subject depicted.[60] In *10–6* (1997), Wearing combined different elements of the body, using adult actors to lip-synch the pre-recorded voices of children and adolescents vocalising their personal revelations.[61] The role of the physical body as signifier of depicted protagonists becomes all the more complex in documentary uses of re-enactment. Jeremy Deller's re-enactments in *The Battle of Orgreave* (2001) probe the relation between performance and documentary, and between the actors and the subjects they represent. The original Battle of Orgreave – a violent confrontation between police and pickets – was a pivotal event in the 1984–5 UK miners' strike. In Deller's documentary artwork, actors feature alongside people who had participated in the original battle, and who played miners as well as policemen in the re-enactment, thus confusing both signification and authenticity.[62]

Bunny Rogers' works also circumvent the human body yet allude to it, and thus create an interesting tension between presence and absence. Her 2016 exhibition *Columbine Cafeteria* focused on the 1999 Columbine high school massacre, without using any direct depictions or conventional documentary signifiers of the event. Instead, she showed objects such as a cafeteria table and chairs (in *Cafeteria Set*), which, rather than aiming to relive the tragic events, simply alluded to the victims and to the social conditions that led to their plight in new and often haunting ways. The strong sense of absence in her works suggests a tragedy unfolding, and questions the need for visual signification of an actual body to evoke the desired response.

The 2018 MOMA exhibition *Being: New Photography 2018* also engages with changing representations of the body. Although photography is most associated with the capture of a person's exact likeness, the artists in this exhibition interrogate conventions of photographic portraiture by using surrogates and masks as replacements for the body, which is not necessarily included in the work. Focusing on the political implications of such portrayals, they explore representations of personhood in an era when rights of representation are contested for many individuals.

Experimental artworks that engage with the crossover between documentary and digital culture continue these themes, raising significant questions about the role and representation of the body in today's technoculture. Harun Farocki's *Serious Games: Immersion* (2009) digitally simulates soldiers' combat traumas, using gaming and military simulation technologies to restage events. Experiences that were not necessarily filmed are thus given visual expression in a manner similar to animated documentaries, which triggers deep emotions through a virtual environment where no physical body is seen. This questions the extent of verisimilitude needed to evoke memories of actual events, and demonstrates that animated interactive versions are 'true enough'.[63]

Artists Eva and Franco Mattes, aka 0100101110101101.org, explore the issue of documentation and preservation of performance art through novel technological re-enactment. They question the role of the body in contemporary culture and networked existence in an ongoing series called *Synthetic Performances* (2006–present), in which avatars re-enact important performance artworks in the virtual world of *SL*.[64] In these works, an animated body, rather than the actual physical subject, drains the meaning or effect of the original performance piece, which was based upon the embarrassment, pain, shock,

Figure 3.3 *Serious Games: Immersion*, artwork by Harun Farocki, 2009. Copyright Harun Farocki GbR, Berlin.

Figure 3.4 *Reenactment of Valie Export and Peter Weibel's Tapp und Tastkino* by Eva and Franco Mattes, 2007. Online performance, Galleria Civica di Trento.

fear, danger and even potential death involved. Since performance art is grounded in physical presence and interactions, viewing these re-enactments through digital avatars raises questions about the body today and the meaning of mediated presence.

An additional contemporary – and in this context – technology-related reason to avoid direct representation by circumventing physical appearance is the growing awareness of pervasive surveillance. Artist Douglas Coupland engages with this in his 2015 series *Deep Face*, which explores Facebook's use of facial recognition algorithms, and the privacy invasions they can produce (and that are likely to characterise social media use in the future). Coupland paints purposely distorted portraits of people who look straight at the camera with their faces disguised so that Facebook can no longer recognise them. He thus plays with the idea of photography as documentation that captures and visually mimics appearance versus camouflage that results in unrecognisable portraits. Coupland also created facial de-recognition software, titled *Deep Face: Communicate with Your Future Self*, which allows patrons to pose for photographic glamour shots that are then covered with barcode patterns over the face and sent as de-recognised images to the subjects via e-mail.[65] The barcodes can be interpreted as alluding to the multiple ways in which people are now 'read' as mere data or categorised biometrically, instead of being recognised as human individuals, once again making the body secondary to the data it conjures and according to which the actual 'somebody' is represented. These examples engage with the body as a more fluid visual signifier of the individual depicted, and open the way for the vast stylistic choices used in animated documentaries.

Obviously, the body is not irrelevant, but in a discussion of technocultural representations, I am arguing that especially when discussing technocultural representations, the user's physical *appearance* is not the *only* credible visual reference of the protagonist. The physical body as visual signifier of the 'I' has been replaced by a multiplicity of representations and imagery used in various platforms and mediated realities. The fact that users become accustomed to different signifiers representing the self and their bodies means that diverse indexes can be used in documentaries.[66] This explains why animated images that do not mimic the body's appearance can be seen as an emergent characteristic of contemporary culture; why animation as a documentary aesthetic has recently exploded; why animation's assumed artificiality is diminishing; and why there is growing reception of animation's perceived credibility as plausible documentary aesthetics.

Notes

1. It is important to note that by 'virtual realities' I do not mean VR headgear and the worlds they make accessible, but rather a wider view of screen-based interactive networked platforms.
2. A term he borrowed from artists Monika Fleischmann and Wolfgang Strauss. Hansen, *Bodies in Code*, p. 1.
3. Hansen, *Bodies in Code*, pp. 1–2, quoted from Turner, 'Myron Krueger Live', unpaginated.
4. Paradiso *et al.*, 'Guest Editors' Introduction'. See also Mann *et al.*, 'All Reality'.
5. Hansen, *Bodies in Code*, p. 2.
6. See Honess Roe, *Animated Documentary*.
7. Cubitt, *Digital Aesthetics*, pp. 31–2.
8. Manovich, 'Introduction to Info-aesthetics', p. 340.
9. Elsaesser and Hagener, *Film Theory*, p. 178.
10. Manovich, *Language of New Media*, p. 190.
11. Skoller, 'Introduction to Special Issue', p. 209.
12. Carroll, *Theorizing the Moving Image*, p. 62.
13. Manovich, 'An Archeology', unpaginated.
14. For more on these topics see Simons, 'Pockets in the Screenscape'; Musser, 'Toward a History'; Huhtamo, 'Elements of Screenology'; McQuire *et al.*, *Urban Screens Reader*; Acland, 'The Crack'; Manovich, 'An Archeology'; Friedberg, 'The End of Cinema'; Cubitt, 'Current Screens'.

15. The cultural implications of such changes in an interdisciplinary research domain links Film Studies, Art, Media Studies, Phenomenology and Post-phenomenology, and Sound and Video Game Studies, to name but a few.
16. For more on display spaces and their effect on the viewer's relation to the world on screen, see Leighton, *Art and the Moving Image*, p. 25; Sitney, 'Search for the Invisible Cinema'; Klinger, *Beyond the Multiplex*; Marchessault and Lord, *Fluid Screens, Expanded Cinema*; Verhofen, 'Grasping the Screen'.
17. Huhtamo, 'Screen Tests', pp. 144–5.
18. Collins, 'The 2014 Sochi Opening Ceremonies Recap'.
19. See, for example, https://expandedanimation.net/, accessed 4 August 2020.
20. Nelson, 'The Right Way'.
21. Sarkar, 'Pokémon Go Hits'; Fitzpatrick *et al.*, 'The 50 Best Apps'.
22. See for example: Gepner *et al.*, 'There's a Pokémon'; Ekstein, 'Pokemon Go'; Daye, 'Pokémon Go Helps'.
23. Of course, this is not to claim that reality was ever limited to physical matter in a strict sense, since the former has always included and been shaped by non-physical elements such as concepts, signs, etc. The relation between the real and the intangible raises issues that have vexed major philosophers, and have been examined across a diverse array of disciplines that exceed the scope of this book.
24. Hansen, *Bodies in Code*, p. 93.
25. Cubitt, *Digital Aesthetics*, p. 83.
26. Shields, *Virtual*, p. 11.
27. Bryant and Pollock, *Digital and other Virtualities*, p. 11.
28. Shields, *Virtual*, p. 2.
29. Avatars' carbon footprints are calculated according to the electricity consumption of servers and data centres. For more information see Carr, 'Avatars Consume'; Daniel, 'Energy Consumption'. Cases of physical seizures and even murder and neglect have occurred due to gaming circumstances, as seen in the following example: Salmon, 'Internet Gaming Addiction'; Slotnik, 'Gamer's Death'.
30. Derrida, *Of Grammatology*, p. 144.
31. Shaw, *Technoculture*, p. 1.
32. *Do It Yourself*, film, directed by Eric Ledune (Belgium: Got! Oh my got, Amnesty International and Wallonie Image, 2007).
33. This film was part of *Animating Reality*, a collection of thirteen animated short documentaries, including award-winning works by filmmakers from Sweden, the Netherlands, Japan, Australia, France, Finland, Canada, Belgium and the United States. See https://vimeo.com/12752583, accessed 4 August 2020.
34. Durham Peters, 'Witnessing', pp. 27–31.
35. Østby Sæther, 'Between Hyperrepresentational and Real', p. 54.
36. The history of technology in relation to human sensorium and representation can include embodied media experiences (including 3D imaging, virtual and augmented reality devices), mediation matters, post-humanism, post-phenom-

enology, cyber-psychology and player–avatar relationships, audience bodies, motion-capture technologies, wearable technology, body data visualisation, sensory perception, novel 'bodies' ranging from the organic to the artificial, hybrid, cyborg, prosthetic, robotic and bionic, representation and self-representation in social media, surveillance and face recognition technologies, altered and augmented sensory perception (covered here in relation to machine vision, for example) and much more, clarifying the breadth of the topic and its contemporary relevance.

37. Levitt, *Animatic Apparatus*, p. 2.
38. For important early discussions, see Turkle, *Second Self*; Hayles, *How We Became Posthuman*; Miah, 'Posthumanism'.
39. Nichols, '"Getting to Know You . . ."', p. 177.
40. Ward, 'Drama-documentary, Ethics', p. 192.
41. Although other manipulations are obviously still possible and 'the body' does not necessarily depict the 'truth', as is evident from Grierson's ultra-fabricated 1922 'documentary' *Nanook of the North*.
42. Besmer, 'What "Robotic Re-Embodiment"'. See also work by Kilteni *et al.*, 'Sense of Embodiment'.
43. Quoted in Jones, *Self/Image*, p. 154.
44. Quoted in Rieser and Zapp, *New Screen Media*, p. 208.
45. See Haraway, 'Cyborg Manifesto'.
46. Morse, 'Sunshine and Shroud'.
47. Paul, *Digital Art*, p. 165.
48. Roquet, 'From Animation to Augmentation', p. 237.
49. Del Río, 'Body as Foundation', p. 109.
50. Gunning, 'Truthiness and the More Real', p. 180.
51. Merleau-Ponty, *Phenomenology of Perception*, p. 166.
52. Several key examples are the following experiments: For the Pinocchio illusion (which creates a kinaesthetic illusion that the nose is moving away from the face) see Lackner, 'Some Proprioceptive Influences'; For the Rubber Hand illusion (based on visual–tactile synchronisation) see Ehrsson *et al.*, 'That's My Hand!'. For body swapping illusions see Petkova, 'If I Were You'.
53. Besmer, 'What "Robotic Re-embodiment"', p. 60.
54. Ibid., p. 63.
55. Ibid., p. 68.
56. *Second Bodies*, film, directed by Sandra Danilovic (Canada: Ryerson University, 2009).
57. Extensive research exists about player–avatar relationships: avatars have been theorised as functioning instrumentally – as tools (such as cursors), as virtual puppets (e.g. in-game virtual marionettes controlled by the player), as agency and embodiment (e.g. the prosthetic extensions of the player's own body that extend into the screen space), and as proxies of the player's body in the game world, acting as the player's agency within the on-screen world. For an excellent review of different approaches to theorising the role and significance of the avatar, see

Klevjer, 'Enter the Avatar'. Beyond the physical sense of embodiment that can occur when using avatars, a strong emotional connection can also arise due to the avatar's representation of one's sense of self, sometimes perceived as more 'real' and/or honest than that projected in the 'real' world. As a fascinating early discussion of the issue, see Dibbell, 'Rape in Cyberspace' and, for more contemporary theorisations of the topic see Spence, 'Virtual Rape, Real Dignity'.
58. For an interesting exploration of personal and social identities shaped online at the beginning of the twenty-first century, see photographer Robbie Cooper's *Alter Ego* project, which includes portraits of online gamers and virtual-world participants from America, Asia and Europe who are paired with images of their avatars. Images are available online at www.robbiecooper.org/small.html, accessed 18 September 2014, and in print: Cooper, *Alter Ego*.
59. See Danilovic, 'Virtual Lens of Exposure'. Rune Klevjer similarly explains that in navigable 3D environments, it is not the body of the avatar that becomes an extension of the player, but rather the navigable virtual camera that allows 'seeing' into the game world. See Klevjer, 'Enter the Avatar', p. 32.
60. Respini, 'Cindy Sherman'. Interestingly, the divide between the representation of the self and the mimetic recording of corporeal appearance can also be linked to earlier representational tendencies, such as the Surrealists' conception of the self-portrait. These often substituted the recognisable persona with a metaphorical allusion to an inner or hidden identity, emphasising a state of mind rather than a physical exterior. Though the scope of this book prevents an in-depth analysis of surrealism in these contexts, it is relevant both to animated documentaries' relation to personal-subjective experiences, as well as to my focus on the use of avatars as signifiers of the self. For more information, see Levy, *Surrealism*, p. 9.
61. See Manchester, 'Gillian Wearing'; Krystof, 'Call Gillian'.
62. See Farquharson, 'Jeremy Deller'; Wilson, 'Jeremy Deller'.
63. See Breitwieser, 'Harun Farocki'; Lowery, 'Harun Farocki'.
64. More about the artists and their works are available at http://0100101110101101.org/, accessed 4 August 2020. These re-enactments include Marina Abramovic's and Ulay's *Imponderabilia* (1977), Joseph Beuys's *7000 Oaks* (1982–7), Gilbert & George's *The Singing Sculpture* (1968), Valie Export's *Tapp und Tastkino* (1968), Vito Acconci's *Seedbed* (1972), and Chris Burden's *Shoot* (1971).
65. See Greenberger, 'You Look So Different Online'.
66. The diverse indexes can be either deictic and/or traces of the physical in ways that do not resemble the physical body.

CHAPTER FOUR

Documenting Game Realities

As virtual worlds converge with the physical world and become part of today's mixed realities, it is logical that these worlds and the multifaceted experiences that take place within them should be documented. Online games are fully animated realms of virtual activity, pictorial worlds that use real-time animation to reflect interactive user input, and as such are essential to consider when discussing virtual culture and emerging documentary tendencies. However, the expanding phenomenon of documenting game realities raises ontological questions about technology as well as aesthetic and epistemological issues inherent in the capture, representation and documentation of virtual realities. The following chapters explore the relation between the virtualisation of culture and what I have identified as three kinds of virtual documentaries: documenting animated virtual game realities (Chapter 4); the in-game/virtual depiction of physical realities in ways that converge the two (Chapter 5); and the use of virtual aesthetics to depict physical events, as in documentary games and VR documentary simulations (Chapter 6). This chapter engages with virtual documentaries as the development, techniques and themes surrounding the documentation of digital games as a unique form of contemporary animated virtual realities. Here I will focus on the history, reasons and techniques (with a special emphasis on machinima) that are used to document game worlds, which is an under-researched aspect of animated documentaries.

Who is Drakedog? What is virtual suicide? And why is this important for the discussion of animated documentaries? Well, Drakedog was a well-known Korean player in the *World of Warcraft* (*WoW*) game and *Drakedog's Suicide* (2006) is the in-game footage that documents his virtual self-destruction. As the soundtrack indicates that the end is imminent, Drakedog is seen deleting his online *WoW* user profile, studying his inventory screen and removing one item at a time. The meticulous account of his suicide is embedded with the sense of a slow death, because each item signifies a trophy earned through endless hours of dedicated gameplay, with no option of redeeming the deleted items. For audiences familiar with game culture, this painstaking deletion is not only high-wire drama, but also very emotional. The emotional tension of the film is built through the lingering of the mouse on each item before it is deleted, and culminates in the momentary hesitation of the mouse over the permanent delete button just before Drakedog removes his entire avatar profile. The emotional responses to this film by players, who react to it as if it were a gruesome execution or a funeral, highlight the increasingly blurred boundaries between virtual animated and physical realities.[1]

The emotive aspect of this work should come as no surprise because, as Shields says, avatars and virtual representations are not just stand-ins for people and places in the physical world, they also impact significantly on the lives and well-being of viewers and users.[2] As early as the 1990s, Julian Dibbell acknowledged that what occurs in virtual worlds is, at the very least, 'profoundly compelling and emotionally true'.[3] Indeed, the field of cyberpsychology, which analyses the relation of players to their avatars as extended self-representation, is a growing field of contemporary research. Drakedog's decision to delete rather than sell his hard-earned trophies also symbolises a meaningful political and anti-capitalist choice, made in an era where virtual objects have 'real-world' value, since an entire economic system based on virtual world currency and consumption of virtual goods has developed. Unfortunately, *Drakedog's Suicide* is no longer available for online viewing and all that remains of it are screen-captured still images of the original footage, acting as documents. This emphasises the importance of preserving early accounts of virtual experiences as the history of significant aspects of contemporary culture.

For readers less familiar with the field of gaming, narrative games may seem neither 'real' nor documentary; indeed, they may appear to weaken the concept of documentary explained in these pages. The recent evolution of the gaming industry raises many classificatory and ontological questions about the nature of games as media and cultural production, and about the relation between games and the virtualisation of culture more generally. In fact, games also vary in the extent to which they include structured activity as opposed to open-ended simulations, extending beyond narrative games to more open-ended, fully animated virtual platforms. Many games can be considered 'real' both in terms of their economic, physical, psychological and social aspects, and because of the diverse and complex experiences they offer; moreover, as their status changes, their role in relation to documentary transforms as well. Three characteristics of games are worthy of attention: (1) the need to document the ever-increasing actions that take place in these online animated worlds and grow more important in the lives of users; (2) the new ways in which animated footage of interactive in-game actions, based on various production methods, are transformed into linear cinematic depictions and contribute to the discussion of animated documentaries; (3) documentary games are also included, further blurring the boundaries between the two, as discussed in Chapter 6. Games are a major aspect of contemporary culture, raising new questions about animation's changing role in visual culture generally, and in documentary more specifically.

Computer games are a global industry and a rising medium for entertainment, social commentary and creative expression. The field of gaming has completely transformed in recent decades and now engages with content in endlessly creative ways, resulting in extensive academic research. The gaming industry still divides those who are game-active, or at least aware of the rich field it has become, from those who maintain outdated ideas about digital games being limited to superficial entertainment for young audiences. Games can be viewed in a multitude of different ways, with varying functions and aims. Philosopher Bernard Suits defines games as (the appropriately wide-ranging) 'voluntary attempt to overcome unnecessary obstacles'.[4] As the popularity of computer gaming in contemporary culture skyrockets, its significance in the fields of visual culture, non-fiction and documentary theory is certainly worthy of attention.

Games are also an essential part of education, social interaction, online communities, economic activity, training and simulation; they are truly ubiquitous – a growing field of animated contemporary virtual reality.[5] Gaming worlds characterise a certain feature of virtual culture, but exemplify characteristics shared by virtual domains more widely that are familiar to all internet users, not just gamers. Technologically mediated experiences proliferate as events are constantly witnessed through the media and virtual worlds become more popular. Edward Castranova describes an 'exodus into the virtual', whereby people prefer to inhabit virtual worlds rather than their own.[6] The perception of virtual experiences as equal or similar to those in the physical world becomes evident on platforms such as Facebook, where users include among their profile pictures screenshot images of their avatars engaging in virtual experiences.[7] Digitally virtual experiences are increasingly documented as part of players' actual experiences and memories, which is one aspect of today's multiple mixed realities. A consideration of the theorisation and definitions of games gives rise to a more complex understanding that liberates them from any constraining association with youth and fantasy, or mere escapism.

In his 1961 book *Man, Play and Games*, sociologist Roger Caillois differentiates between play and games. Play activities are unstructured, spontaneous and not bound by rigid rules, like kicking a pebble down the street; games have clear formalised rules, as in soccer. Both play and games are ageless aspects of what it means to be human, developing physical, intellectual and social capacities.[8] Johan Huizinga, a Dutch historian and cultural theorist, described play as an essential element in the formation of culture, paying tribute to the importance of play by naming his 1938 book *Homo Ludens* – Man the Player. He doesn't define games as such, rather he introduces the important concept of the magic circle, which separates the game from the outside world. The magic circle is a place in time, detached from 'real' life, in which all participants agree to a set of customs and rules.[9] However, the boundaries between play worlds of the magic circle and the real world are not always so clear. Football fans and related violence is one example of huge slippage between the two supposedly separate realms of experience. Celia Pearce summarises it succinctly by claiming that the magic circle is, in fact, more porous than people may have believed.[10] The increasingly fluid and difficult-to-decipher boundaries between the worlds of play and non-play are precisely what makes contemporary games so fascinating and relevant to a discussion of non-fiction. This has led to the study of games flourishing in recent years, as researchers explore the growing worlds of contemporary play further, drawing attention to, among others, their aesthetic, psychological, sociological, anthropological, economic, educational, ethical, communications and technological characteristics.[11] Investigating the field of contemporary computer games through the lens of non-fiction sheds new light on the question of games as essential components of virtual realities today; and on animation as an indispensable form of gaming aesthetics, and a vital part of contemporary documentary imagery. Digital games are an example of virtual worlds that take pictorial representation one step further: they are fully animated and, as such, have become an important new aspect of animated documentary research. These platforms require a new visual aesthetic that is dynamic and capable of responding in real time to user input, introducing a new and central role for animation. The field of contemporary gaming introduces a key shift in the role of animation as a documentary language, demonstrating why it should now be considered a central cultural characteristic that can no longer be overlooked.

Statistics show that the gaming industry has become the largest entertainment business to date, influencing and engaging with other aspects of contemporary culture. Although the figures change daily, it has been suggested that the online gaming industry is now larger than the film and music industries;[12] and that as early as 2007, its customer base included over a quarter of the worldwide internet population.[13] The typical game player is thirty-five years old, has been playing video games for an average of thirteen years and, in contrast to many stereotypes, women aged eighteen or older represent a significantly greater portion of the game-playing population (31 per cent) than boys aged eighteen or younger (17 per cent).[14] Perhaps most tellingly, in 2010 statistics showed that 97 per cent of youth under the age of twenty play digital games.[15] These figures illustrate that, in developed economies, the youth of today – the audiences of the future – grow up experiencing these worlds on a regular basis. In an interview with *Time* magazine in 2014, Michael Frazzini, Vice-President of Amazon Games, put it simply: 'At this point . . . on anything with a screen, games are the No. 1 or 2 activity'.[16] These rising numbers all demonstrate that people are growing accustomed to experiences in virtual animated environments, and to seeing themselves represented by avatars.

Douglas Gayeton's 2007 HBO documentary film *Molotov Alva and His Search for the Creator*[17] is labelled as the first virtual documentary, and is a landmark example of the evolution of documentaries about animated game realities. The film begins by explaining:

> In January of 2007 a man named Molotov Alva disappeared from his California home . . . recently, a series of video dispatches by a traveller of the same name have appeared within a popular online world called *Second Life*. What follows is his story.[18]

In the film, Alva constructs a new identity for himself by creating an avatar that explores lifestyles and online communities, meets people, creates personal relationships and investigates the world of *SL*.

Describing Alva as a traveller is an allusion to early historical documentary films, which – in a similar manner to the exploration of new online worlds – were used to capture lesser known destinations and cultures for audiences 'back home'. The film's subtitle, *A Second Life Odyssey*, introduces the main themes in *Molotov Alva*, which reflect those of Homer's *Odyssey*: travel, experiences along the way, and the meaning of 'home'. Having chosen *SL* over the carbon-based world, Alva searches out new territories and, as in *The Odyssey*, the film follows his adventures and discoveries. The idea of 'home' also relates to Edward Castronova's book *Exodus to the Virtual World*, and to the notion that 20 per cent of Massively Multiplayer Online Role-playing Game (MMORPG) players define themselves as residents of a virtual world.[19] This growing migration into the virtual means that the back story of *Molotov Alva*, about a man who disappears from the 'first world' into *SL*, echoes a dominant (and quite real) cultural trend.

Alva chooses an avatar that resembles his physical body, but there are infinite options for self-representation allowing users to mask themselves in ways that may feel more authentic, or that cannot otherwise be shown.[20] Any online profile can be seen as similar to an in-game avatar's, since people can decide to project a self-image that is quite different from their 'real' offline self and life. Self-definition and self-actualisation is a major theme in a virtual world in which everything is potentially possible, and which people can reinvent to fit their needs. The availability of choice enhances immersion. Alva finds the idea that he can be and create anything he wants intoxicating. The sense of a universe without limits raises many questions, about both games and the realities that are constructed and documented within them. The exploration of the game world and its meaning leads Alva to search for its creator, introducing a religious element, which takes an existential turn when Alva realises that in this virtual world everyone is the creator. Indirectly, the constructedness of the virtual world, and its occasional similarity to the physical world, raise larger philosophical questions about the constructedness of realities in general, and their constructed, narrativised and always biased representation, and the individual's role and agency within them.

In his exploration of *SL*, Alva fluctuates between a sense of endless possibilities with no rules, and the impression that the virtual world is a very close reconstruction of the first world. This is reflected in the attempt to add greenery to the virtual environment in order to make a real-life income through virtual economy and in-game capitalism, to moves by corporations to gain control over increasingly larger aspects of *SL* spaces and activities.[21] Whereas *Molotov Alva* may have been the first virtual documentary to address such themes, they have since become prevalent. The film *Life 2.0* (2010),[22] also about *SL*, ponders what happens when the virtual world turns into a person's reality.[23] Although there is a judgemental tone to the film, which can be challenged, it continues the discussion about the difficulty of distinguishing between virtual gaming experiences and non-game existence, when the former threatens to take over the latter. A more recent example is the increasingly popular phenomenon of gamers who stream their gameplay so others can watch it online in real time; some make a living through advertising and subscriptions on these platforms. *The New York Times* recently covered the health risks, and even deaths, that some gamers face after lengthy gaming sessions in a streaming culture that rewards people for playing for hours on end.[24] Thus, in wide-ranging ways, from social connections to incomes and health risks, the realities of game worlds and non-game worlds are increasingly blurred, contributing to their questionable status in ontological debates.

Many virtual game worlds relate to the physical world in various ways. Examples include Barack Obama's 2008 *SL* campaign; Grammy-winning singer-songwriter Michael Bublé's 2011 (digital) appearance in the popular Facebook game CityVille to promote his album and mingle with fans – via their avatars, of course; conferences, educational and commercial activities that have in-game meeting and discussion platforms; re-enactments of Guantánamo Bay, and many more. Since 2013, professional gamers have been awarded athlete visas for entry to the United States which, from a legal perspective, sheds new light on the status of games today as a sport and profession.[25] Indeed, the success of game tournaments, or e-sports, already mirrors the achievements of major-league sports: e-sports are sponsored by top brands, such as Coca Cola and American Express; they offer millions of dollars in prize money, and estimates suggest they are followed by more than 70 million people worldwide via the internet or TV.[26] The Entertainment Software Association's (ESA) 2016 statistics show that 50 per cent of the gamers surveyed were familiar with professional video game competitions, 45 per cent followed e-sports on social media, 40 per cent follow sports coverage on cable TV, and 38 per cent stream live coverage.[27] Since these games enable so many non-game functions, it is inaccurate to think of them merely as entertainment, frivolous or intended for children. As their cultural status changes, they can be seen to constitute another legitimate way of life.

The diversity involved in digital game platforms is hard to grasp and is an independent, constantly expanding field of research. My focus on these gaming worlds as fully animated virtual realities is premised on the idea that digital games must be acknowledged as components of contemporary realities that are central to the study of animated documentaries. Once games begin to be acknowledged as similar to non-game platforms/realities, the animated settings and avatars notwithstanding, the documentary of a game world seems not only logical but even necessary. Animation plays an important role as documentary representation within these worlds. The technological, ontological, epistemological and aesthetic questions about the non-fiction capture of virtual realities and their representation raise issues about their nature as documentaries, which exist somewhere between the ludic, related to game studies and experiences of play, and the cinematic. Documenting the virtual thus exposes animation's redefined relation to documents and documentaries.

Molotov Alva is interesting as both a self-reflexive documentary work, and an introduction to the wider field of documenting virtual activities within game worlds. The protagonist documents his *SL* experiences with his video camera 'to keep a diary, a digital record of my experience here'.[28] While the camera does not record, of course, it nonetheless indicates more traditional modes of documenting, appealing to historical, film-based conventions. Giving an avatar a camera accentuates the film's self-reflexive character as a new form of documentary that documents the virtual. Additionally, some of the images in the film are presented to the viewer from the perspective of the photographer, with a 'recording' sign flashing in the upper left-hand corner. This obviously refers to documentary conventions, indirectly elevating the ontological status of the virtual which, by being 'captured', is made to seem less fictional and closer to the physical world that the viewer is accustomed to seeing represented photographically. Although a camera can theoretically

Figure 4.1 *Molotov Alva and His Search for the Creator,* directed by Douglas Gayeton, 2007.

be a distancing mechanism, in this instance it turns the viewers into photographers of the virtual world, as if they too are filming from 'within' *SL*. By turning the viewer's screen into a camera, the virtual world is equated with the physical. This process of watching virtual events through a figurative camera constructs a gaze that is familiar and that makes the virtual animated world seem less foreign to the viewer, even if she has no previous gaming experience.

Molotov Alva is also significant as a novel form of documentary that uses animation as a non-fiction language of representation in a new manner. The film clarifies the need to create documents which capture new realities that cannot otherwise be preserved, either due to changes in the virtual worlds, or because of the technologies on which they are based. The question of how digital-virtual worlds can be documented is also inscribed into the film on a technical level. *Molotov Alva* reflects developments in the uses of both animation and photography. As Henry Lowood explains, many of the scenes in the film were recorded just like cinema *verité*, with Gayeton pointing a high-definition camera at his own computer monitor.[29] At the time, this was the only way Gayeton could record animation from his computer screen, however, this is no longer the case.

An important early example of the genre is *Diary of a Camper* (1966),[30] an animated short film that captured in-game experiences. It portrays action within the first-person shooter game *Quake*, which was created by the players, or clan, known as the Rangers.[31] The short film was not the first to capture in-game activities, but is acknowledged as establishing digital games as a medium for filmmaking. It was the first of its kind because it transcended what game creators had made possible for players, that is, recording gameplays, which are the specific ways players interact with a game. Using coding skills and hacking the game engine in which it was made, the Rangers produced new options, such as new viewing perspectives of the event and new narratives created by editing the documented game recording.[32] Documentaries are the narrativisation of documents, and with the advent of editing this documentation of events was transformed into documentary, making this form of filmmaking relevant to the discussion of new forms of animated documentaries. The documentation of games and virtual worlds has since evolved significantly. *Diary of a Camper* and the films it inspired were once called *Quake* movies, but as other game engines were used to create similar films of gameplay documentation, the term 'machinima' was coined in 1998.[33]

MACHINIMA

The term machinima is a contraction of 'machine' and 'cinema'. It can be understood as the convergence of filmmaking, animation production and game-development technology through the creation of original content using game engines and recorded gameplay. The Academy of Machinima Arts and Sciences defines machinima as 'the art of making animated films within a real-time virtual 3D environment'.[34] Machinima is therefore a new form of animation technique (the real-time interactive animation characteristic of digital games), and a form of animated filmmaking based on recorded game content. Rooted in new technologies and participatory new media, embedded within hacking culture and associated with digital gaming, machinima has been described as '*the* visual cultural phenomenon of the twenty-first century'.[35] As the visual surface, that is, the real-time computer graphics of games, as well as the interactive occurrence of the game itself and the translation of code into imagery, machinima animation is both representation *and* ludic action.

Artist and game designer Eddo Stern discusses non-fiction machinima as the result of the live nature of online gaming, combined with the technological capacities of machinima that allow the capture of virtual events, somewhat like live-action documentary, cinema *verité* and surveillance video.[36] Used in documentary contexts, machinima thus introduces a new perspective for researching animated non-fiction by blurring the lines between reality and its representation.

Machinima can document online worlds directly as they appear on screen as if from within the documented world. Since *Diary of a Camper* in 1996, the field of machinima creations has gained a huge following. In 2011, machinima.com, an important community forum, listed more than 2.5 billion downloads of machinima films and more than 45 million monthly users. There are now over 2 billion creators of machinima (known as machinimators) who use various game platforms, social media and online channels for the production and dissemination of their work.[37] The need for machinima will surely only increase as we become more virtualised. These records of virtual materials are important because they obtain data for digital ethnographers interested in game communities, and they can be part of gaming tutorials for other players; they are also a means of self-expression, and can be helpful in documenting technologies as they become obsolete.[38] They may thus become part of a historical archive of game worlds, enabling non-gamers to learn about a widespread contemporary sub-culture. Machinima is now recognised as a category in several major film and animation festivals, as well as having increasing impact on the field of contemporary art.[39]

In this virtualised context, then, the gap between referent and representation is different from instances in which animation is used to describe other kinds of non-physical realities. Animation used to portray personal experiences and physical events (that could have been photographed) is an interpretive visual language because the animation depicts events that look different from their animated portrayal, or personal events with no visible form. In machinima recordings of virtual occurrences, however, the animated depiction is a direct capture of events as they appear on the player/user's screen. With machinima, the gap between representation and referent narrows because animation's mediation and constructedness become less prominent. In other words, in the documentation of virtual realities using machinima, animation does not function as an interpretation or a substitute for photography, but rather as a mimetic visual portrayal of events, turning machinima into *documentary capture animation*. By 'documentary capture animation' I mean the direct capture in animated form of animated referents, similarly to 'documentary film', which captures the referents before the camera.

In the past, non-physical realities, such as belief systems, were interpreted and represented differently in diverse media, whereas in today's networked world the visualisation of digital non-physical realities has a uniform appearance familiar to all users. Thus, even though the digitally virtual is non-physical in many ways, it still has a uniform visual appearance that differentiates it from other historical non-physical realities. Animation bestows visibility on these new dynamic digital worlds (such as the GUI), but not in a visually interpretive manner. Machinima acts as footage of the virtual, presenting viewers with what occurred in the virtual environment as seen by its inhabitants. Because recording techniques include what takes place on screen in the online environment, machinima resembles photography in its ability to record non-physical elements. In these cases, animation is a document of the virtual and thus becomes a direct representation of otherwise non-visualisable platforms of contemporary reality. Discussing photography in the digital era, Damian Sutton explains that a photograph can either be interpreted as real or not, purely in terms of whether what it photographs is real: 'two conflicting ontologies appear – the photograph-as-transparent, and the photograph-as-object [as representation]'.[40] In this sense, taking into account the reality of contemporary digital games and the idea that machinima is a direct, rather than an interpretive, visual record of a virtual occurrence, it is transparent, which consequently positions the recorded virtual events as 'real'.

The ontological status of machinima and virtual domains is largely based on the live nature that is characteristic of machinima animation. As discussed previously, some animation techniques used in documentary may produce a sense of absence due to animation's break with the capture and appearance of the physical referent. Raz Greenberg claims absence is a defining characteristic of animation, but as the uses and technologies of animation evolve, this is no longer necessarily the case.[41] Machinima relies on HCI that dictates the actions visualised, as well as on the presence of players who control their avatars and interact with others. Machinima thus signifies a presence, albeit technologically mediated, by visualising real-time player movements and actions.

The issue of presence becomes central when discussing shifting notions of realism as a basis for understanding the changing uses and reception of animated documentary in a highly virtualised culture. In these circumstances, the issue of immediacy and real-time image-production techniques is a salient factor in the believable simulation of presence in virtual domains. In the current networked culture, the real-time results of user input on screen contribute to a sense of vividness and telepresence, which create new forms of 'reality effects' that strengthen the realism of certain representations, as described in the GPS example in Chapter 3. Rather than striving for mimesis, the aesthetics of machinima are often compromised and sacrificed for better real-time performance, in contrast with the graphic quality of other 3D animation techniques with high-definition depictions of human faces, textures, emotions and more. The real-time nature of machinima contributes to its realism, despite its being far removed from photorealism in visual terms.

Some commentators claim that immediacy is created by the sense of presence or 'liveness' and the feeling of presence, in turn, is defined as inhabiting the digital landscape.[42] When discussing virtual computerised platforms, one does not have to be physically 'there' (wherever 'there' is in the virtual) in order to sense some form of presence that results from the smoothness of the interaction, the rapidity of response and the outcomes of the user input. Since actions are no longer performed only within physical spaces, online gaming platforms are not so very different from other computerised environments and virtual domains. Through a sense of telepresence, the digitally virtual acquires space, becoming connected to physical reality through shared time. The issue of presence is thus a vital aspect of contemporary animation, its realism and believability, since viewers can see themselves as 'present' in animated form. Is there any difference, ask Cameron and Carroll, between recording human–computer game interaction and something performed in front of a video camera? They suggest there is not.[43] The animation in these cases works as an indexical trace of users' physical actions and input. In other words, if machinima and other real-time animation techniques symbolise online presence, then capturing these depictions is comparable to photography of the virtual. What is captured in machinima is what was visually available on the screen of the user participating in the online virtual realm, like the photography of physical events, which is arguably similar to whatever a witness to the event would have seen. As such, viewers of the animated capture/machinima see what they would have seen had they been virtually present in that online domain.

Machinima is, therefore, a novel form of animation that challenges existing preconceptions about the use of animation in non-fiction contexts. Machinima's dual status as event and representation means that it has a unique status in relation to documentaries, documents, footage and artefacts. In order to grasp the new possibilities that machinima offers our theoretical consideration of animated documentaries, it is vital to understand the technologically differentiated techniques of machinima filmmaking. This historical context, which relates to the development of animation's use and production in the growing gaming industry, contributes a new historical perspective to animated documentary that is not covered in existing historical surveys of the topic.

MACHINIMA MECHANISMS

The three primary methods of machinima production are based on demo recording, screen capture and asset compositing, which correspond to the three ways of documenting the history of virtual worlds respectively: replay, player's point of view recording, and asset extraction.[44]

Demo Recording and Replay Based on Code

As the earliest form of machinima, demo recordings are not movies *per se*, but rather mathematically modelled code-based visualisations grounded in sequences of commands. In other words, players' actions were recorded in real time as code and could only be replayed using the game itself. The game engine thus repeated the effects of the actions executed by players. Through programming hacks of the code that extended the possibilities of the game, the game was then transformed into a new performance space that created moving imagery. Initially, the production of in-game films required gaming literacy and technological know-how to make the necessary modifications to the game that created original content. These early machinima works are viewable only in the game engines within which they were created, and are sometimes already obsolete, accentuating the dependence on game technology as a replay engine in post-production and distribution. An example of demo recordings machinima is the 1996 example, *Diary of a Camper*, mentioned above.

Screen Capture and Player's Point of View Recording

By 2004, new machinima technologies, which were unrestricted by the original game engine, became more popular. This type of machinima no longer relied on the game engine for replay and distribution, but was solely a tool for production. It is referred to as 'screen capture' because it captured what was on the screen (actually the graphics card) as a video that could not be edited as code and could only be produced and viewed in digital video formats.[45] Although the game was still used as a performance space for virtual puppeteering, a diversification of genres was now possible.[46] This made both production and spectatorship accessible to wider, non-gamer audiences and enabled new mash-ups that further blurred the boundaries between game worlds.[47] In 2004, *Sims 2* by Electronic Arts was one of the first games to include simple movie-making tools, expanding the possibilities of in-game film production immeasurably. Although this ensured greater viewing potential and visibility, it also reduced machinima to a production technique that fed into traditional media formats, putting the emphasis on the image recording rather than the event production.[48] In other words, this technical change effects a shift from the ludic (i.e. recording the event in a demo format) to the cinematic (recording a viewpoint of the event in screen-capture mode).[49] This is precisely the difference between documentary that is based on cinematic editing and consequent narrativisation (since screen capture method can be edited), and a historical document of the virtual action (as occurred in the demo recordings).[50] This distinction opens up new possibilities in the theory of animated documentaries.

Asset Extraction and Compositing: Models and Artefacts of Virtual Worlds

The third form of machinima production does not take place within the game itself but employs game assets and content, including models, characters, sets, costumes, props, maps and textures. These game assets can be imported into the artist's studio and combined with imagery from other visual sources. This allows the creator to extract game elements from their original context, transform them and create varied amalgamations of content. Game worlds thus become sources for the creation of animation and are used as cinematic spaces that enable independent creativity and production. This technique resembles demo in its dependence on game data, but asset extraction is a more complex method of filmmaking that needs a different range of creative skills and professional knowledge, such as video editing, rather than coding (demo) or gameplay and puppeteering (screen capture) skills.[51] Bespoke machinimation is a more recent production method that takes asset extraction and compositing one step further by using software specifically designed for the creation of 3D animated movies within virtual worlds.[52] These modes of production thus break the confines of specific game worlds, and make way for a broader variety of themes which may appeal to wider audiences.

EXPANDING MACHINIMA

As the focus of machinima modes of production moved from coding to visualisation, another transformation from the ludic to the cinematic occurred. Changes in production technologies severed machinima's reliance both on game engines for production and viewing, and on the original game content (through asset extraction). As a result, machinima works now cover a wide variety of genres.

Tracy Harwood describes the existing range of machinima categories that include parody, often based on recognisable game characters, music videos, advertising for the games themselves, pre-visualisation, which is used in mainstream filmmaking to envisage how scenes will be enacted, art, and more. All machinima genres are based on footage captured from virtual worlds (relating them to non-fiction fields more generally); but interestingly, many of the genres Harwood lists are directly based on traditional documentary goals and conventions. These involve providing visualisation/re-enactment of otherwise unavailable photographic footage, conveying a specific message or narrative about an incident, or capturing archival documents of virtual events that would otherwise be lost. Such documentary-related machinima genres include: fan videos, which document fans' gameplay; reportage, which comprises unedited recordings of virtual events that can be seen as historical documents; re-enactment, which is similar to other animated documentaries since machinima reconstructs non-game and/or virtual events, often with the original audio recordings of the event; activism, whereby events are re-created and illustrated as political protest and/or propaganda; education, as a creative way to illustrate information due to the accessibility of animation; and actual documentaries based on the direction, narrativisation and editing of game/virtual world footage.[53]

It is worth emphasising that even machinima works that are not meant as documentary can still embody a form of documentation, since they capture the virtual events recorded, even if these are staged and therefore 'fictional', as in the case of photography. According to Roger Odin, the reception of a film as documentary involves contextual information that indicates viewers should watch it as such. However, spectators can produce a 'documentarizing lecture' of any film, even one that is fictional, because a film can be watched for the material it captures, rather than just for its fictional narrative.[54] In this sense, all machinima works embody potential documentary viewing since they are based on events that occurred in virtual worlds; and some machinima genres are also narrativised and specifically relate to documentary productions.

Consequently, machinima production is growing in different directions under assorted designations. According to Harwood, since 2014 the 'Let's Play' phenomenon – 'the recording of gameplay (as walk throughs or speed runs) using voiceover commentary that may be humorous or instructional' – has become the latest incarnation of machinima, which, due to evolved technologies, has become indistinguishable from other animated formats.[55] Thus, under different titles and in varied visual styles, users with creative or technological backgrounds are now using recorded gameplay content in various ways for interactive cultural production and promotion in fields as wide-ranging as marketing, entertainment, art and instruction. These works can now be viewed on- and offline by the huge audiences they attract, further demonstrating the growing proliferation of machinima.[56]

The web channel Twitch is a useful example of the animated depiction of virtual game realities in non-fiction. Twitch specialises in live videos of regular players as well as professional gamers, who use it to let spectators watch their game sessions. Here gamers' experiences are depicted simultaneously in the physical and virtual worlds, through the juxtaposition of animated and photographed events and actions. The game being played is displayed along with a video feed of the player's face and a chat window for viewers to communicate with the player and watch the action.[57] Far from an esoteric phenomenon, Twitch, which was founded in 2011, had more than 55 million visitors per month by 2014 and was ranked among the fifteen most trafficked websites around the world. In August 2014, it was purchased by Amazon for $1.1 billion.[58] It is described as the world's leading live-streaming platform for gamers.[59] With the rise of the gaming industry and e-sports events, the battle between Google and Amazon over the Twitch purchase clearly suggests that these multi-national companies see the era of video game viewing as just beginning.[60] Reports from 2017 show that live streaming of video game playing on sites like Twitch, has nearly 10 million visitors daily.[61]

Similarly, Gametoon is a worldwide entertainment TV channel focused on gaming worlds and attracting audiences between the ages of thirteen and thirty-five. It is defined as a 'gaming channel made for gamers by gamers', and is part of SPI International, a global media company operating more than thirty television channels on five continents. Gametoon includes content created by renowned streamers, e-sports events partnered with ESL (the world's largest e-sports company), gameplays, game reviews, tips and more.[62] On these platforms professional game streamers (who combine the expertise of an elite player with the banter of a radio disc jockey) can sometimes make a living through advertising, subscriptions and other revenue sources, thereby destabilising the boundaries between fantasy or game and what constitutes 'the real'.[63] The sheer numbers involved underscore the need for documentary aesthetics that include the virtual alongside the non-virtual in today's technologised culture.

To conclude, using animation to portray non-physical realities allows it to visualise virtual realities and actions. The exclusion of animation from contemporary documentaries would therefore result in a diminishing of the scope of documentary in an era defined by its mixed realities. A portable phone enables communication with distant others, but portable smart technology transcends that, acting as an extension of the self and a portal to other realms. One can be active on virtual platforms while crossing the street, for example, and thus 'be' in two places at the same time. Limited documentary visual languages, which are based solely on the capture of the physical, such as photography, fail to grasp today's simultaneous realities and thus fall behind. Conversely, animation easily depicts virtual actions; and whether accompanied by photographic footage of the physical or not, these depictions deliver a fuller, perhaps more accurate, view of realities today.

THE IMPACT OF MACHINIMA ON THEORISATIONS OF DOCUMENTARY

Machinima's technical forms of production completely change animation's relation to theorisations of documentary, and animation as documentary. Understanding how animation can act as a document that provides information or evidence is vital in the consideration of animated documentary and its reception.[64] According to Rosen, a form of capture is not automatically perceived as a document without discursive intervention, such as narrativisation, for example, making insight into the use and reception of new representations such as machinima necessary.[65] Since perceiving something as a document is related to indexicality, it is important to understand how machinima can capture, act as trace and/or denote information. This discussion would benefit from a renegotiation of machinima's relation to photography, and its role as document and documentary. The study of games is helpful in this context, since a recurring issue within the broader field of game studies is the narratology approach, which asks whether games should be examined as narrative works, versus the ludology approach, which views games as unique structural systems with specific characteristics.

To understand machinima's complex relation both to documentary theory and to wider explorations of contemporary non-fiction, machinima must be conceptualised both from a ludic and a cinematic perspective, since both are crucial to the ontological status of the digitally virtual. In this regard, we must differentiate between *machinima as a technique* of real-time interactive animation – the ludic, or the in-game event that is a translation of physical actions and input of the viewer – and *machinima works*, films that are no longer interactive, but rather based on captured footage of game data – the cinematic. Although all of machinima's systems are based in ludic event production, all three machinima production techniques relate to aspects of documentary differently. From a ludic viewpoint, machinima is the event itself, the referent; a form of digital performance in which 'real-world actors [are] mapped into virtual performance spaces'.[66] Machinima is the visual form of in-game actions where players puppeteer their characters inside real-time 3D game engines that combine AI and other players' actions. Hence, machinima is the event of gaming. As ludic events, machinima is the animation that is being documented, that is, document*ing* animation. Therefore, in all three machinima production techniques there are aspects of machinima being the referent and/or event depicted: in demo recording it is the code, in asset extraction it is the artefacts created, in screen capture it is the space that facilitates virtual puppeteering.

Machinima as cinematic is a form of representation, somewhat removed from the event itself. Since the animation in this case is representation rather than referent, it is document*ary animation*. Games operate through image *production*, whereas traditional cinema is grounded in image *recording*. The cinematic aspects of machinima works are based on transforming interactive, non-linear platforms into linear works meant for viewing, which demands editing and sequencing or narrativisation. This is a capture of the virtual, and in that sense, it is comparable to photography.

To reiterate, as ludic, machinima becomes the *event* upon which a documentary bases itself, in which case it is document*ing* animation, since it is the animated world that is being documented, an animated virtual world that is a trace of users' physical actions and input. As cinematic, machinima acts as document or record, and resembles photography, albeit of the virtual, which can also be edited to create meaning. In this case, I refer to machinima as document*ary* animation, the direct capture in animated form of animated referents.

The ludic aspect of machinima is embodied in demo recording, preserving the game code of the human–computer interactions that created the event within its original domain of the game engine. In this case, the machinima is not only visualisation: even though the player may no longer be involved in an interactive role, it is the event itself that is being re-created, not just its visual record. Demo-recording machinima acts both as a technological artefact of the series of actions stored in code to re-create the event, and as its visual footage, as the code is translated into visuals and thus serves as evidence, artefact or a visual document.

Unlike demo recording, which records events as data, screen capture preserves what is seen on screen, thus drawing it towards the cinematic and photographic. In terms of documentary production, screen capture is not only based on artefacts or footage, it also encompasses the specific perspective of the camera view, which is then sequenced to create a cinematic and edited linear work. With the element of editing, screen capture resembles asset compositing, which contains components extracted from game worlds. These components can be acknowledged as artefacts, documents or footage, but because the end product – the final linear segment – is edited and composed from varied sources, it is also like the edited and narratively constructed nature of screen capture. The use of in-game documents or artefacts and their narrativisation is what allows us to theorise machinima both as a form of virtual *animated document* and as documentary.

Changing characteristics of contemporary animation techniques, such as machinima, bring online realities closer in resemblance to the user's off-screen world, even if varied in visual form as in digital versus physical realities. If both spaces are 'real' and we, as users, are present in both the on- and off-screen worlds, documenting our contemporary mixed realities can take different visual forms. This clarifies animation's growing reception as credible documentary aesthetics.

Moreover, the immediacy of real-time visual mapping of one's physical movements onto corresponding avatars lends a sense of realism that, in turn, compensates for animation's non-naturalistic visuals. Users of virtual worlds feel they can be both 'in there', in the digitally virtual, technologically mediated space of the internet, and 'out here', in the physical world. This dual sense of presence negates the claim that in contemporary culture, the virtual and the material are opposed, and re-situates them as complementing facets of a mixed reality. In order to depict realities that are not physical, new visual languages of documentation that surpass the photographic are required.

However, real-time animated visualisation is extending beyond the portrayal of virtual worlds and is also being used increasingly in representations of physical realities, as discussed in the following chapters. This strengthens the idea of convergence between animated worlds and the viewers' physical world, and highlights how animation is being progressively used and accepted as a visual language of non-fiction. As viewers grow accustomed to seeing themselves, their actions and their physical or virtual environments in animated form, animation as a documentary aesthetic for contemporary realities makes more sense.

To conclude, revised documentary theorisation is required to analyse contemporary animation techniques that are prevalent in virtual domains characterised by real-time signification of online presence. Helpful terminology to differentiate between the ludic and the cinematic, the event and its representation, includes 'animated documents', 'document*ing* animation' and 'document*ary* animation'.

While existing research of animated documentaries refers to physical events depicted in animation, or to subjective experiences given visual form, the case here is different. In digitally virtual animated environments, animation is a component of the environment, not a separate representational choice for documentary reasons. This becomes clear when theorising machinima segments as cinematic works, and photography of the virtual where animation is not interpretative, but rather a direct capture, producing *animated documents* of the virtual. Virtual worlds such as games are real-time animated spaces. The documentation of such worlds is, therefore, the act of *documenting animation*. Documentaries of animated virtual worlds do not just happen to be animated; rather, animation is a direct cinematic record of the visual surface of virtual 3D environments, making it *documentary animation*. A crucial differentiation thus emerges between animated documentaries that use animation as a substitute for photography, or as an interpretative visual language for what cannot be photographed, and documentary animation. Once new techniques facilitate new uses of animation, as event as well as direct representation of the virtual, an additional tier is added to the understanding of animation, as well as to its contemporary uses and role in documentary theory and non-fiction representations.

Notes

1. For more information about the work and users' comments to it see Stern, 'Massively Multiplayer Machinima', p. 47.
2. Shields, *Virtual*, p. xv.
3. Dibbell, 'Rape in Cyberspace', unpaginated. A rich research culture on these topics can be seen in a multitude of publications including: *Cyberpsychology – A Journal of Psychosocial Research on Cyberspace* and *Cyberpsychology, Behavior, and Social Networking*.
4. McGonigal, *Reality is Broken*, p. 22.
5. As an example of the diverse uses of digital games and how they have moved to the centre of contemporary culture, see Bogost, *How to Do Things*.
6. See Castronova, *Exodus to the Virtual World*.
7. In this regard, it is also useful to clarify that physical and gaming experiences are obviously inherently different, but not always mutually exclusive. Gamers often experience physical reactions to gaming experiences, such as heightened adrenalin and/or anxiety. For more information see the following journals: *CyberPsychology & Behavior*, *Teleoperators & Virtual Environments* and *Journal of Media Psychology*.
8. Many theorists have engaged with the nature and definitions of games. As the topic exceeds the scope of this chapter, for an introduction to the field see Caillois, *Man, Play and Games*; Sutton-Smith, *Ambiguity of Play*. Sutton-Smith identifies seven categories of play, which include play as progress, fate, power, identity, the imaginary, the self, and frivolity, each of which orchestrates play in different ways and for different ends.
9. See Huizinga, *Homo Ludens*.
10. Pearce, *Communities of Play*, p. 177.
11. For a wider view of the myriad topics now researched in relation to digital games see the many titles of MIT Press' Game Studies category at www.mitpress.mit.edu/category/discipline/game-studies, accessed 4 August 2020.
12. Wingfield, 'Video Games'.
13. McGonigal, *Reality is Broken*, p. 4.
14. 'Essential Facts About the Game Industry: 2016 Sales, Demographic and Usage Data', Entertainment Software Association, 11 April 2017, http://essentialfacts.theesa.com/Essential-Facts-2016.pdf, accessed 22 January 2017.
15. 'Essential Facts About the Game Industry: 2010 Sales, Demographic and Usage Data', Entertainment Software Association, 16 June 2010, www.theesa.com/facts/pdfs/ESA_Essential_Facts_2010.PDF, accessed 14 February 2011.

16. Carr, '$1.1 Billion'.
17. *Molotov Alva and His Search for the Creator*, film, directed by Douglas Gayeton (USA: Submarine Channel and VPRO, 2007).
18. *SL* users, or residents, are represented by avatars that can interact with other users, explore the 'sandbox' game space, and create virtual property. The term 'sandbox' refers to a categorisation of game design that can be placed on a continuum between sandbox, open or free-roaming games, versus more structured game designs where in-game restrictions enforce a certain linearity, gameplay or objectives. In sandbox games players can roam freely through a virtual world with minimal barriers and the freedom to approach objectives and tools with which to create and modify the world and their activities as they choose.
19. See Castronova, *Exodus to the Virtual World*, and interviews with gamers in Juan Carlos Piñeiro Escoriaza's film *Second Skin* (2008).
20. Juan Carlos Piñeiro Escoriaza's 2008 film *Second Skin*, for example, included an interview with a handicapped teenage boy who, when living through his avatar, can walk and even fly like everyone else around him, transcending his bodily limitations. Sandra Danilovic's 2009 film *Second Bodies*, discussed in the previous chapter, also engages with similar themes about identities and what virtual worlds permit *vis-à-vis* self-image and self-acceptance. See *Second Skin*, film, directed by Juan Carlos Piñeiro Escoriaza (USA: Peter Schieffelin Brauer and Victor Piñeiro Escoriaza, 2008); *Second Bodies*, film, directed by Sandra Danilovic (Canada: Ryerson University, 2009).
21. The virtual economy is also called 'the secondary market' or 'virtual currency trade'. For more information on the topic of virtual economies, see Castronova, 'On Virtual Economies'; Weber, 'Virtual Indication'. According to Steve Salyer, a former game developer and now president of Internet Gaming Entertainment, players spend a real-world total of more than $880 million a year for virtual goods and services produced in online games, not counting sales of the games themselves. See Wallace, 'Game is Virtual'. A fascinating example that questions the boundaries between in-game and real-world economy, resources, labour, commodification, race, racism, globalisation and exploitation is the phenomenon of 'gold farming'. 'Gold farming' is the accrual of in-game wealth, items, and prestige by Chinese players to be sold or traded for real-world resources, transferring Chinese labour to other parts of the world, only virtually. By using the game as an economic platform of activity unwelcome to some, instances of virtual racism against the avatars of these Chinese professional gamers have been known to occur, similar to xenophobic reactions to certain cultural groups seen as 'invading' others' turf. For more on this topic see Arnason, 'Regulating Online Games in China'.
22. *Life 2.0*, film, directed by Jason Spingarn-Koff (USA: Andrew Lauren Productions, PalmStar Media and Preferred Content, 2010).
23. The film won Best Documentary Feature at the Philadelphia Film Festival, 2010.
24. Slotnik, 'Gamer's Death'.
25. For more information about the US granting athlete visas to professional

gamers, see Lejacq, 'Score!'. In 2014, Robert Morris University in Chicago was the first academic institution to award more than $500,000 in athletic scholarships to gamers. See Wingfield, 'Video Games'.
26. Wingfield, 'Video Games'.
27. Entertainment Software Association, 2016 Essential Facts About the Computer and Video Game Industry, www.theesa.com/article/2016-essential-facts-computer-video-game-industry/, accessed 30 July 2017.
28. Quote from Douglas Gayeton's 2007 film *Molotov Alva: My Life in Second Life*.
29. Lowood, 'Video Capture', p. 13. Director Joe Goss used a similar technique in his work on *Quad God*. For more on this see Kelland, 'From Game Mod to Low-budget Film', p. 24.
30. *Diary of a Camper*, film, directed by Matthew Van Sickler (USA: United Ranger Films, 1996).
31. Available at: https://archive.org/details/DiaryOfACamper, accessed 4 August 2016.
32. Lowood, 'High-performance Play', pp. 67–8.
33. Marino, *3D Game-based Filmmaking*, pp. 1, 12.
34. Ibid., p. 1.
35. Greenaway, 'Peter Greenaway Speaks', quoted in Harwood, 'Machinima', p. 150. Original emphasis.
36. Stern, 'Massively Multiplayer Machinima', p. 45.
37. These statistics are quoted from Harwood, 'Machinima', pp. 149–50.
38. Henry Lowood is curator for the history of science and technology collections and the film and media collections at Stanford University. His work in the field is important as he has headed several long-term projects at Stanford, including 'How They Got Game: The History and Culture of Interactive Simulations and Videogames in the Stanford Humanities Lab', the Silicon Valley Archives at Stanford University Libraries and the Machinima Archives and Archiving Virtual Worlds collections hosted by the Internet Archive. He is leading Stanford's work on game and virtual world preservation in the Preserving Virtual Worlds project funded by the US Library of Congress and the Institute for Museum and Library Services.
39. Machinima festivals already exist today, and a move toward integrating machinima with officially sanctioned digital art festivals and exhibitions has also begun. Tracy Harwood lists the following digital art festivals and galleries: Atopic, France; Animatu, Portugal; Bitfilm, Germany; Phoenix Square, Leicester, UK. For example, some of the first exhibitions to focus on machinima were: *Bang the Machine*, curated by Henry Lowood and Galen Davis at the Yerba Buena Center for the Arts in 2004; *Alt-Ctrl*, curated by Robert Nideffer and Antoinette LaFarge at the Beall Center for Art and Technology in California in 2004 (www.beallcenter.uci.edu/exhibitions/altctrl.php, accessed 4 August 2020); and *WOW: Emergent Media Phenomenon*, curated by Grace Kook-Anderson with assistance from Blizzard's curator Tim Campbell and Eddo Stern at the Laguna Art Museum in California (www.lagunaartmuseum.org/wow-emergent-media-

phenomenon, accessed 4 August 2020) in 2009. Machinima artists include Eddo Stern, Joseph DeLappe, Jacqueline Goss, Tom Jantol and many others. Also, reviews of machinima works have been covered in academic journals, for example: Johnson, 'Machinima Reviews'. For more information see Nideffer, 'Eight Questions', p. 73; Harwood, 'Machinima'.
40. Sutton, 'Real Photography', p. 163.
41. See Greenberg, 'Animated Text'.
42. King and Krzywinska, 'Cinema/Videogames/Interfaces', p. 4.
43. Cameron and Carroll, 'Encoding Liveness', p. 129.
44. For more information see Lowood, 'Video Capture'; Kelland, 'From Game Mod to Low-budget Film'; Harwood 'Machinima'.
45. Lowood, 'Video Capture', p. 11.
46. Harwood, 'Machinima', p. 157.
47. Salen, 'Arrested Development', p. 47.
48. For more on this see Nitsche, 'Machinima as Media'.
49. Nitsche, 'Claiming Its Space', unpaginated.
50. Harwood, 'Machinima', p. 157.
51. Lowood, 'Video Capture', p. 16.
52. Harwood, 'Machinima', pp. 157–8.
53. For the full list, elaboration and examples of each genre, see ibid., pp. 159–63.
54. Joost Raessens uses Roger Odin's term to explain the way spectators view works through a documentary or fictionalising perspective. This can be produced by individual spectators, depending on the information/experience they wish to gain from the film, or by the textual and contextual instructions indicated by the film, which stimulate certain viewing lectures – watching a fictional film as a documentary of the places the actor visited, for example. See Odin, 'Semio-pragmatic Approach'. Quoted in Raessens, 'Reality Play', p. 220.
55. Harwood, 'Machinima', p. 172.
56. Ibid., p. 171.
    Some creators have achieved celebrity status, such as PewDiePie who has over 34 million subscribers to his channel and has become one of the most influential people on the internet. For more information see Grundberg and Hansegard, 'YouTube's Biggest Draw'; Begley, 'The 30 Most Influential'.
57. Wingfield, 'What's Twitch?'.
58. Wingfield, 'Video Games'.
59. See https://www.twitch.tv/p/about, accessed 8 August 2019.
60. Ibid. Indeed, competitive video game sports have become mainstream; in 2016 a new gaming league – ELEAGUE – began pitting well-known gamers against one another on Twitch. In the same year, SuperData Research estimated there would be 'about 214 million viewers for e-sports competitions globally . . . up from 188 million last year'. See Herrman and Wingfield, 'ELeague Adapts TV'.
61. Slotnik, 'Gamer's Death'.
62. See http://gametoon.com/pdf/Gametoon2018.pdf, accessed 8 August 2019.
63. Slotnik, 'Gamer's Death'.

64. See Oxford Dictionaries definition of 'document': https://en.oxforddictionaries.com/definition/document, accessed 4 August 2020.
65. See Rosen, 'Document and documentary'.
66. Mazalek, 'Tangible Narratives', p. 96.

CHAPTER FIVE

In-game Documentaries of Non-game Realities

As realities become increasingly mixed, and the physical and computerised virtual worlds converge, it comes as no surprise that the aesthetics used for each are employed in new and hybrid ways. This chapter focuses on documentaries that experiment with and purposely fuse the aesthetics used to depict physical and virtual realities, commenting upon the evolving relationship between the two and the consequent need to rethink the role of animation within these current shifts in documentary aesthetics.

'Congratulations, you have stooped lower than any other guild in MMO history.'[1] This quote appears in the opening credits of *Serenity Now* (2008),[2] an animated documentary that raises disturbing questions about the blurred lines that now exist between virtual game worlds and the non-game, physical reality. After a player of the online game *World of Warcraft* (*WoW*) died in real life, her fellow players organised an online in-game memorial service in her honour, where those who knew her could attend virtually, via their avatars, in order to pay their respects. A rival in-game guild decided to use the occasion, showed up and killed everyone. In other words, a real-life death and memorial became an opportunity for an in-game win, defiled due to game-battle rivalry.

The documentary *Serenity Now* is the attacking guild's edited capture of the events, moving between the peaceful memorial and the invading guild's journey until the moment of attack, and the barely disguised glee following its victory. The film includes atmospheric music to build tension, and intertitles at the beginning and end of the film ('Yes, we know we are assholes :D') that also act as social commentary on the events and subsequent online reactions.[3] The incident raises broader questions about the place of morality within the in-game community and its organisation – issues that are dominant in discussions of computer games and the philosophy of technology today.[4]

Julian Dibbell's classic article 'A Rape in Cyberspace', which discusses the on-screen sexual abuse of another player's avatar, illustrated how, early in the construction of these virtual worlds, offensive in-game actions resulted in demands to create in-game codes of ethics and societal structures that borrowed from existing social norms in the non-game world, but which also highlighted the inherent difficulties. How can you punish an avatar?

According to which rules? Who has the authority to decide?[5] This was merely the beginning. As more people participate and a wider range of activities takes place online, virtual experiences and non-virtual expectations or laws increasingly merge and/or conflict. The disturbing phenomena of cyber-bullying, revenge pornography and online shaming are current examples where laws, shaped by the organisation and values of the physical, non-virtual world, are eventually expanded to online conduct and culture. New technologies often give rise to questions of ethics, as they influence the ways in which participants experience the online world, and how virtual societies are constructed. Social structures, acceptable behaviour, authority and punishment are only some of the ethical and social issues re-created and evolving in virtual realms and game worlds. The questions raised illuminate attempts to assemble virtual platforms according to non-virtual values, laws, conventions and structures. The social issues raised in *Serenity Now* shed light on the complex and growing convergence between virtual and non-virtual realms.

An early example of an in-game (and therefore animated) documentary that deals with non-game realities is the machinima work *The French Democracy* (2005),[6] which was produced as a new form of protest against the racism that sparked civil unrest in France that year. This is considered the first major political machinima to be released and reported on worldwide.[7] I will use two case studies that were made a decade apart, Jacqueline Goss's *Stranger Comes to Town* (2007)[8] and Amir Yatziv's *Another Planet* (2017),[9] to illustrate how animation is used in different ways in cinematic works that combine virtual game worlds with non-game physical reality, creating a new kind of animated documentary.

Whereas the previous chapter discussed in-game documentaries, Goss and Yatziv's thought-provoking works, and related examples, use virtual worlds in both form and content in order to engage with realities that go beyond online games. By examining in-game documentaries of non-game realities, it becomes apparent that what may initially seem fictional can actually be a surprising, precise and poignant way to reveal, comment and reflect upon 'the real', potentially shaping and influencing it as a result. The combination of in-game worlds with non-game 'actual' content adds another layer to the research of animated documentaries in a virtualised culture.

TROLLS AND OTHERS: SELF-REPRESENTATION, PRIVACY AND SURVEILLANCE

Jacqueline Goss's 2007 documentary video artwork, *Stranger Comes to Town*, deliberately blurs the boundaries between virtual gaming and non-virtual non-gaming worlds, and the extent to which they are interconnected. Unlike documentaries such as machinima works that are clearly based on in-game imagery and production methods, my study of *Stranger Comes to Town* engages with the idea of mixed realities by using aesthetics of both virtual and non-virtual worlds to emphasise the inter-changeability and, at times, confusingly indistinguishable nature of the virtual and the physical. Goss's work highlights previously discussed topics including mixed realities, animated documents, machinima and contemporary theorisations of the physical body. Through her multifaceted engagement with virtual worlds, Goss comments on central characteristics of contemporary culture that exceed gaming and virtual realms, specifically self-representation, racial profiling, privacy and surveillance, as well as shifting spaces, borders and geography.

Although not the first of its kind, Goss's work is interesting because, through multiple and combined forms of representations, it adds complexity to the intersection of game and non-game realities. The virtual elements have a metaphoric significance, but are also used to reflect upon documentary techniques and to critique existing social and political systems. In this work, six people are interviewed about their experiences of entering the US and of using the biometric systems that collect physical data about immigrants and visitors at the border. In order to maintain the anonymity of her protagonists, Goss's interviews are based on animated avatars that the interviewees designed for themselves in the *WoW* online role-playing game. The characters we see, therefore, are semi-humanoid creatures. The interviews are accompanied by various visual sources, including Google Earth imagery and *US Visit*, an animated video created by US Homeland Security and used in airports to instruct visitors. The informational video shows people's black silhouettes undergoing the processes of immigration control and biometric tests; it is intended to explain what is expected of immigrants and visitors in the clearest possible manner. The combinations of imagery in Goss's work create fascinating and original mash-ups that further blur the boundaries between virtual game and non-game worlds and representations, thus weakening the conception of virtual worlds as closed systems of their own.

The instructional *US Visit* film explains:

> the US is launching a new program, called 'US Visit' where in [US] ports of entry advanced technology is used to verify the identity of in-coming visitors. This does not apply to US citizens. Using biometrics ... enhances security while facilitating legitimate travel and trade.[10]

By using this video, Goss does not refer to animation as an interpretive visual language, but rather acknowledges its significance as a contemporary cultural document – the animated imagery viewers now recognise as informatics in public spaces. Second, Goss refers to *US Visit* but does not incorporate it directly into her work. Instead, she uses a rotoscoped version of the animated original. By tracing the already animated clip, Goss creates a second-degree animated representation of an animated primary source, commenting upon animation as a document in its own right and the documentary status of animation as a representation of different documents. While rotoscoping is most often used as a trace of photographic footage, this representational choice unburdens the artist in relation to copyright uses, and also allows more creative freedom since she can then incorporate additional aspects into the referenced original. As I will demonstrate, Goss ends the work by integrating non-human game-based characters into the rotoscoped version of *US Visit*, adding interpretive elements and critique into the referenced original. These novel uses of animation open up new directions for the production and the creative use of animation in documentary.

Goss's use of *US Visit* questions the implications of employing biometrical processes to verify identity. *Stranger Comes to Town* describes the depersonalising nature of the biometric tests that collect information about a person according to external and often secret criteria. The incongruity of collecting information about a person through physical data, and the alienation and depersonalisation this process can evoke, are described by the protagonists. One woman said that the pose she had to adopt when being photographed by the border control staff was unnatural and different to how she normally appears; she also mentioned that the immigration officers wore gloves to eliminate body contact as they guided her physically through the process. While the body is thus the focus of the biometric system, it is a body that is posed, moulded and treated as separate from the human subject. Goss explains that *US Visit* depicts 'stick figures, unmarked surfaces of human beings, deracinated ... an elaborate attempt *not* to identify these people',[11] thus critiquing the growing culture of surveillance that dehumanises individuals while collecting their personal information. This visual representation corresponds perfectly with the work's soundtrack, which plays back interviewees' testimonies of cold, alienated exchanges with the border control staff. A second female interviewee explains:

> [Y]ou cannot see the results [of the biometric tests] yourself, they have a device so that you cannot see ... I think it is for security reasons but I would like to see what is on their screens ... You feel you are not free ... You are being taken as cattle ... The place has a lot of light, but not natural light. You feel observed.[12]

The juxtaposition between being observed yet not being shown one's own data is a major theme of this work, highlighting the discrepancy between what is seen and what significance or meaning visual signifiers have. This subject is introduced at the very beginning where the opening scene includes a blue screen and the spoken question 'so this is anonymous?'. The blue screen, which seems to be on the verge of changing (as if always about to expose more), leaves the viewer uncertain about what, if anything, is actually being shown. This theme continues throughout the work, emphasising the gap between visual signifiers and the meaning assigned to them. The lack of clear imagery underscores the significance of the soundtrack, which serves to strengthen the documentary status of the work as an ostensibly credible recording of the protagonists who are heard but not seen (as discussed in Chapter 2). Thus, while the confusing imagery has a potentially destabilising effect, the soundtrack serves to emphasise the 'authenticity' of the work. The question of anonymity introduces the second major theme of the work, which deals with representation of the self through the dichotomy between exposure and privacy.

The representation of the individual, the body, exposure, privacy and depersonalisation are all apparent in the following example, which illustrates that animation can sometimes be far more revealing than photorealistic modes of representation. In the animated *US Visit*, travellers are depicted in a similar way to that of the material world of airport X-ray machines. New scanning procedures in airports enable immigration officers to see travellers as depersonalised human forms that appear as naked silhouettes, while simultaneously invading their privacy and collecting intrusive information about them. These technologies have generated much concern about personal privacy and, as a result, upgraded scanning devices were installed; these may reduce physical exposure, but the element of depersonalisation is still ominously evident. Following the controversy surrounding full-body scanners, new technologies that display generic body outlines have been in use at US airports since 2013.[13] Automatic Target Recognition software technologies produce less detailed body imaging, and instead offer a generic human image, with specific areas of suspicion highlighted by coloured squares. Passengers are thus literally represented as depersonalised generic humanoids through stick-figure representations. Whereas animation may initially seem non-realistic as representation, it is actually hard to imagine a different documentary language that could have been as successful in dehumanising an individual so powerfully and precisely.

The collection of personal data that is kept hidden from the individual in question highlights the contradiction between surveillance and exposure in the current era. As more information about an individual is exposed, more is kept hidden; subjects do not even know how they are recorded and categorised. Goss asks 'Who are the people beside me in databases? What do we share and by which criteria?'[14] These profiles are used by organisations such as immigration control, the police and even marketing companies, thus contributing to the construction of a social identity based on information about which the individual may know little or nothing at all. Goss's use of non-humanoid game avatars in her interviews accentuates both the idea of online identities that may differ from one's physical sense of self and the topic of profile construction used in racial profiling and data collection. While game avatars are a form of self-representation, surveillance and data collection result in the profile being constructed by a separate 'other' and remaining undisclosed to the subject. In engaging with the question of representation by another as opposed to self-representation, Goss develops a particularly compelling multifaceted visual language in a self-reflexive documentary about contemporary representation.

Goss's exploration of border control and issues surrounding identity resonate with larger issues of national identities and control over them. Globalisation of the internet has also raised concerns about the cultural identities of individual nations. As Jerry Everard explains:

> [I]n recent debates about globalisation and about the global spread of telecommunications, several themes are presented in sets of binary oppositions: sovereignty as against the borderless society [of a wired world]; public access to information as against privacy; the state as against individual interests; the virtual as against the real . . . and so on.[15]

While Everard underscores the simplistic nature of such binary oppositions, they are, nonetheless, useful categories with which to consider those aspects of contemporary culture to which Goss refers in her work. Everard explains that, if states are thought of as collective, albeit multifaceted, identities, they become visible when they are weakest, such as when they are questioned or contested by an internal or external 'other'.[16] Since states are constructed by means of borders, the issue of boundaries becomes a key mechanism of state survival. This was made particularly apparent in the aftermath of 9/11, and more recently as a result of the refugee crisis. Goss explores themes of human rights compromised in the name of the War on Terror, and the attempt to control the massive flow of immigrants and refugees seeking safety abroad.

In *Stranger Comes to Town*, Goss illustrates these oppositions. On one hand, she bases her work on the issue of border control and immigration, which use racial profiling to detect the 'other' who is considered a threat to the identity of the state. On the other hand, she uses virtual world imagery that blurs physical and national identities by emphasising the non-recognisable and the non-human. Virtual worlds are potential spaces for virtual communities that transcend the borders and identity-formation criteria of the state. This is important in today's networked era in which national states have increasingly seized control of their corresponding virtual spaces, by restricting online access. The conceptualisation of space, especially with regard to the physical versus the virtual, is in constant flux. In this context, the non-recognisable individual sitting in undetectable cyberspace symbolises a threat; she may be able to infiltrate, and perhaps destabilise, a state's sovereignty from the external space of the virtual, as is the case with hackers, hacktivists and in the growing field of cyber warfare, often referred to as trolls. Interestingly, since Goss's protagonists use troll-like avatars from *WoW*, the animation used is (1) a means to protect anonymity, as is often used in animated documentaries; (2) direct capture of game elements, using virtual puppeteering as an animation technique; but additionally (3) the use of monstrous, non-human characters also has important metaphoric significance vital to the work's critical content about the unrecognisable or invisible 'other' deemed a threat, which is an important theme in Goss's work. Here the avatar guarantees anonymity, but at the same time also exposes the idea of the immigrant as alien, and the 'other' as potentially monstrous. Animation's multiple uses and meanings thus become apparent.

The emphasis on the dehumanisation of the immigrant-avatar, and the discrepancy between self-representation and state categorisation, are reinforced in an additional interview in Goss's work. Here the protagonist, who is depicted as a massive and masculine bearded purple figure with hidden eyes, discusses the Patriot Act passed after 9/11 in order to enhance law enforcement and state surveillance in the pursuit of suspected terrorists. The protagonist describes a trip with eight other male college friends, all from Muslim countries. He recollects that he was required to go to a special immigration office for Muslims in the basement, where he once had to wait for over three hours, almost missing his flight, without anyone providing him with any information. He identifies himself as an atheist male who grew up in a Muslim country, and describes how he came to realise that the way in which others view a person influences the way that person comes to represent him or herself. 'I am a Muslim because other people see me as such, even if I would not have represented myself that way since I am not religious', he says. The gap between the way in which racial profiling is used to define someone and how they define themselves is the embodiment of the process of depersonalisation so visible in the *US Visit* animated film, and the questioning of visual signifiers more widely, so persuasively critiqued by Goss. Interestingly, animation's ability to 'disguise' the appearance of the interviewee also prevents automatic assumptions by the viewer based on physical appearance. Not seeing the person brings the content of the interview into focus, encouraging viewers to listen more intently instead of basing assumptions on visual prejudice, the exact opposite of racial profiling. Choosing a gaming platform whereby many characters are non-human as a source of animation for her protagonists to design their own avatars/film characters means that Goss's decision to disguise her interviewees as non-human through obviously constructed non-photorealistic animation actually and indirectly makes them *more* human and less easily defined by cultural stereotypes.

In order to comment upon this process of representation, Goss visually accentuates the sense of physical disguise, visual layering and concealment. She represents her interviewees' avatars in three modes – as machinima game imagery (as they would appear in *WoW*), as hand-drawn animated figures and as black silhouettes. She ends by incorporating these non-human silhouettes into the *US Visit* Homeland Security video with which the film began. The decision to use non-human gaming-world avatars to represent her immigrant protagonists enables Goss to critique issues of race and the body in the US Homeland's security racial profiling with its reliance on biometric data.

Goss explains that she wanted to counter the representation of depersonalisation in the official *US Visit* film, and to facilitate self-representation while protecting the privacy of her interviewees.[17] Online game imagery facilitates the use of 'pre-formed' animation created by the game engines. By using game-based animation that enables the protagonists to control their

Figure 5.1 Avatar in three modes of animation, from *Stranger Comes to Town*, directed by Jacqueline Goss, 2007.

Figure 5.2 *World of Warcraft* avatars incorporated into the *US Visit* rotoscoped video, from *Stranger Comes to Town*, directed by Jacqueline Goss, 2007.

own representation, the interviewees are able to design and puppeteer their animated characters themselves.[18] Here the animation acts as a mask that guarantees disguise, while simultaneously exposing the personal preferences of the creators/protagonists. The animation production choice means that game-sourced animation tools that are accessible to non-animators relate the discussion to machinima and to the rapid growth of the animation field as new instruments of self-expression become available and user-friendly.[19] Using game engines as tools for animation purposes allows creators to experiment with the cinematic outcome by experimenting while animating instead of preparing and deciding everything in advance, which makes animation a more fluid and playful tool for cinematic production, allowing immediate editing and adjustments and encouraging spontaneity and creativity, developing new directions in animated documentaries.[20]

Games therefore take on dual significance as spaces – spaces for creation as well as spaces of interactive presence and experience. Interestingly the limits between these online spaces and the viewer's own physical space are confusing in more ways than one.

CONTEMPORARY SPACES

By using online animated game imagery in a work about immigration, Goss indirectly references the growing incursion of immigration into virtual worlds, depicting the latter as additional spaces where today's reality takes place. In *Stranger Comes to Town* she creates a continuous geographical expanse comprised of virtual landscapes and Google Earth images. *Stranger Comes to Town* illustrates the growing 'factional' (as opposed to solely fictional) status assumed of digital game aesthetics. It not only serves to demonstrate that game-oriented animation is sometimes indistinguishable from photographic imagery, but also points to similarities between game worlds and non-game realities. What seems like an uninterrupted view of a single landscape emphasises the convergence of these supposedly separate 'worlds', and the increasing representational difficulty in telling them apart due to changes in hyperrealist animation and computerised machine-vision imagery. While the virtual as 'non-real' can seem fictional or fantasy-related, Goss's representational choices are linked to wider conceptions of space and subjectivity in today's globalised and virtualised culture. By portraying virtual spaces as linked to, and continuous with, the physical non-virtual world, Goss's work reinforces the idea that the digitally virtual is merely one aspect of a mixed and multifaceted reality – one that can no longer be dismissed as 'non-real', either in content or form. By incorporating avatars from online games, and scenes from maps and landscapes, Goss introduces the issue of space and geography, taking the virtual as a contemporary space and portraying it as continuous with the physical.

Globalisation's redefinitions of territorial and cultural characteristics have given rise to discourse about the significance of 'other' culturally or emotionally significant spaces that people create for themselves. The result is a globalised culture in which notions of space have shifted and become more fluid, and are based increasingly on non-physical conceptions. This opens up new directions for the theorisation of the non-physical spaces we inhabit (even if border control, rising nationalism and the refugee crisis paint a very different picture of physical geographical space). Irit Rogoff explains that geography has become less essential as a material basis for subjects' lives, sense of belonging and identity-construction. According to Rogoff's concept of 'relational geography', new tensions and bonds evolve between physical and cultural spaces, material perimeters of territory are avoided, and the space of visual culture instead becomes a key reference point.[21] Echoing even earlier ideas about space and technology, the development of cultural geography explains that geography is no longer a physical construct; instead, it is based on people's understanding, which changes due to factors such as telepresence, ease of communication and the proliferation of expatriate communities. Thus the point made in Juan Carlos Piñeiro Escoriaza's 2008 documentary, *Second Skin* (2008),[22] about gamers who see virtual spaces as their 'places of residence' and spend endless hours playing online games rather than inhabiting their 'real-world' personas and lives, is less peculiar than it may have initially seemed. *Second Skin* moves between the photographed footage of gamers and their in-game avatar depictions and experiences. This representational choice also enables engagement with changing contemporary conceptions of space, the physical body, interactive digital platforms as new realms of activity and presence, as well as 'actual' and virtual immigration, as the realities of today converge on so many levels. These changes in the conception of space, and the move towards mixed realities in contemporary culture, clearly generate a need for new visuals in documentaries.

Considering the digitally virtual as a place enables an analysis of contemporary animation's uses, forms and techniques that raises new questions and theorisations about the current role of animated documentaries and their truth claims in today's networked culture, especially as virtual spaces are not only continuous, in many senses, to physical spaces but also used in their place. Virtual spaces are used to explore the physical *instead* of actual physical presence, giving them a new status that it is important to take note of (and one I continue to engage with in the following chapter). *Another Planet*, as its name hints, engages with issues surrounding space and what are ostensibly 'other' spaces, be they virtual, incomprehensible, intangible or otherwise.

The animated documentary *Another Planet*[23] depicts six CG animated simulations of the Auschwitz-Birkenau Concentration Camp. The film records encounters in virtual worlds that all aim to faithfully simulate the concentration camp (despite their obviously non-photorealistic animated styles) and revive something of the historical event by offering new insights and interactive experiences for viewers. The simulations in the film range from photorealistic animation used as a VR experience, to a black and white architectural reconstruction, a 360-degree investigative forensic model, an online role-playing game and a Minecraft music video. The film includes interviews with each of the creators (by using avatars that the filmmaker generated, mostly in external software and incorporated into the pre-made virtual simulations, and also highlighting new game-based animation production methods). Bringing these different virtual simulations together, the film is an exploration of reconstructed memory and the role of animation as a visual aesthetic that deals with the past in today's digital culture.

Although it would be impossible to cover the entire spectrum of phenomena that characterise contemporary digital culture when examining memory construction and shifting notions of evidence, the new structures of mass communication have rewritten how memory is formed. As a result, institutions such as museums no longer have the central or final say but instead a multiplicity of narratives and representations have flourished. This occurs both through sharing personal stories in endless new ways, such as on social media, and through varied individual attempts to represent historical places, events and stories in novel forms, as evident in *Another Planet*. The changing accessibility of information and archives has allowed amateurs to use source materials in new ways and endlessly experiment with representation, resulting in simulations of concentration camps created for varied purposes, for example. Wulf Kansteiner differentiates between 'big' (commercial) memory and 'small' (non-commercial) memory, and defines two cultures of memory construction: the formalised, institutionalised and regimented one of analogue culture versus the emergent, confrontational and fragmented one of the digital, that remediates analogue memory and analogue institutions of memory.[24]

The centrality of interactive media and the rise of animated representations of non-fiction raise new questions about memory construction in a digital age. For example, the status of many holocaust museums and sites is changing in an era where increasing numbers of internet users become comfortable with the replacement of physical space with virtual space. A generational paradigm shift thus emerges where the aura of a physical place and object changes as more people become accustomed to visual and online representations of events, people and things. This means that contemporary media witnesses 'visit' places differently and receive information in new manners. Defined as virtual witnessing, this phenomenon, whereby places, events and personal stories are re-created for online users to explore individually and interactively, will be explored further in the next chapter. It changes the relation between virtual and physical spaces, using the virtual in order to understand the physical, replacing it in a certain way. *Another Planet*, in other words, also examines themes like those incorporated in *A Stranger Comes to Town*, but in a different manner.

Like Goss's interesting uses of animation, what is interesting in *Another Planet* is that the animation in this case study is *both* the visual language used in *each* Auschwitz-Birkenau simulation (i.e. as part of the inherent appearance of the referent), and also the cinematic representational choice (i.e. this is an animated documentary *about* these simulations). This means that the way animation is used is multi-layered. First of all, as a documentary, *Another Planet* directly captures the appearance of the reconstructions as they appear to users through animation, instead of using animation as an interpretive visual language. Whereas Goss uses the animated *US Visit* film as a document from the physical world, and then animates it, making second-degree animation, in *Another Planet* the animation is used in the virtual reconstructions as an interpretive depiction of physical space. However, since these reconstructions are depicted through captured footage, *Another Planet* is also a direct document of a virtual occurrence and space. As explained in earlier chapters, animation in such cases can be equated with photography, only capturing the visual appearance of the virtual rather than the physical. The film even ends with credits that the film was 'filmed' in the following virtual locations, emphasising the blurred boundaries that now exist between animation and photography and what *can* be photographed. As discussed in this book's introduction, animation used in virtual worlds and then captured and defined as photographs demonstrates the blurred boundaries that exist today. Not only are real and virtual experiences combined in these contexts, the aesthetics used, how they are defined and how this influences viewer expectations regarding the imagery's functions and believability are also unclear. New debates are thus clearly essential. The different uses of animation in these case studies contribute to the discussion of animation as a document, as raised in Chapter 2 through indexicality.

As explained, according to Rosen, if a document is intended both to inform and record, this is exactly what the animation in *Another Planet* does, albeit in a complex and dual manner.[25] Animation in a documentary that directly captures the animated simulation can be seen as evidence similar to photographic capture, whereas animation used in re-enactments to convey a historical event is a form of teaching. According to this view of what a document is, animation in both cases then can be seen as a new form of document, a proof of a re-enactment and a wider form of informational conveyor about historical events. The combination of the two is what creates a contemporary mode of believable memory construction built on a complex understanding of what a document may be. I will return to this case study in the final chapter.

To conclude, the divide between animated worlds and the physical space of the viewer is based on the idea that animation does not exist in physical reality; that it is only visible on screen and breaks stylistically with physical appearance. One presumed 'problems' of animated documentary images is, therefore, that 'they cannot objectively represent reality or depart from their innate facticity', and 'that they are ontologically dissimilar with respect to [material-based] indexicality'.[26] These characteristics of animation contradict more traditional documentary conventions, which demand an 'objective' and 'direct' depiction of realities, i.e. photorealistic imagery, while animation inherently highlights its constructed nature. In other words, photographic representation's truth status relies on a physical imprint of the referent and the visual imitation of its physical attributes. This helps to legitimise photography as a believable non-fiction aesthetic (one that tries to erase traces of its own production process). In comparison, animation emphasises its constructed nature, and thus its relation to the 'real' that it depicts is unclear, raising suspicion of its role as trustworthy signifier. With regard to animated documentary, the insurmountable difference from representations of the physically 'actually real' creates an unbridgeable gap, conceptualising animation and 'the real' as essentially contradictory. However, this assumption collapses as both the 'actual', as well as conventions of non-fiction representation, change. The role, richness, and complexity of the virtual and today's ubiquitous screen culture shatter binaries that determine the virtual as non-real, and re-situate it as an additional facet of contemporary realities. Consequently, as distinctions between the virtual and the 'real' dissolve, it is only logical that the aesthetics of today's mixed realities will converge in documentary-related depictions engaging with these realities.

Goss's representational choices in *Stranger Comes to Town* and Yatziv's documentation of online simulations of physical spaces highlight tendencies in contemporary culture. Their work explores a globalised and virtualised world in which the non-physical is as 'real' as the physical, and can be used to reflect upon representations assumed to be authentic or 'direct' in new ways. These issues push the issue of reliable documentary aesthetics away from more conventional reliance upon photography, and raise many questions related to self and cultural representation as explored in racial profiling and fluid conceptions of space.

These case studies illustrate several tendencies new to the theorisation of animated documentaries: the use of game spaces as animation production tools used to create cinematic depictions that shatter the 'magic circle', to use Joan Huizinga's term, and point to the growing convergence between game and non-game realities. Each case study demonstrates different uses of animation as documents and varied documentary aesthetics, be it direct capture of the virtual, metaphoric, second-degree animation and more. Although animation may at first seem an unusual visual choice for non-fiction works, it actually serves to convey important points about realities that extend beyond virtual domains in an incredibly succinct and powerful manner. As an in-game documentary of a non-game reality – and/or a mixture of the two – such documentary works demonstrate that new forms of visualisation can depict what cannot otherwise be shown in traditional documentary imagery, representing the multiplicity and complexity of contemporary realities, while engaging with them differently. This is an important achievement in an era in which photography and documentary are thrown into question, as we seek increasingly to represent realities in new and experimental ways in order to address complexities and reach new insights.[27]

While the virtual in these two case studies was used as a creative space with which to produce a film through virtual puppeteering and in-game animation techniques, the following chapter analyses additional aspects of converging aesthetics and mixed realities by focusing on non-cinematic (i.e. ludic and interactive) works in virtual realms that engage with non-virtual events, e.g. documentary games and VR. These shed new light on, and raise additional questions about, the relationship between virtual aesthetics and the characteristics of virtual worlds, non-virtual realities, animation, believability and documentary.

Notes

1. MMO stands for a massively multiplayer online game, which is capable of supporting large numbers of players on the same server.
2. *Serenity Now*, online capture, 2008.
3. The film is available at www.wn.com/Serenity_Now_bombs_a_World_of_Warcraft_funeral, accessed 4 August 2020.
4. For more information see Sageng *et al.*, *Philosophy of Computer Games*; Sandler, *Ethics and Emerging*.
5. Dibbell, 'Rape in Cyberspace', unpaginated. For an interesting and more recent review of the amalgamation between real-world laws and laws pertaining to virtual actions, see Webber, 'Law, Culture'.
6. *The French Democracy*, film, directed by Alex Chan (France: Atomic Prod, 2005).
7. The machinima is available at https://www.youtube.com/watch?v=stu31sz5ivk, accessed 4 August 2020.

8. *Stranger Comes to Town*, film, directed by Jacqueline Goss (USA, 2007).
9. *Another Planet*, film, directed by Amir Yatziv's (Israel: Amir Yatziv and Jonathan Doweck, 2017).
10. Quoted from the soundtrack of the *US Visit* video as represented in Goss's work.
11. Goss, 'Jacqueline Goss' (artist's presentation of her work at the 2009 *WoW: Emergent Media Phenomenon* exhibition at the Laguna Art Museum, Laguna Beach, California, 26 July 2009).
12. Quoted from *Stranger Comes to Town*, 2007, by Jacqueline Goss.
13. Ahlers, 'TSA Removes Body Scanners'.
14. Goss, 'Jacqueline Goss'.
15. Everard, *Virtual States*, p. 4.
16. Ibid., p. 5.
17. Skype conversations with the artist, July 2010.
18. The free reign that Goss gives her interviewees, due to her choice of animation that is almost a form of puppeteering, is interesting to consider in relation to Samantha Moore's writing on the collaborative frame in her research about the collaboration between animators and protagonists in documentary works: Moore, 'Does This Look Right?'
19. This is relevant to my discussion of the reasons for the proliferation of animated documentaries. For more on machinima as an easy-to-use, low-budget animation tool that provides new opportunities for film making techniques, see Kelland, 'From Game Mod to Low-budget Film'.
20. Hodgkin, 'Animating with a Game Engine'.
21. Rogoff, *Terra Infirma*, p. 4. Rogoff focuses more on the capitalist economy as the basis for the distribution of culture, but sheds light on new conceptualisations of space. For more on this, see Guerra, 'Negatives of Europe'.
22. *Second Skin*, film, directed by Juan Carlos Piñeiro Escoriaza (USA: Peter Schieffelin Brauer and Victor Piñeiro Escoriaza, 2008).
23. Amir Yatziv, 2017
24. Kansteiner, 'Holocaust in the 21st Century'.
25. Rosen, 'Document and documentary', pp. 65–6.
26. In theorising documentary games, Joost Raessens addresses the 'problems', some of which are shared by animated documentaries due to their constructed nature and visual form. Raessens, 'Reality Play', p. 220.
27. Related examples of in-game documentaries that engage with non-game realities are Joseph DeLappe's project *Dead in Iraq* (2006–11), an online memorial and protest taking place within the US Army recruiting game *America's Army*, about the Iraq war.

CHAPTER SIX

Interactive Animated Documentaries: Documentary Games and VR

There are different kinds of animated documentary works that engage with the virtual. Chapter 4 examined the cinematic and linear documentation of interactive virtual worlds, as evident in machinima. Chapter 5 looked at cinematic works that document in-game events intended to engage with, or comment upon, non-game realities, further blurring the boundaries between the two. This chapter focuses on the sub-genre of interactive animated documentaries, or VR documentaries/immersive journalism and documentary games, which employ the characteristics of virtual culture, including telepresence, immersion, avatars, real-time animation and interactivity, in order to portray physical realities.

The *Kuma War Games* website features re-creations of actual events relating to the War on Terror under the strapline, 'Real War News. Real War Games'.[1] The games reconstruct real-world military events in which players are cast into various re-created conflict zones.[2] Three elements of the site are noteworthy: the missions are indeed accurate re-creations of real military operations; the interface is graphically designed to mimic a news channel; and the imagery is based on visual reference materials, recalling *TomoNews*'s use of media reports and imagery in animated reportage. Tracy Fullerton claims that warranting devices such as reference materials and a text crawl at the bottom of the screen announcing new missions based on recent headlines and signify Kuma's arrival at the 'game equivalent of the nightly news'.[3] This is another aspect of the muddled informational spaces that now exist, in which actual worlds converge with game simulations, creating playable re-enactments intended to reinforce the viewer's sense of participation in, and experience of, the event. But sites such as Kuma can also make it difficult to see clearly what *kind* of information is being provided by these sources and they raise a number of salient questions. Are these facts or merely highly persuasive fictions? Can these new informational platforms be considered documentary, and if so, how do they correspond to the investigation of animated documentaries in a virtual culture? What authentication strategies do they use to evoke credibility and documentary viewing? What kind of realism is fashioned in such works, and how does it relate to a growing break with photorealistic imagery in documentary? If we accept that realism is the believable articulation of reality, and that documentary is defined as its being seen as such by viewers,[4] the new directions taken by contemporary documentary and non-fiction need careful consideration.[5]

Simulations combining non-fiction content and news coverage with gaming and VR platforms are proliferating in spheres such as journalism, education, political activism, forensics, documentaries and as training exercises and recruiting tools.[6] They all portray physical realities, but they do so using animation together with elements of virtual platforms. As we saw earlier, animation is used in cinematic documentaries, *inter alia*, to visualise what was not photographed, or to protect subjects' anonymity. The reasons it is used in this context are similar to those that explain its prominence in virtual worlds and games, namely: the creation of dynamic spaces that can react to user input in real time, and the construction of virtual spaces for exploration based (varyingly) on real-world locations to facilitate a different kind of experience and understanding of the events depicted. Since the immersive and/or interactive features are crucial in such works, this is a new documentary form that links contemporary virtualised culture to emerging directions in documentary.

VIVIDNESS AND VIRTUAL WITNESSING

As we saw in Chapter 1, Grierson and Flaherty anchored documentary to a tradition of realism that creates the illusion of reality for viewers. In this regard, there was less of an attempt to capture reality in its authentic form, and more of an intention to use art to imitate it to the point where viewers would no longer even think about it.[7] Although elusive, this idea expands the view of what is accepted as realistic representation beyond the confines of the visual to something based on the overall experience of the viewer.[8] Once truthiness becomes omnipresent and the visually mimetic loses credibility, a 'reality effect' offers a different kind of documentary experience that doesn't strive for directness, transparency or authenticity, but merely seeks to persuade the viewer. I suggest that a 'reality effect' is engendered by a more inclusive sensory experience, based on the simulation of presence rather than on visual mimesis and photographic techniques. This leaves more leeway in the discussion about realism. What, then, is necessary for the creation of such an experience, and where is animation located in this respect?

The fields of VR and digital games are too large to cover fully here, but I will introduce them as examples of new directions in contemporary animated documentaries. These developing documentary forms demonstrate that realism and believability can be achieved despite, or perhaps due to, a lack of visual mimesis, thus strengthening the case for the growing credibility of animated imagery in contemporary documentary works. Although the animated imagery is non-photorealistic, interactive animated documentaries produce new 'reality effects' that enrich evolving documentary aesthetics and theorisations. In other words, new technologies introduce new authentication strategies so that the non-mimetic animation is not perceived as disrupting the work's credibility. On the contrary, the new forms of realism achieved through interaction design enable a move away from photorealistic visual representations.

Tom Gunning identifies an expectation of contemporary media to create a sense of transparency, or the illusion of immediacy, by creating a medium so vivid that it disappears in order to maximise the sense of perceiving a reality.[9] 'Vividness' signifies intensity, liveliness, presented in a distinct and realistic manner that forms striking mental images, such as a memory or imagination.[10] Charles Hill, who believed that more 'vividness' inhered in imagery than in verbal or written description has created a continuum of vividness shown below. The continuum ranges from the most vivid information to the least vivid information. This is also useful in an analysis of animation's possible reality effects, in terms of their being realistic and credible, and thus having potential documentary value.[11]

Most Vivid Information
Actual experience
Moving images with sound
Static photograph
Realistic painting
Line drawing
Narrative, descriptive account
Abstract, impersonal analysis
Statistics
Least Vivid Information

Figure 6.1 Continuum of vividness (source: Hill, 'Psychology of Rhetorical Images').

Hill's vividness continuum provides a new perspective through which to consider animated documentaries, since the closest form of representation to actual experience is moving images with sound. Animated documentaries are just that, and although Hill may have been referring predominantly to photography, moving images nonetheless appear higher on his list than still photographs and realist paintings. As realism is dissociated from visual mimesis and new technologies are used to reproduce the 'actual experience' of, say, movement, real-time depiction or interactivity as much as possible, different combinations of elements that elevate vividness can result in new forms of vivid representations currently missing from Hill's continuum. This relates vividness to contemporary characteristics of the networked information age, involving new forms of (tele)presence in a virtualised world that are meant to simulate witnessing.[12] In what follows, I will analyse evolving representational ways of evoking a sense of presence through immersion that transcends visual mimesis and creates what I describe as a *documentary experience*.

In today's media culture there is a persistent gap between what is experienced and what is acquired through mediated means. John Durham Peters refers to a 'veracity gap', which designates the problem of mediation as a process whereby 'the *experience* of a person present at an event is transmuted into *discourse* about that experience for others who were not present'.[13] Bridging the epistemological gap between experiences and the opacity of discourse or representation is difficult and, as technologies and forms of representation change, the mediation of realities changes as well. It comes as no surprise, then, that interactive digital culture has led to a growing interest in modes of knowledge and memory construction that emphasise viewers'/users' participation. Aiming for media that enhances immersion raises many questions about absence versus presence, or the seeming co-presence of past and present in interactive media, such as games and VR simulations. Such media also contribute to the lack of clarity between actual witnesses as opposed to media witnesses, which leads us to an intense interest in the concept of witnessing today.[14] A key factor has been the attempt to make mediated events seem so vivid that the spectator feels she was actually a first-hand witness. This issue requires an exploration of the concept of witnessing, which links vivid representations, believability and the varied forms of realism that can be deployed as documentary authentication strategies.[15] Tamar Ashuri and Amit Pinchevski distinguish between two central approaches in studies of witnessing in media scholarship: the 'vicarious witness', who receives information through various media, and the 'implicated witness', who receives it through her physical presence at the event.[16] In the current mediatised culture, there is a persistent gap between what is experienced personally by an 'implicated witness', and that which is acquired by the 'vicarious witness' through mediated means and represented in a variety of forms.[17] Bridging the divide between one's own experiences and the opacity of representation is difficult. For this reason, Tom Gunning has argued that contemporary media expect to close that gap by creating representations so vivid that they give more direct access to reality, and thus the viewer feels personally present, like the 'implicated witness'.[18] If credibility is based on what the viewers believe, the reliability of new documentary aesthetics are contingent upon this kind of experience. This leads me to virtual witnessing and immersive animated documentaries.

What does it mean to 'be present' on a virtual platform? How is this sense of presence evoked, and what implications does it have for animation and documentary theory? A central principle of phenomenology is that one's sense of presence is intimately tied up with one's material body, and being physically embodied in a particular location. However, contemporary real-time and interactive technologies of telepresence, such as VR and digital games, complicate this assumption by creating a sense of presence in a distant location, whether a virtual or real environment, such as in robotics (like an engineer operating a distant robot, for example). For the VR community, presence is defined as the extent to which the user feels that she is 'there' in the environment depicted, with no mediation required.[19] The term given to this sense of dual presence – of being both 'here' and 'there' – is 're-embodiment'.[20]

This returns the discussion back to the issue of the material body discussed in Chapter 3, and the idea that in today's networked era, the self is manifest in multiple, fragmented and simultaneous online platforms so that a person's own sense of self transcends the body and its physical location. Real-time animation used on virtual platforms enables a sense of telepresence in virtual environments by seeing the re-created space respond to one's actions, whether they are merely exploratory or intentionally agential, as will be explained.

Accordingly, a sense of presence can be evoked through immersion in 360-degree 3D virtual environments that enable exploration, simulating to some extent an actual physical space. Alternatively, this feeling of presence can be evoked through interactivity, that is, the feeling of agency within another space (provided, for example, by an avatar).[21] However, interactivity is a complex term. Eric Zimmerman identifies four modes of interactivity: 'cognitive/interpretive', 'functional/utilitarian', 'participation with designed choices' and 'cultural participation'.[22] If there are different ways of being interactive, then surely notions and degrees of simulated presence also vary. Janet Murray suggests that mere interactivity, for example the click of a button, is not sufficient to create agency, which she defines as genuine embodied participation in an electronic environment.[23] Furthermore, according to Murray, immersion refers to a form of engagement whereby the viewer is taken out of her immediate context and brought into the realm of a digital fiction. Agency refers to the ability to feel as if users are participating in the fiction, and transformation is the potential to role-play characters within that fiction.[24] In order to create a heightened sense of immersion rather than a merely interactive experience, environments must be meaningfully responsive to user input.[25]

These are important distinctions to keep in mind because the two categories of works examined here behave in two ways: immersive journalism and VR documentaries use VR technologies to create immersive explorations of 360-degree 3D virtual spaces where the narrative is linear and unchangeable. In contrast, documentary games are not based on the VR exploration of 360-degree virtual environments. They focus more on user agency, through both varying forms of interactivity and transformation by role-play via an avatar, and control over events, which results in a non-linear narrative. It is worth noting that as VR technologies develop and are increasingly used in games, the differences between the categories may diminish; thus, a comparison between games and VR is not the object of this chapter; rather, the focus here is on the effects of the characteristics of these fields and technologies on documentary experiences and theory.

IMMERSIVE JOURNALISM AND VR DOCUMENTARIES

Since the media landscape has transformed in recent decades and storytellers of both fiction and non-fiction are exploring new terrain enabled by developing technologies, a spirit of innovation and new engagement with audiences through immersive designs and new aesthetics have emerged. VR documentaries are a growing phenomenon, capturing the imagination, attention and interest of practitioners, audiences and researchers. Since 2007, *The New Frontier* exhibition at the Sundance Film Festival, for example, has revealed the growing production and popularity of VR in documentary works. Additionally, the 2016 MIT conference titled 'Virtually There: Documentary Meets Virtual Reality' explored the emerging aesthetics and strands of VR documentaries, and their implications for representing reality, defining truths and changing the way we think of documentary.

Researcher, artist and journalist, Nonny de la Peña, is the founder and CEO of Emblematic Group, a company focused on immersive journalistic storytelling that combines traditional reporting with emerging VR technology.[26] As a pioneer of the form, de la Peña aims to incorporate the audience into the story by using VR and thereby enabling users to experience it with the whole body rather than just the mind.[27] The 2014 immersive journalism coverage *Project Syria* (about the Syrian civil war), produced by Nonny de la Peña and Vangelis Lympouridis, was commissioned by the World Economic Forum. The short experience – which can be viewed using Oculus Rift or HTC Vive – begins with a child playing on a street corner as an explosion occurs. The voiceover presents some of the facts surrounding Syrian refugees, in particular children, as the user is dropped into several other scenes that are animated in various ways. By using the VR headset and infrared sensors for body tracking, *Project Syria* enables the user to roam the virtual 3D environment freely. Although interaction only involves walking and looking, de la Peña claims visceral responses and immersion are achieved through what she calls 'spatial narrative'.[28] This is one example of many projects by de la Peña that combine news coverage and factual content with VR technologies.

Although these simulations may seem to contradict journalistic integrity, de la Peña argues that 'virtual reality constructs should be considered in the same light as any documentary or news report, with the relevant factor being the transparency surrounding the sources and research material used to support the factual underpinnings.'[29] In the explosion scene, for example, the viewer/user stands inside a thoroughly researched re-creation of an Aleppo street as a missile strikes. The segment is based on video and audio captured before and after the real event, photographs of the location and Google Earth maps. De la Peña's goal is to allow the audience to enter a virtually re-created scenario that represents the story.[30]

The painstaking effort to achieve accurate aesthetics that re-create photographic imagery reflects the time and rigorous research involved, and may strengthen the perceived validity of the work.[31] Interestingly, whereas the emphasis is placed on what innovative technology enables – namely a sense of presence that changes the viewer's experience – the work nonetheless relies heavily on photography as an authenticating device. In *Project Syria*, de la Peña emphasises the precise recreation of photographic footage and the efforts to achieve photorealism, for example by using 3D models with inbuilt photorealistic pictures and textures taken from people's photographs.[32] This shows that much has changed and developed in the sphere of documentary aesthetics, assumptions and technologies of representation. However, the work relies on authenticating devices based on photographic conventions as markers of authenticity, like those used in *The Sinking of the Lusitania* (see Chapter 1).[33] Thus, although animation can be used in simulations that evoke an as-if-you-were-there presence without detracting from the experience,[34] preoccupation with and reliance upon photography persist, demonstrating again animation's indeterminate status as neither totally fictitious but also not quite fact.

Documentary games and immersive non-fiction/VR documentaries are not intended solely to present the facts, they also seek to experience them.[35] Hence the assumption that by immersing the viewer, impersonal information understood as coming from a 'vicarious witness' is made personal via simulated 'implicated' witnessing. But is this, in fact, really the case? There are different degrees of immersion in VR, ranging from simple head movements to much more extensive interaction; the design of the experience obviously influences the resulting degree of presence felt by the user. In addition, the technology can undermine the experience by being distracting in itself. Similarly, like the notion of the uncanny valley, any glitch in representation or glaring difference between actual and simulated presence, emphasises absence rather than simulating presence.[36] For example, *Project Syria* aims to re-create an explosion so precisely that users experience it as fact. However, the precise photographic footage and use of a vest that are meant to add sensory effects to the moment of explosion notwithstanding, no simulation can replicate the actual experience. In fact, the choice to use VR for the depiction of violence and potential death is challenging precisely because it highlights the contradiction between the predictable impact on an actual victim's body and the non-impact on the user's, thereby emphasising the difference between physical and virtual witnessing where no danger is ever possible.

Research is still inconclusive, but the representation of the user's body in VR also has many implications on the effects of the medium, though different representations may impact differently since they influence the user's identification with the in-game/VR representation. It can be argued that by having no in-game body or agency, one's sense of presence is minimal; even in cases of 360-degree visualisation, is it so different from watching events on TV? The user/avatar has no body in *Project Syria*, and no agency within the linear simulation. This may be experienced as less distracting because representational imperfections do not disrupt the illusion; but it also creates the experience of being an unacknowledged, disembodied witness. Disembodiment in the technologically mediated experience mitigates against any affirmation of one's existence. Rather than seeing one's own body, what emerges is an almost ghostly presence that feels strange, and therefore distracting. In other words, analysing the role and depiction of the user's body, especially in the simulation of physical danger, will emphasise the difference between VR and the actual experience, thereby detracting from the realism achieved. This accentuates distance rather than achieving the hoped-for presence to which VR aspires. The choice of content must match the medium and its characteristics. The user's representation within the game/VR experience is linked to research into player–avatar relationships, cyberpsychology, phenomenology and more. Salient issues for further study might include the resemblance between a represented body and the user's real body, similarities between motion and appearance, and questions of agency in avatar design – all well beyond the scope of this study.

De la Peña claims that rather than just watching content, the VR experience of immersive journalism evokes a sense of empathy.[37] The focus on empathy is clearly worthwhile and serves as a useful marketing pitch for VR, but this approach is somewhat optimistic and has been disputed. Commenting on the display of *Project Syria* at the UN, Janet Murray, for example, questioned whether the esteemed members of this elite were experiencing feelings of empathy or simply excitement with the novel technology.[38] Since VR is a nascent form, its reception, effects and supposedly seamless teleporting abilities are still being widely debated and researched,[39] and no definitive conclusions have yet been reached regarding the use of emerging technologies to induce empathy. However, we can remain attuned to the ambivalent responses and changing reactions that are intertwined with the novelty of the medium. Innovation can induce enthusiastic reactions and a sense of realism that engender empathy in some users; but this will change as people become accustomed to these technologies and the novelty wears off.

We now require the development of a representational language that reflects a nuanced approach to VR and incorporates a deep understanding of what it enables. Animation is highly appropriate for interactive scenarios, but it is important to understand the restrictions inherent in visual depictions; ultimately, we are learning how and why it is best to depict events in new formats. The following example deals differently with VR's limitations, emphasising the gap between actual experience and VR simulation, and encouraging reflection rather than simulating presence.

SEPTEMBER 1955

September 1955 is a 2016 VR documentary by Cagri Hakan Zaman, Nil Tuzcu and Deniz Tortum about the pogrom against the Greek minority of Istanbul on 6–7 September 1955. This documentary situates the viewer in a reconstructed photography studio in the moments preceding the attack. The viewer thus witnesses the events from within as a mob gathers in the street outside. The VR work was displayed as part of an installation that included photographs of the aftermath of the actual event. Rather than attempting to simulate presence at the event, the creators chose to portray the moments before the pogrom in VR, evoking a sense of fear and dread of what was to unfold. Thereafter they presented the pogrom's aftermath in photographs.

As in most VR works, *September 1955* also includes distracting elements that may disrupt the illusion and detract from a sense of presence, such as subtitles that appear on the studio wall and the lack of any reflection in a mirror, which emphasises the user's ghostly presence. Aesthetics for VR are still being developed and it is fascinating to explore examples of what creates credible experiences in order to understand which of the new authentication devices evoke belief in a novel representation, and which rely instead on more traditional means such as photorealism.

September 1955 is interesting because it exemplifies awareness of VR's strengths and limitations. Violence can only be experienced physically, so trying to reproduce it in a virtual space and evoke feelings of danger can backfire and result in reinforcing the absence of violence instead. Although VR aims for a convincing sense of presence, this documentary's creators made an astute decision to avoid the actual pogrom, and focus instead on creating the sense of fear provoked by impending danger.

Creator Deniz Tortum claims that the work 'gains its own reality when you can move within it'. Mobility is one form of representational realism; to achieve maximum believability, mobility is combined with other strategies, some of which are based on more traditional documentary conventions.[40] Indeed, there are recurring references to photography in *September 1955*, ranging from the photography studio setting, customers having their portraits taken, and photographs of former customers on the walls – both inside the VR experience and as part of the installation. However, rather than trying to re-create photorealism, the customers posing for photographs are portrayed as faceless, bubblegum-pink, latex-like humanoids that move realistically and with texture resembling flesh. Whereas *Project Syria* used a vest to augment sensory perception, the creators of *September 1955* opted for visual design choices that evoke visceral reactions and the potential for haptic viewing.[41] Evoking physical reactions that transcend the visual contributes to a fuller sense of presence since the entire body can be aroused. The way the creators of the work depicted the studio customers represents a conscious decision to choose realistic movement rather than using CGI to achieve photorealistic appearance. Once the camera click is heard, the pink-bubblegum characters transform into photographs of real people in the same pose. This emphasises the connection to photography – used here as an authenticating device – and gives the people, who are assumed to be victims of the pogrom, faces that personalise them. This could be a metaphor for how civil war turns people who were neighbours into faceless others in the eyes of their persecutors. Moreover, the work sometimes forgoes photorealistic appearance, for example by depicting the mob outside the studio as black silhouettes; but nonetheless the mob mentality is clearly conveyed.

Thus *September 1955* uses photography as an interesting representational anchor, an authentication device to make this new representation more familiar and believable and to enhance its documentary status. However, photography is also used to indicate how the break with photorealism adds additional layers of meaning to the work. It comes as no surprise to discover that the creators' goal was to experiment with different layers of reality and realism, rather than to strive for a precise recreation of events and photographic footage.[42]

The experience of *September 1955* is potentially powerful. The choice to locate the experience inside a studio with a threatening mob outside engenders feelings of confinement that perfectly correspond to the sense of control-and-surround offered by VR. The solitary nature of the VR experience that can evoke loneliness – often seen as a drawback with this technology – is used in this case to enhance the sense of isolation and entrapment generated by the mob. Like an invisible, powerless witness, the viewer is struck by the lack of ability to control or influence the unfolding events. Thus the characteristics of the technology are deployed in ways that augment the experience inherent in the event depicted.

This is a rapidly evolving field where further research is needed, and it will be interesting to see which aesthetic languages are developed and how these changes will impact the issues raised here. Instead of telepresence, perhaps the closest to realism this medium can come at this stage is the sensation of a personalised experience, convincing enough to be memorable. In an era of truthiness, based on things 'felt to be true', and an emphasis on the viewer as

Figure 6.2 Mob gathering outside the photography studio, from *September 1955*, an installation by Cagri Hakan Zaman, Deniz Tortum, Nil Tuzcu, 2016.

validator of a work's documentary status and credibility, it is understandable that the focus on the viewer/user's experience in contemporary documentaries has become so central.

Documentary Games

Documentary games are digital, interactive, non-linear simulations of events that occur in the material world. Animated documentary games, also known as serious games, are a rapidly growing genre in the field of documentary.[43] Digital games predate VR and it is impossible to cover the vast amount of recent research into game experiences and user–avatar cyber-psychological connections. However, in the context of the rise of animated documentaries, documentary games as interactive, non-linear works that combine virtual characteristics and aesthetics with facts about actual events and protagonists, merit consideration.

Whereas VR documentaries and immersive journalism rely on new technologies to simulate presence as the user explores and witnesses an unfolding narrative, the notion of documentary games might seem incongruous. First of all, as a popular source of entertainment, games may not seem suitable as platforms for documentary content. Second, the documentary status of games would appear to be challenged by interactivity and non-linear narratives that might undermine the documentary retelling of an event as it occurs. Third, the role-playing element in games can be confusing since the player is both there and not there: is simultaneously herself and the documentary protagonist usually represented by an avatar. In short, documentary games raise issues that would seem to contradict documentary expectations.

To broach this issue, let us consider the changing status, popularity and complexity of games today, and the diverse expressive platform they have become. Although some animated games have been criticised for being morbid, they do engage viewers with content in new ways, using media-specific methods. The early documentary game *9/11 Survivor*, for example, made in 2003 by University of California students John Brennan, Mike Caloud and Jeff Cole, received massive media attention and provoked an immediate outcry against the depiction of real-world casualties in gameplay form. However, such objections associate gaming with children's entertainment, implying misplaced enjoyment in the re-enaction of real-life tragedy. Today, however, games have assumed a different function: as a new platform for conveying information. The animated visuals and cultural associations may appear child-like, but their cultural role and complexity have been entirely transformed.

9/11 Survivor was never planned for commercial release; it was an art-class project created with the aim of transplanting a historic event into the medium most familiar to its creators, namely computer games. Having become desensitised to the images of 9/11, the creators believed that they could 'restore immediacy to the day's horrors' in an immersive, interactive version of events.[44] It is worth examining how this was achieved. First, since games are interactive, users must engage in order for the narrative to progress – an interesting challenge given the prevailing inundation of endless waves of information. Second, the gaming platform strengthens viewers' initial confrontation with these images by making them relive the experience virtually from a new perspective; in this case, the events are depicted from *within* the World Trade Centre, though no such documentation actually survived. This is one aspect that illuminates the huge potential of animation in such representations. The game re-enacts the experiences of a trapped protagonist, using imagery based on the well-known photographic footage of people jumping/falling from the towers, made possible by animation that documents the event from the perspective of someone watching from within. The imagery's believability is enhanced by its reliance on familiar photographs and thus, indirectly, by photography's status and indexicality. However, the game has the advantage of

Figure 6.3 Screenshot from documentary game *9/11 Survivor*, by John Brennan, Mike Caloud and Jeff Cole, 2003.

being a new, compelling and de-familiarising form of documentary representation that engages users by means of its virtual characteristics and animation.

Third, the interactive, non-linear or open-ended narratives of documentary games would seem to contradict documentary convention. However, this is reflective of the new ways in which technology users engage with information; it is very likely that, as technologies develop, documentary traditions and theories will change accordingly. Since digital data can be customised in response to viewer input, the entire online process is based on interactivity and variability, as on any personalised website or social media.[45] Thus the flexible variability of the documentary narrative in these games reflects wider cultural tendencies where the agential aspect of the user is centre stage. Rather than just being an explorer in a 360-degree virtual space, where the story is linear and impervious to user input – which is comparable to watching TV in a 360-degree environment – in documentary games the player becomes a quasi-director, calling upon information parcels and in-game choices; she is an active user and navigator of information in the networked age. Since documentary definitions are also becoming more viewer-oriented, situating the viewer as arbiter, documentary forms that emphasise the viewer's central role correspond perfectly to wider cultural phenomena and trends.

Furthermore, whereas VR documentaries and immersive journalism are exploratory spaces and linear works, games are not. The interactivity of games requires some form of open-endedness in order to give shape and meaning to user input in the game experience. This may detract from the games' credibility and documentary value. Since games are inherently rule-based structures with clear goals that allow varying degrees of flexibility to players, one can argue that they cannot function as documentaries since the latter aim to narrativise events, whereas games permit freedom of action, which is non-linear. Conversely, the non-linearity and open-endedness of game narratives arguably make games an interesting and important form through which to explore current events and their possible outcomes. This adds to our understanding of the complexities involved and of the different possible trajectories.

Moreover, although the inclusion of multiple potential outcomes may appear to complicate the documentary status of the work, depending on the player's in-game choices, such open-ended narratives do not necessarily mitigate against its basis in fact. The degree of open-endedness necessarily varies and depends on the design of the game. Although different trajectories of events are potentially possible, if the game is designed well it will convey the intended information and message. As Ian Bogost explains, 'interesting choices do not necessarily entail *all* possible choices in a given situation; rather, choices are selectively included and excluded in a procedural representation to produce a desired expressive end'.[46] The open-endedness of games provides players with choices that increase the sense of agency and, therefore, transformation within the game parameters, thus heightening a sense of immersion.[47] The game is so attuned to player input that the visuals can reflect multiple choices and a dynamic experience. Since animation (unlike photography) can visualise any choice of content and action, even in real time, and does so using moving imagery, employing animation to maximise vividness, dynamism and the centrality of a user's input is a perfect match.

Finally, the role-playing element in documentary games can strengthen documentary viewing and enhance the realism of the work. According to Bill Nichols, re-enactments create the sense of a fold in time, 'breathing life into the lived experiences of others'.[48] In the case of a game as a re-enactment of an event, the interactive aspects facilitate the transformation of the then-and-there into the player's here-and-now, thus breathing new life into the event and its interpretation. The term 'procedural rhetoric', coined by Bogost, is applicable in this regard. It describes the ability of games as rule-based representations and interactions to use processes persuasively, reconstructing circumstances in a way that enables players to gain understanding-through-experience that cannot be gained using linear narrative, the spoken word, writing, images or moving pictures.[49] In her analysis of the 2003 Playstation 2 game *Medal of Honor: Rising Sun*, Fullerton claims that procedural rhetoric refers to players becoming 'virtual veterans' of events that they would not otherwise have experienced.[50] She argues that, in the case of documentary games, the player is not only connected to an avatar, he is also reconnected to a historical or current event.

Over the past two decades, it has become increasingly problematic to view avatars solely as representational proxies in virtual realms. It is now acknowledged that a more holistic approach is required, which combines the player, the representation and the medium.[51] Agency in interactivity, or meaningful participation through role playing, can thus be seen as a form of realism, endorsing a connection between a person's self in non-game experiences and that person's role in game environments. Since the player's online actions and experiences are part of 'the real' (see Chapter 3), as well as part of his or her self, when similar virtual aesthetics are used in documentary works, they, too, seem real. This can evoke credibility that enhances the documentary status of this new form of documentary experience.

These serious games, also called news games or games for change, transcend mere entertainment and are used for education, training and politics, among others.[52] Although some serious games use static and photographic imagery, in my opinion animated sequences are imperative, for they can be used to bring the user input to life, changing the game dynamically and vivifying the content and its immersive potential. Susana Ruiz, co-founder of Take Action Games, which specialises in games for change, explains that the design methodology of documentary games is intended to enable the player to become emotionally involved, and to offer a broader informational context for complicated issues.[53] Both VR and documentary games thus convey factual information by constructing a personal experience through varied forms of simulations and virtual presence.

If a documentary experience entails personalising the information and involving the viewer so as to evoke vividness and a reality effect, animated games are a new form of realism developing in documentary works today. This is especially true since realism is also determined by the sociopolitical objective in varied forms of representation, as discussed below.

DARFUR IS DYING

The 2006 documentary game *Darfur is Dying* illustrates the power of an interactive animated documentary to handle a politically sensitive topic.[54] An in-depth analysis of an example of a developing genre, that has already engendered statistical research, is useful to reveal how documentary games can impact the spectator/player.

Darfur is Dying is defined as a documentary game whose creators travelled to refugee camps near Sudan and worked closely with experienced humanitarian aid workers.[55] The game is described as a 'narrative-based simulation where the user, from the perspective of a displaced Darfurian, negotiates forces that threaten the survival of his or her refugee camp. It offers a faint glimpse of what it's like for more than 2.5 million who have been internally displaced by the crisis in Sudan.'[56] The game creators do not attempt telepresence, but rather a faint glimpse of a personal understanding. They define it as an 'informational entryway to the humanitarian crisis in the Sudan [which] weaves uncomplicated and immediate mechanisms into the gameplay that seek to effect real world change'.[57]

The game has several segments that depict information differently. The player chooses an avatar to role-play from eight optional avatars representing female and male refugees of varied ages; the names and details personalise the people presented, though they are not depicted photographically. Deciding which avatar to adopt is one among several choices made by the player – an important element in the construction of player identification and engagement, as explained above. *Darfur is Dying* presents textual information about the conflict in Darfur and the living conditions in refugee camps in order to set a documentary tone. This is done in two ways. First, the player can explore and get additional background information about the refugee camp and its inhabitants by clicking on question marks in the image. This information is based on the personal narratives of Darfurian refugees, and on statistical data about living conditions in the camp. The virtual exploration of the camp is accompanied by a 'threat metre' and measures of village health, water and food supplies that dictate when the player must continue to a different facet of the game, foraging for water outside the camp boundaries. Second, the darfurisdying.com website includes links to further background material about the genocide in Sudan, providing additional sources of information about issues that are not game-oriented.

Foraging for water is a segment of the game whereby, due to insufficient water supplies, the player-as-Darfuri-refugee must leave the camp and search for a well while fleeing the heavily armed and vehicle-aided Janjaweed. Thus, the common videogame power fantasy is inverted and the player is cast in the role of the powerless rather than the powerful actor in the struggle.[58] Although the game makes certain choices available to users, its eventual outcome is the player's failure to avoid the Janjaweed, thus negating the notion that an interactive non-linear framework, such as a game, cannot function as a documentary, that is, tell a story with a clear ending, or make a salient point.

Furthermore, an interesting form of signification takes place that further complicates the me/not-me binary, the viewer's sense of self, and her relation to the documentary protagonist. In interactive games, the avatar acts as a simultaneous and double index: on one hand, it is a deictic index signifying the documentary protagonist, in this case the Darfurian refugee. On the other hand, the avatar is the player's in-game representation, which is also an index as trace of the player's physical actions and input, similar to real-time animation used in games. Through the prism of indexicality, interactive games and their role-playing elements create additional and interesting links between the viewer/player and the depicted protagonist, blurring the boundaries between the two.[59] Such effects disrupt the diegesis of the game, removing the distancing effect, or supposedly fictional and artificial 'screen' of animated representation. Instead, political urgency and documentary knowledge are inscribed into the ostensibly fictional animated world and experience of play.

THE DOCUMENTARY EXPERIENCE AS CONTEMPORARY AUTHENTICATION STRATEGY

In my wider investigation of contemporary animated documentaries, their varied authentication strategies and the multiple forms of realism they evoke, I felt it important to take into account of the emerging forms of interactive animated documentaries now proliferating, and their varied reality effects.

VR documentaries and the related field of immersive journalism and documentary games use digital-virtual environments to simulate real-world events where a sense of presence is key; they also adopt different approaches to engaging with non-fiction content in new, interactive ways.

I use the term 'documentary experience' to describe the process whereby the viewer-user is convinced of the authenticity of the representation through a sense of telepresence and an as-real-as-possible personal experience. Interactive animated documentaries aim to simulate a sense of virtual witnessing, by reducing the gap between the 'vicarious witness', who receives information through various media, and the 'implicated witness', who is physically present. At this stage, research into the success of VR in recreating presence is inconclusive since the medium is constantly changing and improving.[60] However, as Martine Beugnet explains, embodied experiences and visceral reactions to representations that focus on wider sensory impact rather than solely on visual cues can lead to new forms of immersion.[61] For this reason, even if interactive animated documentaries are still emergent, a mere glimpse into what it is like to be present in the situations portrayed may be a sufficient reality effect (for now) to create heightened immersion in the content displayed.

The obvious differences between real physical experiences and virtual simulations notwithstanding, there is often a palpable tension between a user/player's awareness of the artificiality of simulations and the very visceral fear and anxiety that such experiences evoke: people tend to respond to virtual situations and events as if they are real, despite knowing that they are not.[62] Hence the suitability of using immersive virtual worlds to depict non-fiction. Drawing from game studies, where animation is the prevalent visual form, the response-as-if-real (RAIR) to virtual situations occurs nonetheless – despite the fact that interactive animated documentaries introduce new notions of realism because they rely on animation rather than trying to look 'real'. An 'emotional truth', differs from factual certainty, but it can contribute to understanding what strengthens the believability aspect of documentary experiences in interactive documentaries.[63] This is reinforced in an age of truthiness, in which facts are secondary to what one feels, or wishes to be true.

Regardless of where games and VR are headed, interactive animated documentaries are able to evoke powerful reactions. They employ new authentication strategies as new technologies introduce new forms of vividness to contribute to a representation's perceived realism. Interestingly, many creators of these documentaries forgo photorealistic imagery; they do not see non-mimetic animation as an impediment to the simulation of presence, or to the goal of realism. Instead, they *choose* it as their preferred documentary aesthetic.

Animation can be used in documentary works for many reasons, including: heightened representational vividness evoked by dynamic moving imagery that responds to user input in real time; defamiliarisation, which captures attention; new forms of indexicality that involve the viewer in new ways; the ability to re-create events that were not photographed; creation of simulations while maintaining creative freedom and choice for the creators; the depiction of a body (an avatar) for the player to inhabit in simulated worlds; the preservation of anonymity, and more. The distancing effect of animation as an aesthetic that does not look real can also help reception by mitigating against any horrific content in the work and making it more digestible.

Thus we see the development of new forms of realism that articulate reality or set a political goal, and reality effects that accentuate the departure from photorealistic aesthetics using animation without detracting from the documentary status or the credibility of these new representations. The rise of animation in our culture, specifically in games and virtual environments, highlights the development of new documentary sub-genres in which verification devices based on immersion and interactivity increasingly accustom users to receiving non-fiction content through animated imagery. The growing use of non-photographic and non-photorealistic imagery further elevates animation's documentary status and increasingly distances it from any presumption of artifice. Engagement and immersion contribute significantly to believability and are thus a potential alternative to mimetic visuals.

As the gap between on-screen environments and the physical world of the viewer shrinks, interactive animated documentaries illustrate how virtual environments and aesthetics are increasingly used to explore non-virtual events. Following the ideas introduced in Chapter 3, as the animated on-screen and off-screen physical worlds converge, the boundaries between them, and between the viewer/user's virtual and physical environments, become increasingly blurred. But we must consider how these new documentary forms compare and contrast with existing documentary conventions, and what new questions they raise. For example, what is the relation between these virtual experiences and the non-virtual reality and events they portray? Can they be considered documentaries and are they realistic, both in the sense of believably articulating reality and in their potential ability to influence, rather than just reflect, reality?

Nonny de la Peña claims that documentary games are based on viewer choices, but that they do not attempt to delineate any individual case. She therefore suggests that games reproduce the circumstances of events better than the actual details and for her this difference brings immersive journalism more in line with the practice of traditional journalism or documentary.[64] Indeed, the documentary status of games can vary; this makes the field thought-provoking and rich, if difficult to neatly categorise. It is clear, for example, from the list of documentary games created by MIT's Game Lab between 2011 and 2015, that each game can relate differently to documentary.[65] Questions raised by MIT's researchers include, for example: 'Should a documentary game include specific details about real lives? What if it's about an incident, a place or just an idea? Are broad strokes about the human condition sufficient to describe a game as a documentary? What about games that have documentary intent but falter at their goal?'[66] Despite the difficulty of positioning new and interactive sub-genres of documentary – both VR and games – within strict taxonomies of documentary theory, in order to understand the documentary value of these interactive animated documentaries, it is useful to revisit Michael Renov's explication of the purposes of documentary filmmaking.

According to Renov, the functions of the documentary are to record, reveal or preserve; to persuade or promote; to analyse or interrogate; and to express.[67] Although interactive animated documentaries do not directly record physical realities, they can, in a similar manner to time-based animated documentaries, *reveal* information by depicting aspects otherwise not visualised, for example, war experiences where dangerous circumstances preclude photography, and they can *preserve* the information by raising awareness of those situations depicted. Interactive animated documentaries can *persuade* by promoting specific perspectives of an event, and, by facilitating first-hand experience of a simulation, they can do so convincingly. By creating the character of a modern-day refugee, the game developers of *Darfur is Dying*, for example, strive to present refugees not as illegals or threats, but as real people, heroes who fled life-threatening situations only to become victims of immigration systems, thus *promoting* a specific ideological stance. With regard to Renov's third function of documentaries, *analysis* and *interrogation*, many interactive animated documentaries, unlike most digital games, are not commercially distributed. But they are available online for free download, and include forums, discussion areas and external links about the topic presented. Both *Darfur is Dying* and *Project Syria* are available online, free of charge; the latter was used at the UN to promote the urgency of the refugee crisis and the Syrian civil war. As VR technologies become more affordable, more people will be able to experience them. Interactive animated documentaries thus create new experiences for information representation, but they are also part of larger platforms for learning, discourse and action; as such, they serve as informational portals to larger databases for further analysis of the topic. The combination of data with an engaging interface forges a new relation between truth-value and credibility. Dealing with a familiar topic that has already been covered extensively by the media in a new and interactive way, for example the refugee crisis, indicates that the truth-value of the work is influenced both by being based on well-known information from other sources, and by the additional technology-mediated immersion and personal familiarisation generated by a new kind of documentary experience.

After a VR or game-based documentary experience, the player will remember her own experience of the simulated events. Thus, the experience not only contributes to general knowledge, but to simulated participatory knowledge as well. Relying on one's own choices to reach a certain understanding encourages believability through the emergence of a personalised truth narrative based on a personal analysis of the sources and personal memories of the experience.

Renov's final function of documentaries is *expression*. The immersive interactive experience can empower viewers as active agents and, by virtue of being highly stylised and interpretive, they also facilitate prominent expressive power to evoke emotions or create a perspective on the events depicted.

To conclude, depending on the view and definition of documentary and its goals, there is endless possible value in the new developing trends in documentary practice. Clearly, the growing emphasis on situating the viewer centre stage as arbiter of what constitutes a documentary is the starting point for interactive animated documentaries. Although the combination of animation with the immersive experiences of these new documentary sub-genres may appear to distance the viewer from 'real-world' events, we have seen that this is not necessarily the case. Interactive animated documentaries aim to persuade the viewer/user of the validity of the representation by designing documentary experiences that are intended to feel as real as possible, using the personal experience of the viewer to induce credibility. The fact that these experiences are animated does not seem to diminish their potential to simulate presence. These new directions of animated documentaries thus exhibit a new form of realism in documentary that uses interactivity and simulations of presence as vivid representational strategies that, in turn, act as authentication techniques. It will be interesting to see how these fields change and mature, the kinds of interactivity and aesthetic languages that develop, and how they will impact on notions of presence and believability. This also applies to realism's socialpolitical goal to shape reality rather than just depict it. Animated documentaries' multiple forms of realism lead us into the final part of the book.

Notes

1. *Kuma* War Games, www.kumawar.com/, accessed 4 June 2013.
2. Ibid. Interestingly, re-creations here can be understood as re-enactments as well as recreational pastimes.

3. Fullerton, 'Documentary Games', p. 12.
4. Vaughan, *For Documentary*, pp. 84–5. For additional theorists who advocate a viewer-oriented approach to documentaries, see Ellis, *Documentary Idea*, p. 7; Raessens, 'Reality Play', p. 220; Odin, 'Semio-pragmatic Approach'.
5. Dealing with spectatorship demands clarification that I am not aiming to interpret *how* the work is perceived since all viewers cannot be generalised or assumed to interpret similarly. What I am interested in is the *authoritative role* the viewer is given to create a personalised truth narrative and define the documentary value of the work.
6. See also, for example, *America's Army*, a game-based simulation of military operations used for training and recruiting.
7. Aufderheide, *Very Short Introduction*, p. 26.
8. Discussing the notion of 'the contemporary', Alberro similarly claims that a new construction of the spectator is taking place, shifting from the cognitive aspects of a work of art to the affective, focusing on 'the experience-based knowledge that requires an active participation on the part of the public'. See Alberro, 'Questionnaire on "The Contemporary"', p. 60.
9. Gunning, 'Truthiness and the More Real', p. 181.
10. Oxford English Dictionary, www.oed.com, accessed 20 March 2013. Interestingly, Dictionary.com also describes 'vividness' as 'animation'.
11. Hill, 'Psychology of Rhetorical Images', pp. 31, 34.
12. See Hansen, *New Philosophy*, p. 105, about a more rounded, embodied view where vision is part of other senses, important in an era of the loss of markers of the real in images.
13. Frosh, 'Telling Presences', pp. 51–2. Emphasis in the original.
14. See Frosh and Pinchevski, *Media Witnessing*, p. 134.
15. This chapter does not address the holocaust, trauma studies or memory, even though they often overlap with the study of witnessing; nor does it cover language as opposed to the visual. I am more interested in how the topic of witnessing relates to contemporary documentary discourse, and the act of witnessing as a way to contemplate new aspects of representation and its reception.
16. Ashuri and Pinchevski, 'Witnessing as a Field', p. 134.
17. Ibid.
18. Gunning, 'Truthiness and the More Real', p. 181.
19. See Bolter *et al.*, 'Liveness, Presence, and Performance'.
20. Besmer, 'What "Robotic Re-embodiment"', p. 55.
21. Roberts states that 'interactive art . . . is concerned with the distribution of the human presence'. See Roberts, *Art of Interruption*, p. 223.
22. Eric Zimmerman identifies four modes of interactivity as follows: 'Cognitive' or 'interpretive' interactivity emphasises the psychological, emotional, hermeneutic and semiotic 'reading' of content. 'Functional' or 'utilitarian' interactivity involves the total experience of reading (or in this case, viewing) interaction. 'Participation with designed choices' is the most obvious sense of 'interaction', and is based on choices made within dynamic simulations. 'Cultural participation'

is the interaction outside the experience of a single text, or what exceeds the work's limits, such as fan culture: Zimmerman, 'Narrative, Interactivity, Play, and Games', p. 158. Similarly, Cynthia Poremba asks, '[i]f traditional documentary viewing can already be conceptualised as a sublime intersection between an inaccessible past and contemporary embodied audience, what does a game do differently? Games take what is a cognitive interaction construct in traditional documentary, and extend it into explicit interaction': see Poremba, 'Real/Unreal', p. 141.
23. Murray, *Hamlet on the Holodeck*, p. 128.
24. Ibid., pp. 97–128.
25. Ibid., pp. 127–9.
26. For more, see www.emblematicgroup.com/, accessed 4 August 2020.
27. See https://www.ted.com/talks/nonny_de_la_pena_the_future_of_news_virtual_reality, accessed 4 August 2020.
28. Tortum, 'How Virtual Reality'.
29. De la Peña, 'Physical World News', p. 1.
30. Ibid.
31. Although discussing CGI spectacles in animated documentaries, this idea is inspired by Leon Gurevitch, 'The Documentary Attraction'.
32. Taken from a clip of Nonny de la Peña shown as part of Ralph Vituccio's talk 'Well Played: Project Syria' at the 13th annual Games for Change Festival in New York, 2016, www.youtube.com/watch?v=EIf4495EcIM&feature=youtu.be&t=207, accessed 16 May, 2017.
33. *The Sinking of the Lusitania*, film, directed by Winsor McCay (USA: Jewel Productions, 1918).
34. Slater, 'Place Illusion and Plausibility'. Also see de la Peña *et al.*, 'Immersive Journalism'.
35. De la Peña *et al.*, 'Immersive Journalism', p. 301. Emphasis added.
36. Masahiro Mori's hypothesis from 1970 about the Uncanny Valley, a theory in the field of human and robotic aesthetics claiming that when human features look and move almost, but not exactly, like those of actual human beings, it causes a response of fear or revulsion among some human observers. This theory is important in animation practice and reception because, rather than evoking identification, different degrees of mimetic visualisation might have the opposite effect. It is for this reason that 'human enough' or 'realistic enough' representations may evoke easier viewer identification than hyper-realistic animated imagery. See Mori, 'Uncanny Valley'.
37. De la Peña, 'Future of the News?'.
38. Murray, 'VR as Empathy'.
39. See, for example, the 2016 MIT conference Virtually There: Documentary Meets Virtual Reality at http://opendoclab.mit.edu/virtuallythere/, accessed 4 August 2020.
40. Skype conversation, 9 March 2017.
41. See Marks, *Skin of the Film*.

42. Skype conversation, 9 March 2017.
43. Other names include serious games, persuasive games, interactive games, digital games, educational games, virtual reality, alternative purpose games, edutainment, infotainment, digital game-based learning, immersive learning, simulations, social impact games, games for good, synthetic learning environments, new media documentaries, digital documentaries, interactive films, database narratives, online forums, digital art pieces, news games, 3D worlds, educational products and more.
44. Mirapaul, 'Online Games Grab'.
45. For more on variability as a characteristic of new media, see Manovich, *Language of New Media*.
46. Bogost, *Persuasive Games*, p. 45. Original emphasis.
47. This is based on Murray's differentiation between interactivity, immersion and agency. Research into target audiences for serious games development has also shown that '[potential players] wanted a lot of control . . . Choice is important . . . they were not playing like mindless sponges. They applied a lot of their own agency in the [playing] process.' More information can be found in Gunraj *et al*., 'Power to the People', p. 262.
48. Poremba, 'Real/Unreal', p.141.
49. Bogost, *Persuasive Games*, p. x.
50. Fullerton, 'Documentary Games', pp. 220–1.
51. James Paul Gee has described the relation between players of digital games and their avatars as a 'tripartite identity' that includes the real person playing, the virtual character and a 'projective identity'. The latter signifies both the actual person projecting herself onto the virtual character (the scripted character and the actualisation of that avatar in each instantiation), as well as the virtual being as a work in progress, defined and shaped with time. See Gee, *What Videogames*, pp. 54–5.
52. For more see Neys and Jansz, 'Political Internet Games', p. 230.
53. Gunraj *et al*., 'Power to the People', p. 259.
54. *Darfur is Dying* was created in 2006 by Susana Ruiz, Ashley York, Mike Stein, Noah Keating and Kellee Santiago of the University of Southern California.
55. *Darfur Is Dying* is available online at www.darfurisdying.com (accessed 4 March 2013), and was the winner of the Darfur Digital Activist Contest launched by MTV in partnership with the Reebok Human Rights Foundation and the International Crisis Group at the G4C conference in October 2006.
56. *Darfur is Dying*, www.darfurisdying.com/aboutgame.html Accessed 6 October 2012.
57. Taken from the work samples portfolio of Susana Ruiz, sent to author via email on 20 December 2013.
58. Bogost, *Persuasive Games*, p. 96.
59. This is discussed further in the next chapter.
60. Each sub-genre has advantages and limitations, but since these emergent fields are still developing and continually merging, research into the effects and success

of telepresence is still inconclusive. The convergence between games and VR is seen by the growing use of VR in games, the development of different forms of in-game representation, technologies and newer forms of interactivity that influence the potential of a simulation of presence differently.

61. See Beugnet, *Cinema and Sensation*.
62. Slater, 'Place Illusion and Plausibility'. Also see De la Peña *et al.*, 'Immersive Journalism'.
63. As early as the 1990s, Julian Dibbell acknowledged that what occurs in virtual worlds is, at the very least, 'profoundly compelling and emotionally true'. See Dibbell, 'Rape in Cyberspace', unpaginated. A rich research culture on these topics can be seen in the multitude of publications including: *Cyberpsychology – A Journal of Psychosocial Research on Cyberspace*; *Cyberpsychology, Behavior and Social Networking*.
64. De la Peña, 'Physical World News', pp. 8–9.
65. For example, despite being a historical fiction action-adventure game, one can engage with *Assassin's Creed* (Alex Hutchinson, Ubisoft Montreal, 2012) as a form of documentary that aims to produce an accurate representation of the historic cities it features. Autobiographical diary/journal games, such as *Dys4ia* (Anna Anthropy, 2012), about the experience of the creator's transition as a trans woman, uses intentionally frustrating and disorienting game mechanics to convey confusion and discomfort. *Papers, Please* (Lucas Pope, 2013) simulates the experience of an immigration officer: http://docubase.mit.edu/playlist/documentary-games/#projectitem-1, accessed 4 August 2020.
66. See http://docubase.mit.edu/playlist/documentary-games/#projectitem-1, accessed 4 August 2020.
67. Renov, *Theorising Documentary*, pp. 21–5.

Part III

The Power of Animation: Disputing the Aesthetics of 'the Real'

CHAPTER SEVEN

Encounters, Ethics and Empathy

This book covers animated documentaries that engage with virtual worlds, portray physical realities and raise questions about documentary and non-fiction representation and conventions. Having discussed how virtualisation influenced the rise of animation in contemporary visual culture and the proliferation of new kinds of documentaries that engage differently with virtual worlds and virtual aesthetics, this chapter returns to animated documentaries that depict physical realities. The last part of this book examines the potential ramifications of animation's changing uses and contemporary cultural role in non-fiction. Animation is flourishing and its reception is changing accordingly, so the key questions I will ask here are, what are the potential effects of animation on viewers and what are the consequent ethical implications, especially when animation is used to depict difficult sociopolitical realities?

Bernard Stiegler and Mark B. N. Hansen examine the media landscape in which information structures transcend human perception because of machine-to-machine communication, machine vision, unseen code and the sheer mass of data, among other factors. Joel McKim draws on their work when he suggests that digital animation might remain as a 'representational last stand and a viable form of resistance' against the various forms of dehumanising digital calculation.[1] Animation's ability to evoke a humane, ethical viewing of non-fiction in an era when it is pervasively used as 'dry' data visualisation is important to consider. To what extent does animation dehumanise? Since animation portrays protagonists in varied visual styles, it could overshadow content, make serious events appear removed and fantastical and fictionalise the actual protagonists. Curator Okwui Enwezor argues that the amalgamation of arts and politics tends to aestheticise ethical concerns and is unlikely to lead to change.[2] If he is right, animated documentaries could have dire ethical ramifications, including desensitising viewers. In this chapter, I will question this assumption, and demonstrate how animation can achieve the opposite effect, creating new viewing positions that work differently, re-sensitising apathetic viewers. More specifically, based on the idea that ethical viewing involves empathy, this chapter examines whether, and how, animated protagonists in documentaries can evoke empathy.[3]

In contrast to the assumptions that the novelty of animation outshines content and that it is hard to empathise with animated protagonists, there are different mechanisms that actually facilitate empathic viewing in animated documentaries. Guided by the notion that empathy occurs when an inter-subjective encounter is evoked through representation so that the viewer experiences events through the protagonist's eyes, both protagonist and viewer must be 'present' for empathy to occur and identification between them emphasised. To examine how this is achieved in animated as opposed to photorealistic documentaries, I use examples from previous chapters, namely *Slaves* and *Darfur is Dying*, and address the following questions: (1) Do animated images evoke the presence of people who are normally under-represented and unseen, or do they obliterate them? (2) Can animated documentaries produce encounters in which the viewer feels present and engaged? (3) How is the viewer drawn in to acknowledge the similarity and humanity of the protagonist, and to see events through his or her eyes?

Empathy and Ethics as a Basis for Documentary Viewing

Following a long philosophical tradition that sees empathy as central to discussions of ethics, my premise is that ethical viewing of a documentary is grounded in a sense of empathy.[4] According to Vivian Sobchack, the issue of ethics is what fundamentally differentiates identification with non-fictional protagonists from identification with fictional characters, thus acting as a basis for documentary viewing.[5] In this respect, the ability to evoke empathy in order to guarantee that ethical viewing becomes central to the study of animated documentaries. Empathy is a form of receptivity to the 'other'. Unlike sympathy, which denotes feeling compassion, sorrow or pity for the hardships that another person encounters, empathy is defined as standing in the other's shoes.[6] In other words, documentary representations that aim to evoke ethical viewing must succeed in developing empathic emotions among viewers towards the protagonists. To achieve this, it is essential to bring viewer and viewed together to create an empathic mode of viewing.

This premise is shared by Enwezor, who describes a mode of viewing that, rather than confronting the viewer with 'un-negotiable facts', creates instead a place that facilitates an ethical encounter between viewer and viewed.[7] Enwezor describes these encounters as being based on human rights and creating a shared space in a world unevenly impacted by globalisation.[8] He emphasises the need for documentaries to act as spaces of contemplation that make the viewer approach and face the protagonists at eye level, as equals, to acknowledge their shared humanity and engender responsibility for them.[9] A 2016 article in *The New York Times* about Syrian refugees encapsulates this need:

the photographs and videos have made it out. The faces of the besieged, staring into the camera, at us, and at death, pleading for help, baffled by our indifference to the slaughter ... Pictures of war and suffering have pricked the public conscience and provoked action before ... What's happening in Aleppo is almost unbearable to look at. But that's the point. [The faces of the besieged] look us straight in the eye and ask us to save [them], please. We have done nothing to help. The very least we should do is look back.[10]

Can animated documentaries achieve this kind of empathic encounter? What difficulties might arise in the process? Can animation use mechanisms that evoke empathy in ways that differ from photography? Sobchack's views on the relation between empathy, ethics and documentary viewing help to develop these ideas. Whereas she, too, argues for similarity between the viewer and the on-screen protagonist, she also introduces two aspects that may question animation's capacity to evoke empathy. First, in her work on embodiment in moving-image culture, Sobchack claims that empathic identification requires a sense of continuity between the film space and the world of the viewer in order to evoke the realisation of similarity and consequent ethical responsibility. This is the basis for documentary viewing, which she describes as transforming the space of the 'irreal' into the space of the real, connecting on-screen imagery with the viewer's physical environment.[11] It might initially seem that animated documentaries (which may still be associated with fantasy) cannot create empathy since the on-screen world is perceived as distant and detached from the viewer's. However, in light of my discussion about the proliferation of mobile screens as portals to omnipresent digitally virtual platforms, the mixed realities of today and the growing trend of seeing oneself and one's actions represented by on-screen animation, the apparently separate on- and off-screen worlds are increasingly converging. Thus what may originally seem like an obstacle to animated representations creating empathy is no longer so problematic.

Second, Sobchack focuses on how the physical body functions as a point of reference, which induces the realisation of resemblance between spectators and protagonists. She claims that an ethical view of events on screen develops through the spectator's corporeal identification with the protagonist, based on shared materiality and mortality, and thus differentiating documentary spectatorship from the experience of watching a fictional representation.[12] As the viewer comes to comprehend the shared corporeal limitations and potential for physical pain, she creates a connection with the protagonist on-screen that in turn leads to a sense of responsibility, and thus ethical awareness.[13] This is pertinent to the study of animated documentaries' ability to evoke empathy, because it asks whether animation creates a distanced form of viewing by virtue of visually concealing the physical appearance of the protagonists. If identification is based on the realisation of shared corporeality, do depictions of protagonists in myriad visual forms, which diverge from one's own physical appearance and may not even be human, preclude a sense of similarity between oneself and 'the other' on-screen, thus thwarting any possibility of empathy? If they do, then perhaps visual mimesis is required for identification and empathy. This relates back to the tension between mimetic photorealistic imagery versus non-photorealistic animation in documentaries – an issue that is discussed throughout this book. According to this view, the use of animation's novel aesthetics rather than photorealistic imagery risks overshadowing the political urgency of many documentaries. On the other hand, are novel aesthetics really to blame for the lack of empathy? Is the more traditional documentary aesthetic of photography necessarily a better means of conveying horror and urgency, and thus producing change? I would say not. In the same vein, Susan Sontag's formidable book, *Regarding the Pain of Others*, explored visual representations of atrocity and their effects on viewers, concluding that the ethical and political meaning received from photographic and naturalistic imagery has less impact on viewers.[14] Thus people are seen as they appear physically, yet their materiality does not necessarily evoke a sense of empathy. In fact, seeing someone's physical frame while withholding empathy goes beyond documentary representation; it characterises contemporary culture in experiences of civil indifference.[15] Thus, if a mimetic depiction of protagonists in horrific situations no longer necessarily evokes an empathic response, there are grounds for experimenting with new forms of representation, such as animation, and evaluating their potential to evoke empathy. Although animation may initially seem problematic as a documentary aesthetic for ethical viewer reception, this is not necessarily the case. Using new forms of representation, animated imagery can evoke an empathic connection between viewer and viewed, thereby posing no obstacle to ethical viewing. In order to understand what forms of representation these might be, let us examine further the empathic encounter between viewer and viewed and answer the following questions: How do animated documentaries guarantee the 'presence' of a protagonist depicted in stylised form and not seen directly? How is the presence of the viewer inserted into the viewing processes of animated documentaries? How is the viewer drawn to engage with the content so as to achieve empathic recognition and thus an ethical encounter? The following demonstrates how animation can evoke identification, empathy and ethical viewing, without portraying the physical bodies of the protagonists.

Animated Protagonists – Presence or Absence?

In order to establish a sense of encounter, all parties must be 'present'. This may seem obvious, but questions arise regarding how animation portrays its protagonists. Since animation can be used to visualise what cannot be or was not photographed, it can expand what is shown in documentaries to include people who are under-represented, and reveal aspects of their lives that are not usually depicted; this emphasises presence that would otherwise be difficult to achieve. Pertinent examples include the many animated documentaries that address the topic of refugees.[16] Since these do not rely on photographic footage, they are able to depict events in the refugees' homelands, or in dangerous conflict areas, that are rarely portrayed visually. This arguably makes the individual subjects *more* present in the viewers' consciousness, by highlighting their situation and what they had to endure during their migrations. Conversely, the invisibility of refugees, portrayed by animation that disguises their physical appearance, also symbolically alludes to their incarceration in detention centres and the legal invisibility of people deprived of political representation – as described by Giorgio Agamben in *Bare Life*.[17]

Animation that masks protagonists' appearance beyond recognition, however, can be seen as eliminating them. This is not necessarily the case, but it is important to acknowledge that varied theorisations about the *production of animation* reinforce such views, expressed in the observation that, whereas photography captures realities, animation generates them. According to animation scholar Raz Greenberg, this leads to a definition of animation that situates absence as central, because whereas photography bases imagery on the *presence* of physical objects (that is, indexicality as a trace of the physical), animation can create them from nothing.[18] Animation can thus be seen as a form of obliteration, both through production methods but also aesthetically, by depicting protagonists in ways that make them appear less real. Although viewers may be apathetic to photographic images of atrocity, by severing the link to the visual appearance of the physical body, its pain and expressions, animated depiction risks losing the realisation of shared materiality that Sobchack claims is essential to documentary viewing. This may potentially obviate any sense of moral responsibility and identification on the part of the viewer.

Nevertheless, several aspects of animated representations actually undermine the idea that animation is epitomised by absence. First, as discussed in Chapter 2, animation is used increasingly in virtual worlds and on-screen as the users' representation, thus signifying her actions and presence. In this regard, animation is actually a contemporary representation of presence and digital activity; in the prevailing virtualised culture, with new animation production technologies, it ceases to signify absence. Furthermore, the claim that absence – not seeing the physical body – obliterates the protagonists is undermined by the fact that their voices are heard. The soundtrack acts as index of their embodied existence, which retains its palpable trace of physical presence. Documentary studies have often overlooked the important aural link between documentary film and physical realities, emphasising only the visual aspects of representation.[19] For example, *Slaves* is an animated documentary about two Sudanese children who, like thousands of others, were kidnapped by government-backed militia and taken into slavery. The film is largely composed of interviews showing the subjects speaking concurrently with the soundtrack, creating an aural link to the visually depicted reality. *Slaves* fluctuates between what Eric Patrick terms 'sound-based structure', which relies on unmanipulated sound recordings, and 'narrated structure', which uses voiceover to narrativise,[20] and disputes the notion that animation as imagery necessarily creates absence in animated documentaries.

Second, not seeing the protagonists does not automatically imply an ethical problem; visual disguise is not always negative, and animation can protect the speaker's identity. However, unlike pixelated or blacked-out depictions, which have the same anonymising, protective purpose, animation is a more expressive aesthetic that can provide insight into a subject or event. In *Slaves*, even though mimesis is not attempted stylistically, a highly expressive and realistic representation of the children is still evident. For example, the younger child, Abuk, is portrayed blinking frequently, which adds a degree of human naturalism. In this context it is useful to consider Masahiro Mori's hypothesis of the Uncanny Valley, whereby 'human enough' or 'realistic enough' representations evoke easier viewer identification than hyper-realistic animated imagery.[21] In other words, animation styles can indeed reduce individual protagonists to generic human symbols, but additional elements and character design can evoke identification and prevent the protagonist from being perceived merely as an animated figure in a fantastical realm. Animation potentially offers enough representational realism to evoke a sense of presence and existence with which the viewer can identify.

It is also worth noting that although one-sided disclosure can create a voyeuristic audience and engender a sense of 'ownership' of the depiction of minorities, the protagonist's anonymity is nonetheless preserved and his or her dignity maintained through animation. This is a central topic in visual culture and identity politics.[22] If, as Enwezor argues, an ethical encounter between viewer and viewed is based on a sense of equality and human rights, then one-sided exposure can be seen as problematic, but animated depictions can be seen as fairer and more balanced.

Visual stylisation is a central element in the reception of animated documentaries. Honess Roe claims that although animated documentaries do not directly represent the physical appearance of their protagonists, they do not disempower them or detract from their political significance. Instead, they use symbolism and styles of representation to convey their message and offer something additional to what we hear on the soundtrack.[23] This is clearly the case in *Slaves*, when Abuk describes the way her enslaver insults her. The visuals illustrate Honess Roe's concept of non-mimetic substitution, whereby an event that could have been photographed is rendered more meaningful by the style of animation used. Abuk's diminutive size is emphasised by her cowering in a corner of the frame, the rest of which is filled by a graphic form of the insult – a derogatory term for her ethnic group, the Dinka. The word, depicted as twice the size of the child, in capitalised garish red and black letters, portrays the fear and violence in the situation, despite its utterly unrealistic depiction.

Third, obscuring identity can be symbolic. In *Slaves*, the two children are the only characters whose eyes are covered by a dark horizontal line that resembles a Zorro-like disguise. This suggests a double masking, since the characters are literally masked by character design as well as by the non-photorealistic animation. As a result, the act of concealment not only hides the protagonists' identities, it is itself highlighted. This topic will be developed in the next chapter. Obscuring a person's face can be protective, but may also suggest invisibility – a way to depersonalise and dehumanise the individual. In a film that describes enslavement, the dehumanisation of victims is certainly crucial. However, in this case, the faces of the enslavers are presented as silhouettes, and this adds further layers of significance: since the cruel and inhumane actors are also represented as faceless, both victims and offenders can be anyone and everyone. This contributes to the film's significance since the facelessness of the protagonists points to the thousands of children still in captivity, as well as to the fact that, under certain circumstances – as history has repeatedly proved – anyone can be dehumanised. The masked representation can be seen as alluding to the grotesque behaviour that all human beings are potentially capable of, rather than referring to specific individuals, thereby recalling the notion of the banality of evil.[24] Animated masking thus creates a 'generic person', creating distance and de-sensitisation on the one hand, yet evoking an understanding of general truths that transcend the documented individual, on the other.

It is clear from the above that the tension between absence and presence in animated depictions can have multiple meanings and effects. Different forms of representation are a central element of animated films as they expose underlying messages about the people presented, the moral questions raised and the filmmaker's role as portrayer of the events. To conclude, rather than assuming that animation obscures or obliterates protagonists' identities, we see how it can actually evoke a sense of presence, and consequently deliver various ethical considerations as documentary representation. The next section focuses on the viewer and considers whether there is sufficient sense of encounter in animated documentaries to make the viewer feel present and engaged with the representation.

Ethical Encounters

As Enwezor explains, empathy and identification require an encounter based on a sense of equality and similarity; but first the viewer must be engaged so that she feels connected, involved and present – only thus can she 'come into contact' with the protagonist.[25] This can be achieved differently in interactive and non-interactive animated documentaries, and in both cases is based on the idea that animation is used to re-enact situations in ways that cannot be achieved by photography.

Animated re-enactments have great power. For example, although animation eliminates certain visual aspects that would be visible in photographic representations, this can actually contribute to the effect on viewers. Whereas many theorists have commented on the privileged role of sight for orientation in Western culture,[26] the possible disorientation in animation, where certain elements remain unseen, offers the spectator a more active viewing role since there is more freedom for associative interpretation. It is comparable to the difference between reading a book and watching a film. In their analysis of Ari Folman's *Waltz with Bashir*, Ohad Landesman and Roy Bendor claim that the use of animation intensifies the somatic experience of war for viewers, because it places them in a particular situation while still allowing room for their own interpretations.[27] What is depicted in *Waltz with Bashir* in visceral hand-drawn images and strange movement is distant enough from direct photographic representation so that viewers can be released into their own imaginations. The film thus becomes a mnemonic device that activates the viewer's embodied engagement and 'constitutes an active participation in the war's collective perception'.[28] This is echoed by Honess Roe, who claims that animated documentaries invite us 'to imagine, to put something of ourselves into what we see on screen, to make connections between non-realist images and reality'.[29] The absence of photorealistic visuals leaves a gap to be filled, with the potential of actively involving the viewer's imagination and interpretation, and demanding enhanced cognitive interaction in order to create meaning. What remains is to listen to the soundtrack featuring the individual depicted; this requires the viewer to 'flesh out' the representation, which, in turn, creates a connection between viewer and viewed.

Allowing the viewer to fill in the gaps results in a personalised version of the content. This can arguably undermine non-fiction, but it can also further engage integration of the viewer's self into the cognitive construction of the one(s) being viewed, creating a link between the two. Both viewer and viewed thus become implicated in the animated visuals; this enhances immersion and potentially results in a sense of believability towards a work deemed 'true enough'. As explained in Chapter 1, in an era of truthiness, where viewers are key arbiters of what is deemed 'true' and definable as 'documentary', animation's ability to involve the viewer is crucial. Enhanced engagement in representation and content can prevent 'image only', desensitised, non-ethical spectatorship, thereby meeting the ethical demands of Sobchack and Enwezor. Thus, what may initially seem like a form of protagonist obliteration can also serve to implicate and empower viewers, encouraging them to delve deeper and to satisfy the curiosity provoked by what is referred to, yet not shown.

This co-presence also exists between players and avatars in interactive animated documentaries, which create re-enactments where users can perform an active role (see Chapter 6). It can transform the then-and-there into the user's here-and-now, breathing new life into the event and its interpretation, and creating what Fullerton calls 'virtual veterans' of events that would not otherwise have been experienced.[30] Fullerton explains that documentary games create a connection for the player both to the avatar and to a historical or current event, such that documentary protagonists and players are momentarily present in the same realm. This prevents distanced viewing and facilitates instead a sense of encounter, as both characters become part of a larger, shared system. It has been well established that games can create a bond between player and avatar; through the same mechanisms, documentary games create this bond between the player and the protagonist whom the avatar represents. Through the avatars, documentary games situate players in someone else's real-world role, enabling them to experience what would otherwise remain distant and inaccessible.[31] Rather than a spectator, the player is an actor in the protagonist's re-enactment, adopting the other as herself. As Katie Salen and Eric Zimmerman explain, these re-enacted experiences are moments when that which is 'not me' becomes 'me' without losing its 'not-me-ness'.[32] Many experiments have explored this identification between player and avatar: how viewers perceive their location as that of their virtual rather than their physical selves; how they register a physical sense of menace and anxiety when their avatar is under threat.[33] This corresponds with my earlier discussion in Chapter 3 about the multiplicity of the self in an era of the endless technological non-physical platforms in which we are active daily. Thus new forms of interactivity, immersion and participation are possible, and give rise to the identification of player with avatar/protagonist. The player's sense of self is what connects the player's physical world to the non-physical screen world of the documentary work. This echoes Sobchack's view that documentary viewing requires connecting 'irreal' space on screen with the 'real' physical environment inhabited by the viewer. This sense of duality on the part of the player is what establishes the foundation of an ethical encounter: shared space, shared body, shared experiences.

In *Darfur is Dying*, described in Chapter 6, the 'game over' screen reads: 'You have been captured by the militia. You will most likely become one of the hundreds of thousands of people already lost to this humanitarian crisis.' Depending on the age and gender of the avatar selected, probable outcomes of the capture – rape, abuse, kidnapping and murder – are listed on screen. The word 'you' addresses the player, but also acts as an interpellation that deliberately converges player and avatar. As explained in Chapter 6, a further blurring of avatar and player is engendered by the dual indexicality of the avatar, which simultaneously signifies player and protagonist: the avatar acts as an indexical trace of the player's actions and game input, but is also a deictic index that signifies the Darfurian refugee/protagonist. The avatar is like a shifter in language, able to indicate different and multiple individuals, depending on context. By embodying both user/player and documented protagonist, the animated sign brings the two together in an interesting representational strategy: if the documentary's ability to evoke a sense of encounter – an inter-subjective meeting of viewer and viewed – is seen as essential to the creation of an ethical gaze and documentary view of a work, then this is an important aspect to consider.

The user/player/viewer of documentary games evokes a multifaceted mode of spectatorship: as a detached user engaging with an on-screen application; as a player identifying with the selected avatar and engrossed in the mission of the game; as a viewer in 'documentary mode', who is familiar with the content from other media sources, and is aware of the complexity between the game's subject matter and its representation. The opening screen of *Darfur is Dying* addresses these three different roles: the title 'Darfur is Dying' is both the name of the game and an address to the documentary viewer, introducing and contextualising the game's subject matter; 'Start your experience' refers to the player who is about to engage in the personalised experience of the game; 'Help stop the crisis in Darfur' addresses the 'removed' user whose power extends beyond the game and who can, through links provided on the darfurisdying.com website, act to aid the situation represented.

This introduces a level of cultural interactivity to the game, exceeding the work's limits and connecting it to larger systems that break the game's 'magic circle'; this is significant when contemplating the ethical implications of these

Figure 7.1 Screenshot from *Darfur is Dying*, Take Action Games, 2006.

documentary representations.[34] The player's powerlessness in the game (as she forages for water and is inevitably captured by the Janjaweed), is also an indirect message to the viewer, who is *not* as powerless as the depicted protagonist. The gap between the two thus emphasises the user's potential agency to impact the situation, prompting action or at least facing the choice of inaction.

There is a close relationship between drawing the viewer in by having him or her play in someone else's shoes, and the idea that representation can and should lead to ethical understanding, and from there to political action. In this sense, representation can both reflect and also shape realities. This is highlighted in many online documentary games and works that include calls to action for those viewers who feel the need to act after seeing the information, and thus a clear connection between the two is drawn. In *Darfur is Dying*, the 'Take action' segment offers options to send a message to US Congress, to join the growing divestment movement, or to donate, as well as to find more ways to get involved.[35] The creators sought to provide players with an emotional and personal experience, a broader context of the issue, and an immediate way of making a difference in the real world.[36] Indeed, this seemed to work:

> According to mtvU's traffic numbers, more than 800,000 people have played the game over 1.7 million times since its launch on April 30 [2006]. Of those, tens of thousands have participated in the activist tools woven into the

gameplay – such as sending emails to friends in their social networks inviting them to play the game and become informed about Darfur, as well as writing letters to President Bush and petitioning their Representatives in Congress to support legislation that aids the people of Darfur.[37]

These statistics reveal that playing political documentary games does impact players' knowledge and opinion of the subject matter, and that expressing a 'political self' by playing a political game may actually produce outcomes in the real world.[38] Opposing Enwezor's idea that novel aesthetics may overshadow politics and 'transform ethical concerns into aesthetic devices',[39] these statistics illustrate the potential of such games to expose systems, to encourage a sense of agency and engender various forms of activism – or at least effect a change in the players' way of thinking. Animated aesthetics in documentaries, with their innovative forms of representation, also have the potential to disrupt apathy in a culture numb to images of atrocities.

Clearly, the field of interactive animated documentaries is a growing platform for experimentation, production, activism and academic research. Founded in 2004, Games for Change (G4C), for example, is a movement and non-profit organisation dedicated to using digital games for social change. In 2017, the annual G4C conference (which featured over 100 speakers) joined forces with a VR For Change Summit, the first of its kind, on the use of immersive virtual technologies to advocate real-world causes. It will be interesting to see how these new sub-genres of interactive animated documentaries will develop.

Once an encounter between viewer and viewed in animated documentaries is established, an additional step is necessary for ethical viewing: the creation of empathy, which is based on recognition of resemblance and equality, and putting oneself in the shoes of another. Although this was addressed in my discussion of the viewer's 'presence', the next section asks how empathy is engendered – how the viewer is drawn in to acknowledge the similarity and humanity of the protagonist, and to see events through the latter's eyes.

CAN ANIMATED DOCUMENTARIES EVOKE IDENTIFICATION AND EMPATHY?

Identification and empathy take shape in different ways. One important aspect, described by Sobchack, is the physical sense of identification. The relationship between the body on screen and the body of the viewer is an ongoing field of research, often relating to notions of truth and evidence.[40] Nichols places particular emphasis upon the role of violence in documentary viewing, claiming that '[t]he sight of brutal violence, or its extreme manifestation, brutal death, engages us quite differently in documentary. This is not a simulation... The imprint of history registers on the flesh.'[41] Nichols focuses on the undeniable status and truth-value accorded to the injured body, and raises the issue of viewer engagement with the imagery of the wounded or violated body, thus introducing the role of the viewer's body into the reception of documentary. His assertion that 'history registers on the flesh' is true both for the viewed as well as the viewing body, who realises that what is viewed is not a simulation. The truth-value of the represented physical body thus becomes intertwined with the credibility of the image of violence as measured through its effect on the viewer and her body. My question is, can the body presented in animated documentaries emerge through the animated image and reverberate in the viewing body, thus arousing empathy and believability?

My answer is yes, viewers can identify with animated bodies, even when they look nothing like their own. Studies of the physical reaction to animated on-screen bodies, both in animated pornography and VR simulations, find the response is similar to photographed cinematic bodies.[42] This comes as no surprise since, as Deborah Levitt notes, in our current era it becomes impossible to differentiate between intimate and media spaces, between images and bodies.[43] She gives the example of the Sleep Together App, where users can immerse themselves in the illusion that they are actually sharing a bed with Hatsune Miku, a virtual animated character with many fans, as they slowly drift to sleep. Similarly, returning to an example given in Chapter 1, in 2014 *The Guardian* produced a horrifying exposé about slave labour in the Thai fishing industry. *Globalised Slavery: How Big Supermarkets are Selling Prawns in Supply Chain Fed by Slave Labour*[44] tells the story of Burmese refugees who fled to Thailand where they were abducted and enslaved. The coverage contains photographic footage and animated sequences portraying victims' testimonies of their experiences, which include gruesome conditions including twenty-hour shifts, regular beatings, torture and execution-style killings. Even though the interviewed protagonists may not be seen, the soundtrack retains a trace of physical presence. It is noteworthy that *The Guardian* website includes an introductory warning that the video contains scenes some viewers might find disturbing, implying that these images still have the power to shock and disturb the viewer, despite being animated. This also demonstrates the proximity of animation to the viewer's corporeal sense of self, and its ability to evoke corporeal identification.

People are accustomed to seeing themselves represented by animated depictions, such as avatars, and to identifying with them. An important part of the documentary aesthetic is, as Sobchack argues, acceptance of the similarity between one's own body and mortality and that depicted on screen. Whatever doubts were expressed initially, it is now clear that animation can evoke this sense of identification and empathy in the viewer, and facilitate ethical viewing.

In terms of emphasis on the body, Sobchack explains that the ability to feel another's pain arises out of one's own capacity to suffer and bleed.[45] She emphasises the body as lived, rather than merely seen, and acknowledges its ability to make meaning in ways that transcend vision.[46] She claims that lived experience in our era has been reduced to a two-dimensional superficiality that reduces viewing others and their bodies to a spectacle.[47] This superficiality means that we have an alienated epistemological relation to our own and others' bodies.[48] Sobchack argues that what we need to do to counteract this is not to get rid of images but rather to understand them in more detail, 'to flesh them out' in her words.[49] This implies that, in contemporary visual culture, realism transcends naturalistic visual depiction, thus requiring a new conceptualisation of the term. Whereas great emphasis is put on the physical body as a basis for identification and ethical documentary viewing, it is not necessarily visuality and the physical *appearance* of the body that bring about that effect. Animation is therefore an illuminating aesthetic in this regard. It is thus vital to explore identification that is not only based upon mimesis, especially as animated aesthetics proliferate in contemporary documentary depictions.

It is for this reason that images need to be fleshed out in order to restore our reactions to others and to ourselves. Can this only be done through naturalistic depictions? Not necessarily. As we have seen, animated depictions can elicit the right kind of response from viewers – this is 'identification' in the broader sense, not necessarily based on mimesis. Let us now consider what form this identification could take.

Empathy is also evoked through identification on a personal, emotional level. In 1993, Nichols observed that, whereas in the past 'documentary' suggested complete, final disembodied knowledge and facts, more recently documentaries have dealt increasingly with embodied knowledge that is corporeal, specific, subjective and commonplace.[50] Animation has the potential to expose subjective accounts of events that would otherwise remain unrepresentable. Thus themes depicted in animated documentaries are often very personal and include memories, dreams and subjective interpretations, as exemplified in John Canemaker's *The Moon and the Son: An Imagined Conversation* (2005)[51] about the filmmaker's father; Ruth Lingford's *Little Deaths* (2010)[52] about experiences of orgasm; Signe Baumane's *Rocks in My Pockets* (2014)[53] about battles with depression and suicide, and Alex Widdowson's *Music & Clowns* (2018)[54] about a family's communication with an autistic son. Where emphasis is on the personal, animation provides visualisation where no other perceivable visualisation exists, as Wells, Patrick and Honess Roe have noted before.[55] The ability to portray unusual and multiple perceptions of realities is an established characteristic of animated documentaries that focuses on multiple outlooks, or those that are difficult to depict visually, such as experiences of autism, trauma, synaesthesia and more.[56] Examples include *Tying your Own Shoes* (2009)[57] about autism; *Ryan* (2004)[58] about drug- and alcoholism-related deterioration; *Quiet Zone* (2015)[59] about wave refugees (people who suffer from electromagnetic hypersensitivity), and many others. This aspect of realism in animated documentaries indirectly questions what realism is, since experiencing the world through someone else's eyes requires new forms of realism that may indeed have to transcend mimesis, as developed further in Chapter 8. Animation is more successful than photography in conveying a broader spectrum of the protagonist's reactions; although the camera can record external events, it cannot necessarily portray how those events are perceived and experienced. Thus, animation provides additional insights into what cannot be photographed, giving the viewer a more comprehensive sense of the depicted experience. The way animation is stylised not only provides visualisation, it can also add many layers of meaning. Animated representations thus allow viewers to see the event through the eyes of those who experienced it, portraying not only the event itself but also one's personal interpretation and reaction to it. This characteristic of animation is similar to the previously described mechanisms that facilitate a sense of encounter, but it emphasises empathy since the viewer is literally being presented with information as seen through the eyes of the protagonist.

This is apparent in *Slaves*, in a scene depicting the child's nightmare about

Figure 7.2 *Music & Clowns* by Alex Widdowson, 2018.

Figure 7.3 *Slaves*, directed by David Aronowitsch and Hanna Heilborn, 2008.

the loss of his mother. Here, the animated style used for the interview sequences is replaced by elementary colours and basic shapes symbolising a human form. The harsh contrast between the almost blindingly white head shape and the black background manages to visually render the tension and anxiety of the dream, while the elementary colours and shapes befit the primal horror of losing a mother. The shapes of the scar on the protagonist's face act as visual metaphors for the pain and trauma described. One need not be shown all the protagonist's physical characteristics; on the contrary, visual masking, the lack of distinctive features and the creation of generic humans make it all the easier to identify – to project oneself onto these representations – and thereby increase the sense of empathy. In fact, metaphoric representation can create a sense that viewers are stepping into the protagonists' innermost thoughts. This contributes to the work's believability and its documentary status, because it enables empathy and a novel sense of inter-subjective encounter between viewer and viewed.

REPRESENTATIONAL BOOMERANGS

As an aesthetic that aims to depict sociopolitical realities, animated documentaries embody complex and multiple viewing effects in a way that evokes empathy, a sense of encounter and ethical viewing. The ethical implications of animated documentaries and their reception thus depend on a more nuanced reading of individual animated documentaries: on their character design, content, additional visuals, audio, the context in which they are shown, as well as their interactivity, vividness and specific reality effects. Each of these aspects can evoke different forms of representation, and varied possibilities for viewer reception and potential encounters between viewer and viewed.

As a documentary aesthetic, animation can have varied, and at times conflicting, ethical implications and effects on viewers. On one hand, the novel aesthetics of animation used in non-fiction can create a *re*-sensitised mode of viewing. In today's apathetic viewing culture in which viewers are largely numb to images of atrocities and the pornography of horror, perhaps an impactful visual experience with innovative aesthetics will succeed in having a powerful effect.[60] On the other hand, if animation is associated with fiction, it may result in *de*-sensitisation in documentaries where protagonists and events may be perceived as fictional. However, de-sensitisation can also occur even if animation is no longer associated with fiction – if it becomes *too* widespread in non-fictional contexts, it will be just another form of representation among many in our era of information saturation. As animation in documentary proliferates, its unique characteristics – its potential representational contribution – will diminish, unless used wisely. When considering the ethical impact of using varied forms of visual representation, this has immense significance as it makes the difference between apathetic viewing and a socially aware, ethically responsible spectatorship.

Does the use of novel aesthetics disrupt an apathetic viewing culture and evoke more empathic spectatorship? Or does it distance the content all the more, making it seem less real due to its non-photorealistic visual portrayal? It is precisely this multi-layered, sometimes conflicting aspect of animation as a documentary language that makes it a powerful tool for representation. It is also increasingly important to explore as its effects may vary, depending on how it is used. This explains why, as viewers, producers and researchers of visual culture, it is vital to understand animation so that its potential as a documentary aesthetic is maximised and its capacities appreciated. These issues will be developed further in the next chapter. Here, in light of this twofold aspect of animation, I want to consider how best to approach animation in documentary contexts so as to maximise its potential ethical effect on viewers.

Preserving animation's ability to evoke ethical viewing requires a profound engagement with what it can contribute to the representation of information through additional layers of meaning and insights. So, it would be unhelpful to use it solely as the visualisation of a soundtrack, for example. Creators will surely aspire to a balance between fact and fiction, generating a documentary experience that enables what I call in this context a 'boomerang effect'. Emerging technologies and novel representations, such as animation, produce a boomerang effect when they are used in ways that engender interest and distancing by using unusual representations, yet avoid overly engrossing portrayals that diminish the documentary status of the work. Creators can also emphasise the sociopolitical content by disrupting the excitement over the novelty of the representation so that it does not overshadow the subject matter. Ideally, viewers of animated documentaries will undergo a 'circular' experience: the animation allows a certain distancing to occur through novel representation, but viewers are then brought full circle back to the subject matter at hand, though only after engaging more deeply and personally with the content and the protagonists' experiences. Rather than obliterating protagonists or situations, intelligent and creative use of animation in documentary can thus return the viewer to the urgency inherent in the events depicted, so that the information is internalised in new and perhaps more powerful ways.

Initially, it may be effective to 'pack' information in animated imagery in order to convey a message. Animation can summarise and simplify information, making it more digestible for viewers. Additionally, the association with fantasy and the artificial appearance that breaks with photorealism, enable animation to create another world that may be seen as distancing, but can help engage viewers in ways that photographic depictions cannot. The distancing that may result from animation's association with fiction and its departure from the physical appearance of protagonists and places do not necessarily lead to obliteration or diminished credibility. Instead, an interesting paradox arises whereby this distancing actually facilitates and even enhances engagement with the content of animated documentaries since viewers can engage with the information in new ways.

In light of the above, how do creators work to ensure that viewers do not disregard animated content as fictional, and thus fail to create the link between the on-screen world and their own? The answer lies in what Sobchack, writing in the context of film, has termed 'ferocious reality'. This occurs when the reality of one death is made clear through juxtaposition with another, fictionalised death.[61] Sobchack discusses Jean Renoir's *Rules of the Game* (1939),[62] in which the actual death of a filmed rabbit disrupts the fictional nature of the film, and defines the different orders of an existential and a cinematic space.[63] The realisation of a 'ferocious reality' is related to documentary consciousness, since the disruption is caused by the realisation that the death is not just fictional, but occurs in the world of the viewer.[64] This can be achieved in different ways through the depiction of a real and a fictionalised death that appear in the same storytelling frame, fluctuating between fiction and fact. The use of photographic imagery at the end of *Waltz with Bashir*, for example, had the same effect; so, too, does the interpellation of player and documentary protagonist in *Darfur is Dying*. Avoiding a seamless and thus overly engrossing VR simulation, breaking the magic circle in games, or rupturing a fictional sphere in film are important devices in conveying real-world, non-fictional information. These ruptures facilitate an understanding of the protagonists as real and alive, and any fictional associations give way to a documentary consciousness.

Nonetheless, aiming for a boomerang effect in animated documentaries also potentially prevents what Kate Nash sees as the risk of improper distance, especially in VR and interactive documentaries, whereby the 'other' depicted becomes 'indistinguishable from ourselves'. As a result the user/viewer is actually self-occupied rather than really engaging or thinking about the represented other.[65] By combining both a sense of identification with distancing elements through representation, the user/viewer of animated documentaries will be less prone to develop an ironic morality where the 'self' of the viewer is elevated over the experience of others portrayed, prioritising their own experience and interpretation of the representation over engagement with the testimony of the other.[66] Animation's ability to combine distancing with identification thus has important potential moral spectatorial implications.

The shifting cultural status of animation, which can be received in relation to both fiction and fact, and the resulting impacts on viewers, will be the focus of what follows. Chapter 8 will examine how these unique characteristics of animation make it such an interesting and complex contemporary aesthetic to explore, and how the discrepancies that it raises actually embody and reflect much wider trends in current documentary and information culture. These trends invite further consideration of the production and reception of non-fiction representation and how realism may be perceived today in relation to animation.

Notes

1. McKim, 'Speculative Animation', p. 294.
2. Enwezor, 'Documentary/Vérité', p. 77.
3. For a related study from a pedagogical perspective, see Nåls, 'Drawing the Unspeakable'.
4. See Hume, *Treatise*; Smith, *Theory of the Moral Sentiments*; Slote, *Ethics of Care*; Darwall, 'Empathy, Sympathy, and Care'.
5. Sobchack, *Carnal Thoughts*, pp. 178, 283–4.
6. Oxford Dictionaries and Dictionary.com
7. Lind and Steyerl, *Greenroom*, p. 19.
8. Ibid., p. 20.
9. The notion of an encounter may be confusing as it can allude to the actual simultaneous physical presence and interaction of all parties. However, as Enwezor refers it to photographic and moving-image documentary-oriented

contemporary art, the one-sidedness of it is implied, focusing on the viewer's reception of the work.
10. Kimmelman, 'Critic's Notebook'.
11. Sobchack, *Carnal Thoughts*, p. 261.
12. Ibid., p. 173.
13. Ibid., pp. 178, 283–4.
14. Sontag, *Regarding the Pain of Others*. Other writers have subsequently emphasised the lack of connection between viewers and viewed. For more, see Jonsson, 'Facts of Aesthetics', p. 182.
15. Frosh, 'Telling Presences', p. 67. See Bauman, 'Effacing the Face', p. 25.
16. For example: *Hidden/Gömd* (2002), by the filmmakers of *Slaves*, about Giancarlo, a hidden refugee child who has no permit to stay in Sweden, describing what it is like to be chased by the police; *It's Like That* (2003) by SLAG (Southern Ladies Animation Group) (http://vimeo.com/31071014, accessed 4 August 2020); *1000 Voices* (2010), by Tim Travers Hawkins, visualising real testimonies recorded secretly by phone with asylum seekers detained indefinitely in the UK, and revealing their psychological trauma and isolation (http://www.iloobia.com/1000-Voices, accessed 4 August 2020); *Makun (Don't Cry)* (2018) by Emilio Marti (Spain: 2018), about an immigration detention centre in the Canary Islands, animating the drawings made by hundreds of anonymous hands and the messages left on the walls with testimonies by immigrants and human rights activists. A key part of the UK's National Refugee Week in June 2012 was the series of animated documentaries *Seeking Refuge* by Mosaic Films for BBC exploring the experiences of young refugees living in the UK (http://www.youtube.com/watch?v=syPlfzEf3Oo, accessed 4 August 2020).
17. Agamben, *Means without End*, p. 22.
18. Greenberg, 'Animated Text', p. 5.
19. Renov, 'Animation'.
20. In his 2004 examination of the storytelling aptitude of animated documentaries, Eric Patrick proposes four different categories, which are detailed in the Introduction, note 46. See Patrick, 'Representing Reality'.
21. Mori, 'The Uncanny Valley'. This theory from the field of robotics and human aesthetics claims that when human features look and move almost, but not exactly, like those of natural human beings, it causes a response of fear or revulsion among some human observers. This theory is important in animation practice and reception, as rather than evoking identification, different degrees of mimetic visualisation might have the opposite effect.
22. For further reading on the identity politics of representation, see Araeen *et al.*, *Third Text Reader*.
23. Honess Roe, *Animated Documentary*, pp. 111–13.
24. Arendt, *Eichmann in Jerusalem*.
25. Lind and Steyerl, *Greenroom*, p. 19.
26. Chion, *Voice in Cinema*, p. 17.

27. Landesman and Bendor, 'Animated Recollection', p. 367.
28. Ibid.
29. Honess Roe, 'Absence, Excess and Epistemological Expansion', p. 217.
30. Fullerton, 'Documentary Games', pp. 220–1.
31. Witter Turner, *From Ritual to Theatre*, p. 140.
32. See Schechner, *Between Theater and Anthropology*, p. 110. On virtual experiences becoming part of the 'I' of the player see also Dibbell, 'Rape in Cyberspace'.
33. For more on this see De la Peña, 'Physical World News', p. 6; Bigna Lenggenhager *et al.*, 'Video Ergo Sum'; Ehrsson, 'Experimental Induction'; see also work by Kilteni *et al.*, 'Sense of Embodiment'.
34. The term 'magic circle' is accredited to Huizinga, *Homo Luden*. Huizinga argued that playing a game meant entering into a 'magic circle', a separate sphere or second-order reality. The use of the term in the context of virtual realities and online games belongs to Salen and Zimmerman, *Rules of Play*.
35. *Darfur is Dying*, www.darfurisdying.com/takeaction.html, accessed 6 October 2012.
36. Gunraj *et al.*, 'Power to the People', p. 259.
37. Parkin, 'Interview'.
38. Neys and Jansz, 'Political internet games', p. 227.
39. Enwezor, 'Documentary/Vérité', p. 77.
40. Linda Williams discusses 'body genres', film genres that influence the body (horror evokes screaming, drama crying and porn arousal), and 'produce' on the bodies of the spectators an almost involuntary mimicry of emotion or sensation of the body on-screen: Williams, 'Film Bodies', p. 4. See also Foster, *Return*, in which engagement with the real is described as traumatic and exemplified by art involving an abject and brutal focus on the body, which can cause visceral physical reactions in the viewer. See also Eisenstein, 'Montage of Film Attractions', p. 49. Sergei Eisenstein considered emotional responses and theorised about what film does to the body of the politicised spectator as well as about the powers of imitative practices. He claimed that the bodily senses *lead* the spectator, whose involvement is not strictly intellectual but also emotional. See also Gaines, 'Political Mimesis', p. 90. Gaines uses the term 'political mimesis' to explain scenes of struggle that impact the bodies of the spectators who view similar bodies on screen before them.
41. Nichols, '"Getting to Know You . . ."', pp. 189–90.
42. José B. Capino finds that in animated pornography, animated bodies are able to provoke physical responses in viewers, who recognise and relate to the corporeality depicted, despite its different appearance. See Capino, 'Filthy Funnies', pp. 55–6 and Mel Slater's work on interactive contexts shows that users can identify with animated bodies, even if they bear no resemblance to their own. See Slater, 'Virtual Self'.
43. Levitt, *Animatic Apparatus*, p. 109.
44. *Globalised Slavery: How Big Supermarkets are Selling Prawns in Supply Chain Fed by Slave Labour*, video ('Modern-Day Slavery in Focus' series), *The Guardian*, www.the

guardian.com/global-development/video/2014/jun/10/slavery-supermarket-supply-trail-prawns-video, accessed 8 July 2014.
45. Sobchack, *Carnal Thoughts*, p. 173.
46. Ibid., p. 187.
47. Ibid., pp. 181–2, 187.
48. Ibid.
49. Ibid., p. 187.
50. Nichols, '"Getting to Know You . . ."', pp. 174, 181.
51. *The Moon and the Son: An Imagined Conversation*, film, directed by John Canemaker (USA: John Canemaker Productions, 2005).
52. *Little Deaths*, film, directed by Ruth Lingford (USA: Harvard University, 2010).
53. *Rocks in My Pockets*, film, directed by Signe Baumane (USA and Latvia: Rocks In My Pockets and Locomotive Productions, 2014).
54. *Music & Clowns*, film, directed by Alex Widdowson, 2018.
55. This emphasis on the personal, for example, is characteristic of what Wells describes in his 'subjective and fantastic modes', Patrick describes in his 'extended structure', and Honess Roe defines in her 'interpretive function'. See Wells, 'Beautiful Village and True Village'; Patrick, 'Representing Reality'; Honess Roe, 'Absence, Excess and Epistemological Expansion', p. 215.
56. For more on animated documentaries and the expression of subjectivity, see Honess Roe, *Animated Documentary*, pp. 106–55. The recurring connection between animation and the depiction of varied states of mind led in 2011 to the establishment of the annual event Animation on Prescription as part of the Bristol Short Film and Animation Festival.
57. *Tying your Own Shoes*, film, directed by Shira Avni (Canada: National Film Board of Canada, 2009).
58. *Ryan*, film, directed by Chris Landreth (Canada: Copperheart Entertainment, 2004).
59. *Quiet Zone*, film, directed by Karl Lemieux and David Byrant (Canada: National Film Board of Canada, 2015).
60. For more on the inured nature of contemporary spectatorship, viewer reception of the visual representation of atrocity in modern life, and the theorisation of imagery as potential shock therapy, see Sontag, *Regarding the Pain*.
61. Sobchack, *Carnal Thoughts*, p. 283.
62. *Rules of the Game*, film, directed by Jean Renoir (France: Nouvelle Édition Française, 1939).
63. Sobchack, *Carnal Thoughts*, p. 268–70.
64. Ibid., p. 283.
65. Nash, 'Virtual Reality Witness', pp. 128–31. Kate Nash draws on the work of Lilie Chouliaraki: see Chouliaraki, 'Improper Distance' and Chouliaraki, *Ironic Spectator*.
66. Nash, 'Virtual Reality Witness', pp. 126–9.

CHAPTER EIGHT

Conflicting Realisms: Animated Documentaries and Post-truth

Part III, *The Power of Animation: Disputing the Aesthetics of the Real*, discusses the status of truth as a discourse and assesses the potential political and ethical implications of using animation in contemporary documentary. What exactly are animated aesthetics of documentary, and how do they relate to current debates surrounding realism and post-truth? Since 'the real' is always mediated through representation, realism is always based on conventions. Although theorists such as Bill Nichols and Michael Renov have engaged with the problematic nature of documentaries and their fluid forms of realism, these questions endure and have become more urgent in the post-truth era.

The demand for documentaries to present facts while their intention and ability to do so are thrown into doubt reflects contemporary culture in which the surplus of constant information has created pressure for exposure and a demand for knowledge along with a persistent sense of uncertainty and distrust. In an era of post-truth characterised by increasingly blurred boundaries between fiction and non-fiction, the truth claims of a documentary are replaced with the more elusive sense of truthiness and the changing paradigms of credibility regarding varied forms of information delivery.

As explained in Chapter 1, the American Dialect Society defines truthiness as 'the quality of preferring concepts or facts one wishes to be true, rather than concepts or facts known to be true'.[1] In an era of murky conceptualisations of truth based more on belief than fact, the role of the viewer as arbiter of a work's documentary status becomes increasingly central. Believability thus becomes key and it is for this reason it is crucial to understand realism as based on changing conceptions of what we believe representations are, and what they may be. Culturally then, current views of truth and its varied representations and explorations explain why it is important to explore confusing representational forms such as animated documentaries. Since realism is linked to credibility and to viewers' understanding of reality as shaped by documentary representation, this has varied ethical, epistemological and political ramifications.

The omnipresent visibility of animation in diverse contexts and mundane situations means that viewers are becoming accustomed to animations that are used, uncritically, to represent or express real events, feelings, processes and interactions. Esther Leslie and Joel McKim state that, as animation proliferates in today's digital culture, it 'is increasingly fundamental to processes of knowledge production'.[2] Consequently this also contributes to the blurring of boundaries between fields of non-fiction.

Animation's recent and exponential rise in non-fiction indicates that in today's visual culture it is at an interesting turning point, poised between fiction and fact – perhaps combining the two.[3] Animation's traditional association with fiction has become less dominant, though animation is still a form of spectacular (and often childhood-oriented) entertainment; as the introduction to this book suggests, something of animation's assumed link to fiction, childhood, humour and light-heartedness persists. Thus, there is an enduring tension between animation as it was most often used in the past, in relation to fiction, and its growing use today, in non-fiction.

Animation literally means 'bringing to life' and thus it expands the aesthetics of documentary by giving life to sounds and images that could not be recorded. Rethinking what animation is and how it is used in documentary today is a perfect lens through which to examine bigger questions about the credibility of imagery, image referentiality and realism today. The shift in the imagery used to depict factual content is an essential aspect of what we now call the post-truth era. What kind of engagement with information do non-photorealistic animated documentaries currently induce, and how is this related to fluid theorisations of realism as the believable articulation of the real?

This shift demands a reconsideration of the status and uses of animation in contemporary visual culture as imagery that is increasingly being used to depict factual information, raising questions about animation's relation to realism. Animation's in-between status, linked to both fiction *and* non-fiction, signifies that in the current cultural-historical moment, animation embodies two contradictory forms of realism. Animated documentaries on the one hand simplify information and create truth claims meant to project authority and to be consumed uncritically; and on the other they create multilayered meaning, confusion and uncertainty, potentially leading to more critical viewing. These two modes of animation reception relate to two contradictory theorisations of realism, one based on familiarity and the other on defamiliarisation. Animated documentaries interestingly (and perhaps only temporarily) embody both. This, I find, is part of its contemporary allure. By exploring these contradictory notions of realism, I wish to demonstrate how and why non-photorealistic animation is an important, self-reflexive and realistic documentary aesthetic that strongly reflects today's post-truth media.

As animation flourishes in documentary and covers horrific content such as war and the plight of refugees, the main questions are: (1) Can and will animation de- or re-sensitise viewers in an era of post-truth, epistemological mistrust and uncertainty? (2) If animation's links to actuality are fluid and unclear, do (and will) viewers potentially believe nothing or everything; and can these binaries be broken down as representations continually change?

I argue that animated documentaries are masked, self-reflexive documentary aesthetics that both hide and expose information, and foreground issues of truth verification versus disinformation, and thus they act as a perfect form of representation for the zeitgeist.

TRUTH PROCESSES OR TRUTH WITH A CAPITAL T?

Realism is a vast, unresolved field. As explained in Chapter 1, the complexity of realism is indicated by the immense and multiple philosophical questions it raises, ranging from the ontological to the epistemological, moral, semantic, physical, technological and many more.[4] Here I refer to realism as the believable articulation of the real, highlighting that the status of representations' veracity is constantly changing. Realism in animation has been covered in varied and enriching ways.[5] I explained the plurality of realism, which can refer to the capturing of 'a close approximation of . . . the world exterior to the representation', or be judged against what 'has already gained the status of the "realistic" (a particular form of cinematography, for example)'.[6] In other words, realism can be understood in terms of its relation to direct vision, technology or ideology; thus realistic representation must always be in flux. The issue of direct capture and the equivalence between representation and referent (as opposed to falsification), are central to the discussion of realism. Thus animation as a direct capture of virtual realities visible only in animated form (as explained in Part II) can be seen as realistic and as a window to on-screen realities.

Alternatively, when depicting photographable physical realities, animation can be seen as mediated and potentially distorting. Highly relevant to non-photorealistic animation in non-fiction, the confusion surrounding realism is explained by Bruno Latour as a tension between viewers' expectations and what representation can hope to offer.[7] Latour suggests that the relation between representation, reality and verifiable truth claims leads to unrealistic expectations whereby viewers desire a so-called direct grasp of 'truth' through transparency, or 'representation *without* any *re*presentation'. This, he explains, is impossible since there is no such thing as transparent presentation; there is no access to reality other than through *re*presentation. The centrality of the topic of transparency and opacity in debates about realism is clear; but the fact that animation emphasises its opacity through obviously constructed visuals that do not attempt photorealism complicates the issue further. To understand what aspects of realism appear in animation as a contemporary documentary aesthetic we must examine how animation is perceived today, and what it seeks to achieve.

Realism is both an aesthetic associated with mimesis (realistic) and a political goal (realist). I have dealt with the aesthetic aspect of animation's realism throughout the book. Here I focus on the political goal of realism, which takes the form of an activism that seeks not only to know and reveal reality but to change it as well, and aims to appeal by creating art that speaks to the masses.[8] Animation is used in entertainment, advertisements and escapist amusement; it is also used to depict the subjective and personal. Theorising animation as an aesthetic that does not aim to entertain, and that is depersonalised and objective, is thus a difficult task. From childhood, we are familiar with animation and its popularity in many forms of entertainment; in this respect, it is non-intimidating and this may facilitate its mass appeal. So, can we also view animation as a realistic aesthetic? The duality persists, depending on the goals of the representation. From a Marxist perspective, representation aiming to engage with 'the real' either complies with ideology, and may therefore be complicit with an oppressive system, or aims to subvert and reveal underlying structures. Animation does both.[9]

Since documentaries present factual information meant to persuade viewers, what kind of reception or engagement with their truth claims do they aspire to? Whereas novel aesthetics may overshadow content, they can also engage viewers in varied ways. Okwui Enwezor argues that novel documentary artwork can create a 'truth process' that 'doesn't confront the spectator with un-negotiable facts . . .' but rather encourages reflective and analytic spectatorship.[10] Undoubtedly, animation falls into this category; it creates multi-layered representations that require active engagement and viewer interpretation, as demonstrated in *Darfur is Dying* and *Slaves* in Chapter 7.

However, animation can also do the opposite. Although the contemporary networked mediascape requires active users that participate in knowledge production and dissemination, the excess of information also leads to fatigue and detachment. As Fred Ritchin explains, the result is that contemporary media often do not engage viewers in thoughtful and serious conversation, but rather bombard audiences endlessly with competing and trivialising imagery that aims at the automatic establishment of authenticity rather than through collaboration with the audience.[11] In this sense, animation is the perfect visual language to create supposedly final truth claims – or 'Truth with a capital T' – since it simplifies complex systems and large amounts of data until these are dumbed down, easy to digest and received as fact with no questions asked. This in itself is characteristic of the post-truth era in which 'what matter[s] [is] not veracity, but impact . . . the triumph of the visceral over the rational, the deceptively simple over the honestly complex'.[12] Thus, as non-photorealistic animation in non-fiction contexts is increasingly used as a summary of information that depicts events and topics as non-nuanced and supposedly straightforward, animation's abundance as visual representation of complex processes and information is an essential part of the post-truth media environment.

Do animated documentaries encourage 'truth processes' as complex and perceptive engagement with information, or do they present information as 'Truth with a capital T', meant to be consumed uncritically as simplistic fact? This depends on animation's transforming uses and cultural role, which play a large part in the reception and consequent theorisations of realism most suited to the sub-genre of animated documentaries: is realism the familiar, or is it defamiliarising?

REALISM AS THE FAMILIAR

This book began with a description of *Waltz with Bashir*, which garnered wide critical acclaim and stimulated much interest in the then relatively unknown field of animated documentaries.[13] It is perhaps unsurprising that, despite animation's long and complex history, at the time of *Waltz with Bashir* the concept of an animated documentary sounded to many like an oxymoron.[14] This is not to say that animation didn't appear in earlier non-fiction filmmaking, for example in education and propaganda, albeit often infrequently and marginalised,[15] but its proliferation since 2008, when *Waltz with Bashir* was made, has changed its status and reception (see Chapter 1). In *Waltz with Bashir*, the animated imagery was indirectly used to question the difference between animation and photography, and to reflect upon different modes of representation that are accepted as credible, legitimate documentation.

What makes recent animated documentaries 'new' or 'contemporary' as an aesthetic of factual information? First, the staggering growth in the quantity of animated documentaries since 2008 demonstrates that the collective creative recourse to animated modes and imagery is more characteristic of the last decade than any earlier period. In Chapter 1, I discussed the reasons for animation's proliferation in contemporary visual culture, which included the growing ease of animation production, documentary and surveillance culture, info-aesthetics and the information age, machine vision, omnipresent screens and the virtualisation of culture. Second, whereas past uses of animation in non-fiction often relied on animation's traditional association with fiction and fantasy, today such allusions have lessened considerably. Third, changing technological production methods alter animation's inherent qualities and consequently also their relation to documentary theorisations and evidentiary status, distinguishing contemporary animation from its earlier forms, and defining it as entirely contemporary. In 2008, the realism of animated documentaries may have intuitively seemed more problematic because non-photorealistic animation emphasises its own constructed nature, distancing it from any direct capture of events and the more traditional documentary aesthetic, photography.[16] Simply because animation was a relatively unfamiliar documentary language in 2008 that emphasised its own constructedness, and was less readily 'readable' or comprehensible, it may initially have been considered less realistic.

It is important to remember that what viewers recognise as realistic depiction is based on familiarity and conventions of representation. Nelson Goodman contends:

> the realism perceived in a picture arises not from the quantity of information provided but from the ease with which it is read ... the more stereotypical and familiar the ... modes of representation that generate an image, the more natural and true it seems.[17]

Thus, as animation proliferates and its uses in contemporary visual culture vary, users will become increasingly accustomed to seeing it in myriad fields. The reception of animation as realistic will consequently continue to rise, based on its changing uses and popularity in the contemporary media sphere.

The exponential rise of animated documentaries in recent years shows that viewers are more familiar with the sub-genre and the use of animation in factual, rather than fictional contexts. By becoming accustomed to receiving information in stylised animated imagery, animation has become familiar, standard and mainstream, thus enhancing its reception as realistic. As this trend leads to animation becoming a regular form of representation in ever-wider non-fiction contexts, such as news segments, infographics, medical, geographical and scientific visualisations, educational and explanatory platforms, animation's epistemological capability is changing. This popularity in non-fiction consequently makes animation so commonplace that it goes unnoticed as a representational choice; so normalised that it seems almost invisible. Returning to Latour's emphasis on *re*presentation, it is precisely this kind of change in viewer reception that makes certain *re*presentations seem transparent, incorrectly perceived as direct presentation. When considering the epistemological effects this can have on viewers, it is also what defines animation as a de-sensitising aesthetic because viewers may accept it uncritically, when information is presented as 'Truth with a capital T'.

This is often the case in animated simulations on the news, in re-enactments where the animated sequence is meant to show viewers what took place and how the event unfolded. An example is a video by the Dutch Safety Board showing the probable path of a Buk missile that caused the fatal crash of Malaysia Airlines flight MH17 in July 2014.[18] The animation gains credibility by being shown on the BBC, an authoritative media source that encourages unquestioning reception of the information as fact. In cases such as this, the animation is simple and straightforward, with a dry confident voiceover explaining the course of events, and emphasising 'evidence' and 'proof'. The outcome is that the representation is posited as a direct presentation of authoritative fact, rather than one interpretation among many.

Furthermore, as animation's popularity rises, it has great marketing potential. As a result, many documentaries now use animation, but not necessarily in ways that explore what the aesthetics can contribute, or what layers of meaning they might add; rather, the animation is hurried and superficial, merely visualising what is heard on the soundtrack.[19] It begs the question, why use animated documentary when a radio soundtrack or podcast would achieve the same outcome? With the growing visibility of animation in nonfiction, this may be creating uncritical spectatorship. In other words, viewers are becoming desensitised to the multi-layered possibilities of complex visual information transferal through animated representations that offer no additional meaning of their own.

This de-sensitisation has various ramifications: rather than contemplating animation's signifying capabilities, the relation between audio and visual content,[20] truth-value and persuasiveness, or the multiple ways animation can depict subject matter, viewers become apathetic and uncritical, leaving viewing open to misinformation and manipulation. Furthermore, as the uses of animation flourish in contemporary visual culture in general, and in nonfiction specifically, is it only a matter of time until animation becomes so widely accepted and familiar that it is not questioned at all? Is animation becoming invisible? Due to the familiarity of animation from childhood and its growing use in informational contexts, I would say that it is quickly approaching that point. Once the aesthetics of representation are no longer perceived as aesthetics, they become transparent because the representation is read as if it were reality itself.[21] This has important political outcomes: once representation is no longer seen as such, what is represented can be viewed as 'real' rather than cultural and constructed, thus making it 'invisible' and complicit with existing ideology.

The question that remains is, are we there yet? Or are we still at the point where photography continues to be central in documentary and in animated documentaries, where it supposedly adds credibility to the documentary aesthetic of animation, which is seen as almost-credible-yet-not-quite? *Animating Truth* has followed what I see as a transformation in animation's role in visual culture. Nonetheless, is animation so familiar and mainstream that it is accepted uncritically in non-fiction, or does the use of animation still raise questions about its validity as a truth-telling representation? Until the process of fully accepting animation is complete, this tension in animation's contemporary cultural role is part of its appeal and significance as a subject of research. It is important to consider what implications such acceptance may have on the consumption of information and on the political role of animated documentaries as shapers of reality rather than mere reflections of it. This leads me to the second form of realism as defamiliarisation.

REALISM AS DEFAMILIARISING

Since realism is so intertwined with ideas of transparency, opacity and therefore also deceit, it may be animation's overt constructedness that makes it more rather than less realistic. Indeed, when many experimental documentaries are engaging with the problematic nature of truth-telling in the documentary field (both animated and live-action), several theorists have claimed animation is a more honest approach to documentary.[22] Interestingly, 'truthiness', according to Tom Gunning, is that which seems real because it is recognised and depicts the world in familiar ways that reassure viewers that reality is as they think it is.[23] Therefore, what seems transparent is, for Gunning, the biggest form of deceit. In contrast to what seems real, realism, or the 'more real', involves defamiliarisation and indicates a breakthrough to a fresh perception that involves a multiplicity in one's understanding of reality.[24] Therefore, new modes of representation have the potential to evoke a self-reflexive spectator stance. The issue of construction versus transparency – or the illusion of such – led to a realisation of the need for anti-illusionistic, alienating or rupturing techniques, such as those developed by Bertolt Brecht in the 1920s–1940s. According to Brecht, 'our conception of realism needs to be broad and political, free from aesthetic restrictions and independent of convention . . . Reality alters . . . to represent it, the means of representation must alter too.'[25] In other words, realism is theorised in a contradictory manner; not as easily readable and transparent, but rather as a form of defamiliarisation that makes viewers see realities anew through innovative representation that breaks with conventions.

In this context it is also useful to consider surrealism, another form of realism contemporaneous with Brecht. At times aligned with communism and anarchism, surrealism proposed that freeing the mind was directly linked to liberation from repressive social structures. By creating strange and sometimes shocking juxtapositions, and breaking conventions and/or expectations, the 'surreality' of the works often causes a sense of bewilderment.[26]

This precludes any direct interpretive reading or fixed explication and creates instead manifold signification, explained below in my analysis of animated documentaries as crystal images. The potential reactions of bewilderment and confusion make surrealist representations more than pictorial and poetic methods of investigation, and ensure they also act as politically operative tools for social subversion through antagonism and conflict.[27]

These Brechtian and surrealist ideas shed light on current discussions about the growing uses of animation in non-fiction. As long as animation is noticed, questioned and/or deemed 'strange' in documentary, or until such time as it becomes more fully integrated into the mainstream and becomes transparent or invisible, animation's unique and endless visual potential affords it the ability to destabilise existing conventions and expectations, if used imaginatively. In this section, my focus is on animated documentaries that question representational choices by foregrounding varied and shifting styles and/or discrepancies meant to raise questions and prevent complacent viewing.

Novel and stylistically infinite aesthetic regimes like animation can raise doubts about the truth-value of more conventional aesthetics. This is not because one aesthetic is necessarily more truthful or better than another, but because the use and presence of both returns attention to the aesthetics themselves.[28] By emphasising the aesthetics used to portray the content, they are denied any illusion of transparency; thus the representation is made visible as one specific choice among many, rather than assuming equivalence between the representation and its referent. This, in turn, underscores the idea that all languages of representation are constructed and mediated, an awareness that is a cornerstone in maintaining and promoting criticality.

According to Fred Ritchin, in order to prevent complacency, disruptions are often used and constructedness is emphasised.[29] Annabelle Honess Roe similarly analyses the different forms of animated imagery used in live-action documentaries, explaining that animated interjections, which deliberately interrupt the otherwise live-action film, have the potential to create more critical viewing and consequently also the potential for stronger political messages.[30] Indeed, research into forensic animation concludes that mixing visual metaphors and modes can be potentially disorienting to some viewers.[31] This conclusion reinforces the idea that changing visual styles results in disruption for viewers, who must repeatedly readjust and find their bearings in the visual world represented. This form of spectatorship is important if the goal is to induce viewing that is alienated and critical, rather than immersed and complacent. Although not all animated documentaries take this approach, many non-photorealistic animated documentary works, such as *Snack and Drink* (1999),[32] *Ryan* (2004),[33] *In the Same Boat* (2007),[34] *Waltz with Bashir*

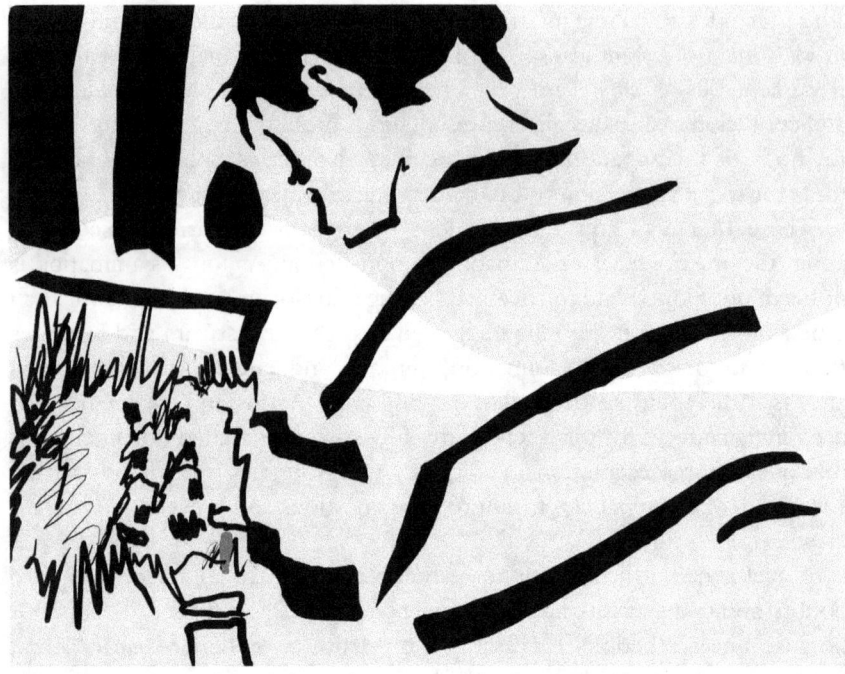

Figure 8.1 *Snack and Drink*, directed by Bob Sabiston, 1999.

(2008), *Slaves* (2008), *I was a Child of Holocaust Survivors* (2010),[35] *The Wanted 18* (2014),[36] *Tower* (2016)[37] and *Another Planet* (2017)[38] alternate between varied styles of animated imagery, and/or include the photographed alongside the animated in ways that emphasise rather than downplay the cut from one to the other. This is mostly done through the use of strikingly different stylistic choices meshed together, accentuating the movement from one scene to the next. The shifts in representational styles are often used to signify a transition between different stages or aspects of the narrative, such as memories, dreams and actual events; but the results show that the entire representation could have taken on different forms, emphasising its constructedness.

The intermediate status of animation between fiction and fact, and the endless visual styles and juxtapositions of animation facilitates in representation make it a thought-provoking documentary aesthetic when used wisely and creatively. This was the case, for example, in Jacqueline Goss's 2007 *Stranger Comes to Town*,[39] discussed in Chapter 5, about national borders, biometrics and racial profiling. Integrating virtual gaming aesthetics with content referring to non-virtual physical realities, *Stranger Comes to Town* combines multiple animated styles and representational origins, including animated documents used in US airports, Google Earth imagery, the game

WoW, machinima recordings, hand-drawn animations and more. The work thus moves between different modes of representation and interchangeably represents physical and virtual worlds until the viewer is no longer sure what is represented, and how. Thus, the work draws new conclusions about the indistinguishability of the two realities, physical and virtual, the use of one to explore and understand the other, and the overall complexities of what constitutes reality today.

Similarly, the film *Tower*, discussed in the book's introduction, is a rapidly paced collage of varied imagery. Here, too, animation is combined with live action; the animation is used to interrogate the difficult question of memory, and to emphasise the trauma and surreal quality of the events, like the portrayal of war in *Waltz with Bashir*. Unlike *Waltz with Bashir*, however, in which the stark contrast between animation and photography only appears in the last scene, in *Tower* the varied documentary aesthetics change repeatedly. The visuals in *Tower* shift from black and white and coloured photographic footage from the actual 1966 shooting event to contemporary photographic colour footage of the location today. This footage then changes into psychedelic, colourful animation, rotoscoped animation (based on actors re-enacting the survivors' experiences) in black and white, to similarly styled colour animation, and then combined with animated silhouettes or interspersed blocks of colour, or a combination of all of the above. The film also includes contemporary footage of interviews with survivors and often juxtaposes manifold visual styles in sharp, frequent cuts, as well as interesting combinations of different visualisations, such as animated characters shown against a background of photographic footage. Thus in *Tower*, the distinction between animation and photography is blurred from the start, unlike the glaring contrast created in *Waltz with Bashir*, which underscores the ostensibly contradictory status between fantasy-animation and fact-photography.

This demonstrates the diversity and endless possibilities of documentary aesthetics today. It is the ceaseless visual changes that create a new type of whole that is greater than the sum of its many, fragmented parts, the many visual depictions used in the film. By emphasising the multiple visual choices and the creative re-enactment of the events, *Tower* indirectly makes the viewer wonder how the narrative was revisited and constructed anew, constantly refocusing on the representational decisions and choices. As a representational decision, this kind of documentary is vital in the post-truth era. As Lee McIntyre explains, although it may be easier to identify a truth that others refuse to see, it is not always simple to doubt information that we ourselves would like to believe. In order to do so we must diversify our sources of information.[40] *Tower*, in this sense, is the kind of documentary that not only emphasises constructedness but also highlights its many sources, and indirectly reminds us that in order to evaluate information critically we must also expand our newsfeed.

The multiple, rich and at times baffling representational choices in these examples emphasise the bewilderment that certain animated documentaries can induce. Once again, these examples show that the vast variety of animated styles, each of which depicts realities differently, exemplifies that no transparent representation is ever possible. This drives the discussion back to credibility and realism, and the ongoing search for the best way to articulate reality.

Creating confusion, or at the very least ensuring that viewers are attentive, by using myriad unusual representational choices, is important in maintaining animation's potential to defamiliarise and evoke critical viewing as it becomes increasingly popular and familiar. Gilles Deleuze's crystal image is a helpful conceptual tool. According to Deleuze, understanding the present is based upon recognition and recollection of prior knowledge, which is the past apparent in the present. According to Deleuze's definition, the present is our perception and is always actual, whereas the future and past, the future-past, are virtual (not to be confused with 'virtual' in the digital sense).[41] Since the past, like potential futures, is embodied in the present, and the present is destined to become the past, our existence duplicates itself, being both actual and, simultaneously, virtual.[42] The virtual is external to the actual image, but it indicates meaning, since meaning is always outside of the film or cultural creation. The actual is not necessarily intelligible in itself, only through virtual approaches to it. Since interpretation influences the meaning of the image, the virtual is constantly touching upon and influencing the actual, the one constantly becoming the other.

Crystal images, which simultaneously incorporate the actual and the virtual, keep twisting within themselves so that the viewer's perception is destabilised, thus complicating interpretation. In the crystal image, viewers' ability to distinguish actual from virtual is suspended, and the relation between the two keeps fluctuating and changing, creating disruptions and uncertainty. The animated documentary image, when used to defamiliarise and evoke questions, potentially highlights this complex confrontation, in which viewers try to negotiate a larger system of meaning to interpret these new forms of referentiality and representation. Whereas photography captures a present, animation references in a way that embodies interpretation in its stylisation (think of the representation of subjective experiences, for example). Animation emphasises this since it can easily indicate more than one possible referent or context. In other words, the constructed nature of the animated image permits the creator to control and insert meaning into it in myriad ways. As such, animated representation embodies many contradictory aspects.

Using Deleuze's ideas about the present as actual and the future-past used to indicate meaning as virtual, we see how animated documentaries embody both. Any animated documentary of an event is meant to show the present depicted, and the present is actual; thus, the animated images serve to actualise events that viewers would not otherwise witness. However, animated imagery in documentaries is also virtual because it is creatively interpreted for the viewer. Since animation's relation to realities is still morphing, Deleuze's virtual is a shifting aspect of animation. Because animation can be stylised and interpreted in varied ways, what is embodied in the images and what is part of the interpretation morphs endlessly. The virtual aspects of interpretation are far from fixed and the relation between the actual image perceived and its virtual 'flip-side' of interpretation constantly changes, returning us to Deleuze's crystal image. Animation's recent rise in visibility in fields of non-fiction as well as its potentially endless visual styles and interpretational abilities require viewers to keep working out the relation between the actual and virtual, the referent and its sign. Like the crystal image, it is never absolutely clear what is actually seen in animated documentaries. Each animated documentary chooses to highlight this characteristic or downplay it, depending on the kind of realism and viewer reception it is aiming for.

Confusion caused by disruption, uncertainty, allegory and constructedness all question assumptions, raise suspicions and thus prevent complacency. This reflects the political aims of representation, which seek to subvert and/or reveal underlying systems and power structures. In this regard, Paul Wells explains that animation's exposed constructedness leads to a questioning of grand narratives, as animation comments indirectly upon the constructedness of reality itself.[43] As a result, the inherent and established 'reality' behind the animated documentary is destabilised. In other words, animation enables viewing the familiar world in a different light and, as a result, invokes contemplation that rejects acceptance of information as a statement of fact. Stressing the constructedness of representation requires the viewer to delve deeper: aware that she is only receiving part of the picture, she is compelled to 'fill in' the contours herself, or at least question the truth-value of the representation in its entirety. In an era of misinformation and post-truth, a constant reminder to viewers to question all and any information presented is in itself an important political position.

Awareness of the *re*presentational aspect of a work means that nothing is accepted 'as is', as if it were 'Truth with a capital T'; but rather that it is only one version of that truth, a representation that embodies varied positions, agendas and consequent representational choices. Understanding and being reminded of the fact that what one sees is *re*presentation, rather than presentation, can help maintain viewer criticality. Confusing representations whose interpretations continually morph, as with crystal images, prevent any single 'truth' being perceived as the only authoritative 'objective' view. It is for this reason that the very complexity of animated documentaries that shift between visual languages underscores their role as contemporary representations that emphasise heterogeneity, complexity, uncertainty and multiple narratives.

Indeed, uncertainty and instability are one way of characterising the contemporary, through the concept of precariousness, which is defined as vulnerability, uncertainty and dependence on chance or circumstance.[44] This same uncertainty exists in the realm of representation and questions how best to gain access to 'the real', which relates the discussion to documentary aesthetics. This ongoing uncertainty and confusion about believability raises further questions about what has become the barely discernible line between a sense of transparency, seeing things 'as they are' in a believable manner, and deception and misinformation. The tension between knowing and not knowing, between being informed and being misinformed is, therefore, timelier than ever in the contemporary post-truth era. What does this signify for the role of documentaries today?

Carrie Lambert-Beatty confronts this issue and coins the term 'parafiction' to address the advantageous effects that such ambiguous documentary works may have. Lambert-Beatty writes about a body of contemporary art practice that is presented as fact, in which artists investigate issues of truth in new ways, and thus 'draw attention to the relativism and subjectivity of truth', or are oriented towards the search for truth.[45] She explains parafiction as part of a deception, a 'gotcha' moment of being fooled, in which, 'with various degrees of success, for various durations, and for various purposes, these fictions are experienced as fact. They achieve truth status.'[46] Combining fact with fiction so that the two become indistinguishable creates more critical consumers of information because '[b]eing in on the trick' is an incentive to upholding criticality; it advocates the need to be on the lookout so as not to be duped.[47]

Analysing animated documentaries in relation to Deleuze's crystal image denies a single clear vantage point from which to view and interpret the constantly shifting meanings of the image, and positions animation in documentaries as part of this wider field of disorienting aesthetics. Thus, as Ward asserts, what is presented as factual and straightforward information, rather than as argument, is in fact covert, not overt because viewers are encouraged to take what is presented as truth.[48] When animated documentaries emphasise their many and often conflicting representational choices, they bring the viewer in on the truth-production process, creating defamiliarisation and precluding any one objective or authoritative view.

Animated Documentaries as Masking and as a Sign of the Post-Truth Era

Examining the double and contradictory forms of realism inherent in contemporary animated documentaries reveals that animation's realism is multi-layered. Realism itself embodies several conflicting lines of thought and can thus be considered both as an easily legible transparent form of representation, and one that destabilises existing assumptions and generates new ways of seeing. These opposing notions of the familiar and easily understandable versus the new and strange are central to the discussion of animation in non-fiction, which in different ways illustrates both. Animation's relation to realism is also continuously shifting, based on its changing status and myriad uses in contemporary visual culture.

Since documentary practice is the 'quest for ever more authentic representations of the real',[49] analysing documentary aesthetics questions the nature of contemporary reality and how best to articulate it. An exploration of animated documentaries as realistic (or not) requires us to recognise whether and how animation in non-fiction captures and expresses the present and conveys it in a way that 'rings true'. Although it is impossible to define 'the contemporary' precisely, the accelerated mistrust of the media in an era of post-truth and fake news is central to a discussion of the varied forms of realism in animation as a contemporary documentary aesthetic. Animated documentaries are, in several ways, an appropriate and self-reflexive documentary aesthetic that functions very much as a sign of the times, reflecting central issues surrounding truth claims, the media and visual culture in the second decade of the twenty-first century.

The following features cannot be overlooked. First, the visual image has become central in the creation and distribution of information about current realities. Animation's endless styles and rapidly evolving production techniques reflect the very visual nature of today's screen culture which is saturated with visual stimuli, and highlight the consequent need to find ways of attracting attention.

Second, incorporating myriad styles in single representations and highlighting constructedness, animation emphasises the multiple ways reality can be portrayed and consequently shaped. A possible legacy of postmodernism and poststructuralism is suspicion of single perspectives in a world too complex to be thus reduced and unified. In this sense then, the goal of experimental documentaries has shifted away from the attempt to portray ostensibly objective truths or highlight epistemological and ontological debates. Instead, the field of documentary that often deals with current realities primarily attests to a diversity and complexity of forms, paradoxes and discrepancies, where organising complexities is prioritised over documenting reality.[50]

Third, in the current information climate of image manipulation and fake news, viewers are highly aware of the possibilities of misinformation (the unintentional dissemination of false or inaccurate data) and disinformation (the manipulative, deceitful and deliberate dissemination of false information). The contemporary tension between information that is visible and available and that which is invisible and disguised has become a major feature of the times. This duality and tension are embodied in animated documentaries through the concept of masking. The post-truth atmosphere of information availability and the contemporary unclear truth status of information are particularly conducive, as explained below. Animated documentaries either emphasise constructedness through varied visual choices and shifts in order to raise awareness of, and battle against, uncritical spectatorship in an era of fake news (realism as defamiliarisation), or they steer clear of that kind of viewership and opt instead for easily digestible and supposedly authoritative animated representations (realism as the familiar). This dichotomy, and the fact that animated documentaries both reveal *and* disguise, as well as encourage either complacent *or* critical viewing, make animated documentaries a perfect form of representation and signifier of the contemporary zeitgeist. This would define animation as realistic in the sense that it is indeed 'a close approximation of . . . the world exterior to the representation'.[51]

In order to examine animation's current epistemological uses and status as documentary imagery, it is useful to think of animated documentaries as a complex and at times contradictory form of masking, whereby exposure and disguise converge.[52] Animation can be used to reflect upon wider cultural characteristics and mistrust of data, both when information is omnipresent and continuously displayed and when it is concealed and misrepresented. By examining animated documentaries as a sub-genre that reveals as much as it hides, the viewing effects that this duality can have on consumers of information become apparent. Animated documentaries simplify information and create truth claims intended to project authority and be consumed uncritically, on the one hand; they can also create multi-layered meaning, confusion and uncertainty – which may lead to more critical viewing – on the other. These two modes of animation reception relate to the two contradictory theorisations of realism described. By addressing central characteristics of contemporaneity and these conflicting modes of realism, one based on familiarity and the other on defamiliarisation, animated documentaries interestingly (and perhaps only temporarily) embody both. Through the prism of masking, therefore, animation can be understood as an important, self-reflexive, and realistic documentary aesthetic entirely attuned to contemporary culture.

Masking is a valuable and central device with which to assess animated documentaries. As objects, masks have multiple roles: they both conceal and reveal; they can cover the wearer's face, or they can 'give face', that is, provide a visual representation that protects memory, as with death masks and representations of deities, thereby exposing the wearer's beliefs, wishes and cultural associations. Masks transform and empower change by breaking with everyday life, status and conduct, and replacing one identity with another. The idea of masking contributes to the field of animated documentaries because masks, like animation in this context, facilitate a convergence of exposure and disguise.

In the same way, animation can replace live-action footage and conceal through stylised representation what would otherwise be seen directly. The masking effects of animation reflect my discussion of animation as an alternative to photography.[53] Animation creates an alternative stylisation for physical appearance, and a graphic visualisation of the non-physical that cannot be photographed; it both conceals by covering what could be photographed *and* exposes what is not representable by other means.

Animated documentaries serve as a *disguise* when they provide an 'alternative face' for what could have been photographed, for example to protect the anonymity of protagonists, to shield spectators from horrific, live-action imagery, and even as a form of censorship. Conversely, they can serve as a form of *exposure* when engaging with information for which live-action footage is unobtainable. Similarly, the style of the animated imagery may expose or conceal information about the creator or the context of the creation, such as biases and sub-contexts that influence the visual interpretation of events. Animated depictions may appear inauthentic or disguising but can also be used to illustrate what would otherwise remain invisible, such as personal perspectives, memories or virtual worlds. As discussed in Part II, the development of digitally virtual, non-physical environments use animation like a mask, as a visualising element that reveals dynamic and otherwise invisible platforms. Animation thus creates a 'face' for realities that are not photographable and exposes elements that would not otherwise be included. By expanding the scope of what can be explored in visual documentary practices, animation broadens the concept of 'reality'. Furthermore, in the same way that masks create a break with familiar reality, animation creates entire worlds that differ from those represented in live-action footage. As such, animation represents the multiplicity and complexity of contemporary realities while engaging with them differently, exploring and representing them in original ways that expose new angles, interrogate the representation and reveal what, if anything, lies beneath it. These issues are particularly pertinent in the contemporary fake-news, post-truth era.

Animated depictions of realities also create a sense of distancing and defamiliarisation that change a viewer's perspective, in the same way that masks break with the quotidian and influence behaviour. The theme of masks thus raises many questions about reality today, about the nature of representation that makes claims about this reality, and how it is best achieved. An example is offered in Bonni Cohen and Jon Shenk's *Audrie & Daisy* (2016),[54] a harrowing documentary about the sexual assault of two teenage girls. The documentary includes animated sequences, some of which depict the night of the assault, based on Daisy's own drawings. Creating the animation in this case has special significance: it serves as an empowering process for Daisy by enabling her to 'speak her truth'; it facilitates personal disclosure without any photographic or voyeuristic exposure; and it depicts subjective experiences.[55] The other animated sequences depict an interview with the teenage boys, the perpetrators of the assault on Audrie, who committed suicide after the event. They agreed to this interview as part of the punishment for their crime. The animation obscures the identities of the underage perpetrators, but it uses a specific visual style that maintains the nuances of their body language, resulting in a stronger focus on the body while the faces remain unrecognisable. In this case, animation offers the best of both representational worlds, concealing some elements while highlighting others. When the boys speak, their body language reveals information beyond what is seen – about their mental state, insights and perhaps even remorse. Not being 'seen' paradoxically lends an honesty to the presentation, revealing the perpetrators' version of the assault, and enabling viewers to consider the gap between what is being said in relation to what is being shown. The contrast between hearing and seeing, concealment and disclosure, are among the many juxtapositions evident in animated documentaries, one of many discrepancies between exposure and disguise, and contribute significantly to their allure.

Similarly, Kota Ezawa's 2002 documentary artwork video installation *The Simpson Verdict* also incorporates exposure and disguise. The use of animation is not a result of live-action footage being unobtainable in this case; Ezawa uses it to redraw overexposed media footage of the all-familiar verdict being announced at O. J. Simpson's trial, and incorporates excerpts from the original court audio recordings. By using familiar imagery with the 'twist' of redrawing it in a clearly recognisable animated style, it may be argued that Ezawa obliterates many details visible in the photographic footage of the event. However, the same animated images can be seen to expose more than they hide by accentuating certain aspects that contextualise the event in a new way. In this case, the animated redrawing emphasises skin tone while eliminating detailed facial features, thus highlighting the issue of race, which undermined the entire event and the way it was covered in the media.

Figure 8.2 *The Simpson Verdict*, video installation by Kota Ezawa, 2002.

Karen Beckman asks whether the use of animation, which in *The Simpson Verdict* 'flattens out' the portrayal, actually creates a viewing experience that changes our epistemological approach and allows us 'to look without expecting to know in a way that enables us to look at the live-action footage differently?'[56] By focusing on close-up shots of Simpson when his verdict is declared, Ezawa emphasises viewers' expectations of being able to decipher some fragment of truth, in this case regarding guilt or innocence, from merely looking while simultaneously questioning the ability to actually do so.[57] Such questions and reflexive representational choices foreground the need to understand viewer reception of animated documentaries; the way reality is represented and understood has the power to structure the reality in question. Representing reality, and the potential and consequent shaping of reality, brings me back to realism.

The existing duality of visible and concealed information characteristic of today's media, typifies animated documentaries. Furthermore, masking situates the issue of visibility versus invisibility centre stage: masking the visible may make it invisible or differently visible, while animation as masking can also provide visibility to the otherwise invisible. The tension between exposure and disguise is prevalent in the ubiquitous headlines about manipulated images, fake news and 'alternative facts', as well as in the discourses concerning whistleblowing and exposure (by Wikileaks, Edward Snowden, Chelsea Manning, Anonymous and the darknet, among others). It is noteworthy that whistleblowing has been proposed as a new brand of journalism,[58] a proposition that exemplifies the idea that in the current cultural moment perhaps only disguise facilitates the exposure of information. The convergence of exposure and disguise embodied in animated documentaries as masking can be extrapolated to politics and information more generally. The post-9/11 preoccupation with 'national security' is defined by ubiquitous surveillance, government secrecy and consequent demands for privacy and anonymity. To avoid scrutiny and protect privacy, information must be disguised and encrypted. I propose that there is a connection between these trends and the depiction of information in animated form – as a visual rendition of encrypted messages. For example, as a way to battle face-recognition technologies, animated depictions could act like word-verification systems (see below), based on the premise that a highly stylised font is recognisable to humans but not to technology. This is of central concern to contemporary documentaries, which implicitly reflect upon meta-systems of information and knowledge production. Thus animated documentaries, which both reveal and conceal, have a vital role to play in the field of documentary. The gap between the visible and invisible, which is also inherent in animated documentary as masking, positions animation as a highly relevant and realistic self-reflexive documentary aesthetic that expresses central concerns in contemporary information culture.

By emphasising the act of masking, partial disclosure of information and the constructedness of truth claims, animation highlights the fact that not everything is seen or made available. Animated documentaries can thus undermine any claims to 'Truth with a capital T', while arousing interest and curiosity in the process. Maureen Burns argues that what is hidden holds a higher truth than what is visible. This would suggest that, despite its only partial disclosure of information, animation can still be deemed believable. Burns explains that a sense of the invisible 'evokes what we both don't know and the traces, the excess, the supplement to our established structures of knowledge. It is the crumb line leading us to a suspicion that there must be more to the visual landscape'. According to her, semi-revelation encourages a perpetual desire to uncover what may be hidden.[59] Animated documentaries, which highlight the sense of what is not seen and disclosed as part of their masked visual representation – especially those that emphasise construction and evoke a sense of realism as defamiliarisation – thus evoke a similar sense of the deficiency of the information presented, and heighten awareness of what is lacking. This means that certainty is replaced by a variety of overlapping options and interpretation is always awaiting additional revelation. The ability of animation to tantalise viewers creates an opacity of meaning that precludes satisfaction and thus preserves the search for a so-called 'truth'. In the era of post-truth, the ability and habit of critically evaluating information before accepting it as true is vital in order to create a counter-narrative to stories that appear in the media. This is a crucial aspect of the fight against a post-truth world where 'media fragmentation, information bias, the decline of objectivity . . . [creates a] threat not just to knowing the truth but to the idea of truth itself'.[60] The concept of masking thus embodies major contemporary characteristics of mistrust and confusion. However, it also illuminates the huge potential of animation as a defamiliarising documentary aesthetic that encourages active spectatorship and the ongoing search for additional truths, which in turn leads to a more complex understanding of the limits of knowledge and critical reflection regarding representation more widely.

To conclude, when discussing animated documentaries' engagement with the current information environment and its relation to realism, it is animation's 'in-between' cultural status between fact and fiction, exposure and disguise, overfamiliarity and defamiliarisation, that makes animation so relevant and important as a contemporary documentary aesthetic. Contemplating contemporaneity in terms of the constant tension between revelation and concealment of information makes animation as a documentary aesthetic that embodies precisely this phenomenon an important and useful self-reflexive tool with which to engage with the zeitgeist. These evolving trends in contemporary non-fiction visual culture shape viewers' understanding of 'factual' information and their corresponding worldviews. Animated documentaries that evoke realism as defamiliarisation remind viewers that we cannot be sure of what is being presented and that it is our role to search further and make sense of what we are watching. This form of realism is both an important way to reflect but also shape reality as it is in the process of becoming. In an era of fake news where it is vital to maintain awareness and sharpen criticality in order to prevent *re*-presentation becoming invisible it has become crucial to address these issues.

Notes

1. Armstrong, 'On the Border', p. 34.
2. Leslie and McKim, 'Life Remade', p. 207.
3. For more on animation's intermediate status see Ehrlich, 'Indeterminate and Intermediate'.
4. This is clearly a partial list. For more on the ontological and epistemological aspects of realism and appearances in the theories of central Western philosophers, see Yolton, *Realism and Appearances*. For a social and ethical perspective on realism through representation in recent decades, see Roberts, *Art of Interruption*

and Reinhardt and Edwards, *Beautiful Suffering*. For a semantic discussion of realism, see Wollen, *Signs and Meaning*. For more on perception theory and the changing cultural role and context of the observer, see Crary, *Techniques of the Observer*. For an introduction to the discourse of humanism versus posthumanism and the role of the human–world relation versus other object-oriented ontologies, see Meillassoux, *After Finitude* and Bogost, *Alien Phenomenology*.

5. See, for example, Strøm, 'Animated Documentary'; Rowley, 'Life Reproduced in Drawings'; Sofian, 'Truth in Pictures'; Nichols, 'Documentary Reenactment'; Skoller, 'Introduction to Special Issue'; Kriger, *Animated Realism*; Honess Roe, *Animated Documentary*; Formenti, 'Sincerest Form of Docudrama'.
6. Ward, 'Videogames as Remediated Animation', p. 125.
7. Latour, 'Emancipation or Attachments?' p. 317. Added emphasis.
8. Hauser, *Social History*, p. 182.
9. For more on the politics and animation, see Herhuth, 'Animation and Politics'.
10. Lind and Steyerl, *Greenroom*, p. 19.
11. Ritchin, *After Photography*, pp. 139, 161.
12. D'Ancona, *Post-Truth*, p. 20.
13. For more information see Murray, 'Waltz with Bashir'; Stewart, 'Screen Memory'; Landesman and Bendor, 'Animated Recollection'; Peaslee, 'It's Fine as Long as You Draw'; Stav, 'Nakba and Holocaust'; Ten Brink, 'Animating Trauma'; Honess Roe, *Animated Documentary*; Morag, *Waltzing with Bashir*; Land, 'Animating the Other Side'; Kraemer, '*Waltz with Bashir* (2008)'; Bolaki, 'Animated Documentary'. See also Introduction, note 55, for a list of further academic publications and events in this subject area.
14. See Davidson, 'Waltz and Interview'; Harsin, 'Responsible Dream'; Garrett, 'Screen Memory'; Peaslee, 'It's Fine as Long as You Draw'. This is not to say that animated documentary did not exist prior to *Waltz with Bashir* but, because of its wide critical acclaim, this film was a first for most audiences unfamiliar with the sub-genre's history, which is covered in Annabelle Honess Roe's excellent *Animated Documentary* (2013).
15. For additional details and examples see Honess Roe, *Animated Documentary*, pp. 8–9; Shale, *Donald Duck Joins Up*; Raiti, 'Disappearance of Disney Animated Propaganda'.
16. I am not implying that photography is in any way 'direct' since it too has a long history of manipulation, and photography's truth-value has been destabilised in recent decades, culminating in today's widespread awareness of image manipulation. This is, however, beyond the scope of this chapter. I refer to photography here as still the most visible aesthetic used in documentary, despite the many debates surrounding its authenticity.
17. Gunning, 'Truthiness and the More Real', p. 185.
18. See www.bbc.com/news/av/world-europe-34516436/mh17-crash-dutch-safety-board-animation-shows-path-of-missile, accessed 4 August 2020.
19. Honess Roe, 'Against Animated Documentary?' p. 24.
20. The relationship between sound and image is a huge field in its own right

that exceeds the scope of this book. Here I focus on animation as a visual medium, but for those interested in the aural content, see Honess Roe, *Animated Documentary*.
21. Cramerotti, *Aesthetic Journalism*, p. 23.
22. See Formenti, 'Sincerest Form of Docudrama'; Honess Roe, *Animated Documentary*, p. 171; Ward, 'Animated Realities', p. 19.
23. Gunning, 'Truthiness and the More Real', p. 184.
24. Ibid., p. 178.
25. Brecht, *Brecht on Theatre*, pp. 108–12.
26. Waldberg, *Surrealism*, p. 8.
27. Levy, *Surrealism*, p. 9.
28. Cramerotti, *Aesthetic Journalism*, p. 22.
29. Ritchin, *After Photography*, p. 146.
30. Honess Roe, 'Interjections and Connections', p. 283.
31. Schofield, 'Playing with Evidence', pp. 53–4.
32. *Snack and Drink*, film, directed by Bob Sabiston (USA: Flat Black Films, 1999).
33. *Ryan*, film, directed by Chris Landreth (Canada: Copperheart Entertainment, 2004).
34. *In the Same Boat*, film, directed by Martha Stiegman (Canada: Martha Stiegman, 2007).
35. *I was a Child of Holocaust Survivors*, film, directed by Ann Marie Fleming (Canada: National Film Board of Canada, 2010).
36. *The Wanted 18*, film, directed by Paul Cowan and Amer Shomali (Canada, Palestine and France: Bellota Films, Dar Films Productions, Intuitive Pictures and National Film Board of Canada, 2014).
37. *Tower*, film, directed by Keith Maitland (USA: Go-Valley and ITVS, 2016).
38. *Another Planet*, film, directed by Amir Yatziv's (Israel: Amir Yatziv and Jonathan Doweck, 2017).
39. *Stranger Comes to Town*, film, directed by Jacqueline Goss (USA, 2007).
40. McIntyre, *Post-truth*, pp. 162–3.
41. For more information see Massumi, *Parables for the Virtual*.
42. Deleuze, *Cinema 2*, pp. 76–7.
43. Wells, 'Beautiful Village and True Village', pp. 41–4.
44. Foster, 'On the Art'.
45. Armstrong, 'On the Border', p. 56.
46. Lambert-Beatty, 'Make Believe', p. 118.
47. Ibid., pp. 137, 141.
48. Ward, 'Animated Realities', p. 19.
49. Lind and Steyerl, *Greenroom*, p. 15.
50. Ibid., p. 22.
51. Ward, 'Videogames as Remediated Animation', p. 125.
52. See Ehrlich, 'Animated Documentaries as Masking'.
53. This is similar to Honess Roe's conceptualisation of mimetic and non-mimetic substitution. Honess Roe, *Animated Documentary*, pp. 22–6.

54. *Audrie & Daisy*, film, directed by Bonni Cohen and Jon Shenk (USA: Actual Film, 2016).
55. For more on the production of the film, see Wakeman, 'Life After Sexual Assault'.
56. Beckman, 'Animation on Trial', p. 266.
57. Ibid., p. 267.
58. Leigh and Harding, *Wikileaks*, p. 247.
59. Burns, 'Invisibility', p. 148.
60. McIntyre, *Post-Truth*, p. 153.

Epilogue

This book explored how contemporary technoculture has transformed the relation between animation and documentary. Whereas the discussion started from the point that animated documentary's reception was complex due to a perceived gap between the on-screen animated world and the physical surroundings of the viewer, this should now be reconsidered. My analysis of the rising visibility of animation in non-fiction and shifting documentary conventions (Chapter 1), animation techniques and their potential status as document and/or evidence (Chapter 2), and ubiquitous screen culture (Chapter 3) illustrates that viewer reception of animation as credible is gradually changing. As we have seen in contemporary mixed realities, the animated and physical worlds are converging, so using animation as documentary is not only reasonable and valid, but also essential.

In Chapters 4 to 6, I identified three kinds of virtual documentaries that use animation and blur the boundaries between contemporary mixed realities: documenting animated virtual game realities; the in-game depiction of non-game physical realities wherein the two converge; and the use of virtual aesthetics, such as interactivity and real-time animated visualisation, to depict physical events, as in documentary games and VR simulations. Taken together, these illustrate the immense influence of wider technocultural characteristics on changes in documentary production and reception, and the varied potential ramifications of this phenomenon one must be aware of, as discussed in Chapters 7 and 8.

A recurring theme throughout the book is that realism, as a believable articulation of actuality, is no longer necessarily linked to visual realism/mimesis. Instead, there are cultural reasons why non-photorealistic animation can and should be used to depict realities that are not physical (and therefore would only be limited by photographic and photorealistic imagery), as well as technological developments that support the use of animation to depict contemporary mixed and virtual realities. These include real-time visualisations of user input and/or immersion that supplement non-photorealistic imagery with various other reality effects meant to contribute to a work's credibility.

Here I will focus on a recent thought-provoking animated documentary that reflects several of the central issues covered by this book. *Another Planet* (2017),¹ introduced in Chapter 5, brings together different CG animated simulations of the Auschwitz-Birkenau concentration camp that aim to simulate the camp authentically despite their non-photorealistic appearance and constructed nature, and recover something of the historical events by offering new insights and interactive experiences for viewers. *Another Planet* follows the creators of these different simulations of Auschwitz-Birkenau, which include: a German prosecution office whose 360-degree investigative simulation is meant for forensic purposes in the trial of a ninety-four-year-old defendant; an Israeli historian and German architect who have been surveying the camp for fifteen years in an attempt to create an accurate black and white architectural reconstruction for museum and education purposes; a flight simulation scenario created by Israeli high school students for the purpose of virtually re-enacting the 2003 Israeli Air Force flight over the camp; an Israeli software developer whose belief in reincarnation has inspired him to attempt to re-create his past life experiences as a Sonderkommando during the holocaust in an online role-playing game, Prisoner Revolt;² and a Polish graphic designer who created a photorealistic VR experience of the camp for 'maximum realism'.

The film's montage moves between the different simulations while interviewing the creators, who often appear as avatars, about their reasons for virtually reconstructing the camp. They all discuss the goal of realism, attempting to provide an experience that is as close as possible to the 'real thing': 'Gradually, a deeper layer of the film is revealed: the obsession with reconstructing the "Other Planet" – or the insatiable urge to document and enrich the historical and cultural memory of the Holocaust.'³ However, the film is not about the holocaust. Rather, it is an exploration of contemporary non-fiction representation in digital culture. In an era when many animated documentaries function as eye candy that merely visualises the soundtrack, *Another Planet* emphasises discrepancies in representation and consequently forces viewers to question the limits of what can be shown, what is said to be shown versus what can actually be seen, and what kind of truth claims can be made through animated depictions of non-fiction. What is the role and significance of animation as a representational choice within this documentary and the virtual simulations it depicts, and how does this correspond with the main themes of this book?

Although the book has raised ontological questions about the nature of contemporaneity and 'the real', it is mainly concerned with the issue of visuality, that is, the relation of animation to documentary aesthetics. Contemplating animated documentaries in today's technological settings and the changing role of animation as a contemporary visual language leads back to the three key areas detailed in the introduction, in which the impact of animation on documentary discourse can be most clearly observed and will be demonstrated through the analysis of *Another Planet*. The three main themes, corresponding to the three parts of the book, are: (1) the evidentiary status of animation as documentary imagery, which contemplates animation's truth-value and believability in relation to photography and photorealism/mimesis; this requires an understanding of what animation has become and how it is being used. Redefining animation from a documentary perspective demonstrates just how far animation has come since its earlier uses, techniques and association with fiction; (2) the virtualisation of culture and virtual documentaries, which examines present developments in technoculture and focuses on how these changes have influenced our understanding of evidence, documentation and new uses of animation in documentary. This includes the relation between animation and the augmentation of reality through technology and virtualisation, and the subsequent need for documentary visualisations that capture this enhanced reality; and (3) disputing the aesthetics of 'the real', which questions how animation in documentary relates to issues of believability, and varied notions of realism. Since realism is linked to credibility but also relates to viewers' understanding of reality as shaped by documentary representation, this has varied ethical, epistemological and political ramifications.

THE EVIDENTIARY STATUS OF NON-PHOTOREALISTIC ANIMATION AS DOCUMENTARY IMAGERY

Another Planet uses animation in several multi-layered ways, redefining animation's relation to documents and documentary representation and reflecting upon the role of visual mimesis in representations attempting realism. First, the film begins with the quote 'I remind you to record video, not stills'. Although this raises expectations of photographic footage, viewers are presented with an animated depiction of an Israeli military aircraft. The supposedly contradictory allusion to photography juxtaposed with obviously constructed animated imagery creates uncertainty from the start and corresponds to the recurring comparison between animation and photography in documentary.[4] Thus the best way to capture and commemorate an event immediately becomes the focus of the film, leading us to ask what is the best or most believable visual language to be used. This raises many questions about authenticity of representation and changing assumptions about documentary aesthetics and visual realism.

Each simulation covered in the film was created for different reasons and uses diverse representational choices. Nonetheless, each of the creators interviewed discusses his or her particular goal of realism, attempting to provide an experience that is as close as possible to the 'real thing'. The Bavarian investigator interviewed in the forensic model, for example, claims that it is 'even more precise than Google Earth', whereas the architectural digital model is described by its creators as 'not approximate. It's exact . . . we are covered in terms of historical precision.' Similarly, the creator of the Prisoner Revolt game explains that the sign at the camp entrance is 'based on an original image. Same font, same sign', whereas the VR model is labelled by its creator as 'one of the most accurate reconstructions'. Interestingly, all of the simulations are animated, none of them resemble photorealism, and all are obviously constructed imagery, yet the creators all claim authenticity through visual means. However, it is that very claim that results in a foregrounding of the endless gaps and inaccuracies in the film, and the *in*ability to represent what is supposedly being, or claimed to be, shown. The result of these claims to visual realism is an emphasis on the *lack* of visual mimesis, highlighting the contradiction involved and the consequent questioning of what realism is when it is referred to so inconsistently.

Second, *Another Planet* demonstrates how animation has changed as a representational language in digital culture. As virtual interactive platforms flourish, the use of animation grows and transforms. In current virtualised computer culture, images are used as a symbolic language that renders visible abstract data or processes with which we engage and act upon. Many aspects of contemporary digital virtual culture appear only on screen and, therefore, require representation that enables real-time dynamic visualisation of user

Figure E.1 *Another Planet*, an animated documentary by Amir Yatziv, 2017.

input. Animation is perfect for this role and, as such, features widely online. If I am active in a virtual space, my representation in-screen, whether by cursor/mouse or highly stylised avatar, is an animated reference that embodies my physical actions and input.[5] Thus, animation is a central visual language in contemporary digital culture, and specifically in interactive media, which takes on interesting significance in documentary studies.

As explained in Chapter 5, in *Another Planet*, the use of animation is twofold: it is *both* the visual language used in *each* simulation as part of the inherent appearance of the referent (the virtual and interactive simulation online); and it is also the cinematic representational choice (this is an animated documentary *about* these simulations). It is the virtual platform's façade/GUI but also, and differently, the film's representational choice. It is both document*ing* animation and document*ary* animation. As a documentary, *Another Planet* uses animation as equated with photography (which captures the visual appearance of physical referents), only in this case the animation captures the virtual rather than the physical occurrences depicted. The final credits even state that *Another Planet* was 'filmed' in the following virtual locations, emphasising the blurred boundaries that now exist between animation and photography and what *can* be photographed. Thus, the uses of animation in this film demonstrate animation's new role as document in today's virtual culture.

The centrality of animation in virtualised culture, as a sign that indicates the physical movements and input of users, cements its central representational role in the arena of human–computer interactions. Interestingly, animation as a contemporary index as trace relies on the physical but does not necessarily resemble the referent since it acts as a trace of one's physical actions but does not necessarily look anything like them, as in the case of a game avatar or cursor. Honess Roe proposes that iconicity may take the place of the indexical; she describes an epistemological blurring of icon and index, whereby 'we do perhaps still take the iconic as evidence of witnessable events, illustrated by the use of animation in forensic contexts'.[6] I would, however, emphasise that although recognisability of a sign is important, in animated indices of virtual platforms the trace of movement of the user remains but the image may appear more like an arbitrary symbol than any recognisable icon, since the user's online appearance may vary greatly.[7]

Maintaining the importance of the index as a basis for documents, and thus documentaries, engenders what I refer to as a *post-photographic* mentality. I do not mean this in the sense of a post-photographic era when digital production methods and a growing awareness of potential image manipulation have established digital photography as a new medium. Rather, that in this post-photographic aesthetic, the logic of the photographic based on indexical trace is maintained, though not the photographic aesthetics that rely on resemblance. Honess Roe, whose work I found inspiring, seems to propose a 'pre-photographic' logic whereby what is similar in appearance to the referent is considered sufficient, an observation that views animated documentary in a manner that echoes the attitude to drawing and modes of visualisation that predate photography.[8] Here, the emergence of a post-photographic logic is emphasised since the elements that made photography credible – specifically, its analogue relation as trace of the physical – are maintained, while the aesthetics of photography are modified. This explains the significance of animation as physical trace in a documentary theory based on indexicality. It also allows for visual changes that embrace the symbolic in an increasingly virtualised culture that is less reliant on the appearance of the physical, since presence now also refers to in-screen actions symbolised by myriad, stylised referents.

In other words, as the virtual becomes another aspect of contemporary mixed realities that now include both the physical and the virtual, new aesthetics of documentary that exceed the capacity of photography (that relies on and resembles material reality) are increasingly necessary.[9] It is not that new animation techniques replace photography; rather, the two converge and contemporary animation must be consequently redefined since it maintains aspects of photography's perceived evidentiary value, that is, indexicality as a link to the physical, while introducing new aesthetics that break with photorealism.

The ongoing discussion surrounding the definition of animation is an integral characteristic of the field itself, a growing and dynamic area of theoretical and technical knowledge. Nichols's distinction between documentary and fiction asserts that documentary addresses '*the* world in which we live rather than *a* world imagined by the filmmaker'.[10] As explained in Chapter 2, this corresponds with Wells's definition of animation, which also differentiates between the animated world and that of the viewer. In his attempt to define the key properties of animation, Wells points to those specific characteristics of animation that express its separateness from the lived physical world of the viewer.[11] However, today's technologies demand a reconsideration of key binaries, including the opposition between live action and animation, and between the worlds of the physical and the animated. In brief, this book demonstrates that a redefinition of animation is needed following technological developments, virtualisation and changes in animation's usage, most tellingly in relation to real-time animation in virtual settings, as summarised in Table E.1.

These changes in animation production and theorisation are the basis for the shift from animated documentaries to documentary animation introduced in Chapter 4. To clarify, I use 'animated documentaries' as a more

Table E.1 Comparison of animation in the past with animation today.

Animation in the past	Documentary capture animation today (capture of virtual and mixed realities)
Associated with fiction	Animated realities become part of the contemporary real, which includes the physical and digitally virtual
Lengthy production process	Real-time animation provides immediate visualisation
Visualising the animator's subjectivity	Visualisation of code
Marker of absence	An indication of presence and interactivity by representing users' actions
A physically non-indexical visual language that breaks the link with the physical referent[a]	A deictic index as well as an indexical trace of the physical referent

Note: [a]This does not include theorisations of animation that focus on the creator's traces in the animation but refers to an indexical link to the referent portrayed.

general term that can include animated depictions of physical events as well as any other hybrid form of animation used in documentary. I specifically refer to 'documentary capture animation' as a direct recording of animated realities that have no other visual appearance, such as virtual environments. Thus it is a direct rather than visually interpreted or stylised representation of events that would otherwise appear in a different form. The capturing of events in virtual animated realities produces an entirely new form of animated documentary; and this new form differs from the subjective and fantastical interpretations of events that have formed the focus of existing research into animated documentaries. Whereas past assumptions about, and theorisations of, animation may have challenged its use in documentary contexts, 'documentary capture animation' reshapes these conventions.

THE RELATIONSHIP OF ANIMATION TO TECHNOCULTURE

The merging of physical and virtual realities leads to an augmented view and experience of reality that exceed the merely physical.[12] Enhanced reality is enabled by technology and has become ubiquitous due to personal portable screens and Wi-Fi. These new experiences of contemporary reality must be translated into new and suitable documentary aesthetics. The impact of advanced technology on daily life is such that transcending the limitations of photography in documentary is an inevitable necessity.[13] It is vital for the documentary to remain a relevant and 'realistic' depiction of contemporary realities for two reasons: first, the need for documentary aesthetics which can capture realities that are non-physical; and second, the need for aesthetics which can visually represent the augmented experience of the physical that has emerged from contemporary omnipresent technology. Portable smart technology has become an extension of the self and a portal to other realms, enabling users to 'be' in the physical and virtual worlds simultaneously. Excluding animation from contemporary documentaries would result in their failure to represent these mixed realities. Furthermore, as discussed in Chapters 5 and 6 through the case studies of *Another Planet* and interactive animated documentaries, virtual simulations are increasingly used to represent and even explore physical spaces, reflecting the changing the relationship between the two realms.

Another reason animation is needed is that smart technology increasingly provides augmented views of physical realities. Thus, it is essential to find new means of representing realities that transcend the limitations of photography as the traditional documentary aesthetic; especially as photography only captures partial aspects of contemporary experience. Get Taxi, like Uber, is a useful example of the ubiquitous use of virtual aesthetics to depict physical realities. First developed for military training and communications, real-time 3D computer graphics technology now pervades and guides our lives.[14] The animated, non-physical space on screen merges with the physical world of the user, which is tracked in real time on screen and concludes when the animated icon that users follow as they wait for the cab turns into a real-life taxi. 'Now that you have more X-Ray Vision than Superman, you can kick back and get up only when your taxi pulls up' is how the Get Taxi's app describes its services.[15] The allusion to enhanced or non-human vision this system incorporates echoes this book's engagement with the way technology shapes vision, representation and consequently also conceptions of realism.

Thanks to smart personal technology, reality extends beyond one's immediate vicinity, or what is perceivable 'organically', and includes a fuller augmented view and/or understanding of reality. To quote Fred Ritchin, 'today . . . we have multiple visions through machines . . . each eye watches a different world'.[16] Examples presented throughout the book (such as augmented reality apps and wearable technology) emphasise the constant split between human vision of the physical world on the one hand, and a mediated visual interpretation on the other. The latter enhances one's ability to see and construe the world, combining the technologically mediated with the physical world we inhabit. This augmented experiencing of reality can best be conveyed visually in documentary form by animation's capacity to portray reality as multi-layered, beyond what can be directly perceived or photographed. As today's mixed realities continue to converge, I believe AR will become increasingly prevalent, as will the documentary of future realities in which animation – alongside (and often in equal measure to) the physical – adds layers to what we see and experience. Thus, we will see a growing need for animation in documentary contexts.

Finally, in an era defined by a vast proliferation of data, animation enables the incorporation in documentaries of non-physical aspects based on information that photography cannot capture and users cannot access. In an era of 'big data', it comes as no surprise that documentaries, which aim to reflect, question and shape reality, already make extensive use of animation, dynamic diagrams and data visualisation in the form of instructive films and graphs. These visualisations are needed as simplified summaries of the vast amounts of data that have become part of the way we consume information. These remix the techniques and methods of representation and expression of other media into what Lev Manovich calls a 'meta-medium' that combines 'cinematography, animation, computer animation, special effects, graphic design, and typography'.[17] In the field of forensic animation, such as in the work by Forensic Architecture for example, data demonstration can explore and uncover otherwise imperceptible patterns and evidence, and illustrate what-if scenarios, testing competing hypotheses and possibly exposing inconsistencies and discrepancies in the evidence being examined. This is closely related to the way animation is used to construct broader views of realities, which incorporate several layers of information that would be imperceptible in an unmediated or direct representation. Thus depictions of realities that include the physical as well as the technologically augmented require documentary visualisations exceeding both human perception and photography. The way technology influences the experience of realities impacts the documentary strategies used for representation; this helps to explain the influence of animation on documentary practice more generally. In other words, animation enables the expansion of both reality and documentary aesthetics simultaneously.

Disputing the Aesthetics of the Real

Any discussion of believable documentary aesthetics raises questions about the relation between the actual, or real, and its representation. This entails a consideration of realism, as the believable representation of what constitutes reality – a central theme in documentary theory – and requires us to reflect on the composition of both 'the real' and its document (or a link to the reality portrayed) to evoke a sense of truth-value and credibility. In my analysis of the existing discourse on realism – which is characterised by ongoing tension between reliance on mimesis versus the unending search for new forms of representation to articulate 'the real' – I focused on what could evoke believability for the viewer, regardless of formal qualities (Chapters 1 to 2).

By grounding this project in the technocultural context of current visual culture, it is clear that growing reliance on technology, and on mediated, augmented and machine vision, results in 'synthetic' images to which viewers become increasingly accustomed; these include many 'non-human' views of the world. This multiplicity of viewpoints and aesthetics that represent reality leads to a distancing away from mimesis and towards shifting criteria of realism which, in turn, make way for new documentary aesthetics like animation. Thus, animation is no longer tied to photography as its counterpart as it once was, but is rather open to myriad other emerging representational forms. Moreover, by using new imaging technologies, contemporary animation changes the relation between technological tools and human animators. Not only does it refer to new technologies of image production, it links the stylisation of animation to machine aesthetics rather than to the omnipotent animator as artist/designer; this takes our understanding of animation in new directions and offers potential openings for future research.[18]

If realistic imagery is no longer necessarily tied to mimesis, what contributes to the sense of realism in representation? Animation's realism has been theorised before but analysing the topic in light of today's technological culture sheds new light.[19] This book has illustrated how animation can be deemed realistic in an era of technological augmentation of human perception that changes how 'the real' may appear visually (Chapter 1): as a more direct and less interpretive visual language when used in documentaries of virtual rather than physical realities (Chapter 4); as a dynamic visual language responsive to real-time user input that heightens vividness in interactive documentaries, such as documentary games and VR (Chapter 6);[20] as a defamiliarising representational mechanism that can both de-sensitise and re-sensitise viewers – this has major implications for documentary aesthetics that aim for a political sense of realism as shapers of realities (Chapters 7 to 8). The many faces of animation's relation to realism contribute to the discussion of animation as a documentary aesthetic.

Animated documentaries such as *Another Planet* contribute to these debates by emphasising the potential power of animation while also reflecting upon what the best or most acceptable form of representation is for documentary and commemoration, and who has the authority to decide. *Another Planet* highlights the fact that realism as the believable articulation of reality (and what is deemed culturally acceptable, for that matter) has evolved and been regularly reincarnated, permanently mutating and questioned. For example, the architect and historian who created the architectural model of the camp for education and museum purposes explain their decision to use black and white imagery: 'Auschwitz was not black and white . . . but the museum was concerned it would be like some comic book.' For people familiar with the remarkable evolution of comics and graphic novels, such as *Maus* by Art Spiegelman or *Palestine* by Joe Sacco, this seems a strange stance.[21] However, this book has similarly illustrated the transformation and contradictory reception of animation, demonstrating that despite animation's varied history, exponential rise and wide-ranging content, something of its assumed link to fiction, childhood, humour and light-heartedness persists. As quoted in the introduction, Keith Maitland, the creator of *Tower*,[22] described his hesitation about reaching out to survivors with the idea of portraying their trauma in animated form.[23] This book also demonstrates how varied contemporary media that engage with documentary such as virtual simulations or varied forms of interactive documentary such as VR and games are also continuously evolving.

Another Planet engages with these issues by questioning what is deemed an 'acceptable' form of digital memory construction and why? In a parallel way to comics and animation, the film raises similar questions about games, seen as different from 'serious' re-enactments, and questions the validity of this judgement. By including *Prisoner Revolt*, a pixelated computer game reminiscent of early first-person shooter games such as *Doom* from 1993, which intentionally portrays the prisoners' revolt in the camp in a gory and disturbing way, the film touches upon the evolving field of games, which is also a salient characteristic of digital culture. Once seen as mere entertainment for children and adolescents, the gaming industry today is the largest among all media, spanning all age groups and content, and engendering endless spheres of academic research. Nonetheless, as the film notes, the *only* re-enactment to be attacked by the Anti-Defamation League was the game. Were the League's criteria for appropriateness the source of the representation, its visual style, the violence depicted, or perhaps the traditional view of games as entertainment and thus considered disrespectful in this case? The latter would certainly disregard the major transformation of the serious game industry and the topics it now tackles. Is a forensic model built by the German police so different from a game exploring actual historical events? Who decides what a tolerable and respectful representation is, and what the criteria are for defining it as such? Is it the source that created the game, in this case the Bavarian police, or is it a matter of visual choices such as pixelated versus more realistic animation? Are these valid criteria? As technologies change and new modes of representation develop, these are important questions to explore.

As discussed in Chapter 8, realism is constantly in flux and we need to remember that, despite a desire for transparency, all we ever have access to is representation. *Another Planet* eliminates any illusion of transparency by celebrating the discrepancies of representation, reminding viewers that no representation is transparent or direct but always constructed. *That* is the potential power of animation as a documentary aesthetic that encourages self-reflexive and critical viewing. For example, in *Another Planet*'s seemingly most 'serious' simulations, created by the German police and used in the legal system, the prosecutor describes the trial of a ninety-four-year-old man suspected of collaborating with the Nazis. He had worked in the kitchen, and claims that he did not know what took place in the camp. The simulation was therefore used to ascertain what he could have seen from the kitchen, using the model to check angles of perception and reach a conclusion about what would have been visible. However, as the police investigator describes the investigation into what could be seen from *within* the kitchen, viewers of the film are shown an old man outside of the kitchen *looking in*, thus contradicting the point of the case about what he could see looking *out*. This image questions what we are shown and what we are told versus what we can *really* see? Is the image of a man looking *in* when he should be seen looking *out* a metaphor for the viewers (and the entire legal system), trying to gain insight into something to which we have no access, and thus being reminded of our limited ability to really see or know? By emphasising inconsistencies, the film not only presents the historical simulations but *re*-presents them in a way that questions representation, the construction of memory and truth claims more widely.

The film ends with the creator of the architectural model looking at his avatar and saying that his avatar for the film's interview looks nothing like him (see book cover image). He concludes with 'Do whatever you want', leaving the viewer wondering how much creative freedom Amir Yatziv, the filmmaker, allowed himself, and for what purpose. In fact, what remains unclear throughout the film is the relationship between the virtual platforms as they were generated by their makers, and the way in which Yatziv, the film's creator, uses them for his own purposes. The unclear gaps are generated by, for example, the use of the camp's simulations as ready-made sets open to alterations and opportunities for virtual puppeteering of avatars created externally. In other words, since these are virtual models of the camp meant to enable open-ended exploration for personalised experiences, the filmmaker stretches the boundaries of clear representation by combining conventional documentary strategies such as interviews with more creative approaches to exploring the limits of the virtual camps through his own reconstruction of events within them, for example, using a music video in the pixelated Minecraft version of the camp. What, then, is captured, what is constructed, and what role do these virtual reconstructions and animated representations play in cementing memories for simulation users and viewers of the film (and of the holocaust itself)? The changing cultural roles of animation and its multiple layers in the film act as a reflection about representation more widely. Ending on this note raises more questions than answers, but this is the point of the film. By creating deliberate misrepresentations that make the viewer think, the film questions the role of visual evidence and highlights the viewer's ability both to notice such discrepancies and to take responsibility for contemplating them further. This lays emphasis on the viewer's role, which brings me to the importance of such work and analysis in the post-truth era.

In an era of truthiness where notions of what is true are based on emotion and persuasion more than fact and evidence, the viewer is central. By emphasising the viewer and the shifting roles of animation, films such as *Another Planet* remind us that critical viewing remains vital in order to notice and question information representation and create counter-narratives to what may be deemed as 'truth' by seemingly authoritative sources. Such films allow us to explore the questions that animation raises in relation to visual signification, viewer reception and new forms of aesthetic and political realism, and what some of the implications may be of this paradigmatic shift in visual culture. This is especially important to consider now, as the roles, uses and visibility of animation change and proliferate in digital culture.

WHERE TO FROM HERE?

As animation is increasingly incorporated into non-fiction, during the period covered by this book, the effect on viewers is complex and multi-layered. The unsettling effects of animated documentaries as masks and crystal images have positive spectatorial impact that can lead to defamiliarisation, re-sensitisation and more critical viewing.[24] The contemporary viewer is thus constantly reminded of the mediated nature of information, and of the need to actively consider the problematics of transparency and analysis presented as 'truth'. However, once animation becomes a familiar documentary aesthetic it will lose its potency as an aesthetic that disrupts, raises questions, and mitigates against apathetic viewing, and may return full circle to being associated with fabrication. But until that happens, animation will occupy a contradictory position: although there are now many reasons to accept it as no longer fiction, to maintain its advantages as a documentary visual language that creates alienation, something of the old paradigm must be preserved. If animation were accepted without question, it would be the perfect visual language for disinformation, able to construct any image to then be uncritically accepted as true.[25] Wider, more mundane use of animation and the ubiquity of screens may boost desensitised documentary viewing, and the distancing effect of animated depiction that no longer shocks and re-sensitises may lead to ever-greater indifference *vis-à-vis* the depiction of atrocities.

Figure E.2 Screenshot from *Black Mirror*, 'Fifteen Million Merits' episode, created by Charlie Brooker, 2011.

Some of these concerns are reflected in the dystopian futuristic British television drama series *Black Mirror* (2011–present),[26] created by Charlie Brooker, who has described the series as being, 'all about the way we live now – and the way we might be living in 10 minutes' time if we're clumsy'.[27] The 'Fifteen Million Merits' episode from 2011 describes a society's insatiable thirst for distraction and depicts a world in which almost everything is mediated by animation. Animation is used in this dystopian culture as spectacle, a way to dumb down daily existence through continuous simulations. It depicts what remains of public spaces in which alienated subjects, who are physically shut in cells made of screens, participate only as animated avatars that are individualised through animated merchandise bought with actual currency, or 'merits'. Although this may seem extreme, it is easy to see the resemblance to our own already highly technologised culture characterised by omnipresent attention-capturing animation, lonely alienated people who spend most of their time alone facing screens, interacting only virtually with others, and increasingly represented by avatars.

The global lockdowns following the outbreak of the coronavirus pandemic in late 2019 clarified just how accurate this situation has become. During lockdown many people experienced the centrality of in-screen existence, as screens became vital portals for different experiences when physical space and actions were restricted. In May 2020, for example, since physical attendance at a graduation ceremony became impossible, University of California (Berkeley) students built the virtual Blockeley University in the popular Minecraft video game where more than 100 buildings have been meticulously reinvented. It is in this animated online version of their university that hundreds of graduates held a virtual ceremony that included a speech by the Chancellor and Vice Chancellor along with the conferring of degrees, followed by a two-day Blockeley Music Festival, all livestreamed on Twitch.[28] The captured Twitch footage acts as a document of the event, combining live-action with animation.[29] Similarly, although the online chat services of Zoom (Zoom Video Communications, Inc.) skyrocketed in popularity during the COVID-19 lockdowns, many users felt that the limited options of Zoom led to frustration since professional, personal and entertainment meetings all became unbearably similar in atmosphere. As a result, gaming environments and virtual reality have become strong alternatives to video calls whereby people can feel they are sharing the same space together. These VR spaces can be designed in endless ways for countless atmospheres and events, ranging from socialising to medical simulation training and team collaboration, all using diverse visualisations and avatars.[30] These recent examples demonstrate the growing use and visibility of animated platforms and game worlds for the creation of wide-ranging actual events and actions that may have been experienced in the physical world in the past but have now transformed into mixed reality experiences, visualised in varied animated styles.

As in *Black Mirror*, in Ari Folman's partly animated film *The Congress* (2013),[31] new technology enables people to transform themselves into animated avatars. While they are enjoying themselves in this mutable illusory state, the world is deteriorating around them. This sense of distance and desensitised viewing already exists and may be altered momentarily by new visualisations of information as with masking or crystal images. As animation becomes increasingly widespread and conventionalised, however, will an ever-greater apathy develop? Will apathy increase because any content can be easily disregarded as false as a result of visual signifiers' unclear criteria for truth-value, and the fact that people are not even depicted as human but rather in a variety of animated forms?

There are clearly many reasons for animation's growing visibility and credibility in contemporary non-fiction and documentary, though its changing uses and reception have many potential implications worth considering. What is important to clarify is that in an era when photorealism has lost the privilege of veracity, animation that does not attempt photorealism achieves validity; when what appears real is not necessarily so, mimesis is simply no longer a preferable aesthetic for truth claims. In an uber-visual culture where viewers have become so accustomed to relying on visual information, what happens when all criteria for an image's veracity is destabilised and lost? This is an entirely new paradigm that must be considered. Once mimesis becomes destabilised in the discourse on visual realism, form is no longer fixed. In the current digital media sphere of post-truth, knowing is replaced by believing and reliable truth criteria are unclear. This opens up the field to new theorisations of, and experimentation, with signifiers and representations of the past. If photography can be manipulated and if animation is now becoming an increasingly believable mode of delivery for non-fictional content, despite its unlimited stylisations, one must ask whether viewers will potentially believe nothing or everything and if these binaries can be challenged.

In an era when viewers are so accustomed to visual messages—either as a result of omnipresent screens, ubiquitous advertising or masses of data commonly simplified into digestible visual nuggets—the ability to internalise visual information may be on the rise, but the sheer quantity of such messages accompanied by the fast-paced nature of contemporary life means that viewers may lack the complex tools needed for visual literacy or the willingness to decipher the complexity of how visual signs are designed to convey a particular meaning. The rapid reading of visual messages combined with the lack of patience for serious analysis leaves viewers prone to potential misinformation. Interestingly, since both verbal descriptions and photorealistic images are widely doubted, it is the *non*-photorealistic images that are potentially, and frighteningly, more open to misinformation, for a number of reasons: (1) people pick up messages quickly, but (2) they do not necessarily have the tools and visual literacy (or even the patience) to deconstruct them and the nuances they embody; additionally, (3) viewers may become so accustomed to non-photorealistic imagery that its constructed nature may stop playing a part in its interpretation, as is becoming the case when major news sources use animated visuals in re-enactments or as explanatory graphics.

This becomes even more complicated when additional factors, such as machine vision and machine recognition, enter the visual realm. Following the discussion in Chapter 1 about machine vision through which images created, captured and categorised by machines are increasingly visible in contemporary visual culture and non-fiction imagery, we must ask where that leaves human viewers' ability to make sense of them? We are increasingly offered imagery intended to provide proof and inform, but increasingly this imagery eschews any simulation of human perception. Since realism is the believable articulation of reality, what, then, is the most credible form of imaging to evoke a sense of truth-value? Viewers have no way of knowing whether an image, which looks completely different from how it would appear to a human, has been manipulated, or even what exactly it is they are seeing. So, is it reliable? These are huge questions that go beyond animation and thus future directions of research would benefit from the related study of technology's impact on visual culture and the consequent epistemological value of non-fiction imagery.

To read an image closely and make sense of the subtleties being portrayed, understanding the nuances of the visual message represented, one must be able to analyse imagery in an informed manner. This is not to be taken for granted. For these reasons, art history and visual fields of research have become a new and important lens through which to analyse and reflect upon the contemporary. Unlike other fields that increasingly use images to transfer information (such as the sciences), art history can critically reflect upon images – more so than other disciplines, because no image can be read if one has not read other images before.[32] Enhanced skills of visual analysis are crucial for contemporary consumers of information, especially in an age characterised by media disinformation and evolving aesthetics of representation.

To conclude, in Chapter 2 I explained that the definition of animation has expanded over time and now indicates different aspects of 'life forces', including 'awakening' and 'intensifying'.[33] Animation has two meanings, therefore, a theological one pertaining to the bestowing of life, and a secular one that refers to movement and change. This brings me to the title of this book, *Animating Truth*. First of all, documentary depictions have the potential to shape and influence the reality and 'truth' in question, intensifying or 'giving it life' in a certain way, not to mention potentially causing an 'awakening' or awareness in viewers. Second, to some readers the 'animated truth' concept may itself seem intuitively oxymoronic, alluding to the still unclear and persisting association of animation with the fictional and magical, aspects of animation's cultural reception that are central to this book's analysis.

Third, in an era of fake news preoccupied with the unstable notion of truth, the idea of 'animated truth' conveys movement, or a dynamic notion of truth that is constantly shifting. Since metamorphosis is a central characteristic of animation whereby images often morph into one another, emphasising movement and a constant sense of becoming,[34] using animation to contemplate today's shifting notions of truth in animated documentaries makes perfect sense, especially in works that go beyond mere visualisation of the soundtrack by adding complexity through the visual layers that animation facilitates. Animated documentaries such as Michèle Cournoyer's *The Hat* (1999)[35] and Ruth Lingford's 2017 *Trump Dreams*[36] in which the images constantly mutate, use the visual characteristics of animation to question the stability of meaning, a significant metaphor for the fluidity of what is considered truth claims in the post-truth era and the dangers this encompasses.

In this sense animation is a perfect visual tool with which to engage with the slippery nature of today's truth claims. Animation is a most befitting

Figure E.3 *Trump Dream*s by Ruth Lingford, 2017.

visual aesthetic that shares certain features with this constant dynamic and transformative meaning and the consequent need for heightened awareness and epistemological questioning. The notion of animated truth as a dynamic truth, always in motion and constantly changing, relates both to the deictic index that can potentially signify multiple referents simultaneously, avoiding any fixed meaning, and to the title of this book. The emphasis on movement and change thus seems an appropriate note on which to end. So, what is the truth-value of animation as documentary imagery in today's networked digital era? Is it like being innocent until proven guilty, or true until proven false, or should it be perceived as false until proven true? In today's viewing culture, the viewer is arbiter of a representation's truth-value so ultimately it is all up to you. What do you think, is it 'true enough'?

Notes

1. *Another Planet*, film, directed by Amir Yatziv's (Israel: Amir Yatziv and Jonathan Doweck, 2017).
2. The Sonderkommando were work units often comprised of Jewish prisoners who were forced to help dispose of victims' bodies in the Nazi camps.
3. See https://www.torchfilms.com/products/another-planet, accessed 4 August 2020.
4. For different views on the comparison and convergence of animation and photography see, for example, Paul Wells (*Basics Animation*, p. 12); Lev Manovich ('Post-media Aesthetics', p. 295 and *Software Takes Command*, p. 294); Alan

Cholodenko ('"First Principles" of Animation', p. 99); Tom Gunning ('Animating the Instant').

5. For example, in games, player/users interact with and manipulate items on screen through varied interfaces via gesture recognition. The mouse and all touch screens also embody animated traces of physical actions as the user's finger drags icons across the screen. This is also true of the mouse, which is activated by the user's movement and translated into a moving icon visible on screen. The touch screen is merely a more-up-to-date example that illustrates the trace of movement more directly.
6. Honess Roe, 'Animating Documentary', p. 142.
7. Resemblance based on movement is, of course, maintained in the indexical trace but as imagery it is closer to the symbol than to the icon, which is associated with resemblance in appearance to the referent.
8. Honess Roe, 'Animating Documentary', p. 142.
9. It is important to clarify that I am not discussing techniques such as cel animation or experimental film whereby the relationship between the photographic aspect and the capture of physical referents may vary. Instead I refer to the manner in which photography was used in the more traditional sense within documentary contexts as a counterpart to the recent rise of non-photorealistic animation as documentary imagery.
10. Nichols, *Introduction to Documentary*, p. xi. Emphasis in the original.
11. Wells defines animation as existing 'in a recorded state of being', 'exactly as its creator committed to creating it'. He questions whether animation can exist in the same time and space as its viewers, or if it is relegated to another dimension, 'a dimension of "projected" time and space that one might perceive as "other-timeness" and "other-spaceness" existing parallel to our "real-timeness" and "real-spaceness"': Wells, 'Frame of Reference', p. 24.
12. I do not mean augmented reality in the sense of specific AR technologies, but more a general enhancement of what reality is when it expands beyond the physical, owing to what is made possible through contemporary personal technologies.
13. In her research into the subjective additions that animation makes to documentary, Honess Roe concludes by discussing the *desire* to transcend the limitations of photographic media in documentary. Although I clearly agree, it is important to emphasise that by analysing contemporary technoculture what becomes evident is that such an expectation is not limited to documentaries; it permeates the *actuality* of life in the early twenty-first century and therefore becomes an objective *necessity* rather than a subjective 'desire'. See Honess Roe, 'Animating Documentary', pp. 89–90.
14. For more information on the military origins of these technologies, see Manovich, 'Navigable Space'.
15. See www.gettaxi.com, accessed 12 December 2013.
16. Ritchin, *After Photography*, p. 171.
17. Manovich, 'After Effects', p. 68.

18. See my forthcoming article in *Journal of Visual Culture* in the special issue on Robot Visions.
19. In his examination of what is considered realistic in animated depictions, Stephen Rowley asserts that realism can be described in multiple ways, including visual realism, aural realism, realism of motion, narrative and character realism and social realism. See Rowley, 'Life Reproduced in Drawings', pp. 70–1. Similarly, Gunning argues that 'the index may not be the best way, and certainly should not be the only way, to approach the issue of cinematic realism'. He stresses motion as a form of realism, which is central to any discussion of animation which obviously relies on movement. See Gunning, 'Moving Away from the Index', p. 31. Gunning also quotes Christian Metz's description of a sense of realism through moving imagery as the ability 'to inject the reality of motion into the unreality of the image and thus to render the world of imagination more real than it had ever been'. See Metz, 'On the Impression', p. 15.
20. The work of Charles Hill on the concept of vividness, as well as Lúcia Nagib and Cecília Mello's work on varied reality effects, led me to acknowledge the importance of witnessing an authenticating device that promotes documentary status by simulating presence and directness for the viewer. As long as a sense of presence is established through immediacy and a link to one's physical presence, the imagery used can take on many forms.
21. Spiegelman, *Maus*; Sacco, *Palestine Collection*; Chute, *Disaster Drawn*; Chute, *Why Comics?*; and the Critical Approaches to Comics Artists Series, edited by David M. Ball, published by University Press of Mississippi.
22. *Tower*, film, directed by Keith Maitland (USA: Go-Valley and ITVS, 2016).
23. Ebiri, 'Keith Maitland'.
24. On the one hand, documentaries are more popular than ever, but on the other, they are less trusted in a contemporary culture increasingly characterised by suspicion of the visual. This uncertainty *vis-à-vis* non-fictional representations generates a need for new forms of representation that directly acknowledge this present state of affairs, as does animation as a form of masking. This is discussed in Chapter 8.
25. It is important to emphasise that this potential deceitfulness is one of many possible uses of animation and *not* an inherent characteristic of animation.
26. *Black Mirror*, TV show, created by Charlie Brooker (UK: Zeppotron and House of Tomorrow, 2011–present).
27. Brooker, 'Dark Side'.
28. Kell, 'Unforgotten: COVID-19 Era Grads'.
29. See https://www.youtube.com/watch?v=J9vpoJ1u26o, accessed 30 June 2020.
30. For a list of companies offering tools and platforms see Rogers, 'Coronavirus Has Made WFH the New Normal'.
31. *The Congress*, film, directed by Ari Folman (France, Israel, Belgium, Poland, Luxembourg and Germany: Pandora Filmproduktion, 2013).
32. For more information see Oliver Grau and Thomas Veigl, 'Introduction: Imagery'; Elkins, 'Visual Practices'.

33. This is a partial list. For an elaborated account of the term's etymology and lexicology, see Crafton, 'Veiled Genealogies', pp. 97–8.
34. See Husbands and Ruddell, 'Approaching Animation', pp. 8–9. Nick Miller addressed the issue of metamorphosis in his 2019 Society for Animation Studies annual conference 'Animating the Literary Imagination: Visual and Verbal Metamorphosis' presentation on 20 June 2019 as part of the SAS annual conference, Lisbon, 17–21 June 2019.
35. *The Hat*, film, directed by Michèle Cournoyer (Canada: National Film Board of Canada, 2010).
36. *Trump Dreams*, film, directed by Ruth Lingford (UK: Ruth Lingford, 2017).

Filmography

1000 Voices, film, directed by Tim Travers Hawkins. UK: Ctrl.Alt.Shift, 2010.
Aladdin, film, directed by Ron Clements and John Musker. USA: Walt Disney, 1992.
An Eyeful of Sound, film, directed by Samantha Moore. Canada, Netherlands and UK: Sapiens Productions, 2010.
Animated Introduction to Cancer Biology, film. USA: Cancerquest, 2013.
Another Planet, film, directed by Amir Yatziv's. Israel: Amir Yatziv and Jonathan Doweck, 2017.
Audrie & Daisy, film, directed by Bonni Cohen and Jon Shenk. USA: Actual Film, 2016.
Avatar, film, directed by James Cameron. USA: Lightstorm Entertainment, Dune Entertainment and Ingenious Film Partners, 2009.
Backseat Bingo, film, directed by Liz Blazer. USA: University of Southern California, 2003.
Black Mirror, TV show, created by Charlie Brooker. UK: Zeppotron and House of Tomorrow, 2011–present.
Chicago 10, film, directed by Brett Morgan. USA: Consolidated Documentaries, Participant Productions, River Road Entertainment and Curious Pictures, 2007.
The Colbert Report, TV show, directed by Jim Hoskinson. USA: Spartina Productions, Busboy Productions and Comedy Partners, 2005–14.
The Congress, film, directed by Ari Folman. France, Israel, Belgium, Poland, Luxembourg and Germany: Pandora Filmproduktion, 2013.
The Daily Show, TV show, directed by Paul Pennolino. USA: Ark Angel and Comedy Partners, 1996–present.
Dawn of the Planet of the Apes, film, directed by Matt Reeves. USA: Chernin Entertainment and TSG Entertainment, 2014.
Diary of a Camper, film, directed by Matthew Van Sickler. USA: United Ranger Films, 1996.
Do It Yourself, film, directed by Eric Ledune. Belgium: Got! Oh my got, Amnesty International and Wallonie Image, 2007.
Exposure, TV show, various producers. UK: various production companies, 2011–present.
Family Planning, film, directed by Les Clark. USA: Walt Disney, 1968.
The French Democracy, film, directed by Alex Chan. France: Atomic Prod, 2005.
Globalised Slavery: How Big Supermarkets are Selling Prawns in Supply Chain Fed by Slave Labour, film. UK: *The Guardian*, 2014.
Guantánamo Bay: The Hunger Strikes, film, directed by Mustafa Khalili and Guy Grandjean. UK: Sherbet, Fonic and *The Guardian*, 2013.
The Hat, film, directed by Michèle Cournoyer. Canada: National Film Board of Canada, 1999.
Hercules, film, directed by Ron Clements and John Musker. USA: Walt Disney, 1997.
Hidden/Gömd, film, directed by David Aronowitsch, Hanna Heilborn and Mats Johansson. Sweden and Finland: Story AB and Kinotar, 2002.

Holy Motors, film, directed by Leos Carax. France and Germany: Wild Bunch, Arte Cinema and Pierre Grise Productions, 2012.
Human Growth, film, directed by Eddie Albert. USA: Wexler, 1947.
Inside Out, film, directed by Pete Docter. USA: Walt Disney and Pixar, 2015.
In the Same Boat, film, directed by Martha Stiegman. Canada: Martha Stiegman, 2007.
It's Like That, film, directed by SLAG. Australia: SLAG, 2003.
I was a Child of Holocaust Survivors, film, directed by Ann Marie Fleming. Canada: National Film Board of Canada, 2010.
Kill Bill, film, directed by Quentin Tarantino. USA: A Band Apart, 2003.
Last Day of Freedom, film, directed by Dee Hibbert-Jones and Nomi Talisman. USA: Living Condition, 2015.
Last Week Tonight with John Oliver, TV show, directed by Joe Perota, Christopher Werner, Jim Hoskinson, Paul Pennolino and Bruce Leddy. USA: Avalon Television and Partially Important Productions, 2014–present.
The Late Show with Stephen Colbert, TV show, directed by Jim Hoskinson. USA: Spartina Productions, Busboy Productions and CBS Television Studios, 2015–present.
Life 2.0, film, directed by Jason Spingarn-Koff. USA: Andrew Lauren Productions, PalmStar Media and Preferred Content, 2010.
Life, Animated, film, directed by Roger Ross Williams. USA: Motto Pictures, A&E IndieFilms and Roger Ross Williams Productions, 2016.
Lip Sync – Creature Comforts, film, created by Nick Park. UK: Aardman Animations, 1989.
Little Deaths, film, directed by Ruth Lingford. USA: Harvard University, 2010.
The Lord of the Rings, film series, directed by Peter Jackson. New Zealand and USA: New Line Cinema and WingNut Films, 2001–3.
Magnetic Movie, film, directed by Ruth Jarman and Joe Gerhardt. UK: Semiconductor, 2007.
Makun (Don't Cry), film, directed by Emilio Marti. Spain: 2018.
Mary Poppins, film, directed by Robert Stevenson. USA: Disney, 1964.
Molotov Alva and His Search for the Creator, film, directed by Douglas Gayeton. USA: Submarine Channel and VPRO, 2007.
The Moon and the Son: An Imagined Conversation, film, directed by John Canemaker. USA: John Canemaker Productions, 2005.
Music & Clowns, film, directed by Alex Widdowson. (UK: 2018).
Neighbors, film, directed by Norman McLaren. Canada: National Film Board of Canada, 1952.
Nowhere Line: Voices from Manus Island, film, directed by Lukas Schrank. Australia: Visitor Studio, 2015.
One Iranian Lawyer's Fight to Save Juveniles from Execution, film, *The Guardian* and Sherbet, 2012.
Persepolis, film, directed by Marjane Satrapi and Vincent Paronnaud. France and Iran: Celluloid Dreams, CNC, France 3 Cinéma, The Kennedy/Marshall Company and Région Ile-de-France, 2007.
Powering the Cell – Mitochondria, film by BioVisions Program at Harvard University and XVIVO Scientific Animation, 2012.
Quiet Zone, film, directed by Karl Lemieux and David Bryant. Canada: National Film Board of Canada, 2015.
Ralph Breaks the Internet, film, directed by Rich Moore and Phil Johnston. USA: Walt Disney, 2018.
Rise of the Planet of the Apes, film, directed by Rupert Wyatt. USA: Chernin Entertainment, Dune Entertainment, Big Screen Productions and Ingenious Film Partners, 2011.

Rocks in My Pockets, film, directed by Signe Baumane. USA and Latvia: Rocks In My Pockets and Locomotive Productions, 2014.
Rules of the Game, film, directed by Jean Renoir. France: Nouvelle Édition Française, 1939.
Ryan, film, directed by Chris Landreth. Canada: Copperheart Entertainment, 2004.
Samouni Road, film, directed by Stefano Savona. France and Italy: Dugong Production, Picofilms and Alter Ego Production, 2018.
Second Bodies, film, directed by Sandra Danilovic. Canada: Ryerson University, 2009.
Second Skin, film, directed by Juan Carlos Piñeiro Escoriaza. USA: Peter Schieffelin Brauer and Victor Piñeiro Escoriaza, 2008.
Seeking Refuge, film series, directed by Andy Glynne. UK: MoMo – Mosaic Motion and Mosaic Films, 2012.
Serenity Now, online capture, 2008.
The Sinking of the Lusitania, film, directed by Winsor McCay. USA: Jewel Productions, 1918.
Seven Wise Dwarfs, film, directed by Richard Lyford. Canada: Walt Disney, 1941.
Slaves, film, directed by David Aronowitsch and Hanna Heilborn. Sweden, Norway, Denmark: Story AB, 2008.
Snack and Drink, film, directed by Bob Sabiston. USA: Flat Black Films, 1999.
Snow White and the Seven Dwarfs, film, directed by David Hand. USA: Walt Disney, 1937.
Stranger Comes to Town, film, directed by Jacqueline Goss. USA, 2007.
Tower, film, directed by Keith Maitland. USA: Go-Valley and ITVS, 2016.
Trump Dreams, film, directed by Ruth Lingford. UK: Ruth Lingford, 2017.
Tying your Own Shoes, film, directed by Shira Avni. Canada: National Film Board of Canada, 2009.
VD Attack Plan!, film, directed by Les Clark. USA: Walt Disney, 1973.
Vertigo, film, directed by Alfred Hitchcock. USA: Alfred J. Hitchcock Productions, 1958.
Waltz with Bashir, film, directed by Ari Folman. Israel, Germany and France: Bridgit Folman Film Gang, Les Films d'Ici and Razor Film Produktion, 2008.
The Wanted 18, film, directed by Paul Cowan and Amer Shomali. Canada, Palestine and France: Bellota Films, Dar Films Productions, Intuitive Pictures and National Film Board of Canada, 2014.
The Water Babies, film, directed by Lionel Jeffries. UK and Poland: Ariadne Films and Studio Minitaur Filmowych, 1978.
Watership Down, film, directed by Martin Rosen. UK: Nepenthe Productions, 1978.
When the Wind Blows, film, directed by Jimmy Murakami. UK: Meltdown Productions, British Screen Productions, Film Four International, TVC London and Penguin Books, 1986.
Wonderland: The Trouble with Love and Sex, film, directed by Jonathan Hodgson. UK: Sherbet, 2011.

Bibliography

ABC News, 'TomoNews Uses Animation to Depict News Stories Satirically', *ABC News* (Australian Broadcasting Corporation), 14 October 2015, www.abc.net.au/news/2015-10-5/tomonews-uses-animation-to-depict-news-stories/6855546, accessed 3 November 2015.

Acland, Charles R., 'The Crack in the Electric Window', *Cinema Journal* 51(2), 2012, pp. 167–71.

Adewunmi, Bim, 'UK's Child Refugees Tell Their Unique Stories', *The Guardian*, 18 June 2012, www.theguardian.com/society/the-womens-blog-with-jane-martinson/2012/jun/18/uk-child-refugees-stories, accessed 3 January 2014.

Agamben, Giorgio, *Means without End: Notes on Politics*, Vincenzo Binetti and Cesare Casarino (trans.) (Minneapolis: University of Minnesota Press, 2000).

Ahlers, Mike M., 'TSA Removes Body Scanners Criticized as Too Revealing', *CNN*, 30 May 2013.

Alberro, Alexander, 'Questionnaire on "The Contemporary"', *October* 130, 2009, pp. 55–60.

Alston, William P. (ed.), *Realism and Antirealism* (Ithaca: Cornell University Press, 2002).

Araeen, Rasheed, Sean Cubitt and Ziauddin Sardar (eds), *The Third Text Reader: On Art, Culture, and Theory* (London and New York: Continuum, 2002).

Arendt, Hannah, *Eichmann in Jerusalem: A Report on the Banality of Evil* (New York: Penguin Books, 1994).

Armstrong, Elizabeth, 'On the Border of the Real', in Elizabeth Armstrong (ed.), *More Real? Art in the Age of Truthiness* (Minneapolis: Minneapolis Institute of Arts, 2013), pp. 24–83.

Arnason, Lara, 'Regulating Online Games in China: Policy, Practice, Innovation, and Change', PhD thesis, University of Edinburgh, 2016.

Ashuri, Tamar and Amit Pinchevski, 'Witnessing as a Field', in Paul Frosh and Amit Pinchevski (eds), *Media Witnessing: Testimony in the Age of Mass Communication* (New York: Palgrave Macmillan, 2009), pp. 133–57.

Aufderheide, Patricia, *A Very Short Introduction to Documentary* (New York: Oxford University Press, 2007).

Balsom, Erika and Hila Peleg, *Documentary across Disciplines* (Cambridge, MA: MIT Press, 2016).

Barthes, Roland, *Camera Lucida* (London: Vintage, 1993).

Baudrillard, Jean, 'Metamorphosis Metaphor Metastasis', in Sylvère Lotringer (ed.), *The Ecstasy of Communication* (New York: Semiotext(e), 1988), pp. 45–57.

Baudrillard, Jean, *Cool Memories* (London: Verso, 1990).

Baudrillard, Jean, *Simulacra and Simulation*, Sheila Faria Glaser (trans.) (Ann Arbor: University of Michigan Press, 1994).

Bauman, Zygmunt, 'Effacing the Face: On the Social Management of Moral Proximity', *Theory, Culture and Society* 7, 1990, pp. 5–38.

Bazin, André, *What is Cinema?*, vol. 2, Hugh Gray (trans.) (Berkeley: University of California Press, 1967).

Beckman, Karen, 'Animation on Trial', *Animation: An Interdisciplinary Journal* 6(3), 2011, pp. 259–76.

Begley, Sarah, 'The 30 Most Influential People on the Internet', *Time Magazine*, 5 March 2015.

Benita Shaw, Debra, *Technoculture* (Oxford and New York: Berg, 2008).

Besmer, Kirk M., 'What "Robotic Re-embodiment" Reveals about Virtual Re-embodiment', in Robert Rosenberger and Peter-Paul Verbeek (eds), *Postphenomenological Investigations: Essays on Human-Technology Relations* (London and New York: Lexington, 2015), pp. 55–72.

Beugnet, Martine, *Cinema and Sensation: French Film and the Art of Transgression* (Carbondale: Southern Illinois University Press, 2007).

Blocker, Jane, *Seeing Witness: Visuality and Ethics of Testimony* (Minneapolis: University of Minnesota Press, 2009).

Bogost, Ian, *Persuasive Games* (Cambridge, MA: MIT Press, 2007).

Bogost, Ian, *How to Do Things with Videogames* (Minneapolis and London: University of Minnesota Press, 2011).

Bogost, Ian, *Alien Phenomenology or What It's Like to Be a Thing* (Minneapolis: University of Minnesota Press, 2012).

Bolaki, Stella, 'Animated Documentary and Mental Health', Chapter 6 in *Illness as Many Narratives: Arts, Medicine and Culture* (Edinburgh: Edinburgh University Press, 2016).

Bolter, Jay David, Blair MacIntyre, Michael Nitsche and Kathryn Farley, 'Liveness, Presence, and Performance in Contemporary Digital Media', in Ulrik Ekman (ed.), *Throughout: Art and Culture Emerging with Ubiquitous Computing* (Cambridge, MA: MIT Press, 2012), pp. 323–36.

Bourriaud, Nicolas, 'Altermodern', in Nicolas Bourriaud (ed.), *Altermodern* (London: Tate Publishing, 2009), pp. 11–24.

Boykoff, Pamela, 'The Blurry Lines of Animated "News"', *CNN*, 2 February 2010.

Brecht, Bertolt, *Brecht on Theatre: The Development of an Aesthetic*, John Willett (ed. and trans.) (London: Methuen, 1964).

Breitwieser, Sabine, 'Harun Farocki: Images of War (at a Distance)', *Museum of Modern Art*, www.moma.org/visit/calendar/exhibitions/1196, accessed 15 September 2012.

Bridle, J. *New Dark Age: Technology and the End of the Future* (London and New York: Verso, 2018).

Broad, C. D., *Kant: An Introduction* (Cambridge: Cambridge University Press, 1978).

Brooker, Charlie, 'The Dark Side of our Gadget Addiction', *The Guardian*, 1 December 2011.

Bruckner, Franziska, Nikica Gilic, Holger Lang, Daniel Suljic and Hrvoje Turkovic (eds), *Global Animation Theory: International Perspectives at Animafest Zagreb* (New York and London: Bloomsbury Academic, 2018).

Bryant, Antony and Griselda Pollock (eds), *Digital and Other Virtualities* (New York: I. B. Tauris, 2010).

Bryant, Levi, Nick Srnicek and Graham Harman (eds), *The Speculative Turn – Continental Materialism and Realism* (Melbourne: Re.press, 2011).

Buchan, Suzanne (ed.), *Animated 'Worlds'* (Eastleigh: John Libbey, 2006).

Buchan, Suzanne (ed.), *Pervasive Animation* (New York: Routledge, 2013).

Buchler, Justus (ed.), *Philosophical Writings of Peirce* (New York: Dover, 1955).

Burnett, Graham D., 'In Lies Begin Responsibilities', in Elizabeth Armstrong (ed.), *More Real? Art in the Age of Truthiness* (Minneapolis: Minneapolis Institute of Arts, 2013), pp. 190–209.

Burns, Maureen, 'Invisibility', in James Elkins, Kristi McGuire, Maureen Burns, Alicia Chester and Joel Kuennen (eds), *Theorizing Visual Studies* (New York and London: Routledge, 2013), pp. 146–9.

Caillois, Roger, *Man, Play and Games* (Chicago: University of Illinois, 1961).

Cameron, David and John Carroll, 'Encoding Liveness: Performance and Real-time Rendering in Machinima', in Henry Lowood and Michael Nitsche (eds), *The Machinima Reader* (London: MIT Press, 2011), pp. 127–42.

Capino, José B., 'Filthy Funnies: Notes on the Body in Animated Pornography', *Animation Journal* 12, 2004, pp. 53–71.

Carr, David, '$1.1 Billion: This Isn't Child's Play', *International New York Times*, 1 September 2014.

Carr, Nicholas, 'Avatars Consume as Much Electricity as Brazilians', *Rough Type*, 5 December 2006, www.roughtype.com/?p=611, accessed 5 May, 2013.

Carroll, Noël, *Theorizing the Moving Image* (Cambridge: Cambridge University Press, 1996).

Carroll, Noël, *Engaging the Movie Image* (New Haven, CT: Yale University Press, 2003).

Cartoon Brew Connect, 'How President-elect Donald Trump was Animated in Real-time with Adobe Character Animator', *Cartoon Brew*, 11 September 2016, https://www.cartoonbrew.com/sponsored-by-adobe/president-elect-donald-trump-animated-real-time-adobe-character-animator-144713.html, accessed 8 September 2019.

Castronova, Edward, 'On Virtual Economies', *Game Studies* 3(2), 2003, unpaginated, www.gamestudies.org/0302/castronova/, accessed 12 March, 2012.

Castronova, Edward, *Exodus to the Virtual World: How Online Fun is Changing Reality* (New York: Palgrave Macmillan, 2007).

Cavell, Stanley, *The World Viewed* (Cambridge, MA: Harvard University Press, 1979).

Cheng, Benjamin Ka Lun and Wai Han Lo, 'Can News be Imaginative? An Experiment Testing the Perceived Credibility of Melodramatic Animated News, News Organizations, Media Use, and Media Dependency', *Electronic News* 6(3), 2012, pp. 131–50.

Chion, Michael, *The Voice in Cinema*, Claudia Gorbman (trans.) (New York: Columbia University Press, 1999).

Cholodenko, Alan, 'Who Framed Roger Rabbit, or the Framing of Animation', in Alan Cholodenko (ed.), *The Illusion of Life: Essays on Animation* (Sydney: Power Publications, 1991), pp. 209–42.

Cholodenko Alan, 'Animation (Theory) as the Poematic: A Reply to the Cognitivists', *Animation Studies* 4, 2009, pp. 1–16.

Cholodenko, Alan, '"First Principles" of Animation', in Karen Beckman (ed.), *Animating Film Theory* (Durham and London: Duke University Press, 2014), pp. 98–110.

Chouliaraki, Lilie, 'Improper Distance: Towards a Critical Account of Solidarity as Irony', *International Journal of Cultural Studies* 14(4), 2011, pp. 363–81.

Chouliaraki, Lilie, *The Ironic Spectator: Solidarity in the Age of Post-Humanitarianism* (Cambridge: Polity Press, 2013).

Chow, Kenny K. N., *Animation, Embodiment, and Digital Media: Human Experience of Technological Liveliness* (New York: Palgrave Macmillan, 2013).

Chute, Hillary L., *Disaster Drawn: Visual Witness, Comics, and Documentary Form* (Cambridge, MA: The Belknap Press Harvard University Press, 2016).

Chute, Hillary L., *Why Comics? From Underground to Everywhere* (New York: HarperCollins Publishers, 2017).

Collins, Michelle, 'The 2014 Sochi Opening Ceremonies Recap: The Winter Olympics of our Discontent', *Vanity Fair*, 8 February 2014, www.vanityfair.com/online/daily/2014/02/sochi-opening-ceremonies-recap, accessed 20 April, 2014.

Conlan, Tara and John Plunkett, '"IRA" Footage Was From Video Game, Admits ITV', *The Guardian*, 27 September 2011, www.theguardian.com/media/2011/sep/27/ira-footage-video-game-itv, accessed 15 April 2013.

Cooper, Robbie, *Alter Ego: Avatars and their Creators* (New York: Chris Boot, 2009).

Corner, John, 'Performing the Real: Documentary Diversions', *Television and New Media* 3(3), 2002, pp. 255–69.

Costello, Diarmud and Margaret Iversen, 'Introduction: Photography between Art History and Philosophy', *Critical Enquiry* 38(4), 2012, pp. 679–93.

Crafton, Donald, 'The Veiled Genealogies of Animation and Cinema', *Animation* 6(2), 2011, pp. 93–110.

Cramerotti, Alfredo, *Aesthetic Journalism* (Chicago: University of Chicago Press, 2009).

Crary, Jonathan, *Techniques of the Observer: On Vision and Modernity in the Nineteenth Century* (Cambridge, MA: MIT Press, 1990).

Cubitt, Sean, *Digital Aesthetics* (London: Sage, 1998).

Cubitt, Sean, 'Current Screens', in Oliver Grau (ed.), *Imagery of the 21st Century* (London and Cambridge, MA: MIT Press, 2011), pp. 21–36.

Daniel, 'The Energy Consumption of Avatars', *Life after Oil*, 10 February 2010, www.life-after-oil.blogspot.com/2010/02/energy-consumption-of-avatars.html., accessed 5 May 2013.

Davidson, Russell, 'A Waltz and an Interview: Speaking with *Waltz with Bashir* Creator Ari Folman', *CC2K*, 20 January 2009, www.cc2konline.com/component/k2/item/1654-a-waltz-and-an-interview-speaking-with-waltz-with-bashir-creator-ari-folman, accessed 22 October 2016.

D'Ancona, Matthew, *Post-Truth: The New War on Truth and how to Fight Back* (London: Ebury Press, 2017).

Danilovic, Sandra, 'Virtual Lens of Exposure: Aesthetics, Theory, and Ethics of Documentary Filmmaking in Second Life', in Jenna Ng (ed.), *Understanding Machinima: Essays on Filmmaking in Virtual Worlds* (London: Bloomsbury Press, 2013), pp. 168–86.

Darwall, Stephen, 'Empathy, Sympathy, and Care', *Philosophical Studies* 89, 1998, pp. 261–82.

Daye, Alison, 'Pokémon Go Helps Two Marines to Catch a Murder Suspect in Fullerton', *CNN*, 13 July 2016, http://edition.cnn.com/2016/07/13/us/pokmon-go-helps-marines-to-catch-suspect/index.html, accessed 4 April 2017.

De la Peña, Nonny. 'Physical World News in Virtual Spaces: Representation and Embodiment in Immersive Nonfiction', *Media Fields* 3, 2011, pp. 1–13.

De la Peña, Nonny. 'The Future of the News? Virtual Reality', *TED*, 2015, https://www.ted.com/talks/nonny_de_la_pena_the_future_of_news_virtual_reality/transcript?language=en, accessed 2 January 2016.

De la Peña, Nonny, Peggy Weil, Joan Llobera, Elias Giannopoulos, Ausiàs Pomés, Bernhard Spanlang, Doron Friedman, Maria V. Sanchez-Vives and Mel Slater, 'Immersive Journalism: Immersive Virtual Reality for the First Person Experience of News', *Presence: Teleoperators and Virtual Environments* 19(4), 2010, pp. 291–301.

Del Río, Elena, 'The Body as Foundation of the Screen: Allegories of Technology in Atom Egoyan's *Speaking Parts*', *Camera Obscura* 13(2), 1996, pp. 92–115.

Deleuze, Gilles, *Cinema 1: The Movement Image*, Hugh Tomlinson and Barbara Habberjam (trans.) (Minneapolis: University of Minnesota Press, 1986).

Deleuze, Gilles, *Cinema 2: The Time Image*, Hugh Tomlinson and Robert Galeta (trans.) (London: Continuum, 2008).

DelGaudio, Sybil, 'If Truth be Told, Can 'Toons Tell It? Documentary and Animation', *Film History* 9(2), 1997, pp. 189–99.

Denslow, Philip Kelly, 'What is Animation And Who Needs to Know? An Essay on Definitions', in Jayne Pilling (ed.), *A Reader in Animation Studies* (London: John Libbey, 1997), pp. 1–4.

Derrida, Jacques, *Of Grammatology* (Baltimore: John Hopkins University Press, 1998).

Dibbell, Julian, 'A Rape in Cyberspace', *The Village Voice* [23 December, 1993] 18 October 2005, www.villagevoice.com/2005-10-8/specials/a-rape-in-cyberspace/, accessed 10 June, 2010.

Doane, Mary Ann, 'Indexicality: Trace and Sign: Introduction', *Differences: A Journal of Feminist Cultural Studies* 18(1), 2007, pp. 1–6.

Doane, Mary Ann, 'The Indexical and the Concept of Medium Specificity', *Differences: A Journal of Feminist Cultural Studies* 18(1), 2007, pp. 128–52.

Durham Peters, John, 'Witnessing', in Paul Frosh and Amit Pinchevski (eds), *Media Witnessing: Testimony in the Age of Mass Communication* (New York: Palgrave Macmillan, 2009), pp. 23–41.

Ebiri, Bilge, 'Keith Maitland Gets Animated Discussing his Powerful Documentary *Tower*', *LA Weekly*, 18 January 2017, www.laweekly.com/film/keith-maitland-gets-animated-discussing-his-powerful-documentary-tower-7834226, accessed 20 January 2018.

Ehrlich, Nea, 'Animated Documentaries as Masking', *Animation Studies* 6, 2011, unpaginated.

Ehrlich, Nea, 'Indeterminate and Intermediate or Animated Non-fiction: Why Now?' in Jonathan Murray and Nea Ehrlich (eds), *Drawn from Life: Issues and Themes in Animated Documentary Cinema* (Edinburgh: Edinburgh University Press, 2019), pp. 47–68.

Ehrsson, Henrik, 'The Experimental Induction of Out-of-body Experiences', *Science* 317, 2007, p. 1048.

Ehrsson, Henrik, Charles Spence and Richard Passingham, 'That's My Hand! Activity in Premotor Cortex Reflects Feeling of Ownership of a Limb', *Science* 30(5685), 2004, pp. 875–7.

Eisenstein, Sergei, 'The Montage of Film Attractions', in Richard Taylor (ed. and trans.), *Selected Works*, vol. 1 (Bloomington: Indiana University Press, 1988), pp. 39–58.

Ekstein, Nikki, 'Pokemon Go is Already a Big Boon for Small Museums', *Houston Chronicle*, 14 July 2016.

Elkins, James, 'Visual Practices across the University: A Report', in Oliver Grau (ed.), *Imagery in the 21st Century* (London and Cambridge, MA: MIT Press, 2011), pp. 149–74.

Elkins, James (ed.), *Photography Theory* (New York: Routledge, 2007).

Ellis, Jack, *The Documentary Idea: A Critical History of English-Language Documentary Film and Video* (New Jersey: Prentice Hall, 1989).

Ellis, John, *Visible Fictions: Cinema, Television, Radio* (London: Routledge, 1982).

Elsaesser, Thomas and Malte Hagener, *Film Theory* (New York: Routledge, 2010).

Enwezor, Okwui, 'Documentary/Vérité: Bio-politics, Human Rights, and the Figure of "Truth" in Contemporary Art', in Maria Lind and Hito Steyerl (eds), *The Greenroom: Reconsidering the Documentary and Contemporary Art* (Los Angeles: Sternberg Press, 2008), pp. 62–102.

Enwezor, Okwui, 'Rules of Evidence: Text, Voice, Sight', *Berlin Documentary Forum Web Magazine*, 2010, www.BDF_magazine_web_e.pdf, accessed 4 July 2010.

Everard, Jerry, *Virtual States – The Internet and the Boundaries of the Nation-State* (London and New York: Routledge, 2000).

Farquharson, Alex, 'Jeremy Deller – The Battle of Orgreave', *Frieze* 61, 2001, www.frieze.com/issue/review/jeremy_deller/, accessed 24 July 2012.

Fitzpatrick, Alex, Mandy Oaklander, Lisa Eadicicco, John Patrick Pullen, Matt Peckham, Dan Hirschhorn and Merrill Fabry, 'The 50 Best Apps of the Year', *Time*, 31 October 2016, http://time.com/4549647/best-apps-year-2016/, accessed 4 April 2017.

Formenti, Cristina, 'The Sincerest Form of Docudrama: Re-framing the Animated Documentary', *Studies in Documentary Film* 8(2), 2014, pp. 103–15.

Formenti, Christina, *The Classic Animated Documentary and Its Contemporary Evolution* (London: Bloomsbury, forthcoming).

Foster, Hal, *The Return of the Real* (Cambridge, MA and London: MIT Press, 1996).

Foster, Hal, 'On the Art of the Decade', *Artforum* 48(4), 2009, https://www.artforum.com/print/200910/hal-foster-24264, accessed 16 October 2016.

Frank, Hannah, 'Traces of the World: Cel Animation and Photography', *Animation: An Interdisciplinary Journal* 11(1), 2016, pp. 23–39.

Freedman, Yacov, 'Is it Real ... Or Is It Motion Capture?: The Battle to Redefine Animation in the Age of Digital Performance', *The Velvet Light Trap* 69, 2012, pp. 38–49.

Fried, Michael, *Why Photography Matters as Art as Never Before* (New Haven and London: Yale University Press, 2008).

Friedberg, Anne, 'The End of Cinema: Multimedia and Technological Change', in Marc Furstenau (ed.), *The Film Theory Reader – Debates and Arguments* (London and New York: Routledge, 2010), pp. 438–52.

Frosh, Paul, 'Telling Presences: Witnessing, Mass Media, and the Imagined Lives of Strangers', in Paul Frosh and Amit Pinchevski (eds), *Media Witnessing* (New York: Palgrave Macmillan, 2009), pp. 49–72.

Frosh, Paul and Amit Pinchevski (eds), *Media Witnessing: Testimony in the Age of Mass Communication* (New York: Palgrave Macmillan, 2009).

Fullerton, Tracy, 'Documentary Games: Putting the Player in the Path of History', in Zach Whalen and Laurie N. Taylor (eds), *Playing the Past: History and Nostalgia in Video Games* (Nashville: Vanderbilt University Press, 2008), pp. 215–38, www.tracyfullerton.com/assets/DocumentaryGames_tfullerton.pdf, pp. 1–28.

Furniss, Maureen, *Art in Motion: Animation Aesthetics* (London and Montrouge: John Libbey, 1998).

Furniss, Maureen, *Art in Motion, Revised Edition: Animation Aesthetics* (Bloomington: Indiana University Press, 2017).

Gaines, Jane M., 'Political Mimesis', in Jane M. Gains and Michael Renov (eds), *Collecting Visible Evidence* (Minneapolis: University of Minnesota Press, 1999), pp. 84–102.

Gee, James Paul, *What Videogames Have to Teach Us about Learning and Literacy* (Basingstoke: Palgrave Macmillan, 2007).

Gepner, Abigail, Rosa Jazmin and Sophia Rosenbaum, 'There's a Pokémon in my Restaurant, and Business is Booming', *New York Post*, 12 July 2016.

Goss, Jacqueline, 'Jacqueline Goss at the Laguna Art Museum', *Laguna Art Museum*, http://lagunaartmuseum.org/wow-emergent-media-phenomenon/, accessed 18 November 2010,

Grau, Oliver (ed.), *Imagery in The 21st Century* (London and Cambridge, MA: MIT Press, 2011).

Grau, Oliver and Thomas Veigl, 'Introduction: Imagery in the 21st Century', in Oliver Grau (ed.), *Imagery in the 21st Century* (London and Cambridge, MA: MIT Press, 2011), pp. 1–18.

Greenberg, Raz, 'The Animated Text: Definition', *Journal of Film and Video* 63(2), 2011, pp. 3–10.

Greenaway, Peter, 'Peter Greenaway Speaks at the 48 Hour Film Project Machinima 2010', *Vimeo*, 2010, http://vimeo.com/groups/8472/videos/15253336, accessed 6 February 2012.

Greenberger, Alex, 'You Look So Different Online: Douglas Coupland Debuts Facial De-recognition Software at the Armory', *Art News*, 2 February 2016, www.artnews.com/2016/03/02/you-look-so-different-online-douglas-coupland-debuts-facial-de-recognition-software-at-the-armory/, accessed 10 March 2017.

Grierson, John, *Grierson on Documentary*, Forsyth Hardy (ed.) (Los Angeles: University of California Press, 1996).

Groys, Boris, 'The Topology of Contemporary Art', in Terry Smith, Okwui Enwezor, and Nancy Condee (eds), *Antinomies of Art and Culture: Modernity, Postmodernity, Contemporaneity* (Durham, NC and London: Duke University Press, 2008), pp. 71–80.

Grundberg, Sven and Jens Hansegard, 'YouTube's Biggest Draw Plays Games, Earns $M a Year', *Wall Street Journal*, 16 June 2014.

Guerra, Carles, 'Negatives of Europe – Video Essays and Collective Pedagogies', in Maria Lind and Hito Steyerl (eds), *The Greenroom: Reconsidering the Documentary and Contemporary Art* (Berlin: Sternberg Press, 2008), pp. 144–64.

Gunning, Tom, 'Moving Away from the Index: Cinema and the Impression of Reality', *Differences: A Journal of Feminist Cultural Studies* 18(1), 2007, pp. 29–52.

Gunning, Tom, 'Truthiness and the More Real: What is the Difference?' in Elizabeth Armstrong (ed.), *More Real? Art in the Age of Truthiness* (Minneapolis: Minneapolis Institute of Arts, 2013), pp. 174–89.

Gunning, Tom, 'Animating the Instant: The Secret Symmetry between Animation and Photography', in Karen Beckman (ed.), *Animating Film Theory* (Durham and London: Duke University Press, 2014), pp. 37–53.

Gunraj, Andrea, Susana Ruiz and Ashley York, 'Power to the People: Anti-oppressive Game Design', in Karen Schrier and David Gibson (eds), *Designing Games for Ethics: Models, Techniques and Frameworks* (New York: Information Science Reference, 2011), pp. 253–74.

Gurevitch, Leon, 'The Documentary Attraction: Animation, Simulation and the Rhetoric of Expertise', in Jonathan Murray and Nea Ehrlich (eds), *Drawn from Life: Issues and Themes in Animated Documentary Cinema* (Edinburgh: Edinburgh University Press, 2019), pp. 84–105.

Hansen, Mark B. N., *Bodies in Code: Interfaces with Digital Media* (New York and London: Routledge, 2006).

Hansen, Mark B. N., *Feed-Forward: on the Future of Twenty-First-Century Media* (Chicago: University of Chicago Press, 2015).

Hansen, Mark B. N., *New Philosophy for New Media* (Cambridge, MA: MIT Press, 2004).

Hanson, Hilary, 'You Won't Believe These Images Aren't Photographs. And You Shouldn't, Because They Are Photographs', *Huffington Post*, 5 March 2015, www.huffingtonpost.com/2015/03/05/hyperrealcg-hoax-cg-images-photographs_n_6808928.html, accessed 20 January 2017.

Haraway, Donna, 'A Cyborg Manifesto: Science, Technology, and Socialist-feminism in the Late Twentieth Century', in *Simians, Cyborgs, and Women: The Reinvention of Nature* (New York: Routledge, 1991), pp. 149–81.

Harman, Graham, *Quentin Meillassoux: Philosophy in the Making* (Edinburgh: Edinburgh University Press, 2011).

Harsin, Jayson, 'The Responsible Dream: On Ari Folman's *Waltz with Bashir*', *Bright Lights Film Journal*, 2009, unpaginated, http://brightlightsfilm.com/the-responsible-dream-on-ari-folmans-waltz-with-bashir/#.V72x8JN940p, accessed 22 October 2016.

Hartshorne, Charles and Paul Weiss (eds), *Collected Papers of Charles Sanders Peirce*, vol. 2 (Cambridge, MA: Harvard University Press, 1932).

Harwood, Tracy, 'Machinima: A Meme of Our Time', in Andy Connor and Stefan Marks (eds), *Creative Technologies for Multidisciplinary Applications* (Pennsylvania: IGI Global, 2016), pp. 149–81.

Hauser, Arnold, *The Social History of Art*, vol. 2 (London and New York: Routledge, 1989).

Hayles, Katherine, *How We Became Posthuman* (Chicago and London: Chicago University press, 1999).

Herhuth, Eric (ed.), 'Animation and Politics', special issue, *Animation Journal*, 11(1), 2016.

Herrman, John and Nick Wingfield, 'ELeague Adapts TV to the Gaming Sensibility', *International New York Times*, 24 May 2016.

Hight, Craig, 'Mockumentary: A Call to Play', in Thomas Austin and Wilma de Jong (eds), *Rethinking Documentary* (Maidenhead: Open University Press, 2008), pp. 204–16.

Hill, Charles A., 'The Psychology of Rhetorical Images', in Marguerite Helmers and Charles A. Hill (eds), *Defining Visual Rhetorics* (Mahwah, N. J.: Lawrence Erlbaum Associates, 2004), pp. 25–40.

Hodgkin, Gary, 'Animating with a Game Engine: A Very Digital Sense of Place', paper presented at the 31st Conference of the Society for Animation Studies, Universidade Lusófona de Humanidades e Tecnologias, Lisbon, Portugal, 17–21 June 2019.

Holliday, Christopher and Alexander Sergeant (eds), *Fantasy/Animation: Connections Between Media, Mediums and Genres* (New York: Routledge, 2018).

Honess Roe, Annabelle, 'Animating Documentary', PhD thesis, University of Southern California, 2009.

Honess Roe, Annabelle, 'Absence, Excess and Epistemological Expansion: Towards a Framework for the Study of Animated Documentary', *Animation: An Interdisciplinary Journal* 6(3), 2011, pp. 215–30.

Honess Roe, Annabelle, *Animated Documentary* (Basingstoke: Palgrave Macmillan, 2013).

Honess Roe, Annabelle, 'Against Animated Documentary?' *International Journal of Film and Media Arts*, 1(1), 2016, pp. 20–7.

Honess Roe, Annabelle, 'Interjections and Connections: The Critical Potential of Animated Segments in Live Action Documentary', *Animation* 12(3), 2017, pp. 272–86.

Huhtamo, Erkki, 'Elements of Screenology: Toward an Archaeology of the Screen', *Iconics: International Studies of the Modern Age* 7, 2004, pp. 31–82.

Huhtamo, Erkki, "Screen Tests: Why Do We Need an Archaeology of the Screen?' *Cinema Journal* 51(2), 2012, pp. 144–8.

Huizinga, Johan, *Homo Ludens: A Study of the Play Element in Culture* (Boston: Breacon Press, 1955).

Hume, David, *A Treatise of Human Nature* [1739], Lewis A. Selby-Bigge (ed.) (Oxford: Clarendon Press, 1973).

Hunt, Lynn and Vanessa R. Schwartz, 'Capturing the Moment: Images and Eyewitnessing in History', *Journal of Visual Culture* 9(3), 2010, pp. 259–71.

Husbands, Lilly, 'The Meta-physics of Data: Philosophical Science in Semiconductor's Animated Videos', *Moving Image Review & Art Journal* 2(2), 2013, pp. 199–212.

Husbands, Lilly and Caroline Ruddell, 'Approaching Animation and Animation Studies', in Nichola Dobson, Annabelle Honess Roe, Amy Ratelle and Caroline Ruddell (eds), *The Animation Studies Reader* (New York and London: Bloomsbury Academic, 2019), pp. 5–16.

Janson, H. W., *History of Art* (New York: Harry N. Abrams, 1986).

Jay, Martin, *Downcast Eyes: The Denigration of Vision in Twentieth-century French Thought* (Los Angeles: University of California Press, 1993).

Johnson, Phylis, 'Machinima Reviews Editor's Note', *Journal of Gaming and Virtual Worlds* 3(1), 2011, pp. 83–8.

Jones, Amelia, *Self/Image: Technology, Representation, and the Contemporary Subject* (New York: Routledge, 2006).

Jonsson, Stefan, 'Facts of Aesthetics and Fictions of Journalism', in Maria Lind and Hito Steyerl (eds), *The Greenroom: Reconsidering the Documentary and Contemporary Art* (Berlin: Sternberg Press, 2008), pp. 166–87.

Judd, Wesley, 'A Conversation with the Psychologist behind "Inside Out"', *Pacific Standard*,

Miller-McCune Center for Research, Media and Public Policy, 8 July 2015, https://psmag.com/social-justice/a-conversation-with-psychologist-behind-inside-out, accessed 9 July 2015.

Kansteiner, Wulf, 'The Holocaust in the 21st Century: Digital Anxiety, Transnational Cosmopolitanism and the Memory of Genocide', paper presented at Holocaust Memory in a Digital Generation, Ben-Gurion University of the Negev, Beer-Sheva, Israel, 1 May 2019.

Kell, Gretchen, 'Unforgotten: COVID-19 Era Grads to be Celebrated Virtually this Saturday', *Berkeley News*, 14 May 2020, https://news.berkeley.edu/2020/05/14/unforgotten-covid-19-era-grads-to-be-celebrated-virtually-this-saturday/, accessed 30 June 2020.

Kelland, Matt, 'From Game Mod to Low-budget Film: The Evolution of Machinima', in Henry Lowood and Michael Nitsche (eds), *The Machinima Reader* (Cambridge, MA: MIT Press, 2011), pp. 23–35.

Kilteni, Konstantina, Raphaela Groten and Mel Slater, 'The Sense of Embodiment in Virtual Reality', *Presence Teleoperators &amp Virtual Environments*, 21(4), 2012, pp. 373–87.

Kim, Ji-Hoon, 'Animating the Photographic Trace, Intersecting Phantoms with Phantasms: Contemporary Media Arts, Digital Moving Pictures, and the Documentary's "Expanded Field"', *Animation* 6(3), 2011, pp. 371–86.

Kimmelman, Michael, 'Critic's Notebook', *New York Times*, 14 December 2016, https://www.nytimes.com/interactive/2016/12/14/world/middleeast/kimmelman-images-of-aleppo.html?_r=0, accessed 15 December 2016.

King, Geoff and Tanya Krzywinska, 'Cinema/Videogames/Interfaces', in Geoff King and Tanya Krzywinska (eds), *ScreenPlay – Cinema/Videogames/Interfaces* (London and New York: Wallflower Press, 2002), pp. 1–32.

Kingsley, Patrick, 'The Death of Alan Kurdi: One Year On, Compassion Towards Refugees Fades', *The Guardian*, 2 September 2016, https://www.theguardian.com/world/2016/sep/01/alan-kurdi-death-one-year-on-compassion-towards-refugees-fades, accessed 3 September 2016.

Kittler, Friedrich, *Gramophone, Film, Typewriter*, Geoffrey Winthrop-Young and Michael Wutz (trans.) (Stanford: Stanford University Press, 1999).

Klevjer, Rune, 'Enter the Avatar: The Phenomenology of Prosthetic Telepresence in Computer Games', in John Richard Sageng, Hallvard J. Fossheim and Tarjei Mandt Larsen (eds), *The Philosophy of Computer Games* (New York and London: Springer, 2012), pp. 17–38.

Klinger, Barbara, *Beyond the Multiplex: Cinema, New Technologies and the Home* (Berkley: University of California Press, 2006).

Kracauer, Siegfried, *The Mass Ornament: Weimar Essays*, Thomas Y. Levin (ed. and trans.) (Cambridge, MA: Harvard University Press, 1995).

Kraemer, Joseph A., '*Waltz with Bashir* (2008): Trauma and Representation in the Animated Documentary', *Journal of Film and Video* 67(3–4), 2015, pp. 57–68.

Krauss, Rosalind, *The Originality of the Avant-Garde and Other Modernist Myths* (London: MIT Press, 1985).

Kriger, Judith, *Animated Realism: A Behind the Scenes Look at the Animated Documentary Genre* (Waltham, MA: Focal press, 2012).

Krystof, Doris, 'Call Gillian – Masks, Identity and Performativity', in *Gillian Wearing*, exhibition catalogue (London, Whitechapel Gallery, 2012), pp. 9–20.

Lackner, James, 'Some Proprioceptive Influences on the Perceptual Representation of Body Shape and Orientation', *Brain* Oxford University Press 111(2), 1988, pp. 281–97.

Lambert-Beatty, Carrie, 'Make Believe: Parafiction and Plausibility', in Elizabeth Armstrong (ed.) *More Real? Art in the Age of Truthiness* (Minneapolis: Minneapolis Institute of Arts, 2013), pp. 110–55.

Land, Ellie, 'Animating the Other Side: Animated Documentary as a Communication Tool for Exploring Displacement and Reunification in Germany', in Ian Convery, Gerard Corsane and Peter Davies (eds), *Displaced Heritage: Responses to Disaster, Trauma, and Loss* (Rochester: Boydell Press, 2014): pp. 121–8.

Landesman, Ohad and Roy Bendor, 'Animated Recollection and Spectatorial Experience in Waltz with Bashir', *Animation: An Interdisciplinary Journal* 6(3), 2011, pp. 353–70.

Latour, Bruno, 'Emancipation or Attachments? The Different Futures of Politics', in Terry Smith, Okwui Enwezor and Nancy Condee (eds), *Antinomies of Art and Culture: Modernity, Postmodernity, Contemporaneity* (Durham and London: Duke University Press, 2008), pp. 309–23.

Leigh, David and Luke Harding, *Wikileaks* (London: Guardian Books, 2011).

Leighton, Tanya (ed.), *Art and the Moving Image – A Critical Reader* (London, Tate Publishing, 2008).

Lejacq, Yannick, 'Score! Professional Video Gamers awarded Athletic Visas', *NBC News*, 20 July 2013, www.nbcnews.com/tech/video-games/score-professional-video-gamers-awarded-athletic-visas-f6C10679998, accessed 29 July 2013.

Lenggenhager, Bigna, Tej Tadi, Thomas Metzinger and Olaf Blanke, 'Video Ergo Sum: Manipulating Bodily Self-consciousness', *Science* 317, 2007, pp. 1096–9.

Leslie, Esther, *Hollywood Flatlands: Animation, Critical Theory and the Avant-Garde* (London and New York: Verso, 2002).

Leslie, Esther, 'Cloud Animation', *Animation: An Interdisciplinary Journal* 12(3), 2017, pp. 230–243.

Leslie, Esther and Joel McKim. 'Life Remade: Critical Animation in the Digital Age', *Animation* 12(3), 2017, pp. 207–13.

Levitt, Deborah, 'Animation and the Medium of Life: Media Ethology, An-ontology, Ethics', *Inflexions* 7, 2014, pp. 118–61.

Levitt, Deborah, *The Animatic Apparatus Animation, Vitality, and the Futures of the Image* (Winchester, UK and Washington: Zero Books, 2018).

Levy, Mark, 'From the Real to the More Real: A Brief Historical and Philosophical Sketch of Hyperreality and its Roots in Realism, Impressionism, Surrealism, Pop Art, and Postmodernism', in Elizabeth Armstrong (ed.), *More Real? Art in the Age of Truthiness* (Minneapolis: Minneapolis Institute of Arts, 2013), pp. 84–109.

Levy, Silvano (ed.), *Surrealism: Surrealist Visuality* (Edinburgh: Keele University Press, 1997).

Lind, Maria and Hito Steyerl (eds), *The Greenroom: Reconsidering the Documentary and Contemporary Art* (Los Angeles: Sternberg Press, 2008).

Lowery, Frédérique Joseph, 'Harun Farocki: Touching Distance', *Art-Press* 385, 2012, pp. 47–9.

Lowood, Henry, 'High-performance Play: The Making of Machinima', in Andy Clarke and Grethe Mitchell (eds), *Videogames and Art* (Bristol and Chicago: Intellect, 2005), pp. 59–79.

Lowood, Henry, 'Video Capture: Machinima, Documentation, and the History of Virtual Worlds', in Henry Lowood and Michael Nitsche (eds), *The Machinima Reader* (Cambridge, MA: MIT Press, 2011), pp. 3–22.

Ma, Minhua, Huiru Zheng and Harjinder Lallie, 'Virtual Reality and 3D Animation in Forensic Visualization', *Forensic Sciences* 55(5), 2010, pp. 1227–31.

Mann, Steve, John C. Havens, Jay Iorio, Yu Yuan and Tom Furness, 'All Reality: Values, Taxonomy, and Continuum, for Virtual, Augmented, eXtended/MiXed (X), mediated

(X,Y), and Multimediated Reality/Intelligence', paper presented at AWE 2018, Santa Clara, CA, 31 May 2018, available at http://wearcam.org/all.pdf, accessed 20 July 2019.

Manchester, Elizabeth, 'Gillian Wearing', *Tate*, www.tate.org.uk/art/artworks/wearing-10-6-t07415/text-summary, accessed 20 July 2012.

Manovich, Lev, 'An Archeology of a Computer Screen', *Manovich.net*, 1995, www.manovich.net/TEXT/digital_nature.html, accessed 18 March 2012.

Manovich, Lev, 'Navigable Space', *Manovich.net*, 1998, www.manovich.net/DOCS/navigable_space.doc, accessed 2 February 2013.

Manovich, Lev, 'Post-media Aesthetics', *Manovich.net*, 2001, www.manovich.net/content/04-projects/030-post-media-aesthetics/29_article_2001.pdf, accessed 10 June 2010.

Manovich, Lev, *The Language of New Media* (Massachusetts and London: MIT Press, 2001).

Manovich, Lev, 'After Effects, or Velvet Revolution', *Artifact* 1(2), 2007, pp. 67–75.

Manovich, Lev, 'Introduction to Info-aesthetics', in Terry Smith, Okwui Enwezor, and Nancy Condee (eds), *Antinomies of Art and Culture: Modernity, Postmodernity, Contemporaneity* (Durham and London: Duke University Press, 2008), pp. 333–44.

Manovich, Lev, 'Image Future', in Henry Lowood and Michael Nitsche (eds), *The Machinima Reader* (London: MIT Press, 2011), pp. 73–90.

Manovich, Lev, *Software Takes Command: Extending the Language of New Media* (London: Bloomsbury, 2013).

Marchessault, Janine and Susan Lord (eds) *Fluid Screens, Expanded Cinema* (Toronto, Buffalo, NY, London: University of Toronto Press, 2007).

Marino, Paul, *3D Game-based Filmmaking: The Art of Machinima* (Scottsdale, AZ: Paraglyph Press, 2004).

Marks, Laura, *The Skin of the Film: Intercultural Cinema, Embodiment, and the Senses* (Durham: Duke University Press, 2000).

Martinez, Omar O. Linares, 'Criteria for Defining Animation: A Revision of the Definition of Animation in the Advent of Digital Moving Images', *Animation: An Interdisciplinary Journal* 10(1), 2015, pp. 42– 57.

Massumi, Brian, *Parables for the Virtual* (Durham and London: Duke University Press, 2002).

Mazalek, Ali, 'Tangible Narratives: Emerging Interfaces for Digital Storytelling and Machinima', in Henry Lowood and Michael Nitsche (eds), *The Machinima Reader* (London: MIT Press, 2011), pp. 91–110.

McGonigal, Jane, *Reality is Broken: Why Games Make us Better And How They Can Change the World* (London: Jonathan Cape, 2011).

McIntyre, Lee, *Post-truth* (Cambridge, MA and London: MIT Press, 2018).

McKim, Joel, 'Speculative Animation: Digital Projections of Urban Past and Future', *Animation: An Interdisciplinary Journal* 12(3), 2017, pp. 287– 305.

McQuire, Scott, Meredith Martin and Sabine Niederer (eds), *Urban Screens Reader* (Amsterdam: Institute of Network Cultures, 2009).

Meillassoux, Quentin, *After Finitude: An Essay on the Necessity of Contingency*, Ray Brassier (trans.) (London: Bloomsbury Academic, 2010).

Merleau-Ponty, Maurice, *Phenomenology of Perception* [1962] (London: Routledge Classics, 2002).

Metz, Christian, 'On the Impression of Reality in the Cinema', in Christian Metz, *Film Language: A Semiotics of the Cinema*, Michael Taylor (trans.) (New York: Oxford University Press, 1974), pp. 3–15.

Miah, Andy, 'Posthumanism: A Critical History', in Bert Gordijn and Ruth Chadwick (eds), *Medical Enhancements & Posthumanity* (New York: Routledge, 2007), pp. 71–94.

Mihailova, Mihaela, 'Before Sound, There Was Soul: The Role of Animation in Silent

Nonfiction Cinema', in Jonathan Murray and Nea Ehrlich (eds), *Drawn from Life: Issues and Themes in Animated Documentary Cinema* (Edinburgh: Edinburgh University Press, 2019), pp. 31–46.

Mirapaul, Matthe, 'Online Games Grab Grim Reality', *New York Times*, 17 September 2003.

Mitchell, William J. T., *Iconology: Image, Text, Ideology* (Chicago: University of Chicago Press, 1987).

Mitchell, William J. T., *Picture Theory: Essays on Verbal and Visual Representation* (Chicago: University of Chicago Press, 1995).

Moore, Samantha. '"Does This Look Right?" Working Inside the Collaborative Frame', in Jonathan Murray and Nea Ehrlich (eds), *Drawn from Life: Issues and Themes in Animated Documentary Cinema* (Edinburgh: Edinburgh University Press, 2019), pp. 206–20.

Morag, Raya, *Waltzing with Bashir: Perpetrator Trauma and Cinema* (London: I. B. Tauris, 2013).

Mori, Masahiro, 'The Uncanny Valley', *Energy* 7(4), 1970, pp. 33–5.

Morse, Margaret, 'Sunshine and Shroud: Cyborg Bodies and the Collective and Personal Self', *Media Art Net*, www.medienkunstnetz.de/themes/cyborg_bodies/collective_bodies/, accessed 20 June 2013.

Murray, Janet, *Hamlet on the Holodeck* (Cambridge: MIT Press, 2000).

Murray, Janet, 'VR as Empathy or Novelty', *Inventing the Medium*, 6 January 2016, https://inventingthemedium.com/2016/01/06/vr-as-empathy-or-novelty-continued/, accessed 20 May 2017.

Murray, Jonathan, 'Waltz with Bashir', *Cineaste*, 2009, pp. 65–8.

Murray, Jonathan and Nea Ehrlich (eds), *Drawn from Life: Issues and Themes in Animated Documentary Cinema* (Edinburgh: Edinburgh University Press, 2019).

Musser, Charles, 'Toward a History of Screen Practice', *Quarterly Review of Film Studies* 9(1), 1984, pp. 59–69.

Nagib, Lúcia and Cecília Mello, 'Introduction', in Lúcia Nagib and Cecília Mello (eds), *Realism and the Audiovisual Media* (New York: Palgrave Macmillan, 2009), pp. xiv–xxvi.

Nagib, Lúcia and Cecília Mello (eds), *Realism and the Audiovisual Media* (New York: Palgrave Macmillan, 2009).

Nåls, Jan Erik, 'Drawing the Unspeakable: Understanding "the Other" through Narrative Empathy in Animated Documentary', *International Journal of Film and Media Arts* 1(1), 2016, pp. 28–41.

Nash, Kate, 'Virtual Reality Witness: Exploring the Ethics of Mediated Presence', *Studies in Documentary Film* 12(2), 2017, pp. 119–31.

Nash, Mark, 'Reality in the Age of Aesthetics', *Frieze* 114, 2008, www.frieze.com/issue/article/reality_in_the_age_of_aesthetics/, accessed 9 September 2010.

Nathan, Sara and Paul Revoir, 'ITV Admits It Passed Off Clip from a VIDEO GAME as Footage of IRA Attack on British Helicopter in New Flagship News Show', *The Daily Mail –Mail Online*, 28 September 2011, www.dailymail.co.uk/news/article-2042568/ITV-fake-footage-row-new-documentary-passes-game-IRA-gun-attack-British-helicopter.html#ixzz2cQevwlFq;, accessed 15 April 2013.

Nelson, Ted H., 'The Right Way to Think about Software Design', in Brenda Laurel (ed.), *The Art of Human–computer Interface Design* (Reading, MA: Addison-Wesley, 1990), pp. 235–43.

Neys, Joyce and Jeroen Jansz, 'Political Internet Games: Engaging an Audience', *European Journal of Communication* 25(3), 2010, pp. 227–41.

Nichols, Bill, *Representing Reality: Issues and Concepts in Documentary* (Bloomington: Indiana University Press, 1992).

Nichols, Bill, '"Getting to Know You . . ." Knowledge, Power, and the Body', in Michael Renov (ed.), *Theorising Documentary* (New York and London: Routledge, 1993), pp. 174–91.

Nichols, Bill, *Introduction to Documentary* (Bloomington: Indiana University Press, 2001).

Nichols, Bill, 'Documentary Reenactment and the Fantasmatic Subject', *Critical Inquiry* 35(1), 2008, pp. 72–89.

Nideffer, Robert F., 'Eight Questions (and Answers) about Machinima', *Journal of Visual Culture* 10(1), 2011, pp. 66–73.

Nitsche, Michael, 'Claiming Its Space: Machinima', *Dichtung Digital: Journal für digitale Ästhetik* 37, 2007, unpaginated. www.brown.edu/Research/dichtung-digital/2007/Nitsche/nitsche.htm, accessed 27 January 2010.

Nitsche, Michael, 'Machinima as Media', in Henry Lowood and Michael Nitsche (eds), *The Machinima Reader* (London: MIT Press, 2011), pp. 113–26.

Odin, Roger, 'For a Semio-pragmatics of Film', in *The Film Spectator: From Sign to Mind*, ed. W. Buckland (Amsterdam: Amsterdam University Press, 1995), pp. 201–26.

Odin, Roger. 'A Semio-pragmatic Approach to the Documentary Film', in Warren Buckland (ed.) *The Film Spectator: From Sign to Mind* (Amsterdam: Amsterdam University Press, 1995), pp. 227–35.

Osborne, Peter, *Anywhere or Not at All* (London: Verso, 2013).

Østby Sæther, Susanne, 'Between the Hyperrepresentational and the Real: A Sampling Sensibility', in Damian Sutton, Susan Bird and Ray McKenzie (eds), *The State of the Real: Aesthetics in the Digital Age* (London and New York: I. B. Tauris, 2007), pp. 48–61.

Ostherr, Kirsten, *Medical Visions. Producing the Patient through Film, Television, and Imaging Technologies* (New York, Oxford University Press 2013).

Paradiso, Joseph A. and James A. Landay, 'Guest Editors' Introduction: Cross-reality Environments', *IEEE Pervasive Computing* 8(3), 2009, pp. 14–5.

Parkin, Simon, 'Interview – Darfur is Dying', *Eurogamer*, 4 September 2006, www.eurogamer.net, accessed 5 June 2010.

Parsons, Caroline, 'Why We Need a New Language of Cinema', *The Society for Animation Studies Blog*, 22 July 2013, www.blog.animationstudies.org/?p=397#comment-575, accessed 3 August 2013.

Patrick, Eric, 'Representing Reality: Structural/Conceptual Design in Non-fiction Animation', *Animac Magazine* 3, 2004, pp. 36–47.

Paul, Christiane, *Digital Art* (New York: Thames and Hudson, 2003).

Pearce, Celia, *Communities of Play: Emergent Cultures in Multiplayer Games and Virtual Worlds* (Boston, MA: MIT Press, 2009).

Peaslee, Robert Moses, 'It's Fine As Long As You Draw, But Don't Film: Waltz with Bashir and the Postmodern Function of Animated Documentary', *Visual Communication Quarterly* 18(4), 2011, pp. 223–35.

Petkova V. I. and H. H. Ehrsson, 'If I Were You: Perceptual Illusion of Body Swapping', *PLoS ONE* 3(12), 2008, p. e3832.

Poremba, Cynthia, 'Real/Unreal: Crafting Actuality in the Documentary Videogame', PhD thesis, Concordia University, 2011.

Raessens, Joost, 'Reality Play: Documentary Computer Games Beyond Fact and Fiction', *Popular Communication* 4, 2006, pp. 213–24.

Raiti, Gerard, 'The Disappearance of Disney Animated Propaganda: A Globalization Perspective', *Animation: An Interdisciplinary Journal* 2(2), 2007, pp. 153–69.

Reinhardt, Mark and Holly Edwards (eds), *Beautiful Suffering* (Chicago: Chicago University Press, 2006).

Reinke, Steve, 'The World is a Cartoon: Stray Notes on Animation', in Chris Gehman and Steve Reinke (eds), *The Sharpest Point: Animation at the End of Cinema* (Toronto: YYZ Books, 2005), pp. 9–26.

Renov, Michael, 'Animation: Documentary's Imaginary Signifier', paper presented at Visible Evidence conference X, Marseilles, France, December 2002.

Renov, Michael (ed.), *Theorising Documentary* (New York: Routledge, 1993).

Respini, Eva, 'Cindy Sherman', *Museum of Modern Art*, www.moma.org/interactives/exhibitions/2012/cindysherman/about-the-exhibition/, accessed 20 July 2012.

Rieser, Martin and Andrea Zapp (eds), *New Screen Media – Cinema/Art/Narrative* (Karlsruhe: BFI, 2002).

Ritchin, Fred, *After Photography* (New York: W. W. Norton, 2009).

Roberts, John, *The Art of Interruption* (Manchester: Manchester University Press, 1998).

Rogers, Sol, 'Coronavirus Has Made WFH the New Normal. Here's How Virtual Reality Can Help', Forbes, 26 March 2020, https://www.forbes.com/sites/solrogers/2020/03/26/coronavirus-has-made-wfh-the-new-normal-heres-how-virtual-reality-can-help/#61cf341f61d5, accessed 30 June 2020.

Rogoff, Irit, *Terra Infirma – Geography's Visual Culture* (London and New York: Routledge, 2000).

Ronchi, Alfredo M., *Eculture: Cultural Content in the Digital Age* (New York: Springer, 2009).

Rosen, Philip, 'Document and Documentary: On the Persistence of Historical Concepts', in Michael Renov (ed.), *Theorising Documentary* (New York and London: Routledge, 1993), pp. 58–89.

Roquet, Paul, 'From Animation to Augmentation: Dennō Coil and the Composited Self', *Animation: An Interdisciplinary Journal* 11(3), 2016, pp. 228–45.

Rowley, Stephen, 'Life Reproduced in Drawings: Preliminary Comments upon Realism in Animation', *Animation Journal* 13, 2005, pp. 65–85.

Sacco, Joe, *Palestine Collection* (Seattle: Fantagraphics Books, 2001).

Sageng, John Richard, Hallvard J. Fossheim and Tarjei Mandt Larsen (eds), *The Philosophy of Computer Games* (New York and London: Springer, 2012).

Salen, Katie, 'Arrested Development: Why Machinima Can't (or Shouldn't) Grow Up', in Henry Lowood and Michael Nitsche (eds), *The Machinima Reader* (London: MIT Press, 2011), pp. 37–50.

Salen, Katie and Eric Zimmerman, *Rules of Play* (Cambridge, MA: MIT Press, 2004).

Salmon, Andrew, 'Internet Gaming Addiction Led to Baby's Death', *CNN*, 2 April 2010, www.cnn.co.il/2010/WORLD/asiapcf/04/01/korea.parents.starved.baby/index.html, accessed 20 June 2012.

Sandler, Ronald (ed.), *Ethics and Emerging Technologies* (New York: Palgrave, 2014).

Sarkar, Samit, 'Pokémon Go Hits 650 Million Downloads', *Polygon*, 27 February 2017, www.polygon.com/2017/2/27/14753570/pokemon-go-downloads-650-million, accessed 4 April 2017.

Schäuble, Michaela, '"All Filmmaking is a Form of Therapy": Visualizing Memories of War Violence in the Animation Film Waltz with Bashir (2008)', in Maria Six-Hohenbalken and Nerina Weiss (eds), *Violence Expressed: An Anthropological Approach* (Farnham: Ashgate Publishing, 2011), pp. 203–22.

Schechner, Richard, *Between Theater and Anthropology* (Philadelphia, PA: University of Pennsylvania Press, 1985).

Schofield, Damian, 'Playing with Evidence: Using Video Games in the Courtroom', *Entertainment Computing* 2(1), 2011, pp. 47–58.

Scott, Anthony, 'Inside a Veteran's Nightmare – Waltz with Bashir', *International New York*

Times, 25 December 2008, www.nytimes.com/2008/12/26/movies/26bash.html, accessed 10 July 2016.

Shale, Richard, *Donald Duck Joins Up: The Walt Disney Studio during World War II* (Ann Arbor: UMI Research Press, 1976).

Shay, Christopher, 'The Taiwan Company That's Turning News Into Cartoons', *Time*. 23 August 2010, www.time.com/time/world/article/0,8599,2012166,00.html, accessed 10 November 2010.

Shields, Rob, *The Virtual* (London and New York: Routledge, 2003).

Short, T. L., *Peirce's Theory of Signs* (Cambridge: Cambridge University Press, 2007).

Sieff, Gemma, 'Bertolt Brecht and the Media Today', *Frieze* 148, 2012, pp. 31–4.

Simons, Jan, 'Pockets in the Screenscape: Movies on the Move', paper presented at Stone and Papyrus, Storage and Transmission Massachusetts Institute of Technology, Cambridge, MA, United States, 24–6 April 2009.

Sitney, Sky, 'The Search for the Invisible Cinema', *Grey Room* 19, 2005, pp. 102–13.

Sito, Tom, *Drawing the Line: The Untold Story of the Animation Unions from Bosko to Bart Simpson* (Lexington: University Press of Kentucky, 2006).

Skoller, Jeffrey, 'Introduction to the Special Issue "Making it (Un)real: Contemporary Theories and Practices in Documentary Animation"', *Animation: An Interdisciplinary Journal* 6(3), 2011, pp. 207–14.

Slater, Mel, 'Place Illusion and Plausibility Can Lead to Realistic Behaviour in Immersive Virtual Environments', *Philosophical Transactions of the Royal Society B* 364, 2009, pp. 3549–57.

Slater, Mel, 'The Virtual Self', paper presented at Contextualizing the Self: Creating and Recreating the First person, Tel Aviv University, Tel Aviv, Israel, 24 January 2017.

Slote, Michael, *The Ethics of Care and Empathy* (London: Routledge. 2007).

Slotnik, Daniel R., 'Gamer's Death Pushes Risks of Live Streaming into View', *International New York Times*, 15 March 2017.

Smith, Adam, *The Theory of the Moral Sentiments* [1759] (Indianapolis: Liberty Classics 1969).

Smith, Terry, *What is Contemporary Art?* (Chicago and London: University of Chicago Press, 2009).

Sobchack, Vivian, *Carnal Thoughts* (Berkeley and London: University of California Press, 2004).

Sofian, Sheila, 'The Truth in Pictures', *FPS Magazine*, March 2005, pp. 7–11.

Solon, Olivia, 'The Future of Fake News: Don't Believe Everything You Read, See or Hear', *The Guardian*, 26 July 2017.

Sontag, Susan, *Regarding the Pain of Others* (New York: Picador, 2003).

Spence, Edward H., 'Virtual Rape, Real Dignity: Meta-ethics for Virtual Worlds', in John Richard Sageng, Hallvard J. Fossheim and Tarjei Mandt Larsen (eds), *The Philosophy of Computer Games* (New York and London: Springer, 2012), pp. 125–42.

Spiegelman, Art, *Maus: A Survivor's Tale*, 2 vols. (New York: Pantheon Books, 1986–91).

Stav, Shira, 'Nakba and Holocaust: Mechanisms of Comparison and Denial in the Israeli Literary Imagination', *Jewish Social Studies* 18(3), 2012, pp. 85–98.

Stern, Eddo, 'Massively Multiplayer Machinima Mikusuto', *Journal of Visual Culture* 10(1), 2011, pp. 42–50.

Stewart, Garrett, 'Screen Memory in Waltz with Bashir', *Film Quarterly* 63(3), 2010, pp. 58–62.

Stiegler, Bernard, *Automatic Society*, Daniel Ross (trans.) (Cambridge: Polity Press, 2016).

Stix, Madeleine, 'World's First Cyborg Wants to Hack Your Body'. *CNN*, 2016, https://edition.cnn.com/2014/09/02/tech/innovation/cyborg-neil-harbisson-implant-antenna/index.html, accessed 15 September 2017.

Strøm, Gunnar, 'The Animated Documentary', *Animation Journal* 11, 2003, pp. 46–63.

Sutton, Damian, 'Real Photography', in Damian Sutton, Susan Brind and Ray McKenzie (eds), *The State of the Real – Aesthetics in the Digital Age* (London and New York: I. B. Tauris, 2007), pp. 162–71.
Sutton-Smith, Brian, *The Ambiguity of Play* (Cambridge, MA: Harvard University Press, 1997).
Taylor, Grant D., *When the Machine Made Art: The Troubled History of Computer Art* (New York: Bloomsbury Academic, 2014).
Ten Brink, Joram, 'Animating Trauma: Waltz with Bashir, David Polonsky', in Joram ten Brink and Joshua Oppenheimer (eds), *Killer Images: Documentary Film, Memory, and the Performance of Violence* (New York: Columbia University Press, 2012), pp. 127–35.
Tortum, Deniz, 'How Virtual Reality Technology Is Changing Documentary Filmmaking', *Open Documentary Lab at MIT*, originally featured in Indiewire, 31 January 2015, http://opendoclab.mit.edu/virtual-reality-technology-changing-documentary-filmmaking-deniz-tortum and www.indiewire.com/2015/01/how-virtual-reality-technology-is-changing-documentary-filmmaking-248298/, accessed 2 July 2017.
Turkle, Sherry, *The Second Self: Computers and the Human Spirit* (New York: Simon & Schuster, 1984).
Turner, Jeremy, 'Myron Krueger Live', *C-Theory*, 23 January 2002, http://ctheory.net/ctheory_wp/myron-krueger-live/, accessed September, 9, 2019.
Vaughan, Dai, *For Documentary: Twelve Essays* (Berkley: University of California Press, 1999).
Verhofen, Nanna, 'Grasping the Screen, Toward a Conceptualization of Touch, Mobility and Multiplicity', in Marianne van den Boomen, Ann-Sophie Lehmann, Sybilles Lammes and Joost Raessens (eds), *Digital Material: Tracing New Media in Everyday Life and Technology* (Amsterdam: Amsterdam University Press, 2009), pp. 209–22.
Virilio, Paul, *The Vision Machine* (Bloomington: Indiana University Press, 1994).
Wakeman, Jessica, 'Life After Sexual Assault: Inside Harrowing Doc "Audrie & Daisy"', *Rolling Stone*, 23 September 2016, www.rollingstone.com/culture/features/life-after-sexual-assault-inside-doc-audrie-daisy-w441794, accessed 14 April 2017.
Waldberg, Patrick, *Surrealism* (New York: Thames & Hudson, 1997).
Wallace, Mark, 'The Game is Virtual. The Profit is Real', *New York Times*, 29 May 2005.
Warburton, Alan, 'Goodbye Uncanny Valley', *Vimeo*, 2017, https://vimeo.com/237568588, accessed 3 April 2019.
Ward, Paul, 'Videogames as Remediated Animation', in Geoff King and Tanya Krzywinska (eds), *ScreenPlay: Cinema/Videogames/Interfaces* (London: Wallflower Press, 2002), pp. 122–35.
Ward, Paul, *Documentary: The Margins of Reality* (London: Wallflower Press, 2005).
Ward, Paul, 'Animated Realities: The Animated Film, Documentary, Realism', *Reconstruction: Studies in Contemporary Culture* 8.2.19, 2008, pp. 1–27.
Ward, Paul, 'Drama-documentary, Ethics and Notions of Performance: The "Flight 93" Films', in Thomas Austin and Wilma de Jong (eds), *Rethinking Documentary* (Maidenhead: Open University Press, 2008), pp. 191–203.
Ward, Paul, 'Animating with Facts: The Performative Process of Documentary Animation', *Animation: An Interdisciplinary Journal* 6(3), 2011, pp. 293–305.
Webber, Nick, 'Law, Culture and Massively Multiplayer Online Games', *International Review of Law, Computers & Technology* 28(1), 2014, pp. 45–59.
Weber, Samuel, 'A Virtual Indication', in Antony Bryant and Griselda Pollock (eds), *Digital and Other Virtualities* (New York: I. B. Tauris, 2010), pp. 63–78.
Weizman, Eyal, *Forensic Architecture: Violence at the Threshold of Detectability* (Cambridge: MIT Press, 2017).

Wells, Brian, 'Frame of Reference: Toward a Definition of Animation', *Animation Practice, Process & Production* 1(1), 2011, pp. 11–32.
Wells, Paul, 'The Beautiful Village and the True Village: A Consideration of Animation and the Documentary Aesthetic', in Paul Wells (ed.), *Art and Animation* (London: Academy Editions, 1997), pp. 40–5.
Wells, Paul, *Animation – Genre and Authorship* (London: Wallflower Press, 2002).
Wells, Paul, *Basics Animation: Scriptwriting* (Lausanne: AVA Publishing, 2007).
Williams, Linda, 'Film Bodies: Gender, Genre, Excess', *Film Quarterly* 44(4), 1991, pp. 2–13.
Williams, Raymond, 'A Lecture on Realism', *Screen* 18(1), 1977, pp. 61–74.
Wilson, Andrew, 'Jeremy Deller – The Battle of Orgreave Archive (an Injury to one is an Injury to All)', *Tate*, www.tate.org.uk/art/artworks/deller-the-battle-of-orgreave-archive-an-injury-to-one-is-an-injury-to-all-t12185/text-summary, accessed 24 July 2012.
Wingfield, Nick, 'What's Twitch? Gamers Know, and Amazon Is Spending $1 Billion On It', *International New York Times*, 25 August 2014.
Wingfield, Nick, 'Video Games Go Big League', *International New York Times*, 1 September 2014.
Witter Turner, Victor, *From Ritual to Theatre: The Human Seriousness of Play* (New York: Performing Arts Journal Publications, 1982).
Wollen, Peter, *Signs and Meaning in the Cinema* (London: BFI, 1997).
Woodcock, Rose, 'Capture, Hold, Release: An Ontology of Motion Capture', *Studies in Australasian Cinema*, 10(1), 2016, pp. 1–15.
Yolton, John W., *Realism and Appearances: An Essay in Ontology* (Cambridge: Cambridge University Press, 2000).
Zimmerman, Eric, 'Narrative, Interactivity, Play, and Games', in Richard Schechner, *Between Theater and Anthropology* (Philadelphia, PA: University of Pennsylvania Press, 1985), p. 110.
Zimmerman, Eric, 'Narrative, Interactivity, Play, and Games: Four Naughty Concepts in Need of Discipline', in Pat Harrigan and Noah W. Wardrip-Fruin (eds), *First Person New Media as Story, Performance, and Game* (Cambridge, MA: MIT Press, 2004), pp. 154–64.
Zylinska, Joanna, *Nonhuman Photography* (Cambridge, MA: MIT Press, 2017).

Index

animated documentaries
    contemporary forms of, 35–7, 213–14, 225
    defined, 3
    emergence of, 2, 10, 27
    scholarship on, 3, 19, 46–7
Animated Introduction to Cancer Biology, 36
animation
    comparison of animation in the past with animation today, 229
    crossover of fact and fiction in, 8–9, 199–200, 208–9
    definitions of, 9–10, 59–62, 228, 239
    fantasy/artificiality conception of, 1, 2, 4, 8
    as a form of document, 14, 54, 75, 77–8, 120–1, 127, 137–8, 146–7, 227, 237
    within the human-technological paradigm, 57
    idea of motion, 60, 66
    multidisciplinary approaches, 7–8
    for non-fiction purposes, 11, 32–3, 35, 46
    non-mimetic imagery for non-fiction, 39–43, 167–8
    non-photographic animated imagery, 6
    for non-physical realities, 9, 88–9, 94–5, 120–1, 126, 147
    to portray 'the real,' 2, 56, 60
    presence/absence in, 121–2, 153
    in relation to live-action film, 3–4, 56, 59, 61, 207
    relationship with realism, 16–17
    shifting relationship with photography, 10–11, 13, 27, 57
    term, 59–60, 62
    use of photographs in, 35, 58
animoji, 103
Another Planet (Yatziv), 136, 144–6, 147, 224, 225–7, 232–5
anymation, 62
artificial intelligence (AI), 38

artificial animation, 61
    machine vision, 40–1, 238–9
    mistrust of images, 38
    objectivity of mechanically captured images, 57
Ashuri, Tamar, 153
audio interviews, 54, 55, 139
Audrie & Daisy (Cohen/Shenk), 216
augmented reality (AR), 10, 91, 94
authenticity
    diminished truth-value of photography, 37–9, 44
    in documentaries, 99
    in immersive journalism, 156
    non-mimetic images, 38–9
    perceptions of photographs, 34–5, 156, 159–60
    reactivity of interactive animated documentaries, 167–8
    of virtual reality documentaries, 159
    witnessing and, 153–4
Avatar (Cameron), 10
avatars
    in *Another Planet* (Yatziv), 145, 224
    with cameras, 117–18
    in *Darfur is Dying*, 165–6, 186–7
    in *Drakedog's Suicide*, 111–12
    indexicality of, 166, 186
    moral codes for, 135–6
    non-humanoid game avatars in *Stranger Comes to Town* (Goss), 137, 139, 140, 141–3, *142*
    non-photographic imagery, 102
    for online users, 68, 100, 101, 112, 115–16, 129, 164
    player identification with avatars/protagonists, 112, 164, 165–6, 185–6
    WoW memorial services, 135

Barthes, Roland, 58
The Battle of Orgreave (Deller), 104

Index

Baudrillard, Jean, 44
Bazin, André, 31, 57
Beckman, Karen, 217
Bendor, Roy, 184
Besmer, Kirk, 102
Beugnet, Martine, 167
Black Mirror (Brooker), 236
bodies
  animoji, 103
  Being: New Photography 2018, 105
  biometric testing, 137–40
  body language, 216
  cartoonification of, 102
  corporeal experience of immersive journalism, 155–6
  corporeal identification of the viewer, 179–80
  cyborg bodies, 101
  data collection on, 100
  in digital culture, 99
  in documentaries, 98
  in documentary-related artworks, 103–5
  embodiment in virtual culture, 99
  facial recognition software, 106–7
  non-photographic imagery for, 102–3
  performance art, 105–6
  physical identification in ethical viewing, 179, 188–9
  presence in a VR platform, 154
  re-embodiment, 100, 154
  representations of the self, 6, 101–3, 107, 154, 185
  role of the body and physical movement, 63
  and the sense of self, 98–9, 100–1
  as signifiers of truth, 98–100, 188–9
  viewer identification with animated bodies, 189–92
  in virtualised culture, 100–7
  see also physicality
Bogost, Ian, 163–4
Brecht, Bertolt, 205
Brennan, John, 161
Bridle, James, 40–1
Brooker, Charlie, 236
Buchan, Suzanne, 56, 61
Burns, Maureen, 217

Caillois, Roger, 113
Caloud, Mike, 161
Cameron, David, 122
Carroll, John, 122
Carroll, Noel, 90

Castranova, Edward, 113, 115
Cholodenko, Alan, 60
Chow, Kenny, 62, 67
Cohen, Bonni, 216
Cole, Jeff, 161
Columbine Cafeteria (Rogers), 104–5
The Congress (Folman), 237
coronavirus pandemic, 236–7
Coupland, Douglas, 106–7
Crafton, Donald, 59–60
Crary, Jonathan, 46
Cubitt, Sean, 95

Danilovic, Sandra, 103, *104*
Darfur is Dying (Ruiz et al.)
  avatar selection, 165–6, 186–7
  documentary games, 165–6, 169, 186–7
  player/protagonist interpellation, 194, 202
data
  animated data visualisations, 8–9, 11, 14, 40, 69–73
  biometric testing, 137–40
  corporeal data collection, 100
  data-driven art, 40, 69–70, *70*, 73
Deep Face (Coupland), 106
deixis, 64–5, 66, 67, 69–75, 76
Deleuze, Gilles, 72, 211–13
Deller, Jeremy, 104
Denslow, Phillip Kelly, 62
Derrida, Jacques, 97
Diary of a Camper, 119, 120, 123
Dibbell, Julian, 112, 135
digital culture
  animation as the visualisation of code, 74–5
  bodies in, 99
  digital virtual, defined, 88
  indexicality in, 29, 63, 65, 74
  machine vision, 40–1, 238–9
  memory construction, 145–6, 233
  non-photographic animated imagery, 10
  role of the physical in, 6, 14–15, 17, 42, 65
  use of non-photorealistic animation, 2
  see also gaming; technoculture; virtual culture
Do It Yourself (Ledune), 97–8, *98*
Doane, Mary Ann, 65
documentaries
  authenticity in, 99
  defined, 12, 27, 29, 30, 31, 56, 72, 75–6, 77
  documentary artworks, 103–5
  narrative games as, 112–13, 115, 117–18

documentaries (*cont.*)
  non-physically mimetic imagery of people, 99
  realism of, 6–7, 45, 151
  role of the body, 98
  role of violence, 188–9
  visual footage, 39–40
  warranting devices, 54–5
documentary animation, 7, 128, 129–30, 227, 228–9
documentary experiences
  concept of, 167
  emotional connections with virtual worlds, 167–8
  within existing documentary conventions, 168–70
  new forms of realism, 168
  response-as-if-real (RAIR), 167
  on-screen/off-screen convergence, 168, 186
documentary games
  Darfur is Dying, 165–6, 169, 186–8, 194, 202
  within existing documentary conventions, 168–70
  expressions of the political self, 187–8
  games for change, 164–5
  genre of, 161
  interactivity or, 162–3
  news games, 164–5
  open-ended narratives, 163–4
  player identification with avatars/protagonists, 112, 164, 165–6, 185–6
  role-playing element, 164
  witnessing in, 157
documentary studies
  documentary/document relationship, 75–7
  index as trace, 75–6
  referentiality in, 58
  representations of 'the real,' 16
  veracity narratives, 6–7
Dove, Toni, 100–1
Drakedog's Suicide, 111–12

Elsaesser, Thomas, 42, 89
empathy
  animated imagery and, 180, 193–5
  from animated protagonists, 177–8
  and animation's novel aesthetic, 193–5
  documentary viewing and, 179–80
  ethical encounters in animated documentaries, 178–9, 182, 184, 192
  within ethical viewing, 177, 178
  in immersive journalism, 158
  physical identification for, 188–9
  protagonists in horrific situations, 180
  spectator's corporeal identification, 179–80
  viewer identification with animated bodies, 189–92
  visual mimesis for, 180
Enwezor, Okwui, 58, 177, 178, 182, 184, 185, 202
ethical viewing
  animated imagery and, 180, 184–5, 193–5, 205
  depictions of reality, 11–12
  desensitised, non-ethical spectatorship, 185, 205, 235–6
  empathy and, 177, 178
  ethical encounters in animated documentaries, 178–9, 182, 184, 192
  non-fictional protagonists vs fictional characters, 178
  physical identification for, 179, 188–9
Everard, Jerry, 137
Ezawa, Kota, 216–17

fake-news, 29, 30, 38, 213, 214, 239
Farocki, Harun, 105, *105*
Flaherty, Robert, 45, 151
Flight Patterns (Koblin), 69–70, *70*, 73
Folman, Ari, 237; see also *Waltz with Bashir* (Folman)
Fullerton, Tracy, 150, 164, 185
Furniss, Maureen, 60

games, concept of, 113–14
games for change, 164–5
Games for Change (G4C), 188
Gametoon, 126
gaming
  as alternative to video calling, 237
  animation production in, 15, 36
  boundaries between play/non-play, 113–14, 116, 126, 144
  the capture of online game activities, 74–5, 111
  Diary of a Camper, 119, 120, 123
  digitally virtual experiences, 113
  documentary animation within, 129–30
  graphic user interface (GUI), 75
  the industry of, 15, 96, 113, 114–15
  interactions with 'the real' world, 96–7, 112–13

'Let's Play' phenomenon, 125
Medal of Honor: Rising Sun, 164
morality and the in-game community, 135–6
narrative games as documentaries, 112–13, 115, 117–18
online streaming of players, 116, 125–6
professionalisation of, 116–17, 126
real-time animation, 15
see also avatars; documentary games; in-game documentaries; machinima
Gayeton, Douglas, 15, 115–16, 117–19, *118*
Globalised Slavery: How Big Supermarkets are Selling Prawns in Supply Chain Fed by Slave Labour, 34, 46, 189
Goodman, Nelson, 204
Goss, Jacqueline see *Stranger Comes to Town* (Goss)
Greenberg, Raz, 121, 181
Grierson, John, 27, 30, 31, 45, 76, 151
Groys, Boris, 35
Guantánamo Bay: The Hunger Strikes, 33–4
The Guardian, 33–4, 35, 46, 189
Gunning, Tom, 64, 152, 154, 205

Hagener, Malte, 89
Hansen, Mark B. N., 63, 74, 87–8, 177
Haraway, Donna, 101
Harbisson, Neil, 41
Harwood, Tracy, 124–5
Hill, Charles, 152–3
Holy Motors, 66
Honess Roe, Annabelle, 34, 36, 58, 68, 183, 184, 190, 228
Huhtamo, Erkki, 92
Huizinga, Johan, 113–14, 148

immersive journalism
audience participation and, 155–6
empathy in, 158
physicality and, 157–8
Project Syria (de la Peña), 156, 157, 158, 169
in relation to journalism, 168
virtual reality constructs, 156
indexicality
of animation, 58–9
animation as deictic index of the non-physical, 74–5
animation as deictic index of the physical, 69–73
animation/physical connections, 62–3
of avatars, 166, 186
defined, 13, 58

in digital culture, 29, 63, 65, 74
documentary conventions and, 75–7
icon, symbol, index trichotomy, 63–4, 65, 66, 67, 72
index as deixis, 64–5, 66, 67, 69, 76
index as trace, 72, 75–6
indexical traces of the physical, 13, 37, 62–3, 64, 65, 66–8
photographic referents, 13–14, 37–8, 56, 58, 64, 65, 66
post-photographic logic, 13–14, 65, 68, 78, 227–8
infotainment, 30
in-game documentaries
Another Planet (Yatziv), 136, 144–6, 147, 224, 225–7, 232–5
characteristics of, 112–13, 119, 148
Drakedog's Suicide, 111–12
factional game aesthetics, 143
see also machinima; *Stranger Comes to Town* (Goss)

Jantol, Tom, 62

Kansteiner, Wulf, 145
Kill Bill (Tarantino), 1, 2
Kittler, Friedrich, 74
Koblin, Aaron, 40, 69–70, *70*, 73
Kuma War Games, 150

Lambert-Beatty, Carrie, 212
Landesman, Ohad, 184
The Late Show with Stephen Colbert, 39
Latour, Bruno, 201, 204
Ledune, Eric, 97–8
Leslie, Esther, 28, 69, 200
Levitt, Deborah, 60, 98–9
Life, Animated, 36
Lind, Maria, 29
Lingford, Ruth, 239, 240
Lipkin, Steven, 54–5
live-action film, 3–4, 56, 59, 61, 207
Lowood, Henry, 118–19
Lympouridis, Vangelis, 156

McCay, Winsor, 34, 36
machinima
as animated documents, 127–8
animation technique of, 68, 119, 121
asset extraction and compositing, 124
defined, 119
demo recordings, 123, 128
Diary of a Camper, 119, 120, 123

268 *Animating Truth*

machinima (*cont.*)
  as documentary capture animation, 120–1
  The French Democracy, 136
  in gaming, 68, 119–20
  genres of, 124–6
  ludic/cinematic distinctions, 124, 127–8, 129
  real-time nature of, 121–2
  representation/referent gap, 69, 120
  screen capture, 123, 128
  theorisations of documentary and, 125, 127–9
McIntyre, Lee, 209
McKim, Joel, 28, 61, 69, 74, 177, 200
Maitland, Keith, 5, 233; see also *Tower* (Maitland)
Manovich, Lev, 46, 59, 88, 91
Mattes, Eva, 105
Mattes, Franco, 105
Medal of Honor: Rising Sun, 164
Mello, Cecilia, 45
Merleau-Ponty, Maurice, 102
Milk, Chris, 40
mimesis
  diminished truth-value of photography, 37–9
  in machinima, 120
  mimetic photorealism, 180, 237–8
  non-mimetic imagery, 38–43, 69, 167–8
  visual mimesis and empathy, 180
  visual realism and, 16–17, 31–2, 56, 191
MIT's Game Lab, 169
mixed realities
  contemporary forms of, 3, 54, 78, 88
  of in-game documentaries, 137
  GPS systems and, 87–8, 89
  screen culture, 42, 179
  in *Stranger Comes to Town* (Goss), 136–7, 140–1, 143–4, 147, 208–9
  of virtualised culture, 16
MoCap (motion capture) animation, 10, 66–7, 69
Molotov Alva and His Search for the Creator (Gayeton), 15, 115–16, 117–19, *118*
Mostafaei, Mohammad, 33
Murray, Janet, 154–5, 158
Music & Clowns (Widdowson), 190, *191*

Nagib, Lucia, 45
Nash, Kate, 195
Nelson, Theodor H., 93
New Media Animation (NMA), 28–9, 30
news games, 164–5

news media
  animation in, 33–4, 204–5
  fake-news, 29, 30, 38, 213, 214, 239
  Globalised Slavery: How Big Supermarkets are Selling Prawns in Supply Chain Fed by Slave Labour, 34
  Guantánamo Bay: The Hunger Strikes, 33–4
  Kuma War Games, 150
  One Iranian Lawyer's Fight to Save Juveniles from Execution (Mostafaei), 33
  simulations, simulacra and hyper-reality, 150–1
  still photographs for authenticity, 34–5
  Tomonews (NMA), 28–30, 32–3, 40, 44
  see also immersive journalism
Nichols, Bill, 56, 99, 164, 188, 199, 228
9/11 Survivor (Brennan/Caloud/Cole), 161–2
nomophobia, 101
non-photorealistic animation
  in contemporary culture, 2, 6
  as documentary image, 12–14, 225–9
  vs mimetic photorealism, 180, 237–8
  new forms of realism, 152, 168, 207, 223
  in non-fiction fields, 39–43, 193
  in the post-truth era, 200, 203, 238
  the spectator and, 12
  truth-value of, 10
Nowhere Line: Voices from Manus Island, 36

Odin, Roger, 125
One Iranian Lawyer's Fight to Save Juveniles from Execution (Mostafaei), 33

parafiction, 212
Patrick, Eric, 182, 190
Pearce, Celia, 114
Peirce, Charles Sanders, 63–4, 65, 66, 67, 72, 76
Peña, Nonny de la, 155–6, 158, 168
Peters, John Durham, 98, 153
Petrov, Aleksandr, 93
photography
  animation to live action shifts, 3–4
  authenticity of still photographs, 34–5, 156, 159–60
  Being: New Photography 2018, 105
  digital photography, 65, 121
  indexicality of photographic referents, 13–14, 37–8, 56, 58, 64, 65, 66
  meaning and interpretation of, 56–7
  mimetic visual style, 37–8, 56
  non-mimetic images, 38–9

post-photographic logic, 13–14, 65, 68, 78, 227–8
presence of the object, 181
realism of, 31
shifting relationship with animation, 10–11, 13, 27, 57
still photographs and authenticity, 34–5, 156, 159–60
stop-motion animation, 66
truth-value status of, 37–9, 44, 147
use of photographs in animation, 58, 207–10
in *Waltz with Bashir* (Folman), 194, 203, 209
see also non-photorealistic animation; photorealism
photorealism
concept of, 4
mimetic photorealism, 180, 237–8
non-photographic animated imagery as alternative to, 10, 180, 225, 237–8
theoretical photorealism, 11, 71
see also non-photorealistic animation
physicality
animation and the physical referent, 10–11, 13, 58–9
animation as deictic index of the non-physical, 64, 74–5
animation as deictic index of the physical, 64, 69–73
animation for non-physical realities, 9, 88–9, 94–5, 120–1, 126, 147
within digital culture, 6, 14–15, 17, 42, 65
as explored through virtual spaces, 144, 145–6
in-game/virtual depiction convergence, 16, 135
GPS systems and, 87, 89
immersive journalism and, 157–8
indexical traces of the physical, 13, 37, 62–3, 64, 65–8
photography and the physical referent, 13–14, 37, 58, 65, 66
physical representation in documentaries, 65–6
'real' world of the viewer, 9, 58, 62
real-time animated visualisation, 16
role of the body and physical movement, 63
screen images in the 'real' world, 93–4
of virtual geographical spaces, 143–4, 150–1
see also bodies

Pinchevski, Amit, 153
Pineiro Escoriaza, Juan Carlos, 144
play, defined, 113–14
post-truth era
animation in the post-truth era, 2, 6, 201, 214
documentary aesthetics in, 16, 199, 209–10, 211–12
factual content depiction in, 200–1, 202–3, 211–12, 219
non-photorealistic animation in, 200, 203, 238
term, 29
see also truth-value
Powering the Cell – Mitochondria, 71–2
presence/absence
of animated protagonists, 181–4
in animation, 121–2, 153, 181
interactivity, 154–5
in virtual platforms, 154, 157, 167
Project Syria (de la Peña), 156, 157, 158, 169

Ralph Breaks the Internet (aka *Wreck-It Ralph 2*), 8, 9
realism
animation's relationship with, 3–4, 16–17, 191, 200
in *Another Planet* (Yatziv), 224
concept, 31–2, 201
defamiliarisation and, 200, 206–12, 213, 214
as distinct from mimesis, 31–2
in documentaries, 6–7, 45, 151, 168
ethics and depictions of reality, 11–12
familiarity and, 200, 203–6, 213, 214
ferocious reality, 194–5
imagery/reality relations, 6, 44–5
masking function of animated documentaries, 214–19
philosophical debates, 41–2
of photography, 31
reality principle split, 40–1
representations of reality, 4–5, 201–2, 231–5
see also photorealism; visual realism
reality effects, 45, 151–2
real-time animation, 15, 68, 129, 154
Renov, Michael, 72, 75, 169–70, 199
representation
constructedness and, 76, 211, 215
crystal images, 211–13
defamiliarisation through stylistic disruptions, 207–11

representation (*cont.*)
  enhanced engagement, 184–5
  familiarity and conventions of representation, 204
  masking function of animated documentaries, 214–19
  mediated realities, 30–1
  of reality, 4–5, 201–2, 231–5
  *re*presentation, 201, 204, 211–12
  of the self through animated images, 6, 101–3, 107, 154, 185
  of unrepresentable events and perspectives, 190–1, 211
  veracity narratives, 6–7
  of violence, 180
  in virtual platforms, 157
  vividness and, 152–3
  witnessing and, 153
Rio, Elena Del, 101
Ritchin, Fred, 202, 230
Rogers, Bunny, 104–5
Rogoff, Irit, 144
Roquet, Paul, 101
Rosen, Philip, 75–6, 146
rotoscoping, 66, 67, 138, 142
Rowley, Stephen, 18
Ruiz, Susana, 165

Sabiston, Bob, 208
Salen, Katie, 185
screen culture
  animation as only visible on screen, 9, 10, 59, 90
  augmented reality (AR), 10, 91, 94
  within the digitally virtual, 87, 88
  GPS systems, 87, 89
  imagery on, 90–1
  interactive virtual screen worlds, 3
  omnipresence of in virtualised culture, 6, 42, 87, 90, 93
  physical-technological characteristics of, 91–2
  screen images in the 'real' world, 93–4
  screen-mediated daily life, 42, 94, 236–7
  on-screen/off-screen convergence, 3, 10, 13, 62, 87, 90, 92–3, 100, 168, 179, 186
  3D digital projections, 92–3
Second Bodies (Danilovic), 103, *104*
Second Life (SL), 14, 103, 115–16, 117–19
Second Skin (Pineiro Escoriaza), 144
September 1955 (Zaman/Tuzcu/Tortum), 158–61
Serenity Now, 135, 136

Serious Games: Immersion (Farocki), 105, *105*
Serkis, Andrew Clement, 67
Shaw, Benita, 97
Shenk, Jon, 216
Shields, Rob, 95, 96, 112
Sieff, Gemma, 38–9
The Simpson Verdict (Ezawa), 216–17, *217*
Sims 2, 123
The Sinking of the Lusitania (McCay), 34, 36, 156
Slaves (Aronowitsch/Heilborn), 54, 55, *55*, 58, 73, 182, 183, 191–2, 202
Snack and Drink (Sabiston), 208
Snapchat, 103
Snapchat dysmorphia, 6
Snow White and the Seven Dwarfs (Disney), 11–12
Sobchack, Vivian, 178, 179, 181, 185, 188, 189, 190, 194
Sofian, Sheila, 3
Sontag, Susan, 180
soundtracks
  audio interviews, 55, 138, 139, 182
  in *Slaves*, 54, 55, 182, 183
  viewer experiences and, 184
space
  Another Planet (Yatziv), 136, 144–6, 147
  cultural geography, 143–4
  virtual geographical spaces, 143–4, 150–1
  virtual witnessing, 146, 167
spectatorship *see* viewership
Stern, Eddo, 119–20
Steyerl, Hito, 29
Stiegler, Bernard, 177
stop-motion animation, 66
Stranger Comes to Town (Goss)
  biometric testing, 137–40
  cultural identities in, 140–1
  mixed realities in, 136–7, 140–1, 143–4, 147, 208–9
  non-humanoid game avatars, 137, 139, 140, 141–3, *142*
  US Visit (informational video) in, 137–9, 141, 142, 146
  virtual geographical spaces, 143–4
Strom, Gunnar, 59
Suits, Bernard, 113
surrealism, 205–6
Sutton, Damien, 121
Synthetic Performances (Mattes), 105

Take Action Games, 165
Tarantino, Quentin, 1, 2

Index

technoculture
  animation/documentary relationship, 2
  defined, 2, 97
  dominance of visual communication, 6, 61–2
  role of animation in, 3, 229–31
  screen culture, 93
  smart personal technology, 230
technology
  evolution of in animation, 37
  image-production techniques, 39, 61
  machine aesthetics, 61
  objectivity of mechanically captured images, 57
10–6 (Wearing), 104
theoretical photorealism, 71
Tomonews (NMA), 28–30, 32–3, 40, 44, 150
Tortum, Deniz, 158, 159
Tower (Maitland), 5, 209–10, 233
Trump, Donald, 28–9, 239, 240
Trump Dreams (Lingford), 239, 240
truthiness
  depictions of reality, 205, 235
  term, 29, 151
  viewers as arbitrators of, 185
truth-value
  of animated documentaries, 58, 76, 224
  of animation, 13, 16–17, 202–3, 211–12, 239–40
  bodies as signifiers of truth, 98–100, 188–9
  of documentaries, 12–13, 202
  referentiality and, 58, 147
  status of photography, 37–9, 44, 147
  of virtual images, 89–90, 147
  see also post-truth era
Tuzcu, Nil, 158
Twitch, 125–6, 237

US Visit (informational video), 137–9, 141, 142, 146

Vaughan, Dai, 12, 29
viewership
  active role of, 12, 44–5, 184–5
  animated imagery/physical world gap, 58, 62
  avatars with cameras, 117–18
  belief in depictions of reality, 18–19, 29, 151
  defamiliarisation through stylistic disruptions, 207–9
  dehumanisation of viewers, 177
  desensitised, non-ethical spectatorship, 185, 205, 235–6
  ethical encounters in animated documentaries, 178–9, 182, 184, 192
  gaming player's point of view recording, 123–4
  of immersive journalism, 155–6
  player agency in the real world, 187–8
  spectator's corporeal identification, 179–80
  user/player view of documentary games, 163, 185–7
  viewer identification with animated bodies, 189–92
  see also witnessing
Virilio, Paul, 40, 100
virtual, defined, 96
virtual culture
  the body in, 99, 100–7
  contrasted with materiality, 75, 96
  crossover of the physical and the animated, 87–8, 89
  digitally virtual experiences, 113, 144
  emotional connections with virtual worlds, 112
  GPS systems and, 87–8, 89
  image truth-values, 89–90, 147
  importance of animation, 3, 89
  migration to the virtual, 115
  moral codes for, 135–6
  non-physical computerised concepts, 95
  online representations of the user, 101–3, 107, 129
  and 'the real,' 96–7
  technological innovation and, 97
  virtual witnessing, 146, 167
  see also digital culture; gaming; mixed realities; screen culture; technoculture
virtual documentaries
  Molotov Alva and His Search for the Creator, 15, 115–16, 117–19
  narrative games as documentaries, 112–13, 115, 117–18
  see also in-game documentaries; machinima
virtual reality, 167
virtual reality documentaries
  growth in, 155
  the reality effect in, 151–2
  September 1955, 158–61
  witnessing in, 157
visual culture
  animated gifs and emojis, 6, 65, 95, 102–3

visual culture (*cont.*)
  animation's role in non-fiction representation, 39–43, 69–73, 203, 235–40
  crystal images, 211–13
  image significance, 44–5
  mechanical visualisation, 57, 61
  as mediated through screens, 3, 6, 42–3, 59, 87
  non-photographic animated imagery, 10, 14
  role of animation in, 7, 8, 14, 15–16, 61–2
visual realism
  animation as, 60–1
  animation's break with, 16, 27
  human perception and, 32–3, 40–2
  machine vision, 40–2, 57, 238–9
  meaning and interpretation of, 56–7
  see also mimesis; non-photorealistic animation; photorealism
vividness, continuum of, 152–3

Waltz with Bashir (Folman)
  representations of war, 4–5
  significance of, 2, 3, 15, 184

  use of photographic imagery, 3, 194, 203, 209
Wang, Phillip, 38
Ward, Paul, 30
warranting devices, 54–5
Wearing, Gillian, 104
Wells, Brian, 62, 190, 228
Wells, Paul, 59, 211
Widdowson, Alex, 190, 191
Winter Olympics in Russia (2014), 93
witnessing
  in animated documentaries, 153
  in documentary games, 157
  implicated witnesses, 153–4
  vicarious witnesses, 153
  virtual witnessing, 146, 167
Woodcock, Rose, 67
World of Warcraft (*WoW*), 111–12, 135

Xi Jinping, 28, 29

Yatziv, Amir, 136
Yolton, John W., 32

Zaman, Cagri Hakan, 158
Zimmerman, Eric, 154, 185

EU representative:
Easy Access System Europe
Mustamäe tee 50, 10621 Tallinn, Estonia
Gpsr.requests@easproject.com

www.ingramcontent.com/pod-product-compliance
Lightning Source LLC
Chambersburg PA
CBHW052104230426
43671CB00011B/1927